JUMP Math 8.1

Book 8 Part 1 of 2

Contents

jump math™

MULTIPLYING POTENTIAL.

JUMP Math
One Yonge Street, Suite 1014
Toronto, Ontario M5E 1E5
Canada
www.jumpmath.org

Writers: Dr. Anna Klebanov, Saverio Mercurio, Dr. Sohrab Rahbar
Editors: Megan Burns, Liane Tsui, Natalie Francis, Jackie Dulson, Janice Dyer, Laura Edlund, Rachelle Redford, Joe Zingrone
Layout and Illustrations: Linh Lam, Fely Guinasao-Fernandes, Sawyer Paul, Marijke Friesen, Ilyana Martinez
Cover Design: Blakeley Words+Pictures
Cover Photograph: © NASA, ESA, S. Beckwith (STScI), and The Hubble Heritage Team (STScI/Aura)

ISBN 978-1-927457-52-8

Fourth printing June 2021

Printed and bound in Canada

A note to educators, parents, and everyone who believes that numeracy is as important as literacy for a fully functioning society

Welcome to JUMP Math

Entering the world of JUMP Math means believing that every child has the capacity to be fully numerate and to love math. Founder and mathematician John Mighton has used this premise to develop his innovative teaching method. The resulting resources isolate and describe concepts so clearly and incrementally that everyone can understand them.

JUMP Math is comprised of teacher's guides (which are the heart of our program), interactive whiteboard lessons, student assessment & practice books, evaluation materials, outreach programs, and teacher training. The Common Core Editions of our resources have been carefully designed to cover the Common Core State Standards. All of this is presented on the JUMP Math website: **www.jumpmath.org**.

Teacher's guides are available on the website for free use. Read the introduction to the teacher's guides before you begin using these resources. This will ensure that you understand both the philosophy and the methodology of JUMP Math. The assessment & practice books are designed for use by students, with adult guidance. Each student will have unique needs and it is important to provide the student with the appropriate support and encouragement as he or she works through the material.

Allow students to discover the concepts by themselves as much as possible. Mathematical discoveries can be made in small, incremental steps. The discovery of a new step is like untangling the parts of a puzzle. It is exciting and rewarding.

Students will need to answer the questions marked with a  in a notebook. Grid paper notebooks should always be on hand for answering extra questions or when additional room for calculation is needed.

Contents

PART 1

Unit 1: Expressions and Equations: Operations on Rational Numbers

Unit 2: Expressions and Equations: Powers and Exponents

Unit 3: Geometry: Understanding Congruence and Properties of Angles

Unit 7: Statistics and Probability: Patterns in Scatter Plots

PART 2

Unit 1: Functions: Modeling Linear Relationships Using Functions

Unit 2: Geometry: Transformations

Unit 3: The Number System: Real Numbers

Unit 4: Geometry: Pythagorean Theorem

Unit 5: Expressions and Equations: Systems of Linear Equations

Unit 6: Geometry: Volume

Unit 7: Statistics and Probability: Line of Best Fit and Two-Way Tables

EE8-1 Multiplication Review

Multiplication is a short form for repeated addition. Example: $3 \times 5 = \underbrace{5 + 5 + 5}_{\text{add three 5s}}$

1. Write as repeated addition, then calculate.

a) 4×5
$= 5 + 5 + 5 + 5$
$= 20$

b) 5×3

c) 2×4

d) 1×3

2. Write as a product, then calculate.

a) $4 + 4 + 4 + 4 + 4$
$= 5 \times 4$
$= 20$

b) $5 + 5 + 5$

c) $2 + 2 + 2 + 2$

d) $1 + 1 + 1$

3. What do you notice about the answers to 4×5 and 5×4, 5×3 and 3×5, 2×4 and 4×2, and 1×3 and 3×1? ______________________

Multiplication is **commutative**. Example: $8 \times 7 = 7 \times 8$

4. Complete the sentence.

a) $9 \times 6 = 54$, so $6 \times 9 = 54$.

b) $7 \times 6 = 42$, so ________.

c) $8 \times 4 = 32$, so ________.

d) $12 \times 10 = 120$, so ________.

You can use multiplication to find the number of items in an array.

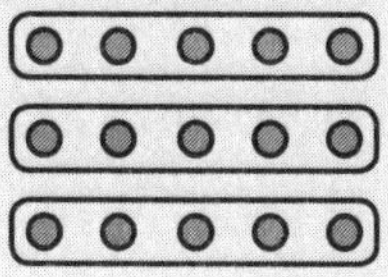

$5 + 5 + 5 = 3 \times 5 = 15$ or

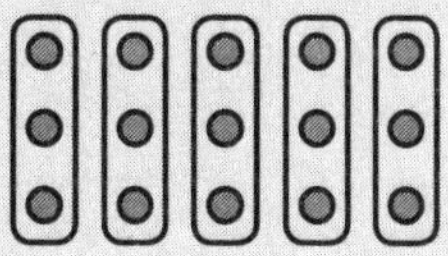

$3 + 3 + 3 + 3 + 3 = 5 \times 3 = 15$

5. Write two multiplication equations to find the number of items in the array.

a) 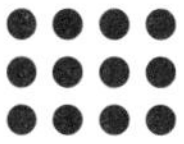

$3 \times 4 = 12$
$4 \times 3 = 12$

b) 

____
____

c) 

____
____

d) 

____
____

You can multiply 234 × 2 using place values or the standard algorithm.

Place values

2 hundreds + 3 tens + 4 ones

× 2

4 hundreds + 6 tens + 8 ones

= 468

Standard algorithm

	2	3	4
×			2
	4	6	8

6. Multiply using the standard algorithm.

a) 213 × 3

b) 212 × 4

c) 2,301 × 3

To multiply 218 × 4, you need to regroup.

Place values

2 hundreds + 1 ten + 8 ones

× 4

8 hundreds + 4 tens + 32 ones

= 8 hundreds + 4 tens + (3 tens + 2 ones)

= 8 hundreds + 7 tens + 2 ones

= 872

Standard algorithm

		3		← 3 tens regrouped
	2	1	8	
×			4	
	8	7	2	

(7: 4 × 1 + 3)

7. Multiply using the standard algorithm. You may need to regroup more than once.

a) 425 × 3

b) 172 × 4

c) 135 × 7

d) 3,145 × 3

e) 6,384 × 9

Bonus ▶ 987,654,321 × 9

8. In football, a touchdown earns 7 points. How many points does a team earn if it scores 43 touchdowns?

A quick way to multiply a whole number by 10, 100, or 1,000 is to write zeros at the end of the whole number.

Examples: $23 \times 10 = 230$ $35 \times 100 = 3{,}500$ $417 \times 1{,}000 = 417{,}000$

9. Multiply mentally.

a) 235×10

$= 2{,}350$

b) 752×100

c) $48 \times 1{,}000$

Bonus ▶ $465 \times 10{,}000$

Multiplication satisfies the **associative property**. Example: $(2 \times 3) \times 4 = 2 \times (3 \times 4)$

We can use the associative property to multiply 31×200 mentally.

Example: $31 \times 200 = 31 \times (2 \times 100)$

$= (31 \times 2) \times 100$

$= (62 \times 100)$

$= 6{,}200$

10. Multiply mentally.

a) 213×30

$= 6{,}390$

b) 413×200

c) 121×40

Bonus ▶ $423 \times 20{,}000$

Multiplication satisfies the **distributive property** over addition or subtraction.

Example: $2 \times (3 + 4) = (2 \times 3) + (2 \times 4)$

11. Rewrite using the distributive property.

a) $25 \times (10 + 4)$

$= (25 \times$ __10__ $)$

$+ (25 \times$ __4__ $)$

b) $32 \times (20 + 7)$

$= (32 \times$ ______ $)$

$+ (32 \times$ ______ $)$

c) $53 \times (40 + 2)$

$= (53 \times$ ______ $)$

$+ (53 \times$ ______ $)$

12. Rewrite the second number, then calculate using the distributive property.

a) 43×21

$= 43 \times (20 +$ __1__ $)$

$= (43 \times 20) + (43 \times$ __1__ $)$

$= 860 + 43$

$= 903$

b) 51×32

$= 51 \times (30 +$ ______ $)$

$= (51 \times 30) + (51 \times$ ______ $)$

$=$

$=$

c) 72×43

$=$ ______ $\times (40 +$ ______ $)$

$=$

$=$

$=$

d) 70×32

$= 70 \times (30 + 2)$

e) 80×47

$= 80 \times (40 + 7)$

f) 90×62

$= 90 \times (60 + 2)$

You can multiply by a 2-digit number in two grids using the distributive property.

56×27

$= 56 \times (20 + 7)$

$= (56 \times 20) + (56 \times 7)$

$= 1{,}120 + 392$

$= 1{,}512$

			4	
			5	6
×			2	7
		3	9	2
+	1	1	2	0
	1	5	1	2

		1		
			5	6
×			2	0
	1	1	2	0

13. Multiply using two grids.

a) 48×32

			4	8
×			3	2
+				

			4	8
×			3	0

b) 123×58

		1	2	3
×			5	8
+				

		1	2	3
×			5	0

You can multiply by a 2-digit number using one grid to save space.

This is the standard algorithm for multiplying a 2-digit number.

		1			
			4		
			5	6	
×			2	7	
		3	9	2	← 56×7
+	1	1	2	0	← 56×20
	1	5	1	2	← $(56 \times 20) + (56 \times 7)$

14. Multiply using the standard algorithm.

a) 38×42

b) 43×79

c) 314×26

EE8-2 Division Review

The division equation $8 \div 2 = 4$ represents two ways of dividing 8 items into equal groups.

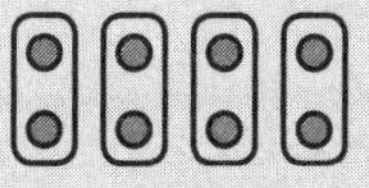

or

8 items with 4 groups of 2 each

8 items with 2 groups of 4 each

1. Write two division equations for the situation.

a) 15 apples are divided into 5 groups of 3 each. *$15 \div 3 = 5$* ______ *$15 \div 5 = 3$* ______

b) 24 pictures are placed on 4 pages.
Each page has 6 pictures. ______ ______

c) $35 is shared among 7 friends.
Each friend gets $5. ______ ______

If we divide 23 items into 4 groups, 3 items are left over.

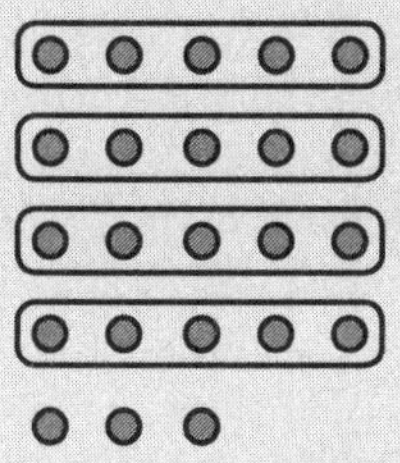

Using **long division** helps you to write a **division equation**.

$$\begin{array}{r} 5 \\ 4\overline{)23} \\ -\underline{20} \\ 3 \end{array}$$

5 ← quotient; divisor → 4; 23 ← dividend; 3 ← remainder

$23 \div 4 = 5 \text{ R } 3$

2. Write a division equation for the long division.

a) $\begin{array}{r} 5 \\ 7\overline{)38} \\ -\underline{35} \\ 3 \end{array}$ ______

b) $\begin{array}{r} 7 \\ 4\overline{)30} \\ -\underline{28} \\ 2 \end{array}$ ______

c) $\begin{array}{r} 9 \\ 6\overline{)58} \\ -\underline{54} \\ 4 \end{array}$ ______

To do long division:

Step 1: Try a digit for the quotient.

Step 2: Multiply the quotient by the divisor. If the answer is greater than the dividend, try a new quotient.

Step 3: Subtract. The remainder must be less than the divisor.

$\begin{array}{r} 8 \\ 5\overline{)38} \\ -\underline{40} \end{array}$ ← too high

$\begin{array}{r} 7 \\ 5\overline{)38} \\ -\underline{35} \\ 3 \end{array}$ ← must be less than divisor

3. Divide using long division on grid paper.

a) $58 \div 7$ b) $76 \div 9$ c) $46 \div 8$

To divide 235 ÷ 5, you will need to regroup:

Step 1: Circle the first group of digits larger than the divisor. 23 is greater than 5, so circle 23 tens in (23)5.

Step 2: Divide the 23 tens into 5 groups.

```
    4      ← 4 tens in each group
5)(23)5    ← 23 tens to be divided into 5 groups
 −20
   3       ← 3 tens left over
```

Step 3: The leftover is 3 tens and 5 ones = 35 ones.

```
    47     ← 7 ones in each group
 5)235
  −20↓
    (35)   ← 3 tens + 5 ones = 35 ones
   −35
     0
```

4. Divide using long division, then write the division equation.

a) 426 ÷ 6

b) 356 ÷ 8

c) 289 ÷ 4

d) 1,371 ÷ 3

e) 3,120 ÷ 5

f) 1,602 ÷ 9

5. Find the number of weeks in 1,095 days.

EE8-3 2-Digit Division Review

To round to the nearest ten, **round up** if the ones digit is 5 or greater, and **round down** if the ones digit is less than 5.

Examples: $3\underline{8} \approx 40$ $3\underline{2} \approx 30$ The $\approx$ symbol means "approximately equal."

1. Round to the nearest ten.

a) $47 \approx$ ______ b) $81 \approx$ ______ c) $29 \approx$ ______ d) $65 \approx$ ______

2. Circle the first group of digits in the dividend larger than the divisor. Then round the divisor to the nearest ten.

a) $27\overline{)624}$ (62 circled) ↓ *30*

b) $41\overline{)861}$ ↓ ______

c) $14\overline{)294}$ ↓ ______

d) $75\overline{)1,632}$ ↓ ______

To divide $445 \div 18$:

Step 1: Circle the first group of digits in the dividend larger than the divisor. Round the divisor to the nearest ten.

445 (44 circled) $18 \approx 20$

$$\begin{array}{r} 2 \\ 18\overline{)445} \\ -\underline{36} \end{array}$$

Step 2: Estimate the quotient. Use $44 \div 20$.

Step 3: Multiply the divisor by the quotient. Use $18 \times 2 = 36$.

3. Complete Steps 1–3 of the division.

a) $17\overline{)646}$ (64 circled), quotient *3*, $-\,\underline{51}$

$17 \approx 20$

	2	
	1	*7*
×		*3*
	5	*1*

b) $23\overline{)713}$

______

×		

c) $38\overline{)912}$

______

×		

Step 4: Subtract and find whether the estimate for the quotient was too low, too high, or just right.

$$\begin{array}{r} 1 \\ 47\overline{)987} \\ -\underline{47} \\ 51 \end{array}$$ but $51 > 47$

1 is too low.

$$\begin{array}{r} 3 \\ 23\overline{)644} \\ -\underline{69} \\ ? \end{array}$$ but $69 > 64$, negative number

3 is too high.

4. Subtract and state whether the estimate for the quotient was too high, too low, or just right.

a) $$\begin{array}{r} 2 \\ 27\overline{)924} \\ -\underline{54} \end{array}$$ ______

b) $$\begin{array}{r} 2 \\ 53\overline{)1,045} \\ -\underline{106} \end{array}$$ ______

c) $$\begin{array}{r} 2 \\ 34\overline{)729} \\ -\underline{68} \end{array}$$ ______

d) $$\begin{array}{r} 2 \\ 42\overline{)813} \\ -\underline{84} \end{array}$$ ______

Step 5: To continue dividing 445 ÷ 18, subtract and bring down the next digit.

```
   24
18)445
 – 36↓
   85
```

5. Complete Steps 1–5 of the division. You may have to adjust your estimate if it is too high or too low.

a) 644 ÷ 17

		3	
17)	6	4	4
–	5	1	↓
	1	3	4

b) 952 ÷ 34

		2	
34)	9	5	2
–			↓

c) 868 ÷ 28

28)	8	6	8
–			↓

d) 1,312 ÷ 41

41)	1	3	1	2
–				

e) 1,363 ÷ 29

)				
–				

f) 1,026 ÷ 38

)				
–				

To continue dividing 445 ÷ 18, divide 85 ÷ 18.

```
   24   ← Step 6: Estimate the quotient.
18)445            Use 85 ÷ 20.
 – 36↓
   85
 – 72   ← Step 7: Multiply the divisor by the
                  estimate. Use 18 × 4 = 72.
   13   ← Step 8: Subtract to find the remainder.
```

6. Estimate the next digit in the quotient. Multiply by the divisor and subtract to find the remainder.

a)

		4	2
12)	5	0	9
–	4	8	↓
		2	9
–		2	4
			5

b)

		2	
42)	9	6	7
–	8	4	
	1	2	7
–			

c)

		3	
27)	9	6	8
–	8	1	
	1	5	8
–			

7. Divide using long division. Continue dividing until you have brought down all the digits. Write the division equation.

a) 674 ÷ 32

		2	1
32)	6	7	4
−	6	4	↓
		3	4
−		3	2
			2

674 ÷ 32 = 21 R 2

b) 946 ÷ 27

c) 694 ÷ 46

d) 7,168 ÷ 56

e) 6,152 ÷ 59

f) 3,312 ÷ 72

8. A theater that holds 896 people has 32 rows of seats. How many seats are in each row?

9. One acre is 4,840 square yards. Fred owns one acre of land in the shape of a rectangle. The rectangle is 55 yards wide. How long is the rectangle?

10. A winning lottery ticket for $3,744 is shared by 24 people. How much money will each person receive?

11. One floor of an apartment building is 22,320 square feet. There are 18 apartments on one floor. How many square feet is each apartment?

EE8-4 Fractions Review

A fraction names part of a whole. The pie is cut into 8 equal parts. 5 parts out of the 8 are shaded.

So $\frac{5}{8}$ of the pie is shaded.

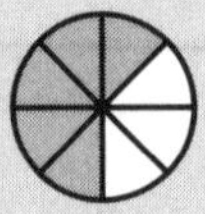

$\frac{5}{8}$

The **numerator** tells you how many parts are shaded.

The **denominator** tells you how many equal parts are in a whole.

1. Write a fraction for the shaded region.

a) 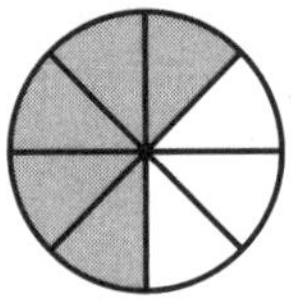 ______

b)  ______

c) 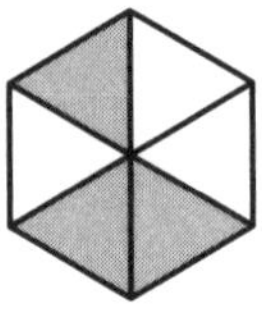 ______

d)  ______

Equivalent fractions show the same part of the same whole.

You can find equivalent fractions by cutting every part of the whole into equal parts.

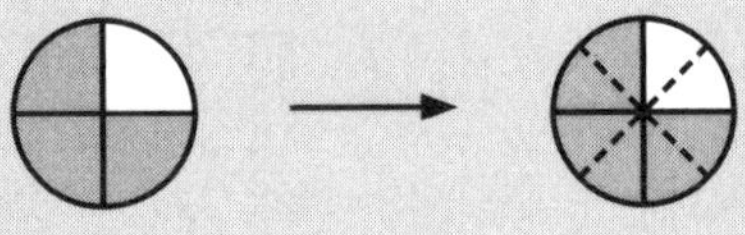

$\frac{3}{4} \begin{matrix} \times 2 \\ \times 2 \end{matrix} = \frac{6}{8}$

2. Draw lines to cut the pie into more pieces. Count the number of shaded parts and the number of parts in the whole to find the equivalent fractions.

a) 6 pieces

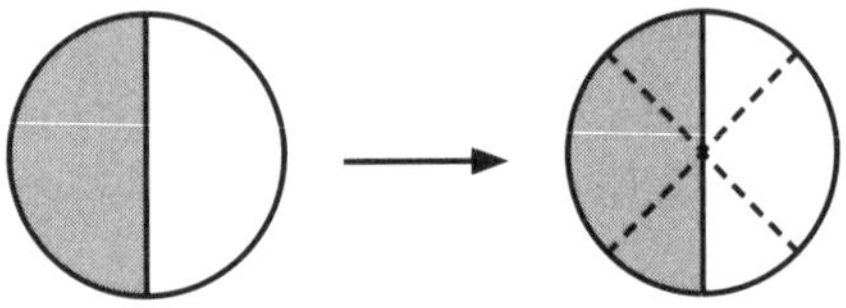

$\frac{1}{2} = \frac{3}{6}$

b) 8 pieces

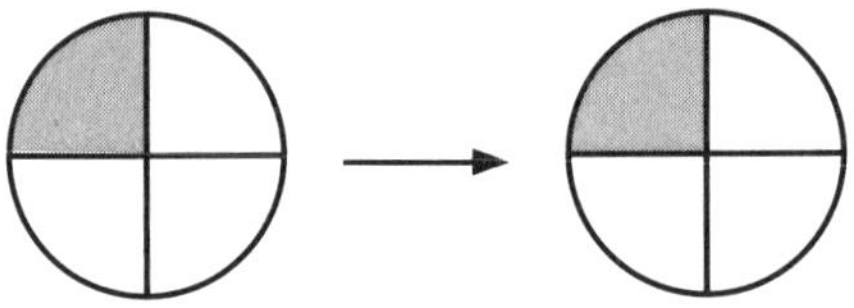

=

c) 9 pieces

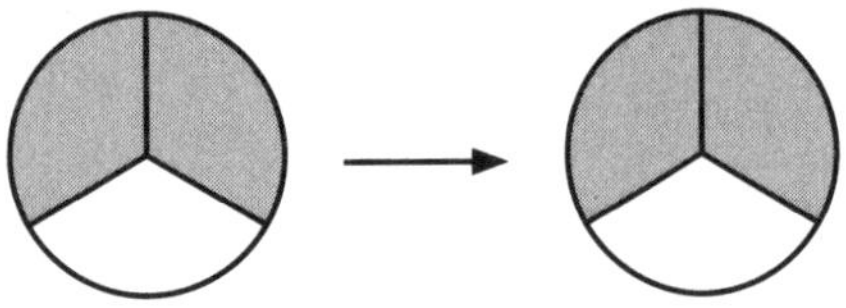

=

d) 10 pieces

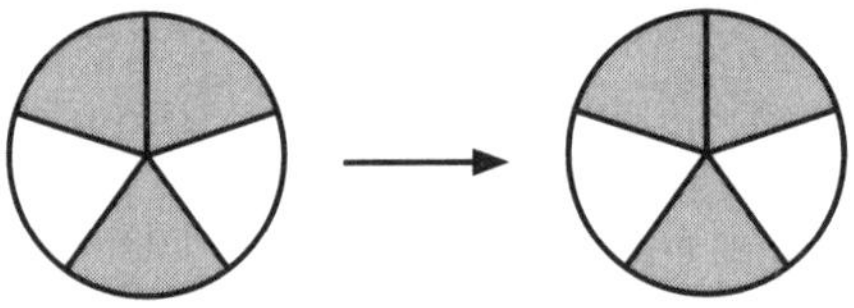

=

3. Use multiplication to find an equivalent fraction.

a) $\frac{3 \times 5}{4 \times 5} = \frac{15}{20}$ b) $\frac{5 \times 2}{6 \times 2} =$ c) $\frac{4 \times 6}{5 \times 6} =$ d) $\frac{5 \times 3}{8 \times 3} =$

4. What number do you multiply the fraction by to get the equivalent fraction?

a) $\frac{5 \times 3}{8 \times 3} = \frac{15}{24}$ b) $\frac{3 \times}{7 \times} = \frac{12}{28}$ c) $\frac{4 \times}{9 \times} = \frac{20}{45}$ d) $\frac{1 \times}{6 \times} = \frac{7}{42}$

4, 8, (12), 16, 20, 24, and so on, are multiples of 4.
6, (12), 18, 24, 30, and so on, are multiples of 6.

The **lowest common multiple** (**LCM**) of 4 and 6 is the first number to appear in both lists.

The LCM for 4 and 6 is 12.

5. Find the LCM of the numbers.

a) 6, 8 *6, 12, 18, (24), 30, 36, ...*
8, 16, (24), 32, 40, 48, ...
LCM = *24*

b) 10, 15 ______
______
LCM = ______

c) 9, 12 ______
______
LCM = ______

d) 2, 10 ______
______
LCM = ______

e) 4, 10

f) 14, 21

To compare fractions with the same denominator, look at the number of shaded parts for each fraction.

So $\frac{5}{8} > \frac{3}{8}$ because 5 > 3.

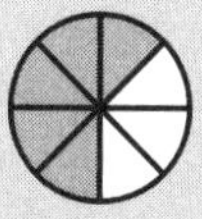
5 shaded parts

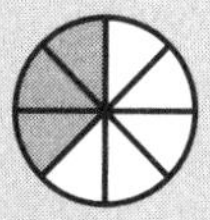
3 shaded parts

6. Circle the larger fraction.

a) $\frac{1}{4}$ and $\frac{3}{4}$ b) $\frac{7}{8}$ and $\frac{5}{8}$ c) $\frac{9}{16}$ and $\frac{11}{16}$ d) $\frac{31}{50}$ and $\frac{11}{50}$

7. Circle the smaller fraction.

a) $\frac{1}{6}$ and $\frac{5}{6}$ b) $\frac{3}{5}$ and $\frac{2}{5}$ c) $\frac{7}{10}$ and $\frac{3}{10}$ d) $\frac{5}{25}$ and $\frac{7}{25}$

To compare fractions with different denominators, you need to find the equivalent fractions.

Example: $\frac{5}{6}, \frac{3}{4}$

Step 1: Find the LCM of the denominators. This is called the **lowest common denominator** (**LCD**).

The LCM of 4 and 6 is 12. So the LCD is 12.

Step 2: Change each fraction to an equivalent fraction with the new denominator.

$\frac{5 \times 2}{6 \times 2} = \frac{10}{12}$ $\frac{3 \times 3}{4 \times 3} = \frac{9}{12}$

Step 3: Compare the equivalent fractions.

Since $\frac{10}{12} > \frac{9}{12}$, then $\frac{5}{6} > \frac{3}{4}$

8. Find the larger fraction by comparing the equivalent fractions.

a) $\frac{7}{10}$ and $\frac{5}{8}$

LCD = *40*

$\frac{7 \times 4}{10 \times 4} = \frac{28}{40}$

$\frac{5 \times 5}{8 \times 5} = \frac{25}{40}$

So $\frac{7}{10} > \frac{5}{8}$

b) $\frac{7}{9}$ and $\frac{11}{12}$

LCD = ______

c) $\frac{7}{10}$ and $\frac{5}{6}$

LCD = ______

d) $\frac{3}{5}$ and $\frac{4}{7}$

LCD = ______

To add (or subtract) fractions with the same denominator, keep the denominator and add (or subtract) the numerators.

Example: 

$\frac{3}{7}$ of the squares are shaded dark.

$\frac{2}{7}$ of the squares are shaded light.

So $\frac{3}{7} + \frac{2}{7} = \frac{5}{7}$ of the squares are shaded.

9. Add or subtract.

a) $\frac{3}{8} + \frac{4}{8} =$

b) $\frac{9}{10} - \frac{2}{10} =$

c) $\frac{3}{16} + \frac{8}{16} =$

d) $\frac{18}{30} - \frac{5}{30} =$

e) $\frac{3}{7} - \frac{1}{7} + \frac{4}{7} =$

f) $\frac{3}{8} + \frac{3}{8} - \frac{1}{8} =$

g) $\frac{4}{9} + \frac{4}{9} - \frac{3}{9} =$

h) $\frac{13}{15} - \frac{4}{15} - \frac{2}{15} =$

To add or subtract fractions with different denominators:

Step 1: Find the lowest common denominator.

Step 2: Find the equivalent fractions using the LCD as the denominator.

Step 3: Add or subtract the equivalent fractions.

Example: $\frac{3}{8}+\frac{1}{6}$

8 ⟶ 8, 16, 24, 32, 40, …
6 ⟶ 12, 18, 24, 30, 36, …

LCD = 24

$\frac{3\times3}{8\times3}=\frac{9}{24}$ $\qquad$ $\frac{1\times4}{6\times4}=\frac{4}{24}$

$\frac{9}{24}+\frac{4}{24}=\frac{13}{24}$

10. Add or subtract.

a) $\frac{7}{9}-\frac{5}{12}$ LCD = *36*

$=\frac{7\times4}{9\times4}-\frac{5\times3}{12\times3}$

$=\frac{28}{36}-\frac{15}{36}$

$=\frac{13}{36}$

b) $\frac{5}{6}+\frac{3}{10}$ LCD = ______

c) $\frac{7}{12}-\frac{3}{8}$ LCD = ______

d) $\frac{3}{8}+\frac{1}{5}$

e) $\frac{3}{4}-\frac{1}{2}$

f) $\frac{7}{10}-\frac{2}{15}$

You can also think of a fraction as division.

Example: $\frac{8}{4}$

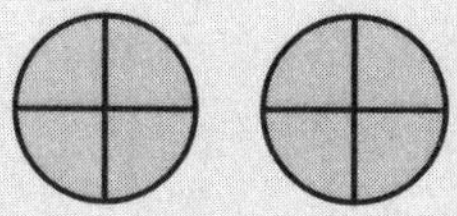

8 parts shaded
4 parts in the whole

There are 8 ÷ 4 = 2 whole pies.

11. Write the fraction as a division.

a) $\frac{8}{4}$ = *8 ÷ 4* $\qquad$ b) $\frac{15}{5}$ = $\qquad$ c) $\frac{3}{4}$ = $\qquad$ d) $\frac{9}{10}$ =

12. Write the division as a fraction.

a) 18 ÷ 6 = $\frac{18}{6}$ $\qquad$ b) 20 ÷ 4 = $\qquad$ c) 7 ÷ 8 = $\qquad$ d) 11 ÷ 16 =

Reducing Fractions

Reduced fractions are equivalent fractions with fewer parts in the whole.

You can reduce fractions by combining equal parts of the whole to make fewer parts.

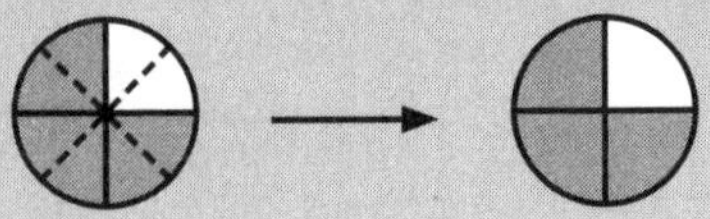

$$\frac{6}{8} = \frac{6 \div 2}{8 \div 2} = \frac{3}{4}$$

1. Use division to find a reduced fraction.

a) $\frac{15 \div 5}{20 \div 5} = \frac{3}{4}$ b) $\frac{15 \div 3}{24 \div 3} =$ c) $\frac{18 \div 2}{20 \div 2} =$ d) $\frac{30 \div 6}{42 \div 6} =$

The factors of 12 are 1, 2, 3, 4, (6), and 12.

The factors of 18 are 1, 2, 3, (6), 9, and 18.

The **greatest common factor (GCF)** is the greatest number that appears in both lists.

The GCF of 12 and 18 is 6.

2. Find the GCF of the numbers.

a) 10, 15 *1, 2, (5), 10*

1, 3, (5), 15

GCF = *5*

b) 8, 12 ______

______

GCF = ______

c) 24, 32 ______

______

GCF = ______

d) 27, 36 ______

______

GCF = ______

A fraction is in **lowest terms** if the GCF of the numerator and denominator is 1.

$\frac{3}{4}$ is in lowest terms because the GCF of 3 and 4 is 1.

$\frac{6}{9}$ is not in lowest terms because the GCF of 6 and 9 is 3.

3. Write the GCF of the numerator and denominator. Circle the fraction if it is in lowest terms.

a) $\frac{9}{12}$ b) $\frac{5}{7}$ (circled) c) $\frac{10}{15}$ d) $\frac{3}{8}$ e) $\frac{9}{14}$ f) $\frac{14}{28}$

GCF = *3* GCF = *1* GCF = ______ GCF = ______ GCF = ______ GCF = ______

To reduce a fraction to lowest terms, divide the numerator and denominator by the GCF.

Example: $\frac{12}{15}$

Step 1: Find the GCF of the numerator and denominator.

12 → 1, 2, (3), 4, 6, 12
15 → 1, (3), 5, 15

GCF = 3

Step 2: Divide both the numerator and the denominator by the GCF.

$\frac{12 \div 3}{15 \div 3} = \frac{4}{5}$

4. Reduce the fraction to lowest terms.

a) $\frac{10}{12}$ GCF = 2

$= \frac{10 \div 2}{12 \div 2}$

$= \frac{5}{6}$

b) $\frac{15}{20}$ GCF = ______

c) $\frac{18}{24}$ GCF = ______

d) $\frac{12}{27}$ GCF = ______

e) $\frac{12}{32}$

f) $\frac{14}{21}$

g) $\frac{27}{45}$

Bonus ▶ $\frac{100}{150}$

5. Add or subtract the fractions. Reduce your answer to lowest terms.

a) $\frac{3}{8} + \frac{3}{8}$

$= \frac{6}{8}$

$= \frac{6 \div 2}{8 \div 2}$

$= \frac{3}{4}$

b) $\frac{7}{12} - \frac{1}{12}$

c) $\frac{4}{15} + \frac{8}{15}$

d) $\frac{7}{9} - \frac{1}{9}$

6. Add or subtract the fractions. You will need to find the LCD of the fractions. Reduce your answer to lowest terms.

a) $\frac{1}{3} + \frac{1}{6}$

b) $\frac{9}{10} - \frac{11}{15}$

c) $\frac{1}{6} + \frac{1}{12}$

Bonus ▶ $\frac{21}{100} - \frac{31}{300}$

7. Zack thinks that a fraction is in lowest terms if he cannot reduce it any further. Is he correct? Explain using the GCF.

EE8-6 Multiplying Fractions

Here is $\frac{1}{3}$ of a rectangle.

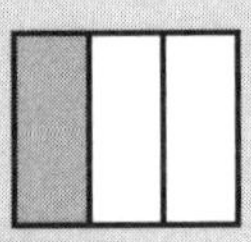

Here is $\frac{1}{2}$ of $\frac{1}{3}$ of a rectangle.

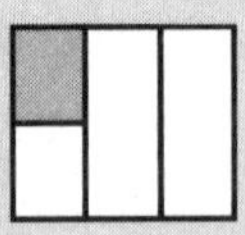

Extend the line to find the fraction that is shaded.

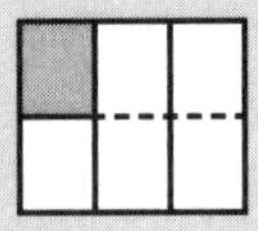

$\frac{1}{2}$ of $\frac{1}{3} = \frac{1}{6}$

The word "of" can mean multiply. So you can write $\frac{1}{2}$ of $\frac{1}{3} = \frac{1}{6}$ as $\frac{1}{2} \times \frac{1}{3} = \frac{1}{6}$.

1. Extend the horizontal lines. Then complete the multiplication equation.

a) 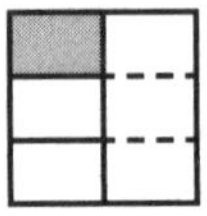

$\frac{1}{3} \times \frac{1}{2} = \frac{1}{6}$

b) 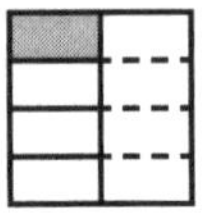

$\frac{1}{4} \times \frac{1}{2} =$

c) 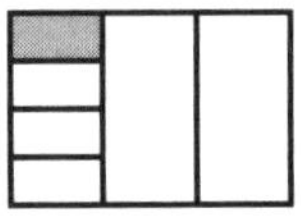

$\frac{1}{4} \times \frac{1}{3} =$

d) 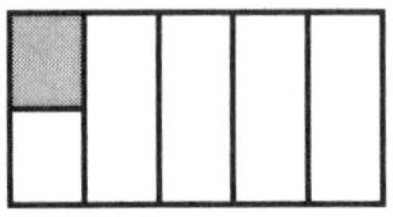

$\frac{1}{2} \times \frac{1}{5} =$

To find the denominator when multiplying unit fractions, multiply the denominators.

Example: $\frac{1}{3} \times \frac{1}{4} = \frac{1}{12}$ ⟵ $3 \times 4 = 12$

2. Multiply.

a) $\frac{1}{3} \times \frac{1}{6} =$

b) $\frac{1}{4} \times \frac{1}{5} =$

c) $\frac{1}{7} \times \frac{1}{3} =$

d) $\frac{1}{9} \times \frac{1}{5} =$

Here is $\frac{2}{3}$ of a rectangle.

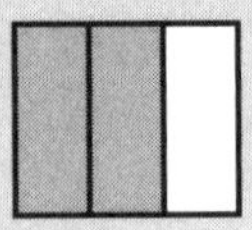

Here is $\frac{4}{5}$ of $\frac{2}{3}$ of a rectangle.

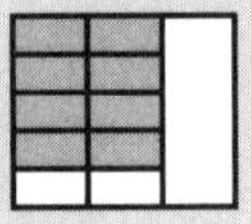

Extend the line to find the fraction that is shaded.

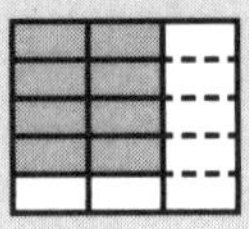

$\frac{4}{5} \times \frac{2}{3} = \frac{8}{15}$

3. Extend the horizontal lines. Then complete the multiplication equation.

a) 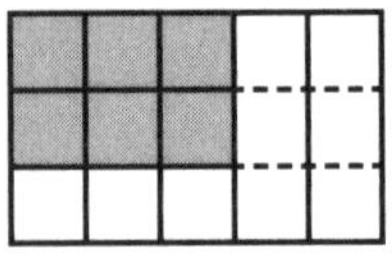

$\frac{2}{3} \times \frac{3}{5} = \frac{6}{15}$

b) 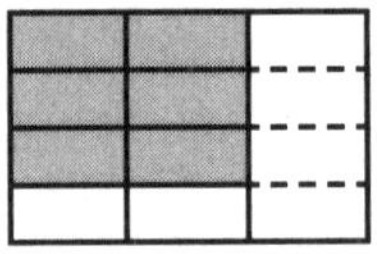

$\frac{3}{4} \times \frac{2}{3} =$

c) 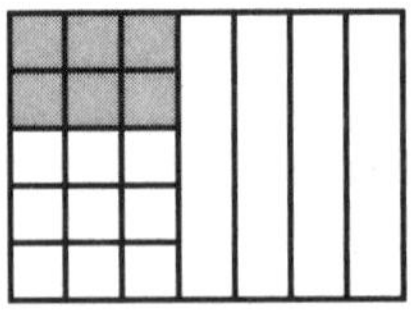

$\frac{2}{5} \times \frac{3}{7} =$

d) 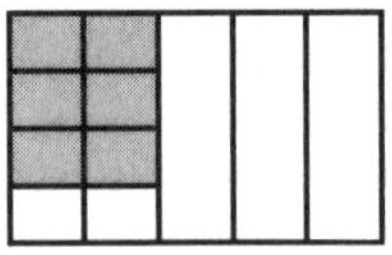

$\frac{3}{4} \times \frac{2}{5} =$

To multiply fractions, multiply the numerators and denominators separately.

Example: $\frac{2}{3} \times \frac{4}{7} = \frac{8}{21}$ ← $2 \times 4 = 8$; ← $3 \times 7 = 21$

4. Multiply.

a) $\frac{3}{4} \times \frac{5}{8} =$ b) $\frac{4}{7} \times \frac{2}{9} =$ c) $\frac{2}{5} \times \frac{4}{7} =$ d) $\frac{2}{3} \times \frac{7}{9} =$

5. Multiply. Reduce your answer to lowest terms.

a) $\frac{3}{4} \times \frac{5}{6}$

$= \frac{15}{24}$

$= \frac{5}{8}$

b) $\frac{3}{5} \times \frac{4}{9}$ c) $\frac{5}{6} \times \frac{4}{7}$ d) $\frac{5}{9} \times \frac{6}{10}$

$\frac{9}{4}$ is an **improper fraction** because the numerator is greater than the denominator.

You can multiply improper fractions the same way you multiply proper fractions. Example:

$\frac{7}{5} =$ 

$\frac{2}{3} \times \frac{7}{5} =$  $= \frac{14}{15}$ ← 7 groups of 2 are shaded; ← 5 groups of 3 in each whole

6. Multiply. Reduce your answer to lowest terms.

a) $\frac{3}{4} \times \frac{5}{3}$

$= \frac{15}{12}$

$= \frac{5}{4}$

b) $\frac{2}{3} \times \frac{9}{4}$ c) $\frac{3}{4} \times \frac{8}{7}$ d) $\frac{9}{4} \times \frac{8}{3}$

7. Claire was given $\frac{3}{4}$ of her weekly allowance on Monday. On Tuesday, she spent $\frac{2}{3}$ of the money she received on Monday.

a) What fraction of her allowance did she spend on Tuesday?

b) What fraction of her allowance is left?

You can simplify the multiplication.

Example: $\frac{5}{6} \times \frac{8}{7} = \frac{5 \times 8}{7 \times 6}$ ← commutative property

Step 1: Find the GCF of one number from the numerators and one number from the denominators.

The GCF of 8 and 6 is 2.

Step 2: Divide one number from the numerators and one number from the denominators by the GCF.

You can divide without switching the order.

$\frac{5}{6 \div 2} \times \frac{8 \div 2}{7} = \frac{5}{3} \times \frac{4}{7}$

8. Simplify the multiplication using the steps above.

a) $\frac{9}{7} \times \frac{5}{12}$ GCF = 3

$= \frac{9 \div 3}{7} \times \frac{5}{12 \div 3}$

$= \frac{3}{7} \times \frac{5}{4}$

b) $\frac{10}{15} \times \frac{7}{8}$ GCF = 5

$= \frac{10 \div 5}{15 \div 5} \times \frac{7}{8}$

c) $\frac{8}{9} \times \frac{6}{5}$ GCF = 3

d) $\frac{10}{12} \times \frac{5}{3}$ GCF = 2

e) $\frac{16}{9} \times \frac{7}{20}$ GCF = 4

f) $\frac{12}{7} \times \frac{5}{18}$ GCF = 6

9. Simplify the multiplication as much as possible, then multiply.

a) $\frac{5}{12} \times \frac{8}{3}$

$= \frac{5}{12 \div 4} \times \frac{8 \div 4}{3}$

$= \frac{5}{3} \times \frac{2}{3}$

$= \frac{10}{9}$

b) $\frac{15}{10} \times \frac{7}{11}$

c) $\frac{8}{12} \times \frac{9}{5}$

d) $\frac{14}{5} \times \frac{3}{21}$

e) $\frac{20}{7} \times \frac{4}{30}$

f) $\frac{15}{9} \times \frac{10}{14}$

EE8-7 Dividing Fractions

To divide $6 \div 2$ using a number line, find the number of steps it takes to get to 6 when counting by 2s.

So $6 \div 2 = 3$

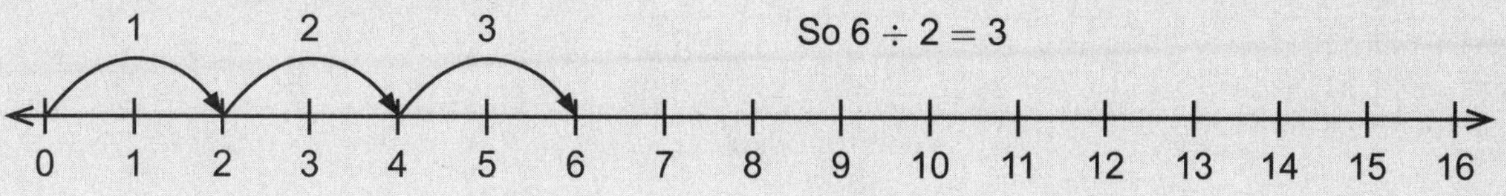

1. Use the number line above to divide.

a) $12 \div 3 =$ b) $16 \div 8 =$ c) $12 \div 2 =$ d) $15 \div 3 =$

2. Label the missing fractions on the number line.

a)

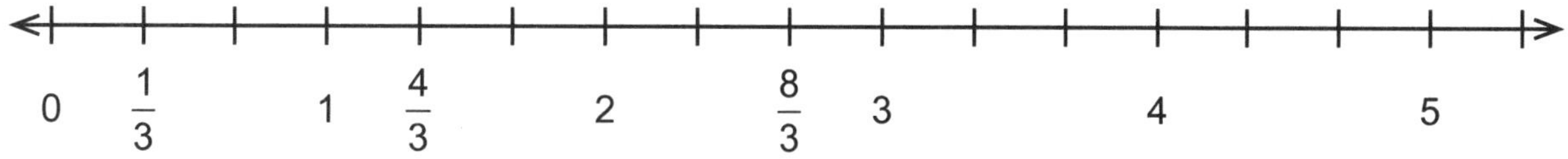

b)

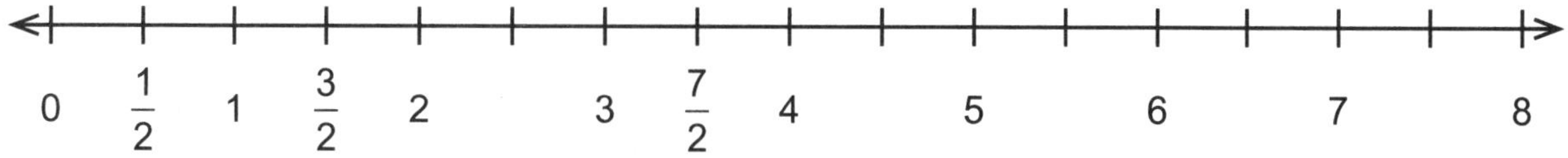

c)

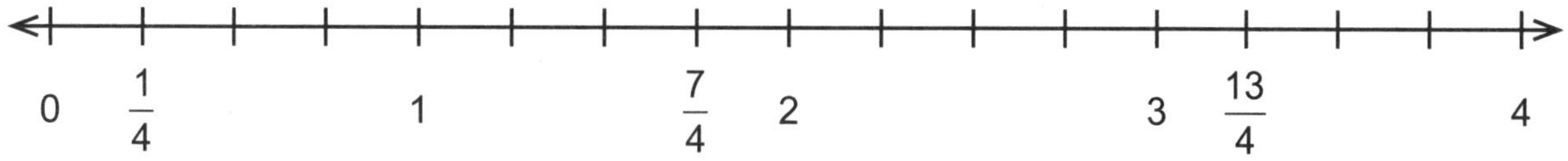

d)

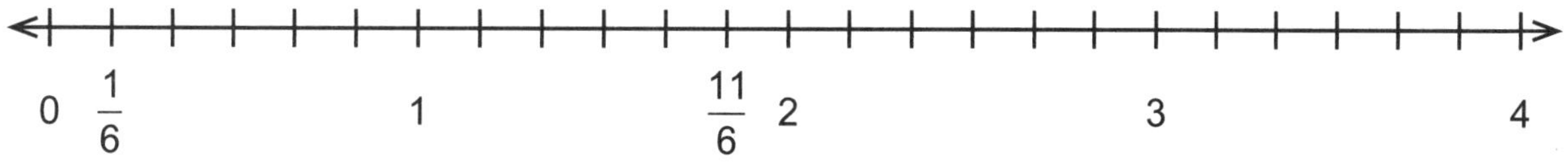

To divide $4 \div \frac{1}{3}$ using a number line, find the number of steps it takes to get to 4 when counting by $\frac{1}{3}$.

So $4 \div \frac{1}{3} = 12$

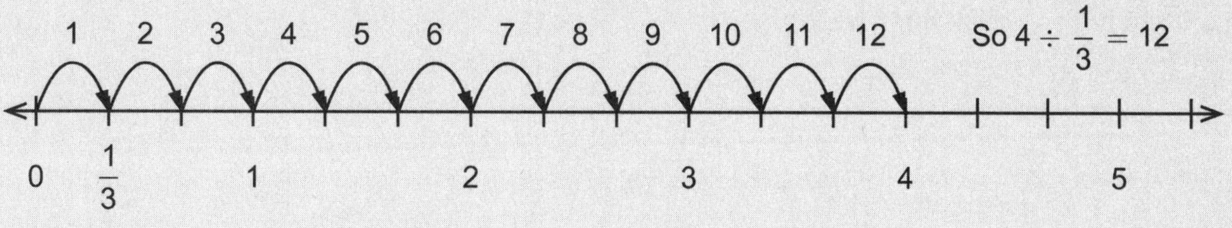

3. Use a number line from Question 2 to divide by the unit fraction.

a) $5 \div \frac{1}{2} =$ b) $3 \div \frac{1}{4} =$ c) $5 \div \frac{1}{3} =$ d) $3 \div \frac{1}{6} =$

e) $5 \div \frac{1}{3} =$ f) $7 \div \frac{1}{2} =$ g) $2 \div \frac{1}{6} =$ h) $4 \div \frac{1}{4} =$

There are 3 thirds in one whole. There are $4 \times 3 = 12$ thirds in 4 wholes.

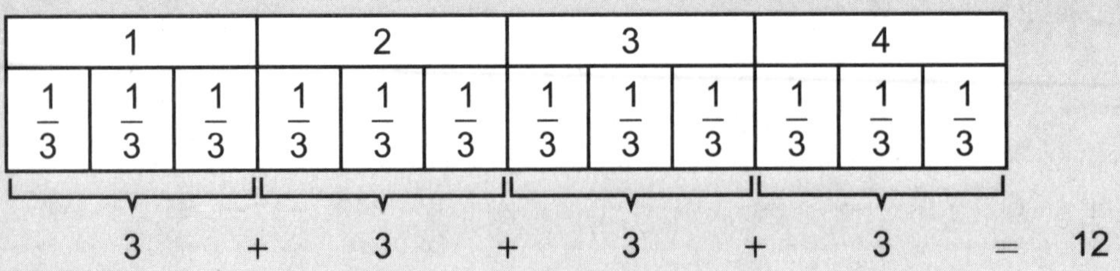

So $4 \div \frac{1}{3} = 12$

4. Use multiplication to divide by a fraction.

a) $4 \div \frac{1}{3}$

$= 4 \times 3$

$= 12$

b) $2 \div \frac{1}{3}$

c) $5 \div \frac{1}{4}$

d) $3 \div \frac{1}{6}$

To divide $4 \div \frac{2}{3}$, count the number of $\frac{2}{3}$ in 4. You can use $4 \div \frac{1}{3}$ to help.

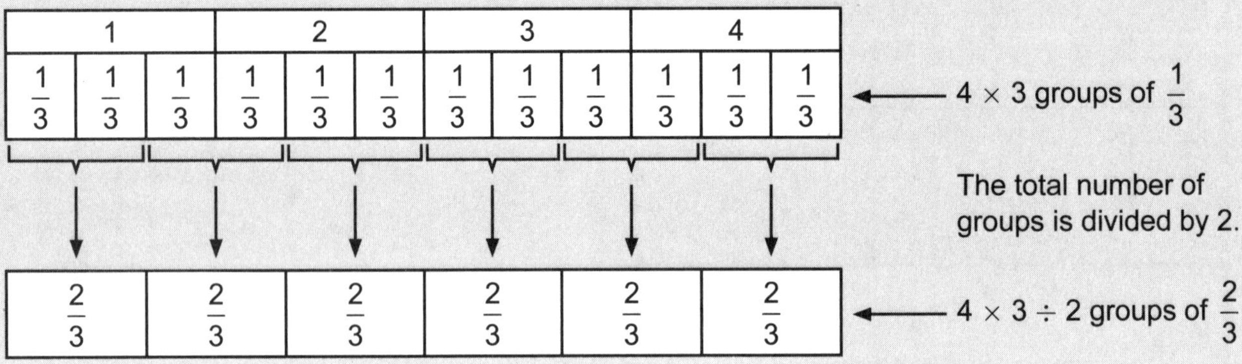

So $4 \div \frac{2}{3} = 4 \times 3 \div 2 = 6$

5. Calculate using multiplication and division.

a) $6 \div \frac{3}{4}$

$= 6 \times 4 \div 3$

$= 8$

b) $9 \div \frac{3}{5}$

c) $12 \div \frac{3}{8}$

d) $10 \div \frac{5}{6}$

e) $6 \div \frac{2}{3}$

f) $10 \div \frac{2}{5}$

g) $16 \div \frac{2}{3}$

h) $15 \div \frac{5}{8}$

REMINDER: You can write $5 \div 4$ as the fraction $\frac{5}{4}$.

6. Rewrite the statement using multiplication by a fraction.

a) $6 \div \frac{3}{4}$

$= 6 \times 4 \div 3$

$= 6 \times \frac{4}{3}$

b) $8 \div \frac{4}{5}$

c) $14 \div \frac{7}{8}$

d) $12 \div \frac{4}{7}$

To find the **reciprocal** of a fraction, switch the numerator and the denominator.

Example: The reciprocal of $\frac{3}{4}$ is $\frac{4}{3}$.

7. Rewrite the statement using multiplication by the reciprocal of the second number.

a) $10 \div \frac{5}{3}$

$= 10 \times \frac{3}{5}$

b) $12 \div \frac{6}{5}$

c) $32 \div \frac{8}{3}$

d) $28 \div \frac{7}{4}$

8. Rewrite the statement using multiplication. Reduce and then multiply to find the answer.

a) $14 \div \frac{7}{3}$

$= \frac{14 \div 7}{1} \times \frac{3}{7 \div 7}$

$= \frac{2}{1} \times \frac{3}{1}$

$= 6$

b) $20 \div \frac{4}{3}$

c) $48 \div \frac{6}{7}$

d) $27 \div \frac{9}{4}$

9. Divide using multiplication by the reciprocal.

a) $\frac{4}{5} \div \frac{8}{3}$

b) $\frac{10}{3} \div \frac{15}{7}$

c) $\frac{12}{5} \div \frac{9}{4}$

d) $\frac{15}{14} \div \frac{10}{21}$

10. In construction, a piece of wood that is called a two-by-four is actually less than 4 inches wide. Nina is building a deck using two-by-fours that are $\frac{7}{2}$ inches wide. How many two-by-fours will she need to place side by side to make a floor $\frac{254}{4}$ inches wide?

EE8-8 Mixed Numbers and Improper Fractions

A **mixed number** is made up of a whole number and a proper fraction.

Example: $2\frac{3}{4}$

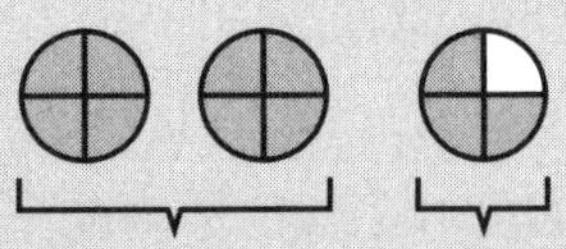

The total number of quarter pieces is $2 \times 4 + 3 = 11$. $2\frac{3}{4} = \frac{11}{4}$

$\frac{11}{4}$ is an **improper fraction** because the numerator is greater than the denominator.

1. Write the mixed number as an improper fraction.

a) $3\frac{1}{4} =$ b) $2\frac{3}{8} =$ c) $4\frac{5}{6} =$ d) $5\frac{1}{2} =$

To change $\frac{11}{4}$ into a mixed number, divide the numerator by the denominator.

$11 \div 4 = 2 \text{ R } 3$

$\frac{11}{4} = 2\frac{3}{4}$

2. Write the improper fraction as a mixed number.

a) $\frac{7}{3} =$ b) $\frac{29}{6} =$ c) $\frac{35}{8} =$ d) $\frac{47}{10} =$

Sometimes you need to regroup the fractional part. To regroup, change the improper fraction to a mixed number and then add the whole parts.

Example:

$5\frac{7}{4} = 5 + 1\frac{3}{4} = 6\frac{3}{4}$

3. Write the mixed number as a mixed number with a proper fraction.

a) $1\frac{5}{3}$ b) $2\frac{11}{8}$ c) $4\frac{11}{6}$ d) $12\frac{9}{5}$

To add mixed numbers, add the whole numbers and fractions separately. Write the answer as a mixed number with a whole number and a proper fraction.

Example:

$2\frac{3}{7} + 8\frac{6}{7} = 10\frac{9}{7} = 10 + 1\frac{2}{7} = 11\frac{2}{7}$

4. Add. Write your answer as a whole number and a proper fraction.

a) $1\frac{3}{5} + 8\frac{4}{5}$ b) $3\frac{5}{8} + 2\frac{6}{8}$ c) $4\frac{5}{7} + 2\frac{6}{7}$ d) $6\frac{5}{9} + 4\frac{8}{9}$

5. Add. You will need to find the LCD (lowest common denominator) of the fractions. Write the answer as a mixed number with a proper fraction.

a) $1\frac{2}{3}+2\frac{3}{4}$

$=1\frac{8}{12}+2\frac{9}{12}$

$=3\frac{17}{12}$

$=4\frac{5}{12}$

b) $4\frac{5}{6}+1\frac{3}{8}$

c) $3\frac{7}{14}+2\frac{5}{21}$

You can subtract mixed numbers by subtracting the whole numbers and the fractions separately.

Example:

$6\frac{5}{7}-2\frac{4}{7}=(6-2)+\left(\frac{5}{7}-\frac{4}{7}\right)=4+\frac{1}{7}=4\frac{1}{7}$

6. Subtract. Write your answer as a whole number and a proper fraction.

a) $8\frac{3}{5}-4\frac{2}{5}=4\frac{1}{5}$

b) $9\frac{5}{8}-2\frac{4}{8}=$

c) $7\frac{7}{9}-6\frac{5}{9}=$

To subtract $6\frac{2}{7}-3\frac{4}{7}$, you need to regroup because we can't subtract $\frac{4}{7}$ from $\frac{2}{7}$.

Step 1: Regroup the first mixed number. $6\frac{2}{7}=5+1\frac{2}{7}=5+\frac{9}{7}=5\frac{9}{7}$

Subtract 1 from 6 and add to $\frac{2}{7}$

Step 2: Subtract the whole numbers and fractions separately. $6\frac{2}{7}-3\frac{4}{7}=5\frac{9}{7}-3\frac{4}{7}=2\frac{5}{7}$

7. Subtract by regrouping the first mixed number.

a) $4\frac{3}{8}-2\frac{6}{8}$

$=3\frac{11}{8}-2\frac{6}{8}$

$=1\frac{5}{8}$

b) $7\frac{1}{5}-3\frac{3}{5}$

c) $4\frac{1}{6}-1\frac{5}{6}$

d) $5\frac{1}{4}-2\frac{3}{4}$

e) $2\frac{5}{8}-1\frac{7}{8}$

f) $1\frac{1}{3}-\frac{2}{3}$

8. Subtract. You will need to find the LCD of the fractions. You might also have to regroup.

a) $7\frac{5}{6} - 2\frac{1}{8}$ b) $5\frac{1}{4} - 2\frac{5}{6}$ c) $9\frac{3}{10} - 3\frac{7}{15}$ d) $10\frac{1}{8} - 2\frac{5}{12}$

9. Add or subtract. Write your answer as a mixed number in lowest terms.

a) $6\frac{1}{2} - 2\frac{5}{6}$ b) $2\frac{1}{10} + 4\frac{3}{15}$ c) $5\frac{1}{8} - 2\frac{3}{4}$ d) $2\frac{4}{9} + 6\frac{5}{12}$

$= 6\frac{3}{6} - 2\frac{5}{6}$

$= 5\frac{9}{6} - 2\frac{5}{6}$

$= 3\frac{4}{6}$

$= 3\frac{2}{3}$

To multiply mixed fractions: Example: $1\frac{3}{4} \times 2\frac{2}{3}$

Step 1: Change to improper fractions. $= \frac{7}{4} \times \frac{8}{3}$

Step 2: Reduce, and then multiply. $= \frac{7}{4 \div 4} \times \frac{8 \div 4}{3} = \frac{7}{1} \times \frac{2}{3} = \frac{14}{3} = 4\frac{2}{3}$

10. Multiply. Write your answer as a mixed number in lowest terms.

a) $4\frac{1}{2} \times 1\frac{4}{9}$ b) $2\frac{4}{5} \times 3\frac{3}{4}$ c) $2\frac{1}{2} \times 2\frac{1}{5}$ d) $3\frac{6}{7} \times 2\frac{1}{3}$

To divide mixed fractions: Example: $2\frac{1}{8} \div 1\frac{3}{4}$

Step 1: Change to improper fractions. $= \frac{17}{8} \div \frac{7}{4}$

Step 2: Multiply by the reciprocal of the second fraction. Reduce, and then multiply. $= \frac{17}{8 \div 4} \times \frac{4 \div 4}{7} = \frac{17}{2} \times \frac{1}{7} = \frac{17}{14} = 1\frac{3}{14}$

11. Divide. Write your answer as a mixed number in lowest terms.

a) $2\frac{5}{8} \div 2\frac{1}{3}$ b) $3\frac{3}{7} \div 2\frac{4}{5}$ c) $4\frac{4}{9} \div 2\frac{6}{7}$ d) $4\frac{7}{10} \div 2\frac{4}{5}$

EE8-9 Order of Operations

Mathematicians use a standard order of operations.

1. Do operations in brackets.
2. Do all multiplications and divisions, from left to right.
3. Do all additions and subtractions, from left to right.

1. Circle the operation you would do first.

a) $6 + (5 \times 2)$ b) $5 \times (8 - 4)$ c) $8 \times 7 - 3$

d) $4 \times 8 \div 3$ e) $9 - 3 + 6$ f) $(6 - 4) \times 9$

g) $12 - 3 - 8$ h) $36 \div 6 \div 3$ i) $42 \div (6 \div 2)$

2. Do the operations one at a time, in the standard order.

a) $6 + 5 \times (7 - 3)$

$= 6 + 5 \times 4$

$= 6 + 20$

$= 26$

b) $24 \div 3 + 7 \times 5$

c) $12 - 15 \div (7 - 2)$

d) $7 \times 2 \div (8 - 6)$

e) $24 - 12 \div (7 - 4)$

f) $(15 + 13) \div (1 + 2 \times 3)$

3. Find the value of the expression using the standard order of operations.

a) $8 + \frac{15}{5}$

$= 8 + 15 \div 5$

$= 8 + 3$

$= 11$

b) $12 - \frac{24}{6} + 5$

c) $\frac{28}{4} + 6 - \frac{35}{5}$

d) $\frac{42}{6} - \frac{10}{2}$

e) $5 \times \left(3 + \frac{8}{2}\right)$

f) $(5 + 4) \times \frac{10}{2}$

The expression $\frac{8+5\times 4}{6-2}$ means $\frac{(8+5\times 4)}{(6-2)}$. Calculate the numerator and denominator separately.

4. Write brackets around the numerator and denominator, then calculate.

a) $\frac{3+4\times 6}{11-2}$

$= \frac{(3+4\times 6)}{(11-2)}$

$= \frac{(3+24)}{9}$

$= \frac{27}{9}$

$= 3$

b) $\frac{27-15\div 5}{2+3\times 2}$

c) $\frac{15+12\div 4}{10-2\times 4}$

Calculations with fractions follow the same order of operations.

5. Calculate using the standard order of operations. Reduce your answer to lowest terms.

a) $\frac{2}{3}+\frac{5}{8}\times\frac{4}{3}$

$= \frac{2}{3}+\frac{5}{8\div 4}\times\frac{4\div 4}{3}$

$= \frac{2}{3}+\frac{5}{2}\times\frac{1}{3}$

$= \frac{2}{3}+\frac{5}{6}$

$= \frac{4}{6}+\frac{5}{6}$

$= \frac{9}{6}$

$= \frac{3}{2}$

b) $\left(\frac{3}{4}+\frac{1}{2}\right)\times\frac{6}{7}$

c) $\frac{3}{2}-\frac{1}{6}\div\frac{2}{9}$

d) $\left(\frac{3}{4}-\frac{1}{6}\right)\times\frac{6}{5}$

e) $\left(\frac{1}{3}\div\frac{1}{4}\right)\div\frac{1}{6}$

f) $\frac{1}{3}\div\left(\frac{1}{4}\div\frac{1}{6}\right)$

g) $\left(\frac{1}{2}+\frac{1}{3}\right)\div\frac{7}{12}$

h) $\frac{2}{3}\div\frac{5}{6}+\frac{1}{5}$

i) $\left(\frac{5}{8}-\frac{1}{4}\right)\div\frac{5}{8}$

EE8-10 Decimal Review

In a **decimal fraction**, the denominator is a power of 10.

10, 100, 1,000, and so on, are powers of 10.

Examples: $\frac{7}{10}$, $\frac{23}{100}$, and $\frac{247}{1{,}000}$ are decimal fractions.

1. Find the missing equivalent decimal fractions.

a) $\frac{7}{10} = \frac{\mathit{70}}{100}$

b) $\frac{35}{100} = \frac{\_\_\_}{1{,}000}$

c) $\frac{\_\_\_}{10} = \frac{900}{1{,}000}$

d) $\frac{3}{10} = \frac{\mathit{30}}{100} = \frac{\mathit{300}}{1{,}000}$

e) $\frac{\_\_\_}{10} = \frac{90}{100} = \frac{\_\_\_}{1{,}000}$

f) $\frac{\_\_\_}{10} = \frac{\_\_\_}{100} = \frac{500}{1{,}000}$

Decimals are a way to record place values based on decimal fractions.

2 7 5 → 2 hundreds + 7 tens + 5 ones

0 . 2 7 5 (decimal point) → 2 tenths + 7 hundredths + 5 thousandths

$\frac{2}{10} + \frac{7}{100} + \frac{5}{1{,}000}$

2. Write the number in expanded form.

a) $2.35 = \underline{\mathit{2}} + \frac{\mathit{3}}{10} + \frac{\mathit{5}}{100}$

b) $3.49 = \_\_\_ + \frac{\_\_\_}{10} + \frac{\_\_\_}{100}$

c) $4.178 = \_\_\_ + \frac{\_\_\_}{10} + \frac{\_\_\_}{100} + \frac{\_\_\_}{1{,}000}$

d) $7.490 = \_\_\_ + \frac{\_\_\_}{10} + \frac{\_\_\_}{100} + \frac{\_\_\_}{1{,}000}$

e) $9.073 = \_\_\_ + \frac{\_\_\_}{10} + \frac{\_\_\_}{100} + \frac{\_\_\_}{1{,}000}$

f) $6.102 = \_\_\_ + \frac{\_\_\_}{10} + \frac{\_\_\_}{100} + \frac{\_\_\_}{1{,}000}$

3. Write the expanded form as a decimal.

a) $2 + \frac{3}{10} + \frac{9}{100} + \frac{1}{1{,}000} = \underline{\mathit{2.391}}$

b) $7 + \frac{2}{10} + \frac{3}{100} + \frac{4}{1{,}000} = \_\_\_$

c) $9 + \frac{3}{10} + \frac{0}{100} + \frac{5}{1{,}000} = \_\_\_$

d) $4 + \frac{0}{10} + \frac{6}{100} + \frac{8}{1{,}000} = \_\_\_$

Bonus ▶

e) $4 + \frac{1}{10} + \frac{6}{1{,}000} = \_\_\_$

f) $2 + \frac{3}{100} + \frac{6}{1{,}000} = \_\_\_$

You can write 0.27 as a single fraction: $0.27 = \frac{2}{10} + \frac{7}{100} = \frac{20}{100} + \frac{7}{100} = \frac{27}{100}$

You can write 0.135 as a single fraction: $0.135 = \frac{1}{10} + \frac{3}{100} + \frac{5}{1{,}000} = \frac{100}{1{,}000} + \frac{30}{1{,}000} + \frac{5}{1{,}000} = \frac{135}{1{,}000}$

4. Write the decimal as a single fraction.

a) $0.37 = \frac{37}{100}$ b) $0.28 = \frac{\quad}{100}$ c) $0.43 =$ ____ d) $0.07 =$ ____

e) $0.219 = \frac{219}{1{,}000}$ f) $0.614 = \frac{\quad}{1{,}000}$ g) $0.438 =$ ____ h) $0.029 =$ ____

Multiplying by 10 moves the decimal point 1 place to the right. $0.37 \times 10 = \frac{37}{100} \times 10 = \frac{370}{100} = 3 + \frac{70}{100} = 3.70$

0	0.	3	7	0	0

5. Multiply by 10 by moving the decimal point.

a) 3.5×10

0	0	3.	5	0	0

= 35.0

b) 0.47×10

0	0.	4	7	0	0

= ________

c) 38.0×10

0	3	8.	0	0	0

= ________

Multiplying by 100 moves the decimal point 2 places to the right. $0.028 \times 100 = \frac{28}{1{,}000} \times 100 = \frac{2{,}800}{1{,}000} = 2 + \frac{800}{1{,}000} = 2.800$

6. Multiply by 100 by moving the decimal point.

a) 2.9×100

0	0	2.	9	0	0

= 290.0

b) 0.36×100

0	0.	3	6	0	0

= ________

c) 52.4×100

0	5	2.	4	0	0

= ________

7. Multiply.

a) $9.28 \times 10 =$ ________ b) $0.063 \times 100 =$ ________ c) $2.367 \times 10 =$ ________

d) $0.0045 \times 100 =$ ________ e) $0.4 \times 10 =$ ________ f) $6.1 \times 100 =$ ________

g) $0.65 \times 10 =$ ________ h) $0.0043 \times 100 =$ ________ i) $8.34 \times 100 =$ ________

Dividing by 10 moves the decimal point 1 place to the left.

$$0.37 \div 10 = \frac{37}{100} \div 10 = \frac{37}{1{,}000} = 0.037$$

8. Divide by 10 by moving the decimal point.

a) 2.8 ÷ 10

0	0	2.	8	0	0

= *0.28*

b) 0.47 ÷ 10

0	0	0.	4	7	0

= ______

c) 75 ÷ 10

0	7	5.	0	0	0

= ______

Dividing by 100 moves the decimal point 2 places to the left.

$$2.7 \div 100 = \frac{27}{10} \div 100 = \frac{27}{1{,}000} = 0.027$$

9. Divide by 100 by moving the decimal point.

a) 9.6 ÷ 100

0	0	9.	6	0	0

= *0.096*

b) 0.67 ÷ 100

0	0	0.	6	7	0

= ______

c) 81.3 ÷ 100

0	8	1.	3	0	0

= ______

10. Divide.

a) 5.18 ÷ 10 = ______   b) 0.63 ÷ 100 = ______   c) 2.36 ÷ 10 = ______

d) 0.048 ÷ 100 = ______   e) 0.3 ÷ 10 = ______   f) 7.4 ÷ 100 = ______

11. Use the grid to calculate.

a)	7.635 × 100	0	0	7.	6	3	5	0	0	*763.5*
b)	0.354 ÷ 10	0	0	0.	3	5	4	0	0	*0.0354*
c)	0.89 × 10	0	0	0	0	0	0	0	0	
d)	23.76 ÷ 100	0	0	0	0	0	0	0	0	
e)	0.0034 × 100	0	0	0	0	0	0	0	0	
f)	0.56 ÷ 100	0	0	0	0	0	0	0	0	
g)	9.23 × 100	0	0	0	0	0	0	0	0	
h)	0.12 × 1,000	0	0	0	0	0	0	0	0	
i)	7.56 ÷ 1,000	0	0	0	0	0	0	0	0	

EE8-11 Operations With Decimals

Decimals can be written as decimal fractions. The number of decimal digits is the same as the number of zeros in the denominator.

Examples: $0.3 = \frac{3}{10}$ $\quad 0.37 = \frac{37}{100}$ $\quad 0.371 = \frac{371}{1{,}000}$

1. Write as a decimal fraction.

a) $0.35 =$ b) $0.7 =$ c) $0.275 =$ d) $0.0249 =$

We can add or subtract decimals as decimal fractions. $0.27 + 0.34 = \frac{27}{100} + \frac{34}{100} = \frac{61}{100} = 0.61$

2. Add or subtract as decimal fractions.

a) $0.5 + 0.3$ b) $0.48 - 0.23$ c) $0.416 - 0.135$ d) $0.01 + 0.02$

To add or subtract decimals without using fractions:

Step 1: Line up the decimal points. Write zeros to the right of the last digit so all numbers will have the same number of decimal digits.

Step 2: Add or subtract the decimals as if they were whole numbers. Place the decimal point in the answer under the other decimal points.

Example: $1.45 - 0.924$

			4		
	1.	~~4~~	~~5~~	0	← extra zero
−	0.	9	2	4	
	0.	5	2	6	

3. Add or subtract.

a) $0.145 + 1.237$ b) $2.35 - 1.18$ c) $13.45 - 9.237$ d) $5.06 + 13.573$

4. Jane spent \$8.45 on lunch and paid with a \$20 bill. How much is her change?

To multiply numbers with decimals, multiply as if they were whole numbers, and then place the decimal point so that there will be the same number of decimal digits.

Example: $1.34 \times 2 = \frac{134}{100} \times 2 = \frac{268}{100} = 2.68$

5. Multiply.

a) 2.34×3

	1	1	
	2.	3	4
×			3
	7.	0	2

b) 4.125×2

c) 12.37×3

d) 8.45×9

To multiply a decimal by a decimal:

Example: $1.3 \times 0.12 = \frac{13}{10} \times \frac{12}{100} = \frac{156}{1{,}000} = 0.156$

Step 1: Multiply the decimals as if they were whole numbers. — $13 \times 12 = 156$

Step 2: Count the digits after the decimal points, then find the total number of decimal digits. — 1.3 has **1** digit after the decimal point. 0.12 has **2** digits after the decimal point. **1** + **2** = **3**

Step 3: Shift the decimal point left that many places. — 0 1 5 6 . So $1.3 \times 0.12 = 0.156$

6. Multiply.

a) 2.34×1.2

		2	. 3	4
×			1	. 2
		4	6	8
+	2	3	4	0
	2	. 8	0	8

b) 32.1×2.4

c) 1.345×2.9

d) 9.84×0.1

e) 9.84×0.01

f) 42.35×21.02

7. To convert temperatures in degrees Celsius to degrees Fahrenheit, multiply the Celsius temperature by 1.8 and add 32. Convert 23.5 degrees Celsius into degrees Fahrenheit.

8. The state tax in New York State is found by multiplying the retail price by 0.075. Find the tax on a sofa with a price tag of $240.

REMINDER: To multiply a decimal by 10, move the decimal point 1 place to the right.
To multiply a decimal by 100, move the decimal point 2 places to the right.

Examples: $2.35 \times 10 = 23.5$ $3.146 \times 100 = 314.6$ $23 \times 10 = 23.0 \times 10 = 230.0$

9. Multiply mentally.

a) 54.67×10 ____

b) 0.345×100 ____

c) $2.76 \times 1{,}000$ ____

d) 0.002×100 ____

e) $0.034 \times 1{,}000$ ____

f) 29.38×10 ____

g) 0.0098×100 ____

h) $4.82 \times 1{,}000$ ____

You can write division as a fraction. You can also multiply the numerator and the denominator by the same number to make an equivalent fraction.

To divide by a decimal, multiply both the dividend and the divisor by the power of 10 that makes the divisor a **whole number**.

Example:

$0.23\overline{)0.828} \rightarrow \dfrac{0.828 \times 100}{0.23 \times 100}$

$0.23\overline{)0.828} \rightarrow 23\overline{)82.8}$

10. Write an equivalent division question so that the divisor is a whole number.

a) $0.3\overline{)0.243}$ b) $0.12\overline{)21.6}$ c) $0.08\overline{)0.0984}$ d) $4.2\overline{)882}$

11. Write an equivalent division question so that the divisor is a whole number, and then divide. Place the decimal point in the quotient directly above the new decimal point in the dividend.

a) $0.5\overline{)1.15}$ b) $0.07\overline{)0.168}$ c) $0.23\overline{)9.43}$ d) $1.8\overline{)6.12}$

$5\overline{)11.5}$

$5\overline{)1\ 1\ .\ 5}$

To change a fraction into a decimal:

Step 1: Write the numerator as a decimal.

Step 2: Divide the numerator by the denominator.

Step 3: Keep dividing until there is no remainder.

Example: $\dfrac{3}{4}$

$= 3.000 \div 4$

$$\begin{array}{r} 0.75 \\ 4\overline{)3.000} \\ -\underline{28\downarrow} \\ 20 \\ -\underline{20} \\ 0 \end{array}$$

So $\dfrac{3}{4} = 0.75$

12. Write the fraction as a decimal.

a) $\dfrac{1}{4}$ b) $\dfrac{3}{8}$ c) $\dfrac{17}{20}$ d) $\dfrac{18}{25}$

13. If 0.75 grams of gold costs $80.31, what is the cost of one gram of gold?

14. In baseball, a batting average is calculated by dividing the number of hits by the number of times at bat. Joey Slugger had 22 hits in 80 at bats. What is his batting average?

EE8-12 Rounding Decimals

To write a number in **expanded form**, multiply each digit by its place value.

Hundreds	Tens	Ones	Tenths	Hundredths	Thousandths
3	2	5	7	9	4

$325.794 = (3 \times 100) + (2 \times 10) + (5 \times 1) + \left(7 \times \frac{1}{10}\right) + \left(9 \times \frac{1}{100}\right) + \left(4 \times \frac{1}{1{,}000}\right)$

1. Write in expanded form.

a) 34.6 = ______________________

b) 127.89 = ______________________

c) 78.408 = ______________________

2. Write in decimal form.

a) $(4 \times 10) + (7 \times 1) + \left(3 \times \frac{1}{10}\right) + \left(8 \times \frac{1}{100}\right) =$ __________

b) $(2 \times 100) + (0 \times 10) + (8 \times 1) + \left(2 \times \frac{1}{10}\right) + \left(7 \times \frac{1}{100}\right) + \left(3 \times \frac{1}{1{,}000}\right) =$ __________

c) $(6 \times 1{,}000) + (3 \times 10) + (2 \times 1) + \left(3 \times \frac{1}{10}\right) + \left(2 \times \frac{1}{100}\right) =$ __________

3. Write the name of the place value to the right.

a) tenths *hundredths*

b) hundreds __________

c) thousands __________

d) hundredths __________

To round to a place value, you need to decide whether to round up or round down.

Step 1: Underline the digit with the place value. Point to the digit on the right.

Step 2: If the digit is less than 5, round down. If the digit is 5 or greater, round up.

Examples: Round to the nearest tenth.

4.<u>6</u>98 (arrow at 9) — **round up (ru)** (circled) / round down (rd)

8.<u>3</u>27 (arrow at 2) — round up (ru) / **round down (rd)** (circled)

4. Underline the place value you need to round to. Then circle whether you would round up or down.

a) tenths

2.<u>4</u>92 (arrow at 9) — **ru** (circled) / rd

b) hundredths

4.7<u>3</u>1 (arrow at 1) — ru / rd

c) thousandths

5.6728 — ru / rd

d) hundredths

3.806 — ru / rd

e) thousandths

1.3421 — ru / rd

f) tenths

7.426 — ru / rd

When you know whether to round up or down to the underlined digit …
- round up by adding 1 to the digit.
- round down by keeping the digit the same.

Remove the decimal digits to the right of the rounded digit.

7 .	4	2	6
7 .	4		

round up (ru)
round down (rd) (circled)

5. Round to the given place value.

a) tenths

2 .	4	3	7
2 .	*4*		

ru
rd (circled)

b) hundredths

3 .	5	6	8
3 .	*5*	*7*	

ru (circled)
rd

c) thousandths

9 .	1	2	4	8
.				

ru
rd

Sometimes in rounding, you have to regroup. Example: Round 2.964 to the nearest tenth.

Step 1: Round up the digit 9 to 10.

2 .	9	6	4
.	*10*		

Step 2: Regroup 10 tenths as 1 ones and add it to the 2 ones.

2 .	9	6	4
3 .	*0*		

6. Round to the given digit. You will need to regroup.

a) hundredth

3 .	8	9	6
		10	
3 .	*9*		

b) tenth

4 .	9	6	8
.	*10*		

c) thousandth

1 .	4	7	9	6
.				

Sometimes when calculating costs, you get fractions of pennies.
We usually round to the nearest penny or **one hundredth** of a dollar.

dimes, pennies
$873.2645
fractions of pennies

7. Round to the nearest penny.

a) $57.348 *$57.35*
b) $65.743 ____________
c) $ 1.745 ____________
d) $9.139 ____________
e) $36.994 ____________
f) $34.996 ____________

8. The state tax in Colorado is found by multiplying the retail price by 0.029.

a) A television set has a retail price of $908.55. Calculate the sales tax to the nearest penny.

b) Calculate the combined retail price and state tax.

EE8-13 Integers

Integers include positive whole numbers, negative whole numbers, and zero.

An integer is any of the numbers: ..., −4, −3, −2, −1, 0, +1, +2, +3, +4, ...

You can represent integers on a number line. Positive numbers do not need to have the + sign

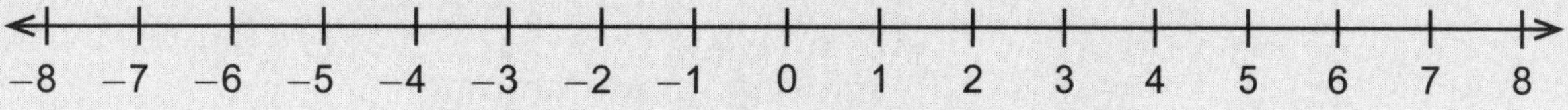

1. Label the integers on the number line with their letters.

U. −5 **E.** 3 **R.** 4 **N.** −7 **M.** −2 **B.** −1 **S.** +6

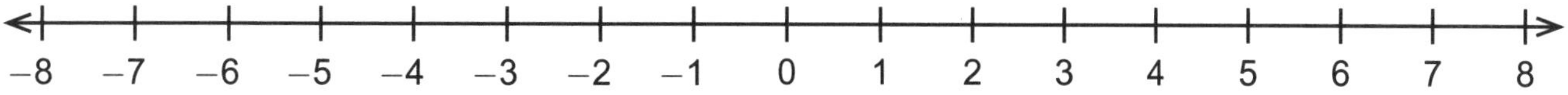

A number line shows how the numbers compare.

2 is **greater** than −3; 2 is farther to the **right** on the number line. We write 2 > −3.

−5 is **less** than −1; −5 is farther to the **left** on the number line. We write −5 < −1.

2. Circle the larger integer.

a) (5), −3 b) −2, 4 c) −3, −7 d) −8, 0

3. a) Circle the integers −5, 3, −7, 4, 0, and −1 on the number line.

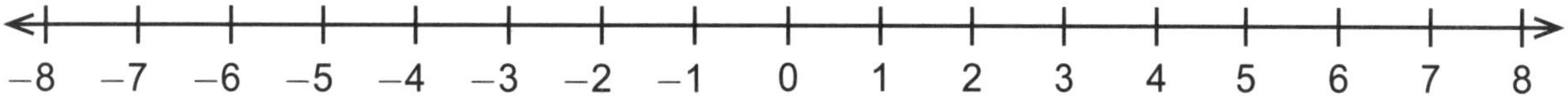

b) Write the integers in order from least to greatest. _____ < _____ < _____ < _____ < _____ < _____

c) Write the integers in order from greatest to least. _____ > _____ > _____ > _____ > _____ > _____

4. Write the integers −15, 23, 0, −8, −17, 14, and −1 from least to greatest.

______ < ______ < ______ < ______ < ______ < ______ < ______

Integers are used in many everyday situations to describe numbers that are compared to zero.

Examples: −30°C is 30 degrees below the temperature at which water freezes (0°C).

+30,000 ft is 30,000 ft above sea level (0 ft).

5. Write an integer for the situation.

a) A gain in weight of 10 lb. ______

b) A decrease of $235 in a bank account. ______

c) A golf score that is 3 strokes below par. ______

d) A gain in the stock market of 250 points. ______

You can use ⊕ to represent (+1) and ⊖ to represent (−1).
Examples: ⊕⊕⊕ represents (+3). ⊖⊖ represents (−2).

6. Draw a diagram to represent the integer.

a) (−3) b) (+2) c) (−4) d) (+5)

A gain of \$1 (+1) followed by a loss of \$1 (−1) is the same as no gain or loss. We write (+1) + (−1) = 0.
You can represent (+1) + (−1) with a diagram: ⊕⊖

To add (+3) + (−5):

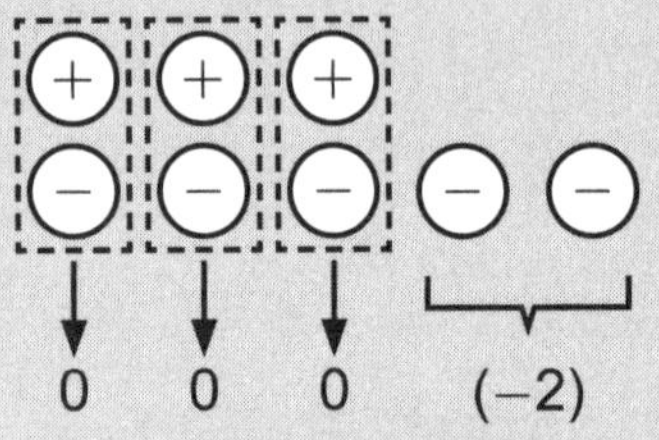

(+3) + (−5) = (−2)

To add (+5) + (−2):

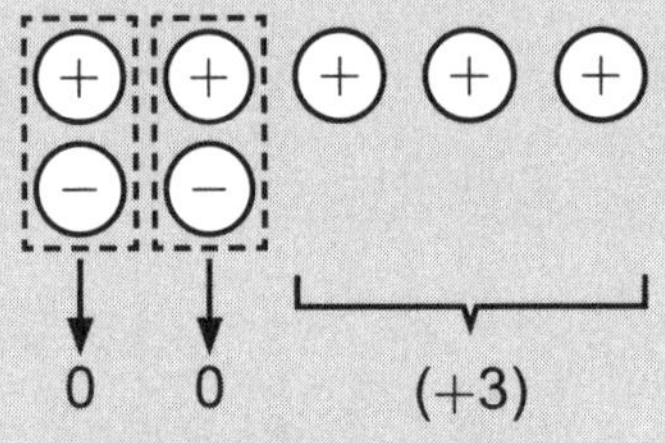

(+5) + (−2) = (+3)

7. Use a diagram to add the integers.

a) (+4) + (−2) b) (+3) + (−7) c) (+4) + (+2) d) (−4) + (−2)

To add integers without a diagram, think of a contest between the positives and negatives.
Who won the contest: the positives or the negatives? By how many did they win?

Question	Who Won?	By How Many?	Answer
(+3) + (−5)	negatives	2	(+3) + (−5) = (−2)
(+7) + (−4)	positives	3	(+7) + (−4) = (+3)
(−3) + (−2)	negatives	5	(−3) + (−2) = (−5)

8. Add without using a diagram.

a) (+7) + (−2) = b) (−8) + (+5) = c) (−6) + (−3) = d) (−5) + (−4) =

e) (+5) + (+4) = f) (−3) + (−6) = g) (−3) + (−3) = h) (+6) + (−8) =

9. Add without using a diagram.

a) (+5) + (−2) + (−4) = b) (−3) + (−2) + (+6) =

c) (+8) + (−3) + (+4) = d) (−3) + (−5) + (+6) =

e) (−1) + (−4) + (−3) = f) (+3) + (−5) + (+2) =

To show how we subtract integers, we remove the integers from the diagram. If necessary, we can add zeros in the form of ⊕ ⊖ so there will be enough positives or negatives to remove.

(+5) − (+2) = (+3)

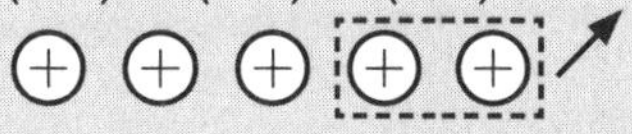

(+3) − (−2) = (+5)

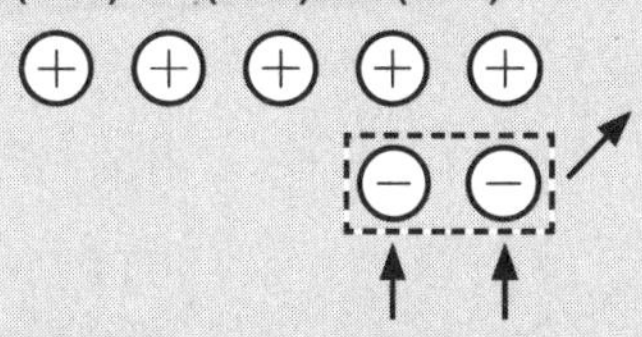

Add 2 groups of zero so we can take away 2 negatives

(−3) − (+3) = (−6)

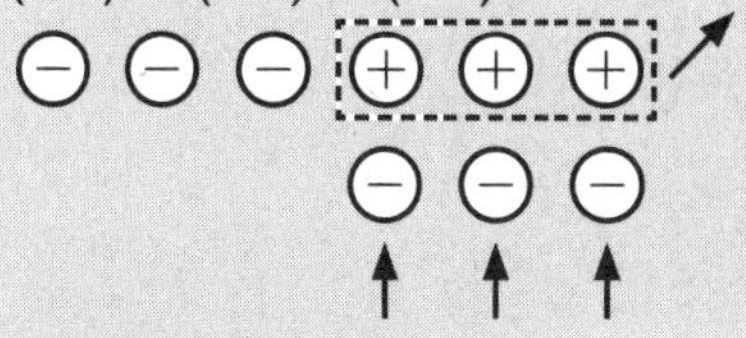

Add 3 groups of zero so we can take away 3 positives

10. Use a diagram to subtract the integers.

a) (+4) − (+5) b) (−2) − (+3) c) (−3) − (−2) d) (−3) − (−4)

Opposite integers are the same distance from 0, but on opposite sides of 0 on the number line.

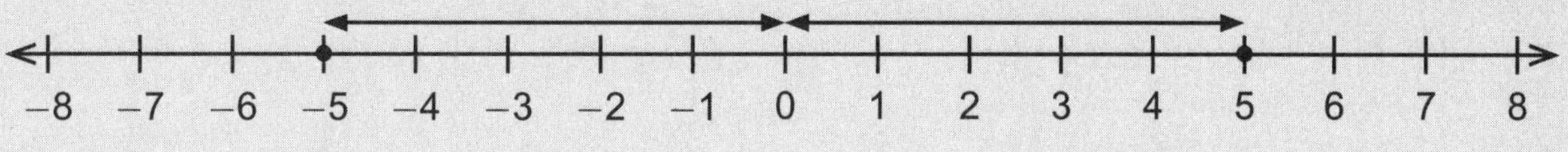

Example: −5 and 5 are both 5 units from 0. They are opposite integers.

11. Find the opposite integer.

a) (−3) ______ b) (+4) ______ c) (+8) ______ d) (−12) ______

Subtracting an integer is the same as adding its opposite integer.

(+3) − (−2) = (+3) + (+2)

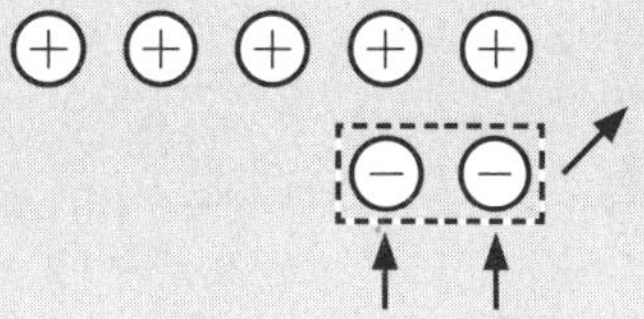

Adding 2 zeros in the form of (+1) + (−1) twice and then taking away the 2 negatives is the same as adding (+2).

(−3) − (+3) = (−3) + (−3)

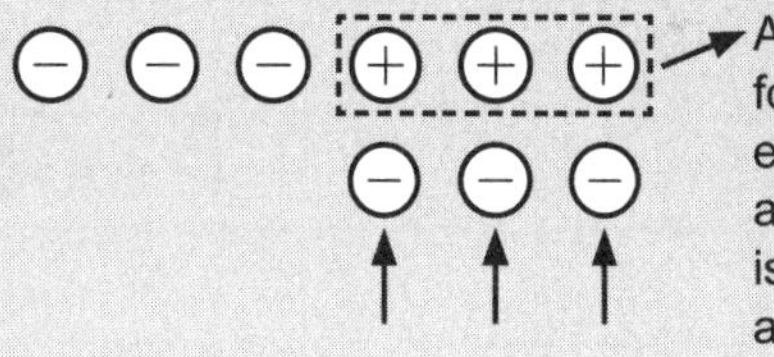

Adding 3 zeros in the form of (+1) + (−1) each and then taking away the 3 positives is the same as adding (−3).

12. Subtract by adding the opposite integer.

a) (+3) − (−4)
= (+3) + (+4)
= (+7)

b) (−4) − (+2)
= (−4) + (−2)
= (−6)

c) (+7) − (−3)

d) (−3) − (−5)

e) (+2) − (+8) f) (−6) − (−2) g) (−1) − (+5) h) (−4) − (−7)

13. After the bank accidentally charged Rachel $5 in service fees, her account balance was $45. The bank corrected the mistake and returned the money to Rachel's account. Use integer subtraction to show that her balance is now $50.

EE8-14 Operations with Integers

Multiplication is a short form for addition. Multiplication is also commutative.

$(+3) \times (-2)$

$= (-2) + (-2) + (-2)$ ← add (-2) three times

$= (-6)$

$(-2) \times (+3)$

$= (+3) \times (-2)$ ← commutative property

$= (-6)$

To multiply integers with opposite signs: $(+) \times (-) = (-)$, $(-) \times (+) = (-)$

So $(+3) \times (-2) = (-6)$ and $(-2) \times (+3) = (-6)$. Both are the opposite of $3 \times 2 = 6$.

1. Multiply.

a) $(+3) \times (-4)$ = ______

b) $(-5) \times (+6)$ = ______

c) $(-8) \times (+7)$ = ______

d) $(+2) \times (-9)$ = ______

e) $(+2) \times (-10)$ = ______

f) $(-9) \times (+9)$ = ______

g) $(-8) \times (+8)$ = ______

h) $(-2) \times 0$ = ______

2. a) Continue the patterns to complete the charts.

i)

	First Integer	Second Integer	Product	
	(+4)	(−3)	(−12)	
−1	(+3)	(−3)	(−9)	+3
−1	(+2)	(−3)		+3
−1	(+1)	(−3)		+3
−1		(−3)		+3
−1		(−3)		+3
−1		(−3)		+3
◯		(−3)		◯
◯		(−3)		◯

ii)

	First Integer	Second Integer	Product	
	(+4)	(−2)	(−8)	
−1	(+3)	(−2)	(−6)	+2
−1	(+2)	(−2)		+2
−1	(+1)	(−2)		+2
−1		(−2)		+2
−1		(−2)		+2
−1		(−2)		+2
◯		(−2)		◯
◯		(−2)		◯

b) What is the sign of the product when one integer is negative and the other integer is positive? ______________________________

c) What is the sign of the product when the first and second integers are both negative?

____

A negative integer multiplied by a negative integer is a positive integer. Example: $(-3) \times (-4) = (+12)$

3. Multiply.

a) $(-3) \times (-5)$ $= \_\_\_\_\_$

b) $(-5) \times (-2)$ $= \_\_\_\_\_$

c) $(-2) \times (-7)$ $= \_\_\_\_\_$

The fact family for $3 \times 4 = 12$ includes $4 \times 3 = 12$, $12 \div 4 = 3$, and $12 \div 3 = 4$.

4. Write the other members of the fact family.

a) $(+5) \times (-2) = (-10)$

$(-2) \times (+5) = (-10)$

$(-10) \div (+5) = (-2)$

$(-10) \div (-2) = (+5)$

b) $(-7) \times (+3) = (-21)$

____

____

____

c) $(-4) \times (-5) = (+20)$

____

____

____

5. Use your answers from Question 4 to fill in the blank.

a) When a negative integer is divided by a positive integer, the answer is __________.

b) When a positive integer is divided by a negative integer, the answer is __________.

c) When a negative integer is divided by a negative integer, the answer is __________.

To multiply or divide integers:

- if the signs are the same, the answer is positive. $(+)(+) = (+)$ $(-)(-) = (+)$
- if the signs are different, the answer is negative. $(+)(-) = (-)$ $(-)(+) = (-)$

6. Multiply or divide.

a) $(-3) \times (+4)$ $= \_\_\_\_\_$

b) $(+5) \times (-3)$ $= \_\_\_\_\_$

c) $(-8) \times (-6)$ $= \_\_\_\_\_$

d) $(+3) \times (+7)$ $= \_\_\_\_\_$

e) $(-24) \div (-6)$ $= \_\_\_\_\_$

f) $(-9) \div (+9)$ $= \_\_\_\_\_$

g) $(+27) \div (-3)$ $= \_\_\_\_\_$

h) $(+5) \div (-5)$ $= \_\_\_\_\_$

i) $0 \times (+5)$ $= \_\_\_\_\_$

j) $0 \times (-5)$ $= \_\_\_\_\_$

k) $0 \div (+7)$ $= \_\_\_\_\_$

l) $0 \div (-7)$ $= \_\_\_\_\_$

To make expressions easier to read, you should ...

- write positive numbers without brackets or signs. $(+3) = 3$
- rewrite subtracting an integer as adding the opposite integer. $3 - 5 = 3 + (-5)$
- use brackets around negative integers if two signs are written together. $3 + -5 = 3 + (-5)$

7. Rewrite the expression to use only addition.

a) $4 - 6$

$= 4 + (-6)$

b) $-3 - 2$

c) $4 - 7$

d) $-7 - (-2)$

e) $4 - 5 + 3 - 6$

f) $7 + 9 - 4 - 2$

g) $-3 - 4 + 6 - 2$

h) $-2 - 3 - 4$

8. Rewrite the expression to use only addition, and then calculate.

a) $5 - 8$

$= 5 + (-8)$

$= -3$

b) $-3 - 4$

c) $6 - (-8)$

d) $-2 - (-5)$

e) $6 - 8 - 3$

f) $-2 + 4 - 7$

g) $-2 - 6 - 7$

h) $6 - 4 + 3$

9. Calculate by adding the positive numbers and the negative numbers separately.

a) $3 - 6 - 4 + 8$

$= 3 + 8 + (-6) + (-4)$

$= 11 + (-10)$

$= 1$

b) $-2 + 6 - 8 + 9$

c) $4 - 6 + 5 - 3 - 8 + 9$

d) $-6 + 5 - 3 - 2 + 7$

10. Find the value of the expression. Remember to follow the correct order of operations.

a) $3 - 5 \times (-2)$

$= 3 + (-5)(-2)$

$= 3 + 10$

$= 13$

b) $-10 + 2 \times 3 \times (-4)$

c) $-24 \div (-8) + (-2) \times (-3)$

d) $14 - 21 \div (-3)$

e) $(-5 + 2) \times (-3 - 4)$

f) $-5 \times 2 - 12 \div (-4)$

11. Liquid nitrogen freezes at $-346°F$. A beaker containing liquid nitrogen at a temperature of $-334°F$ is being cooled at the rate of 2°F per minute. Will it be frozen after 5 minutes?

____

____

REMINDER: You can write a fraction as a division. Example: $\frac{6}{2} = 6 \div 2$

12. a) Rewrite the fraction as a division statement and calculate the answer.

i) $\frac{-6}{2}$

$= (-6) \div 2$

$= (-3)$

ii) $\frac{6}{-2}$

iii) $-\left(\frac{6}{2}\right)$

iv) $\frac{-6}{-2}$

b) What do you notice about your answers to i) to iii), above? Is your answer to part iv) the same?

____

When a fraction has a single negative sign, you can place the sign in the numerator, in the denominator, or outside the fraction.

Example: $\frac{-10}{2} = \frac{10}{-2} = -\frac{10}{2} = -5$

13. Calculate.

a) $\frac{5}{7} + \frac{3}{-7}$

$= \frac{5}{7} + \frac{-3}{7}$

$= \frac{2}{7}$

b) $\frac{-3}{5} + \frac{1}{-5}$

c) $-\frac{1}{8} + \frac{7}{8}$

d) $\frac{1}{4} - \frac{1}{-4}$

14. Find a common denominator and then calculate.

a) $\frac{5}{6} + \frac{1}{-8}$

$= \frac{5}{6} + \frac{-1}{8}$

$= \frac{20}{24} + \frac{-3}{24}$

$= \frac{17}{24}$

b) $\frac{-3}{4} + \frac{5}{-6}$

c) $\frac{7}{-9} - \frac{1}{-6}$

d) $\frac{-7}{10} - \frac{4}{-15}$

EE8-15 Powers Review

A **power** is a short form for repeated **multiplication**.

Example: $3^4 = 3 \times 3 \times 3 \times 3$

The power 3^4 means multiply 3 four times.

The exponent tells you how many times to multiply the base.

base → 3^4 ← exponent

power

1. Write the base and the exponent for the power.

a) 2^5 base = 2 exponent = 5

b) 4^3 base = ______ exponent = ______

c) 7^2 base = ______ exponent = ______

2. Write the power as a product.

a) $2^4 = 2 \times 2 \times 2 \times 2$

b) $8^3 =$

c) $10^4 =$

d) $7^2 =$

e) $10^3 =$

f) $0^2 =$

3. Write the product as a power.

a) $5 \times 5 \times 5 \times 5 = 5^4$

b) $9 \times 9 \times 9 =$

c) $10 \times 10 =$

d) $0 \times 0 \times 0 =$

e) $(-1) \times (-1) \times (-1) =$

f) $2 \times 2 \times 2 \times 2 \times 2 \times 2 =$

4. Evaluate the power.

a) 2^3

$= 2 \times 2 \times 2$

$= 8$

b) 3^2

c) 6^3

d) $(-2)^3$

e) 0^4

f) $\left(\frac{1}{2}\right)^3$

g) 10^2

h) 10^3

Bonus ▶ 10^6

5. a) Evaluate the power.

i) $1^3 =$ ______

ii) $1^5 =$ ______

iii) $1^{10} =$ ______

Bonus ▶ $1^{75} =$ ______

b) Predict the value of any power with the base 1. ______

6. a) Evaluate the power.

i) $8^1 =$ ______ ii) $3^1 =$ ______ iii) $9^1 =$ ______ **Bonus ▶** $235^1 =$ ______

b) Predict the value of a power with any base to the exponent 1. ______________________

7. Write the number as a power.

a) $8 =$ *8^1* b) $5 =$ ______ c) $(-3) =$ ______ d) $\left(\frac{1}{2}\right) =$ ______

> Remember the order of operations with powers: evaluate the power before multiplying or dividing.
>
> Example: $3 \times 2^4 = 3 \times (2 \times 2 \times 2 \times 2)$
> $= 3 \times 16$
> $= 48$

8. Evaluate the power, then multiply.

a) 2×5^2
$= 2 \times 25$
$= 50$

b) 3×6^2

c) 4×10^3

d) 2.8×10^2

9. Evaluate the expression. Use the standard order of operations.

a) $3^2 + 4^2$
$= 9 + 16$
$= 25$

b) $17 - 2^3$

c) $2^4 \times 3^2$

d) $10^4 \div 10^3$

e) $3 + 5^2$

f) $(3 + 5)^2$

g) $\frac{8^2}{2^4}$

h) $(5 \times 2)^3$

10. A **scientific calculator** has a button to evaluate powers. The example shows the buttons to press to evaluate powers.

Use a scientific calculator to evaluate the power.

To evaluate	Press
2^3	[2] [y^x] [3] [=]
5^4	[5] [y^x] [4] [=]

a) $2^5 =$ ________ b) $9^3 =$ ________ c) $6^4 =$ ________ d) $2^{10} =$ ________

11. Ben thinks that $4^3 = 12$ and $8^2 = 16$. Is he correct? Explain your answer.

____

____

EE8-16 Product of Powers

REMINDER: A power is a short form for repeated multiplication. Example: $2^5 = \underbrace{2 \times 2 \times 2 \times 2 \times 2}_{\text{multiply 2 five times}}$

1. Write each power as a product. How many times do you multiply each base?

a) $2^3 \times 5^4$

$= \underbrace{2 \times 2 \times 2}_{} \times \underbrace{5 \times 5 \times 5 \times 5}_{}$

__3__ times __4__ times

b) $7^2 \times 9^3$

____ times ____ times

c) $4^3 \times 6^5$

____ times ____ times

d) $3^2 \times 8^3$

____ times ____ times

e) $6^2 \times 7^2$

____ times ____ times

f) $10^3 \times 2^4$

____ times ____ times

2. How many times do you multiply each base? Write the expression as a product of powers.

a) $\underbrace{2 \times 2 \times 2 \times 2}_{} \times \underbrace{7 \times 7 \times 7}_{}$

__4__ times __3__ times

$= 2^4 \times 7^3$

b) $5 \times 5 \times 6 \times 6 \times 6$

____ times ____ times

$=$

c) $8 \times 8 \times 8 \times 9 \times 9 \times 9 \times 9$

____ times ____ times

$=$

d) $3 \times 3 \times 6 \times 6 \times 6 \times 6$

____ times ____ times

$=$

e) $4 \times 4 \times 4 \times 9 \times 9 \times 9$

____ times ____ times

$=$

f) $5 \times 5 \times 5 \times 5 \times 5 \times 4 \times 4$

____ times ____ times

$=$

3. Write each power as a product. Then write the final product as a single power.

a) $2^3 \times 2^4$

$= (2 \times 2 \times 2) \times (2 \times 2 \times 2 \times 2)$

$= 2 \times 2 \times 2 \times 2 \times 2 \times 2 \times 2$

$= 2^7$

b) $5^4 \times 5^2$

c) $9^2 \times 9^6$

d) $7^5 \times 7^4$

e) $8^3 \times 8^2$

f) $2^7 \times 2^3$

4. a) Use your answers from Question 3 to complete the table.

Question	$2^3 \times 2^4$	$5^4 \times 5^2$	$9^2 \times 9^6$	$7^5 \times 7^4$	$8^3 \times 8^2$	$2^7 \times 2^3$
Answer	2^7					

b) Look at the exponents in each question and answer in the table. How can you predict the exponent in the answer using only the exponents in the question?

____

To multiply powers with the same base, keep the base and add the exponents.

Example: $2^3 \times 2^4$

$= 2^{3+4}$

$= 2^7$

5. Write the product as a single power by keeping the base and adding the exponents.

a) $5^3 \times 5^4$

$= 5^{3+4}$

$= 5^7$

b) $3^2 \times 3^4$

c) $2^5 \times 2^4$

d) $3^5 \times 3^3$

e) $7^3 \times 7^5$

f) $9^7 \times 9^3$

To check that $2^3 \times 2^4 = 2^7$, evaluate each side of the equation separately.

Left Side: $2^3 \times 2^4 = 8 \times 16 = 128$

Right Side: $2^7 = 2 \times 2 \times 2 \times 2 \times 2 \times 2 \times 2 = 128$

Since the left side equals the right side, $2^3 \times 2^4 = 2^7$.

6. Evaluate each side of the equation separately to check that the equation is true.

a) $3^2 \times 3^3 = 3^5$

b) $2^4 \times 2^2 = 2^6$

c) $10^3 \times 10^4 = 10^7$

7. Mona thinks that $2^3 \times 5^2 = 10^5$. Evaluate each side of the equation separately to check. When multiplying powers, what must be true about the bases before you can add the exponents?

REMINDER: A power with 1 as the exponent is equal to the base. Example: $2^1 = 2$

8. Write the product as a single power by keeping the base and adding the exponents.

a) $5^6 \times 5$

$= 5^6 \times 5^1$

$= 5^7$

b) $8^4 \times 8$

c) $7^9 \times 7$

d) 4×4^6

e) 8×8^5

f) 10×10^8

9. Write the product as a single power.

a) $(5^6 \times 5^2) \times 5^3$

$= 5^8 \times 5^3$

$= 5^{11}$

b) $(3^4 \times 3^5) \times 3^6$

c) $2^4 \times (2^5 \times 2^3)$

d) $(6^4 \times 6^2) \times (6^3 \times 6^5)$

e) $(9^3 \times 9) \times (9^2 \times 9^7)$

f) $(5^3 \times 5 \times 5^4) \times 5^6$

10. Write the product of powers as a single power.

a) $2^3 \times 2^5 \times 2^4$

$= 2^{3+5+4}$

$= 2^{12}$

b) $10^3 \times 10^4 \times 10$

c) $(-3)^6 \times (-3) \times (-3)^2$

d) $10 \times 10^7 \times 10$

e) $\left(\frac{1}{2}\right)^2 \times \left(\frac{1}{2}\right)^3 \times \left(\frac{1}{2}\right)$

f) $(0.2)^3 \times (0.2) \times (0.2)^2$

REMINDER: You can only add the exponents if you are multiplying powers with the same base.

11. Multiply powers with the same base.

a) $2^3 \times 2^5 \times 3^4 \times 3^2$

$= 2^{3+5} \times 3^{4+2}$

$= 2^8 \times 3^6$

b) $4^7 \times 4^2 \times 6^5 \times 6^7$

c) $3^5 \times 8^2 \times 3^4 \times 8^3$

EE8-17 Quotient of Powers

A fraction with a product in the numerator and in the denominator can be written as a product of separate fractions.

Example: $\frac{4\times3}{7\times5}=\frac{4}{7}\times\frac{3}{5}$

1. Write the fraction as a product of separate fractions.

a) $\frac{5\times7}{2\times3}=$

b) $\frac{6\times2}{5\times11}=$

c) $\frac{3\times2}{4\times2}=$

2. Write the fraction as a product of separate fractions. Multiply by 1 to make the number of factors in the numerator and the denominator the same.

a) $\frac{5\times6\times8}{2\times3}$

$=\frac{5\times6\times8}{1\times2\times3}$

$=\frac{5}{1}\times\frac{6}{2}\times\frac{8}{3}$

b) $\frac{4\times7\times6\times8}{8\times9}$

$=\frac{4\times7\times6\times8}{1\times1\times8\times9}$

c) $\frac{3\times2\times5\times7\times6}{8\times9}$

d) $\frac{3\times2\times7\times5}{4\times9}$

e) $\frac{8\times5}{4}$

f) $\frac{3\times2\times7\times5\times9}{6}$

3. Write the powers as products and then as the product of separate fractions. Multiply by 1 to make the number of factors in the numerator and the denominator the same.

a) $\frac{2^5}{2^3}$

$=\frac{2\times2\times2\times2\times2}{2\times2\times2}$

$=\frac{2\times2\times2\times2\times2}{1\times1\times2\times2\times2}$

$=\frac{2}{1}\times\frac{2}{1}\times\frac{2}{2}\times\frac{2}{2}\times\frac{2}{2}$

b) $\frac{3^5}{3^2}$

c) $\frac{7^6}{7^2}$

d) $\frac{8^5}{8^2}$

e) $\frac{9^7}{9^3}$

f) $\frac{10^6}{10^2}$

REMINDER: A fraction with the same numerator and denominator is equal to 1. Example: $\frac{5}{5} = 1$

4. Evaluate.

a) $\frac{8}{8} =$ b) $\frac{10}{10} =$ c) $\frac{45}{45} =$

$\frac{4^5}{4^2}$ is called a **quotient of powers**. To divide, write the numerator and denominator as products.

$\frac{4^5}{4^2} = \frac{4 \times 4 \times 4 \times 4 \times 4}{4 \times 4}$ ← multiply four 5 times / ← multiply four 2 times

$= \frac{4 \times 4 \times 4 \times 4 \times 4}{1 \times 1 \times 1 \times 4 \times 4}$

$= \frac{4}{1} \times \frac{4}{1} \times \frac{4}{1} \times \frac{4}{4} \times \frac{4}{4}$ ← $\frac{4}{1} = 4$ $\frac{4}{4} = 1$

$= 4 \times 4 \times 4 \times 1 \times 1$ ← multiply four 3 times

$= 4^3$

Shortcut:

There are 3 more 4s in the numerator than in the denominator, so $\frac{4^5}{4^2} = 4^3$.

5. Find how many more times the base appears in the numerator, then write as a single power.

a) $\frac{6^5}{6^3}$ b) $\frac{8^4}{8^2}$ c) $\frac{2^7}{2^4}$

$= \frac{6 \times 6 \times 6 \times 6 \times 6}{6 \times 6 \times 6}$

$= 6 \times 6$

$= 6^2$

d) $\frac{10^6}{10^4}$ e) $\frac{3^5}{3^2}$ f) $\frac{7^6}{7^2}$

To divide powers with the same base, keep the base and subtract the exponents.

$6^7 \div 6^4 = 6^{7-4} = 6^3$ or $\frac{6^7}{6^4} = 6^{7-4} = 6^3$

6. Divide by keeping the base and subtracting the exponents.

a) $\frac{2^7}{2^4} = 2^{7-4} = 2^3$ b) $\frac{7^9}{7^3} =$ c) $4^9 \div 4^7 =$

d) $\frac{8^6}{8^2} =$ e) $10^7 \div 10^3 =$ f) $\frac{(-2)^4}{(-2)^2} =$

7. Divide, then evaluate the power.

a) $\dfrac{5^8}{5^6} = 5^2 = 25$ b) $6^7 \div 6^5 =$ c) $\dfrac{2^9}{2^6} =$

d) $\dfrac{10^8}{10^5} =$ e) $\dfrac{(-1)^7}{(-1)^5} =$ **Bonus ▶** $\dfrac{4^{187}}{4^{184}} =$

8. Write the quotient as a single power. Hint: $2 = 2^1$.

a) $\dfrac{2^7}{2} = 2^{7-1} = 2^6$ b) $\dfrac{3^5}{3} =$ c) $\dfrac{5^9}{5} =$

d) $\dfrac{4^{11}}{4} =$ e) $\dfrac{(-3)^6}{(-3)} =$ **Bonus ▶** $\dfrac{123^{95}}{123} =$

To check that $2^5 \div 2^2 = 2^3$, evaluate each side of the equation separately.

Left side: $2^5 \div 2^2 = 32 \div 4 = 8$ **Right side:** $2^3 = 2 \times 2 \times 2 = 8$

Since the left side equals the right side, $2^5 \div 2^2 = 2^3$.

9. Evaluate each side separately to check that the equation is true.

a) $3^5 \div 3^3 = 3^2$ b) $4^4 \div 4^3 = 4^1$ c) $10^6 \div 10^4 = 10^2$

10. David thinks that $10^5 \div 5^2 = 2^3$. Evaluate each side of the equation separately to check. When dividing powers, what must be true about the bases before you can subtract the exponents?

For some questions, you will need to use the rules for multiplying powers and dividing powers. Use the rules to rewrite the expression as a single power.

$2^6 \times 2^3 \div 2^4$ ← multiplying powers with the same base

$= 2^9 \div 2^4$ ← dividing powers with the same base

$= 2^5$

11. Rewrite the expression as a single power. Hint: Operations in brackets are done first.

a) $3^5 \times 3^7 \div 3^8$

$= 3^{12} \div 3^8$

$= 3^4$

b) $5^7 \times 5^6 \div 5^{11}$ c) $10^7 \times 10^4 \div 10^8$

d) $6^8 \div (6^3 \times 6^2)$ e) $7^{10} \div (7^3 \times 7^2)$ f) $(4^8 \times 4^4) \div (4^3 \times 4^6)$

EE8-18 Zero and Negative Exponents

REMINDER: A fraction with the same numerator and denominator is equal to 1. Example: $\frac{5}{5} = 1$

1. Evaluate the fraction.

a) $\frac{2^4}{2^4} = \frac{16}{16} = 1$ b) $\frac{3^2}{3^2} =$ c) $\frac{4^3}{4^3} =$

d) $\frac{5^2}{5^2} =$ e) $\frac{2^6}{2^6} =$ f) $\frac{10^3}{10^3} =$

REMINDER: To divide powers with the same base, keep the base and subtract the exponents. Example: $\frac{2^7}{2^3} = 2^4$

2. Divide by keeping the base and subtracting the exponents.

a) $\frac{2^4}{2^4} = 2^{4-4} = 2^0$ b) $\frac{3^2}{3^2} =$ c) $\frac{4^3}{4^3} =$

d) $\frac{5^2}{5^2} =$ e) $\frac{2^6}{2^6} =$ f) $\frac{10^3}{10^3} =$

3. a) In Question 1, what was the answer each time? ________

b) In Question 2, what was the exponent in the answer each time? ________

A power with the exponent zero has the value 1. Example: $2^0 = 1$

4. Find the value of the power.

a) $4^0 =$ ______ b) $9^0 =$ ______ c) $10^0 =$ ______

d) $(-8)^0 =$ ______ e) $\left(\frac{3}{5}\right)^0 =$ ______ **Bonus ▶** $1{,}237^0 =$ ______

5. Evaluate the expression. Use the correct order of operations.

a) $2^0 + 2^3 \times 3^2$

$= 1 + 8 \times 9$

$= 1 + 72$

$= 73$

b) $3^2 + 5^2 \div 4^0$

c) $\frac{5^3}{5^3} + \frac{5^3}{5}$

d) $(8^2 - 4^0) \div (5 \times 2^2 + 7^0)$ e) $(5^2)^0$ f) $(2 + 3 \times 5)^0$

6. Write the quotient of powers as a product of fractions. Multiply by 1 to make the number of factors in the numerator and denominator the same.

a) $\dfrac{2^3}{2^5}$

$= \dfrac{2 \times 2 \times 2}{2 \times 2 \times 2 \times 2 \times 2}$

$= \dfrac{1 \times 1 \times 2 \times 2 \times 2}{2 \times 2 \times 2 \times 2 \times 2}$

$= \dfrac{1}{2} \times \dfrac{1}{2} \times \dfrac{2}{2} \times \dfrac{2}{2} \times \dfrac{2}{2}$

b) $\dfrac{3^3}{3^7}$

c) $\dfrac{4^3}{4^6}$

d) $\dfrac{7^2}{7^6}$

e) $\dfrac{9^4}{9^5}$

f) $\dfrac{10^4}{10^6}$

To divide $\dfrac{4^2}{4^5}$, write the numerator and denominator as a product.

$\dfrac{4^2}{4^5} = \dfrac{4 \times 4}{4 \times 4 \times 4 \times 4 \times 4}$ ← multiply four 2 times / ← multiply four 5 times

$= \dfrac{1 \times 1 \times 1 \times 4 \times 4}{4 \times 4 \times 4 \times 4 \times 4}$

$= \dfrac{1}{4} \times \dfrac{1}{4} \times \dfrac{1}{4} \times \dfrac{4}{4} \times \dfrac{4}{4}$ ← $\dfrac{4}{4} = 1$

$= \dfrac{1}{4 \times 4 \times 4}$ ← multiply four 3 times

$= \dfrac{1}{4^3}$

Shortcut:

There are 3 more 4s in the denominator than in the numerator, so $\dfrac{4^2}{4^5} = \dfrac{1}{4^3}$.

7. Find how many more times the base appears in the denominator, and then write as a single power.

a) $\dfrac{8^3}{8^5}$

$= \dfrac{8 \times 8 \times 8}{8 \times 8 \times 8 \times 8 \times 8}$ multiply 3 times / multiply 5 times

$= \dfrac{1}{8 \times 8}$ 2 more 8s in the denominator

$= \dfrac{1}{8^2}$

b) $\dfrac{6^3}{6^7}$

c) $\dfrac{3^2}{3^6}$

d) $\dfrac{10^2}{10^7}$

e) $\dfrac{9^2}{9^8}$

f) $\dfrac{4^5}{4^7}$

Remember: When dividing powers with the same base, keep the base and subtract the exponents.

Example: $\frac{2^3}{2^7} = 2^{3-7} = 2^{-4}$

$2^{-4} = \frac{1}{2^4}$

But $\frac{2^3}{2^7} = \frac{1}{2^4}$ because there are 4 more 2s being multiplied in the denominator.

8. Write the power as a fraction with a positive exponent in the denominator.

a) $2^{-3} = \frac{1}{2^3}$ b) $8^{-5} = \frac{1}{}$ c) $7^{-3} = \frac{1}{}$

d) $9^{-8} =$ e) $10^{-2} =$ f) $(-3)^{-2} =$

9. Write the fraction as a power with a negative exponent.

a) $\frac{1}{3^5} = 3^{-5}$ b) $\frac{1}{4^3} =$ c) $\frac{1}{6^4} =$

d) $\frac{1}{9^2} =$ e) $\frac{1}{10^4} =$ f) $\frac{1}{(-2)^6} =$

10. Evaluate the power by first writing it as a fraction.

a) 2^{-3}

$= \frac{1}{2^3}$

$= \frac{1}{8}$

b) 4^{-2} c) 5^{-2}

d) 10^{-2} e) 10^{-5} f) $(-3)^{-4}$

11. Evaluate. If the answer has a negative exponent, rewrite it as a fraction.

a) $2^3 \times 2^{-6}$

$= 2^{3+(-6)}$

$= 2^{-3}$

$= \frac{1}{2^3}$

$= \frac{1}{8}$

b) $3^8 \times 3^{-6}$ c) $4^3 \div 4^5$

d) $5^4 \times 5^3 \div 5^9$ e) $8^2 \div 8^6 \times 8^3$ f) $2^5 \div 2^7 \div 2^2$

EE8-19 Introduction to Scientific Notation

To multiply by a power of 10, move the decimal point to the right.

Examples: $2.83 \times 10 = 28.3$ $\quad$ $3.40 \times 100 = 340$

1. Evaluate the power, then multiply.

a) 2.4×10^2

$= 2.4 \times 100$

$= 240$

b) 4.56×10^3

c) 0.94×10^4

d) 0.345×10^3

e) 1.23×10^4

f) 0.094×10^5

To multiply by a power of 10 with a positive exponent, move the decimal point to the right as many places as the exponent.

Examples: $0.2357 \times 10^3 = 235.7$

2. Multiply by moving the decimal point.

a) $0.345 \times 10^2 = 34.5$

b) $1.8193 \times 10^3 =$

c) $9.4 \times 10^2 =$

d) $82.3 \times 10^4 =$

e) $0.045 \times 10^2 =$

f) $0.0354 \times 10^5 =$

To divide by a power of 10, move the decimal point to the left.

Examples: $283.4 \div 10 = 28.34$ $\quad$ $7.48 \div 100 = 0.0748$

3. Evaluate the power first.

a) $2.48 \div 10^3$

$= 2.48 \div 1{,}000$

$= 0.00248$

b) $45.67 \div 10^2$

c) $94.87 \div 10^4$

d) $375.8 \div 10^2$

e) $1.23 \div 10^3$

f) $0.097 \div 10^4$

To divide by a power of 10 with a positive exponent, move the decimal point to the left as many places as the exponent.

Examples: $93.57 \div 10^3 = 0.09357$

4. Divide by moving the decimal point.

a) $82.3 \div 10^2 = 0.823$

b) $28.34 \div 10^3 =$

c) $9.4 \div 10^2 =$

d) $145.2 \div 10^3 =$

e) $0.25 \div 10^2 =$

f) $98.2 \div 10^3 =$

5. Use the grid to multiply or divide.

a) 2.38×10^3	0	2 •	3	8	0	0	*= 2,380*
b) $3.58 \div 10^2$	0	0	3 •	5	8	0	*= 0.0358*
c) 56.7×10^2	0	5	6	7	0	0	
d) $45.9 \div 10^3$	0	0	4	5	9	0	
e) $0.571 \div 10^1$	0	0	5	7	1	0	
f) 0.056×10^4	0	0	5	6	0	0	
g) 65.3×10^3	0	6	5	3	0	0	
h) $467.8 \div 10^4$	0	4	6	7	8	0	

REMINDER: To divide by a fraction, multiply by the reciprocal.

Examples: $6 \div \frac{3}{4} = 6 \times \frac{4}{3}$ $\quad 5 \div 8 = 5 \times \frac{1}{8}$

6. Write the division statement using multiplication.

a) $2.3 \div 10$

$= 2.3 \times \frac{1}{10}$

b) $3.46 \div 100$

c) $42.687 \div 1{,}000$

7. Write the multiplication statement using division.

a) $5.6 \times \frac{1}{10}$

$= 5.6 \div 10$

b) $8.214 \times \frac{1}{100}$

c) $7.2 \times \frac{1}{1{,}000}$

8. Write the power of 10 as a fraction, then write the multiplication as a division.

a) 8.5×10^{-2}

$= 8.5 \times \frac{1}{10^2}$

$= 8.5 \div 10^2$

b) 8.419×10^{-3}

c) 1.27×10^{-5}

d) 6.73×10^{-1}

e) 4.25×10^{-2}

f) 7.1×10^{-3}

To multiply by a power of 10 with a negative exponent, move the decimal point left.

Example: $4.35 \times 10^{-2} = 4.35 \div 10^2$
$= 0.0435$

9. Multiply by moving the decimal point left.

a) $456.9 \times 10^{-2} = 4.569$

b) $93.4 \times 10^{-3} =$

c) $4.16 \times 10^{-1} =$

d) $32.96 \times 10^{-4} =$

e) $0.034 \times 10^{-2} =$

f) $5.873 \times 10^{-3} =$

Numbers that are very, very large or very, very small are difficult to work with. They may not even fit on your calculator!

To help deal with these numbers, we use **scientific notation**.

In scientific notation, numbers are written as the product of a decimal greater than or equal to 1 but less than 10 and a power of 10.

Example: 237,000

2.37×10^5

decimal number   power of 10

10. Circle the number if it is written in scientific notation.

a) 2.74×10^{23} b) $3.14 + 10^{-5}$ c) 1.09×10^{-7}

d) $4.1 \div 10^3$ e) 8.7×10^{12} f) 10.34×10^{-8}

To change from scientific notation to decimal form, move the decimal point ...

- right if the power of 10 has a positive exponent.
- left if the power of 10 has a negative exponent.

Examples: $3.12 \times 10^4 = 31,200.0$

$9.45 \times 10^{-3} = 0.00945$

11. Change from scientific notation to decimal form.

a) $2.13 \times 10^4 =$ *21,300*   b) $8.74 \times 10^3 =$ c) $1.98 \times 10^5 =$

d) $7.2 \times 10^{-3} =$ *0.0072*   e) $5.146 \times 10^{-2} =$ f) $1.03 \times 10^{-4} =$

g) $9.4 \times 10^{-2} =$ h) $1.9 \times 10^3 =$ i) $2.03 \times 10^{-1} =$

12. A light year (the distance light can travel in 1 year) is approximately 9.5×10^{15} m. Write the distance in decimal form.

13. The mass of an electron is approximately 9.1×10^{-31} kg. What is the mass in decimal form?

14. a) The land area of Earth is approximately 1.49×10^8 km^2. What is the land area written in decimal form?

b) The water area of Earth is approximately 3.61×10^8 km^2. What is the water area written in decimal form?

c) How much greater is the water area than the land area of Earth in km^2?

EE8-20 Scientific Notation

REMINDER: In scientific notation, numbers are written as the product of a decimal greater than or equal to 1 but less than 10 and a power of 10.	Example: 8.1×10^{-4} (decimal number: 8.1; power of 10: 10^{-4})

1. Circle the number if it is written in scientific notation.

a) 18.4×10^2 b) 2.39×10^{-4} c) 0.37×10^8

d) 534,000 e) 0.003456 f) 1.07×10^1

To change from decimal form to scientific notation:	Examples:	
Step 1: Find the decimal number for the scientific notation.	238,040,000	0.006502
a) Put the decimal point after the first non-zero digit.	2.38040000	0006.502
b) Remove all zeroes at the beginning or end.	2.3804	6.502

2. For the numbers in Question 1 that are not written in scientific notation, explain why.

3. The number has been changed to scientific notation. Find the decimal part of the answer.

a) 260,300
$= $ *2.603* $\times 10^5$

b) 0.004518
$= $ ______ $\times 10^{-3}$

c) 65.3400
$= $ ______ $\times 10^1$

d) 0.000005800
$= $ ______ $\times 10^{-6}$

e) 1,000,457,000
$= $ ______ $\times 10^9$

f) 182.34
$= $ ______ $\times 10^2$

Step 2: Find the exponent for the power of 10.	Examples:	
a) Count the number of places between the decimal point and its original position.	2.3804	6.502
	2 3 8,0 4 0,0 0 0	0.0 0 6 5 0 2
b) If you counted to the right, the exponent is positive. If you counted to the left, the exponent is negative.	$= 2.3804 \times 10^8$	$= 6.502 \times 10^{-3}$

4. The number has been changed to scientific notation. Find the power of 10.

a) 6,204
$= 6.204 \times$ *10^3*

b) 0.00038
$= 3.8 \times$ ______

c) 92,000,000
$= 9.2 \times$ ______

d) 0.5809
$= 5.809 \times$ ______

e) 3,060,010
$= 3.06001 \times$ ______

f) 0.0854
$= 8.54 \times$ ______

g) 0.0074
$= 7.4 \times$ ______

h) 0.15
$= 1.5 \times$ ______

Bonus ▶ 9.8
$= 9.8 \times$ ______

5. Perform **Step 1** and **Step 2** from the previous page to change the number to scientific notation.

a) 248,000,000

$= 2.48 \times 10^8$

b) 0.00354

$= 3.54 \times 10^{-3}$

c) 91.356

d) 123,987

e) 0.0048

f) 0.87

g) 9.73

Bonus ▶ 52,040,000,000,000,000,000

> Scientific calculators have a button for scientific notation. The button might be [EE] or [EXP].
> To change 1.56×10^3 to decimal form, press [1.56] [EE] [3] [=]. The answer is 1,560.

6. Use a scientific calculator to change to decimal form.

a) 6.57×10^8

b) 9.41×10^{-1}

c) 2.83×10^4

d) 7.45×10^{-5}

e) 1.052×10^4

f) 6.04×10^{-3}

7. Change to scientific notation. Then use a calculator to check your answer by changing the number back to decimal form.

a) 0.00624

$= 6.24 \times 10^{-3}$

b) 45,037,000

c) 0.000034

d) 15,803

e) 0.205

f) 38,000,000,000

8. A nanosecond is 0.000000001 s. How many seconds is a nanosecond written in scientific notation?

____

9. A picometer is a unit of length equal to 0.000000000001 m. What is the length written in scientific notation?

____

10. The star Mizar, in the Big Dipper, is approximately 741,000,000,000,000,000 m away from Earth. Write the distance in scientific notation.

____

To compare numbers written in scientific notation:

- if the exponents are different, the number with the larger exponent is the larger number.
- if the exponents are the same, the number with the larger decimal is the larger number.

Examples:

$2.3 \times 10^{-2} > 9.4 \times 10^{-8}$

$9.2 \times 10^{5} > 7.3 \times 10^{5}$

11. Circle the larger number.

a) 4.5×10^{7} or 6.1×10^{9} b) 1.73×10^{4} or 5.1×10^{4} c) 5.06×10^{-4} or 1.99×10^{-2}

12. Circle the smaller number.

a) 1.9×10^{-4} or 2.8×10^{-2} b) 5.7×10^{3} or 4.8×10^{3} c) 3.9×10^{-2} or 9.38×10^{-1}

A number is not in scientific notation if the decimal part is not in the right range.

Example: 0.746×10^{3}

Not in the right range

13. Change to scientific notation by first changing to decimal form.

a) 0.746×10^{3}

$= 746$

$= 7.46 \times 10^{2}$

b) 834.6×10^{-4}

c) 0.024×10^{-3}

d) $7{,}459.2 \times 10^{-2}$

e) 0.0056×10^{-4}

f) 0.00056×10^{7}

If the decimal part is not in the right range, we can:

Step 1: Write the decimal part in scientific notation.

Step 2: Use the power rules to multiply the powers with the same base.

Example: 0.046×10^{5}

$(4.6 \times 10^{-2}) \times 10^{5}$

$= 4.6 \times 10^{-2+5}$

$= 4.6 \times 10^{3}$

14. Use the power rules to change to scientific notation.

a) 0.0813×10^{7}

$= (8.13 \times 10^{-2}) \times 10^{7}$

$= 8.13 \times 10^{5}$

b) 0.000172×10^{-3}

c) 536.12×10^{-5}

d) 482.1×10^{4}

e) 0.9×10^{-1}

f) 14.09×10^{-4}

EE8-21 Operations with Scientific Notation

To multiply or divide a number in scientific notation by a decimal, multiply or divide the decimals, and then multiply by the power of 10.

Examples: $(2.0 \times 10^3) \times 2.3$
$= (2.3 \times 2.0) \times 10^3$
$= 4.6 \times 10^3$

$(8.4 \times 10^5) \div 4.0$
$= (8.4 \div 4.0) \times 10^5$
$= 2.1 \times 10^5$

1. Multiply.

a) $(2.0 \times 10^4) \times 3.2$ b) $(3.0 \times 10^{-5}) \times 2.1$ c) $(3.0 \times 10^7) \times 1.2$

2. Divide.

a) $(6.3 \times 10^4) \div 3.0$ b) $(4.4 \times 10^{-3}) \div 4.0$ c) $(7.8 \times 10^{-3}) \div 2.0$

REMINDER: If the decimal part of a number is less than 1 or greater than or equal to 10, use the power rules to rewrite the number in scientific notation.

3. Write in scientific notation.

a) 132.4×10^3
$= (1.324 \times 10^2) \times 10^3$
$= 1.324 \times 10^5$

b) 0.075×10^5

c) 56.7×10^{-4}

d) 0.0034×10^{-2} e) 0.0185×10^{-1} f) 0.874×10^2

4. Multiply, then write the answer in scientific notation.

a) $(5.0 \times 10^4) \times 3.1$
$= 15.5 \times 10^4$
$= (1.55 \times 10^1) \times 10^4$
$= 1.55 \times 10^5$

b) $(3.0 \times 10^{-4}) \times 4.3$

c) $(9.1 \times 10^8) \times 7.0$

d) $(4.0 \times 10^4) \times 2.1$ e) $(6.0 \times 10^{-2}) \times 2.5$ f) $(8.3 \times 10) \times 3.0$

5. Divide, then write the answer in scientific notation.

a) $(0.4 \times 10^{6}) \div 5.0$

$= 0.08 \times 10^{6}$

$= (8.0 \times 10^{-2}) \times 10^{6}$

$= 8.0 \times 10^{4}$

b) $(3.6 \times 10^{-2}) \div 4.0$

c) $(4.2 \times 10^{-4}) \div 6.0$

d) $(0.06 \times 10^{-2}) \div 2.0$

e) $(0.09 \times 10^{8}) \div 3.0$

f) $(0.42 \times 10^{-4}) \div 7.0$

To multiply a number in scientific notation by a power of 10, use the power rules to find the product of the powers.

Example: $(2.6 \times 10^{3}) \times 10^{4}$

$= 2.6 \times (10^{3} \times 10^{4})$

$= 2.6 \times 10^{7}$

6. Multiply.

a) $(3.4 \times 10^{5}) \times 10^{3}$

$= 3.4 \times (10^{5} \times 10^{3})$

$= 3.4 \times 10^{8}$

b) $(8.12 \times 10^{-4}) \times 10^{7}$

c) $10^{-2} \times (4.28 \times 10^{-3})$

d) $(9.8 \times 10^{-4}) \times 10^{-3}$

e) $(2.04 \times 10^{-2}) \times 10^{6}$

f) $10^{3} \times (5.78 \times 10^{7})$

7. The Earth takes one year to travel around the Sun. It travels approximately 9.4×10^{8} km during one orbit. Approximately how many kilometers does it travel in 5 years? Write your answer in scientific notation.

8. Five grains of rice have a mass of 1.4×10^{-4} kg. Find the mass in grams of one grain of rice. Write your answer in scientific notation.

9. A virus cell used in an experiment has a mass of 1.5×10^{-15} g. What is the mass of 300 virus cells? Write your answer in scientific notation.

10. A grain of sand has a mass of approximately 2.4×10^{-3} g. There are approximately 10^{9} grains of sand in a cubic meter of sand. Find the approximate mass in grams of a cubic meter of sand. Write your answer in scientific notation.

11. There are approximately 10^{9} people in China. If the average weight per person is approximately 6.0×10^{4} g, what is the approximate weight in grams of all the people in China? Write your answer in scientific notation.

EE8-22 More Operations with Scientific Notation

To multiply two numbers in scientific notation:

Step 1: Multiply the decimals and multiply the powers.

Example: $(4.0 \times 10^3) \times (3.0 \times 10^5)$
$= (4.0 \times 3.0) \times (10^3 \times 10^5)$
$= 12 \times 10^8$

1. Multiply the decimals and multiply the powers.

a) $(5.0 \times 10^{-2}) \times (7.0 \times 10^4)$ b) $(4.0 \times 10^2) \times (3.0 \times 10^5)$ c) $(7.0 \times 10^{-4}) \times (6.0 \times 10^{-3})$

Step 2: If the decimal part of a number is not in the correct range, rewrite it using scientific notation and use the power rule to multiply powers with the same base.

Example: 12×10^8
$= (1.2 \times 10^1) \times 10^8$
$= 1.2 \times 10^9$

2. Write the number in scientific notation.

a) 283.4×10^3 b) 0.375×10^4 c) 623.7×10^{-3}

3. Multiply the numbers and write the answer in scientific notation.

a) $(7.2 \times 10^4) \times (2.0 \times 10^3)$ b) $(2.3 \times 10^{-2}) \times (5.0 \times 10^6)$ c) $(4.2 \times 10^{-2}) \times (3.0 \times 10^{-3})$

$= 14.4 \times 10^7$

$= (1.44 \times 10^1) \times 10^7$

$= 1.44 \times 10^8$

To divide two numbers in scientific notation:

Step 1: Divide the decimals and divide the powers.

Example: $\frac{2.8 \times 10^5}{4.0 \times 10^2} = \frac{2.8}{4.0} \times \frac{10^5}{10^2}$
$= 0.7 \times 10^3$

4. Divide the decimals and divide the powers.

a) $\frac{9.6 \times 10^6}{3.0 \times 10^4}$ b) $\frac{3.6 \times 10^4}{9.0 \times 10^7}$ c) $\frac{8.4 \times 10^4}{4.0 \times 10^{-1}}$

Step 2: If the decimal part of the number is not in the correct range, rewrite it using scientific notation and use the power rule to multiply powers with the same base.

Example: 0.7×10^3

$= (7.0 \times 10^{-1}) \times 10^3$

$= 7.0 \times 10^2$

5. Divide, then write the answer in scientific notation.

a) $\dfrac{4.2 \times 10^4}{7.0 \times 10^7}$

$= 0.6 \times 10^{-3}$

$= (6.0 \times 10^{-1}) \times 10^{-3}$

$= 6.0 \times 10^{-4}$

b) $\dfrac{2.8 \times 10^8}{4.0 \times 10^4}$

c) $\dfrac{4.5 \times 10^7}{9.0 \times 10^2}$

6. A dripping faucet leaks 5.0×10^{-4} L of water every second. There are approximately 3.2×10^7 seconds in a year. Approximately how many liters of water does the faucet leak in a year? Write your answer in scientific notation.

7. In 2012, approximately 2.6×10^9 cases of bottled water were sold in the United States. There are 6.0×10^3 mL of water in a case. Approximately how many milliliters of bottled water were sold that year? Write your answer in scientific notation.

8. In 2013, the population of the United States was approximately 3.2×10^8. The total cost of health care in 2013 was approximately $\$2.88 \times 10^{12}$. What was the approximate cost of health care per person? Write your answer in decimal form.

9. In 2013, the population of India was approximately 1.25×10^9. The population of South Korea was approximately 5.0×10^7. Approximately how many times as many people lived in India as lived in South Korea in 2013? Write your answer in decimal form.

10. In 2013, the population of the United States was approximately 3.2×10^8.

a) If a typical family household has 4 people, how many households were there? Write your answer in scientific notation.

b) The typical family household wastes approximately \$2,200 in food each year. What is the approximate value of the food wasted each year by the entire country? Write your answer in decimal form.

EE8-23 Estimating Using Scientific Notation (Advanced)

1. Round the decimal part of the number to the nearest whole number.

a) $2.7 \times 10^3 \approx$ *3×10^3* b) $8.1 \times 10^{-2} \approx$ c) $4.3 \times 10^{-1} \approx$

d) $5.79 \times 10^8 \approx$ e) $6.03 \times 10^{-5} \approx$ f) $9.86 \times 10^7 \approx$

To estimate a product of numbers written in scientific notation:

Step 1: Round the decimal part of each number.

Step 2: Multiply the whole numbers and multiply the powers.

Example: $(4.23 \times 10^{-5}) \times (2.99 \times 10^2)$

$\approx (4 \times 10^{-5}) \times (3 \times 10^2)$

$= 12 \times 10^{-3}$

2. Round the decimal part of each number, then multiply to estimate.

a) $(3.17 \times 10^{-4}) \times (5.69 \times 10^3)$ b) $(7.89 \times 10^2) \times (2.14 \times 10^{-3})$ c) $(6.8 \times 10^9) \times (3.29 \times 10^{-5})$

Step 3: If the decimal part of an answer is not in the right range, rewrite the answer using scientific notation.

Example: 12×10^{-3}

$= (1.2 \times 10^1) \times 10^{-3}$

$= 1.2 \times 10^{-2}$

3. Estimate the product. Write the answer in scientific notation.

a) $(5.9 \times 10^3) \times (4.12 \times 10^5)$ b) $(2.9 \times 10^{-2}) \times (6.89 \times 10^3)$ c) $(5.14 \times 10^{-3}) \times (9.7 \times 10^{-5})$

$\approx (6 \times 10^3) \times (4 \times 10^5)$

$= 24 \times 10^8$

$= (2.4 \times 10^1) \times 10^8$

$= 2.4 \times 10^9$

To estimate a quotient of numbers written in scientific notation:

Step 1: Round the decimal part of each number.

Step 2: Divide the whole numbers and divide the powers.

Example: $\dfrac{3.89 \times 10^7}{8.1 \times 10^2} \approx \dfrac{4}{8} \times \dfrac{10^7}{10^2}$

$= 0.5 \times 10^5$

4. Round the decimal part of each scientific notation, then divide.

a) $\dfrac{1.99 \times 10^5}{5.2 \times 10^3}$ b) $\dfrac{7.8 \times 10^{-1}}{2.1 \times 10^2}$ c) $\dfrac{5.7 \times 10^3}{7.92 \times 10^{-2}}$

Step 3: If the decimal part of the answer is not in the right range, rewrite the answer using scientific notation.

Example: 0.5×10^5

$= (5.0 \times 10^{-1}) \times 10^5$

$= 5.0 \times 10^4$

5. Estimate the quotient. Write the answer in scientific notation.

a) $\dfrac{3.94 \times 10^3}{4.8 \times 10^5}$

$\approx \dfrac{4}{5} \times \dfrac{10^3}{10^5}$

$= 0.8 \times 10^{-2}$

$= (8.0 \times 10^{-1}) \times 10^{-2}$

$= 8.0 \times 10^{-3}$

b) $\dfrac{2.75 \times 10^2}{5.89 \times 10^{-1}}$

c) $\dfrac{1.9 \times 10^3}{7.9 \times 10^{-4}}$

6. Estimate by first changing each number into scientific notation.

a) $3{,}276{,}745{,}892 \times 0.00592$

$\approx (3.0 \times 10^9) \times (6.0 \times 10^{-3})$

$= 18 \times 10^6 = 1.8 \times 10^7$

b) $\dfrac{83{,}237}{0.0195}$

$\approx \dfrac{8.0 \times 10^4}{2.0 \times 10^{-2}} =$

c) $0.00584 \times 712{,}568$

d) $\dfrac{0.0019}{5{,}387}$

7. 12.01 g of carbon has approximately 602,214,129,000,000,000,000,000 atoms. What is the approximate mass of one atom of carbon?

8. One cubic kilometer of water contains 10^{12} liters of water. Each liter of water has approximately 3.3×10^{25} water molecules. There are approximately 1.4×10^9 cubic kilometers of water on Earth. Find the approximate number of water molecules on the planet.

9. The speed of light is approximately 3.0×10^8 meters per second. There are 31,536,000 seconds in a year. The Antlia Dwarf galaxy is approximately 4.04×10^{22} meters away from Earth. If an astronaut could travel at the speed of light, approximately how many years would it take the astronaut to reach Antlia Dwarf?

EE8-24 Power of a Power

REMINDER: base → 2^5 ← exponent; 2^5 is the power.

$2^5 = 2 \times 2 \times 2 \times 2 \times 2$ (multiply 2 five times)

1. Write the power as a product.

a) $3^4 =$ b) $7^6 =$ c) $9^4 =$

2. Complete the table.

Base	Exponent	Power	Product
2	5	2^5	$2 \times 2 \times 2 \times 2 \times 2$
3	4		
			$4 \times 4 \times 4$
		8^3	
5			1

The base of a power can also be a power. This is called a **power of a power**.

$\left(2^3\right)^4$ is the power.

base $= 2^3$

exponent $= 4$

$\left(2^3\right)^4 = 2^3 \times 2^3 \times 2^3 \times 2^3$ (multiply 2^3 four times)

3. Write the base and exponent for the power of a power.

a) $\left(3^2\right)^5$ base = ______ exponent = ______

b) $\left(7^4\right)^3$ base = ______ exponent = ______

c) $\left(9^8\right)^0$ base = ______ exponent = ______

4. Write as a product of powers.

a) $\left(2^6\right)^4$

$= 2^6 \times 2^6 \times 2^6 \times 2^6$

b) $\left(4^5\right)^3$

c) $\left(9^2\right)^5$

5. Write as a power of a power.

a) $3^4 \times 3^4 \times 3^4 \times 3^4 \times 3^4$

$= \left(3^4\right)^5$

b) $9^2 \times 9^2 \times 9^2$

c) $2^4 \times 2^4 \times 2^4 \times 2^4 \times 2^4 \times 2^4$

REMINDER: To multiply powers with the same base, keep the base and add the exponents.

Examples: $2^3 \times 2^5$
$= 2^{3+5}$
$= 2^8$

$10^4 \times 10^2 \times 10^3$
$= 10^{4+2+3}$
$= 10^9$

6. Write the power of a power as a product of powers. Then multiply powers with the same base.

a) $\left(2^4\right)^3$
$= 2^4 \times 2^4 \times 2^4$
$= 2^{4+4+4}$
$= 2^{12}$

b) $\left(6^5\right)^4$

c) $\left(7^2\right)^5$

d) $\left(9^4\right)^2$

e) $\left(5^3\right)^3$

f) $\left(8^1\right)^5$

7. In Question 6, what do you notice about the original exponents and the exponent in the final answer?

____

To find the power of a power, keep the base and multiply the exponents.

Examples: $\left(2^4\right)^3 = 2^{4\times3} = 2^{12}$ $\quad \left(4^6\right)^5 = 4^{6\times5} = 4^{30}$

8. Write the power of a power as a single power.

a) $\left(7^5\right)^2 = 7^{5\times2}$
$= 7^{10}$

b) $\left(3^8\right)^5$

c) $\left(10^4\right)^7$

d) $\left(8^9\right)^7$

e) $\left(9^6\right)^5$

f) $\left(2^{13}\right)^1$

9. Grace thinks that $5^4 \times 5^3$ and $\left(5^4\right)^3$ are the same. To see if she is correct, write each expression as a product then as a single power. Are they the same? Explain.

____

____

EE8-25 Power of a Product or Quotient

The base of a power can also be a product.

This is called a **power of a product**.

$(2 \times 3)^4 = (2 \times 3) \times (2 \times 3) \times (2 \times 3) \times (2 \times 3)$

power of a product — multiply 2×3 four times

1. Write as a product.

a) $(2 \times 4)^3$

$= (2 \times 4) \times (2 \times 4) \times (2 \times 4)$

b) $(4 \times 9)^2$

c) $(6 \times 8)^4$

2. Write as a power of a product.

a) $(5 \times 6) \times (5 \times 6) \times (5 \times 6)$

$= (5 \times 6)^3$

b) $(9 \times 3) \times (9 \times 3)$

c) $(4 \times 2) \times (4 \times 2) \times (4 \times 2) \times (4 \times 2)$

The associative property of multiplication lets us change the order of the numbers being multiplied.

Example: $(2 \times 4)^3 = (2 \times 4) \times (2 \times 4) \times (2 \times 4)$

$= (2 \times 2 \times 2) \times (4 \times 4 \times 4)$

$= 2^3 \times 4^3$

3. Write as a product. Then use the associative property to write as a product of powers.

a) $(7 \times 2)^3$

$= (7 \times 2) \times (7 \times 2) \times (7 \times 2)$

$= (7 \times 7 \times 7) \times (2 \times 2 \times 2)$

$= 7^3 \times 2^3$

b) $(9 \times 8)^2$

c) $(5 \times 6)^4$

4. In Question 3, what do you notice about the base and exponents in the original question and the final answer?

____

To evaluate the power of a product, apply the exponent separately to each factor, and then multiply.

Example: $(3 \times 5)^4 = 3^4 \times 5^4$

5. Write the power of a product as a product of powers.

a) $(4 \times 5)^3 = 4^3 \times 5^3$

b) $(8 \times 2)^9 =$

c) $(6 \times 12)^7 =$

d) $(7 \times 9)^5 =$

e) $(7 \times 3)^4 =$

Bonus ▶ $(25 \times 8)^{100} =$

6. Write the product of powers as a power of a product.

a) $7^2 \times 8^2 = (7 \times 8)^2$

b) $4^6 \times 5^6 =$

c) $7^4 \times 8^4 =$

d) $3^9 \times 6^9 =$

e) $8^4 \times 9^4 =$

Bonus ▶ $8^{927} \times 3^{927} =$

The base of a power can also be a quotient.
This is called a **power of a quotient**.

Example:

$\left(\frac{2}{3}\right)^4 = \left(\frac{2}{3}\right)\times\left(\frac{2}{3}\right)\times\left(\frac{2}{3}\right)\times\left(\frac{2}{3}\right)$

7. Write as a product.

a) $\left(\frac{3}{4}\right)^3 = \left(\frac{3}{4}\right)\times\left(\frac{3}{4}\right)\times\left(\frac{3}{4}\right)$ b) $\left(\frac{5}{3}\right)^2 =$ c) $\left(\frac{4}{5}\right)^3 =$

8. Write as a power of a quotient.

a) $\left(\frac{5}{7}\right)\times\left(\frac{5}{7}\right)\times\left(\frac{5}{7}\right)\times\left(\frac{5}{7}\right)=\left(\frac{5}{7}\right)^4$ b) $\left(\frac{7}{8}\right)\times\left(\frac{7}{8}\right)\times\left(\frac{7}{8}\right)\times\left(\frac{7}{8}\right)=$ c) $\left(\frac{9}{4}\right)\times\left(\frac{9}{4}\right)=$

We can multiply the numerators and denominators
to write the power of a quotient as a quotient of powers.

Example:

$\left(\frac{4}{5}\right)^3 = \left(\frac{4}{5}\right)\times\left(\frac{4}{5}\right)\times\left(\frac{4}{5}\right) = \frac{4\times4\times4}{5\times5\times5} = \frac{4^3}{5^3}$

9. Write as a product of quotients, then as a quotient of powers.

a) $\left(\frac{5}{4}\right)^3 = \left(\frac{5}{4}\right)\times\left(\frac{5}{4}\right)\times\left(\frac{5}{4}\right)$

$= \frac{5\times5\times5}{4\times4\times4}$

$= \frac{5^3}{4^3}$

b) $\left(\frac{9}{2}\right)^3$ c) $\left(\frac{5}{8}\right)^2$

10. In Question 9, what do you notice about the base and exponents in the original question and the final answer?

____

To evaluate the power of a quotient, apply the exponent to the numerator and to the denominator.

Example:

$\left(\frac{2}{3}\right)^4 = \frac{2^4}{3^4}$

11. Write the power of a quotient as a quotient of powers.

a) $\left(\frac{3}{5}\right)^4 = \frac{3^4}{5^4}$ b) $\left(\frac{5}{7}\right)^6 =$ c) $\left(\frac{7}{3}\right)^5 =$

d) $\left(\frac{8}{3}\right)^9 =$ e) $\left(\frac{7}{3}\right)^2 =$ **Bonus ▶** $\left(\frac{2}{7}\right)^{453} =$

EE8-26 Summary of Exponent Rules

REMINDER:

Power Rule	Example
To multiply powers with the same base, keep the base and add the exponents.	$2^5 \times 2^4 = 2^9$
To divide powers with the same base, keep the base and subtract the exponents.	$2^7 \div 2^3 = 2^4$
A power with exponent zero is equal to 1.	$2^0 = 1$
A power with a negative exponent is equal to a unit fraction with a positive exponent in the denominator.	$2^{-3} = \frac{1}{2^3}$
To rewrite the power of a power, keep the base and multiply the exponents.	$(2^3)^4 = 2^{12}$
To rewrite the power of a product, apply the exponent to each factor.	$(2 \times 3)^4 = 2^4 \times 3^4$
To rewrite the power of a quotient, apply the exponent to the numerator and the denominator.	$\left(\frac{2}{3}\right)^4 = \frac{2^4}{3^4}$

1. Circle the expression if it is a product of powers. Underline it if it is a power of a product. Double underline it if it is a power of a power.

a) $(2^3)^4$ b) $2^3 \times 2^4$ c) $(2 \times 3)^4$ d) $4^3 \times 4^5$ e) $(4 \times 3)^5$

f) $5^6 \times 5^7$ g) $(5^6)^7$ h) $(5 \times 6)^7$ i) $(9 \times 2)^3$ j) $(9^3)^2$

2. Circle the expression if it is a power of a quotient. Underline the expression if it is a quotient of powers.

a) $\frac{5^6}{5^2}$ b) $\left(\frac{5}{2}\right)^3$ c) $\left(\frac{3}{8}\right)^4$ d) $\left(\frac{4}{3}\right)^8$ e) $\frac{3^2}{3^8}$

3. Find the power rule that applies and use the rule to find an equivalent expression.

a) $10^2 \times 10^5$ b) $\frac{8^6}{8^4}$ c) $\left(\frac{5}{2}\right)^4$ d) 5^0 e) 3^{-2}

$= 10^7$

f) $(7 \times 3)^4$ g) $8^2 \times 8^7$ h) 23^0 i) $(4^2)^3$ j) $2^7 \div 2^4$

4. Carlos says that $2^3 + 2^4 = 2^7$. Use your calculator to show he is incorrect. Explain why Carlos cannot keep the base and add the exponents in this example.

5. Write the expression as a power with a single base. More than one power rule may be required.

a) $(2^6 \times 2^3) \div 2^4$

$= 2^{6+3} \div 2^4$

$= 2^{9-4}$

$= 2^5$

b) $(3^4)^2 \times 3^5$

c) $(5^6 \times 5^3) \div (5^2 \times 5^4)$

d) $(2^5)^3 \div (2^3)^4$

e) $\dfrac{(-3)^2(-3)^8}{((-3)^2)^3}$

f) $\left(\dfrac{3}{4}\right)^2 \times \left(\dfrac{3}{4}\right)^5 \div \left(\left(\dfrac{3}{4}\right)^2\right)^3$

6. Evaluate using the power rules and the correct order of operations.

a) $2^3 \times 2^4 - (2^3)^2$

$= 2^7 - 2^6$

$= 128 - 64$

$= 64$

b) $3^7 \div 3^4 + 3^0$

c) $\left(\dfrac{2}{3}\right)^2 - \left(\dfrac{1}{3}\right)^2$

d) $2^{-4} - \left(\dfrac{1}{4}\right)^2$

e) $(8 - 6)^{-3}$

f) $(0.2)^3 - 8 \times 10^{-3}$

7. Write the number as a power of 2.

a) $16 = 2^{\square}$

b) $4 = 2^{\square}$

c) $8 = 2^{\square}$

8. Write as a power of 2 by changing the base and using the power of a power rule.

a) 16^3

$= (2^4)^3$

$= 2^{4 \times 3}$

$= 2^{12}$

b) 4^7

c) 8^5

9. Write the number as a power of 3.

a) $81 = 3^{\square}$

b) $27 = 3^{\square}$

c) $9 = 3^{\square}$

10. Write as a power of 3 by changing the base and then using the power of a power rule.

a) 81^2

$= (3^4)^2$

$= 3^{4 \times 2}$

$= 3^8$

b) 27^5

c) 9^8

11. Write the fraction as a power of 2 with a negative exponent.

a) $\frac{1}{2^3} = 2^{\square}$ b) $\frac{1}{2^5} = 2^{\square}$ c) $\frac{1}{2^4} = 2^{\square}$

12. Write the denominator as a power of 2. Then write the fraction as a power of 2 with a negative exponent.

a) $\frac{1}{8}$ b) $\frac{1}{32}$ c) $\frac{1}{16}$

$= \frac{1}{2^3}$

$= 2^{-3}$

13. Write the fraction as a power of 2 by changing the base and then using the power of a power rule.

a) $\left(\frac{1}{16}\right)^3$ b) $\left(\frac{1}{8}\right)^2$ c) $\left(\frac{1}{32}\right)^{-3}$

$= \left(\frac{1}{2^4}\right)^3$

$= \left(2^{-4}\right)^3$

$= 2^{-4 \times 3}$

$= 2^{-12}$

14. Write the fraction as a power of 3 with a negative exponent.

a) $\frac{1}{3^4} = 3^{\square}$ b) $\frac{1}{3^2} = 3^{\square}$ c) $\frac{1}{3^3} = 3^{\square}$

15. Write the denominator as a power of 3. Then write the fraction as a power of 3 with a negative exponent.

a) $\frac{1}{81}$ b) $\frac{1}{9}$ c) $\frac{1}{27}$

$= \frac{1}{3^4}$

$= 3^{-4}$

16. Write the fraction as a power of 3 by changing the base and then using the power of a power rule.

a) $\left(\frac{1}{9}\right)^4$ b) $\left(\frac{1}{27}\right)^4$ c) $\left(\frac{1}{81}\right)^{-2}$

G8-1 Points and Lines

Object	point	line	line segment	ray
Diagram		 no endpoints	 2 endpoints	 1 endpoint
Name	*A*	*AB* (or *BA*)	*AB* (or *BA*)	*AB* (**not** *BA*)

1. Name the line in two ways.

a)

line <u>*AB*</u> or ______

b)

line ______ or ______

c)

line ______ or ______

2. Is *PQ* a line, line segment, or ray?

a)

PQ is a ______________

b)

PQ is a ______________

c)

PQ is a ______________

3. a) Measure the line segment *EF* to the nearest millimeter.

EF = ______

b) Draw a line segment 5 cm long. Label it *GM*.

Lines and rays can be extended. Rays can be extended only where there is no endpoint. Remember to name a ray with the endpoint *first*.

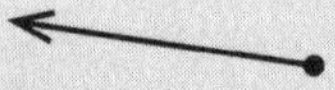
endpoint

4. Circle the endpoint on the ray. Then name the ray.

a)
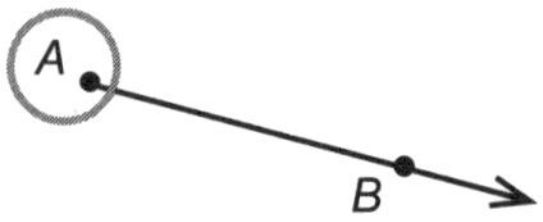

ray <u>*AB*</u>

b)

ray ______

c)

ray ______

5. Extend the rays in Question 4.

6. Name the rays.

a) 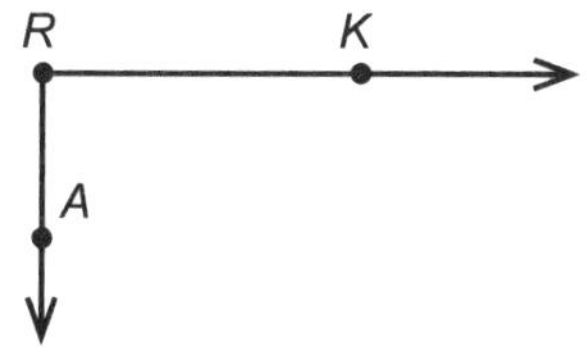

b) 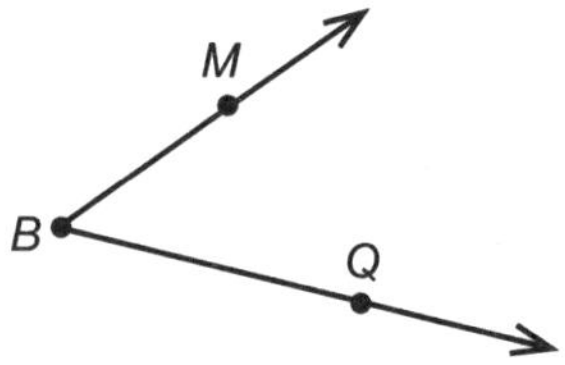

c) 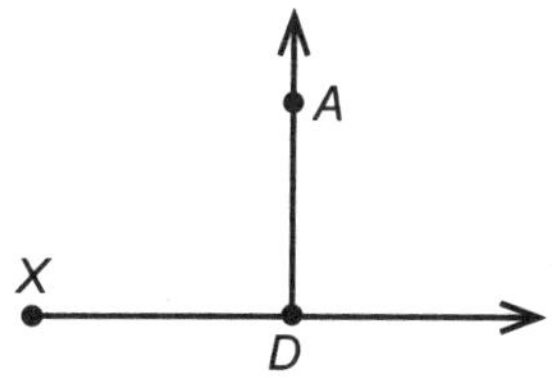

a) <u>RA</u> and ______ b) ______ and ______ c) ______ and ______

A point where lines, rays, or line segments meet is called an **intersection point**.

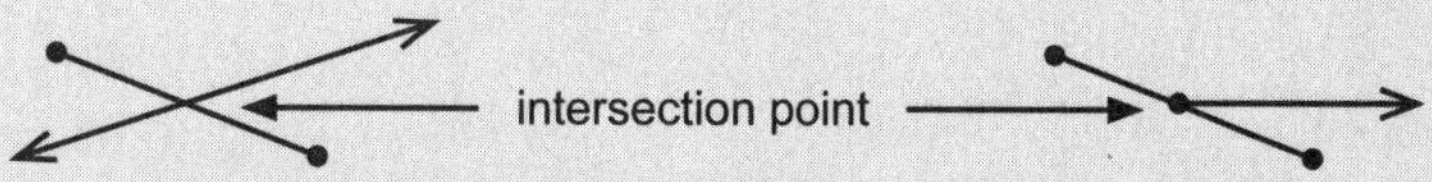

7. Name two intersecting lines, line segments, or rays and the intersection point.

a) 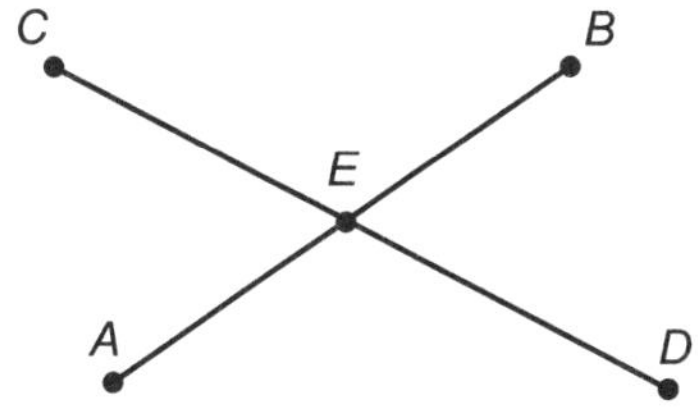

b) 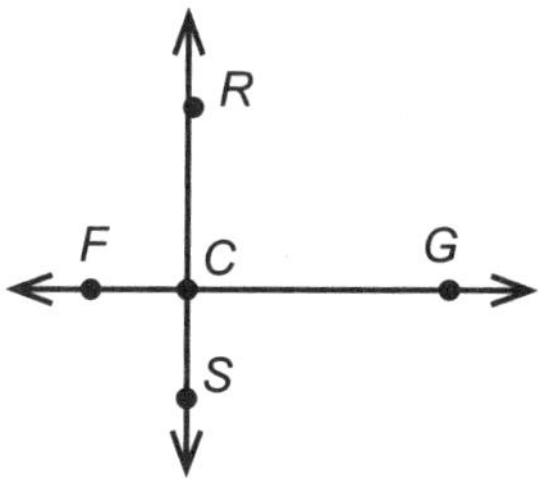

c) 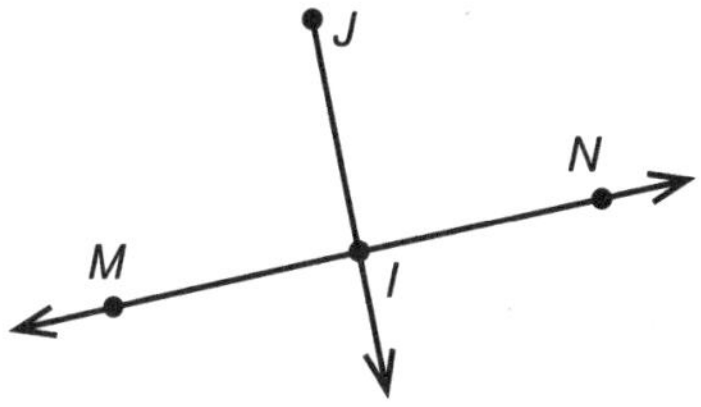

a) <u>CD</u> and ______ intersect at ______

b) ______ and ______ intersect at ______

c) ______ and ______ intersect at ______

8. Circle the intersection point.

a) 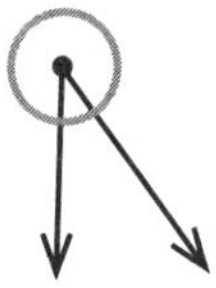 b)  c)  d) 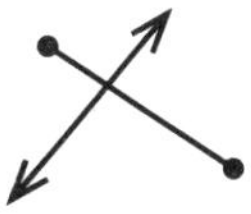 e)  f) 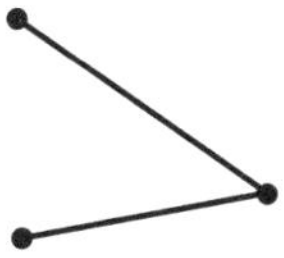

9. a) Draw a point *P* on *AB*.

b) Draw the line segment *XY* that intersects *AB* at point *P*.

Bonus ▶ Name the line in six ways.

<u>AB</u>, <u>AC</u>, ______, ______, ______, ______

Angles and Shapes

When two rays have the same endpoint, they form an **angle**.
You do not have to draw a dot to show the common endpoint.

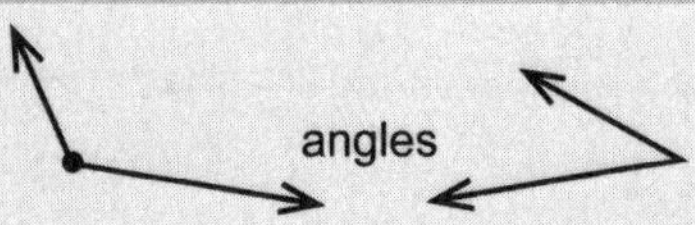

1. Circle the diagrams that show angles.

An angle has a **vertex** and two **arms**. You can extend the arms as much as needed without changing the angle.

When naming an angle, you always write the vertex in the middle.

Example: The angle shown is ∠*XYZ* or ∠*ZYX*.

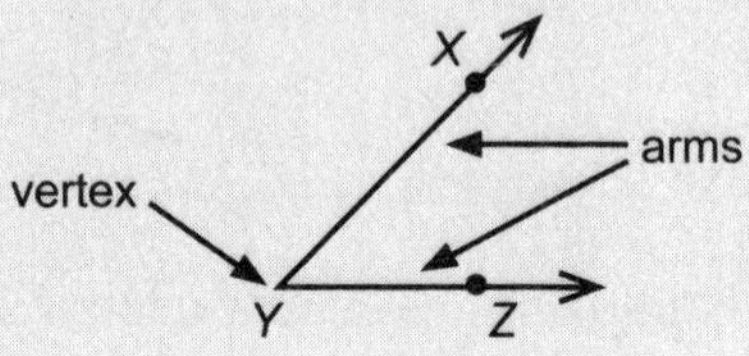

2. Circle the vertex. Then name the angle in two ways.

a)

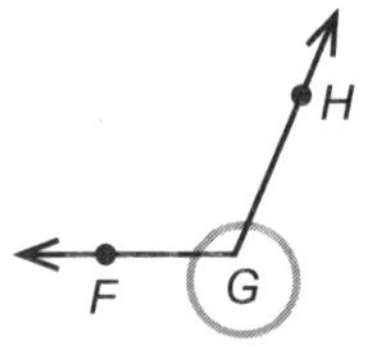

∠ FGH or ∠ HGF

b)

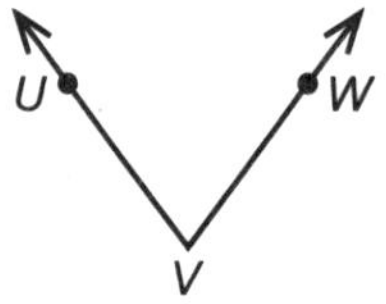

∠______ or ∠______

c)

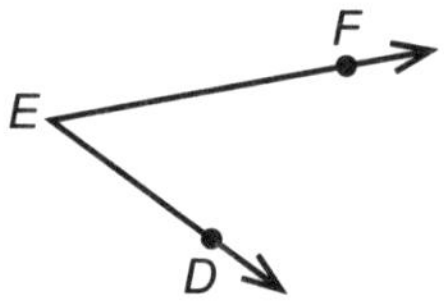

∠______ or ∠______

3. Circle the possible names for the angle in the diagram.

∠*ACT* or ∠*TCA*

∠*ATB* or ∠*BTA*

∠*CBT* or ∠*TBC*

∠*CTB* or ∠*BTC*

∠*BCA* or ∠*ACB*

∠*CTA* or ∠*ATC*

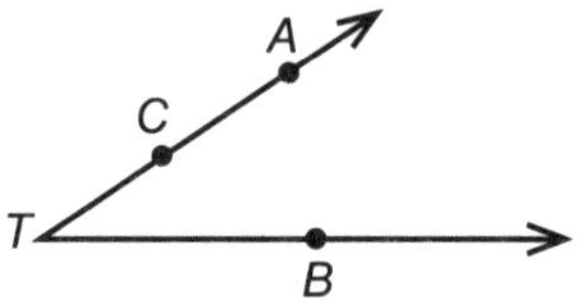

4. Name the angle marked with an arc (⌒).

a)

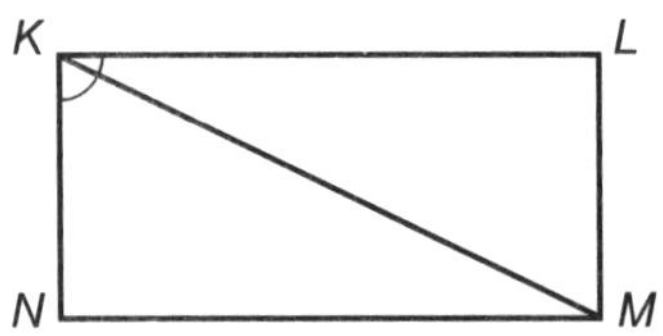

∠NKL

b)

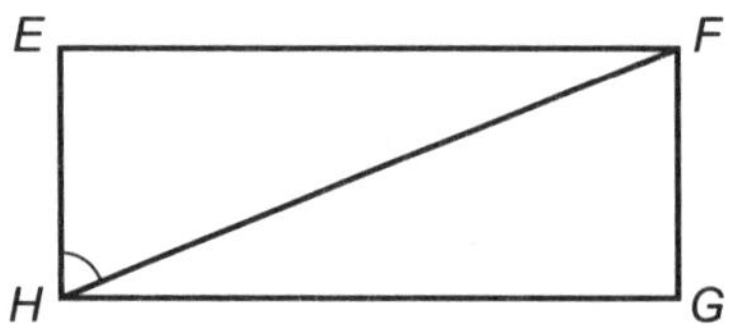

____

c)

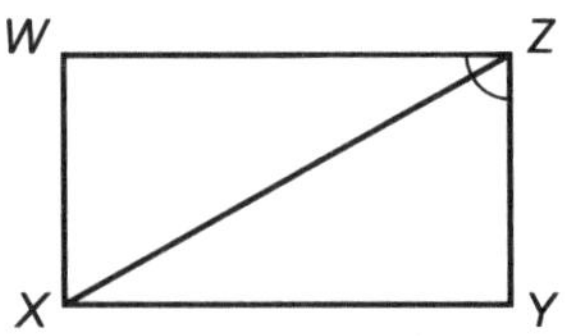

____

Bonus ▶ Name all the angles in the diagram.

____

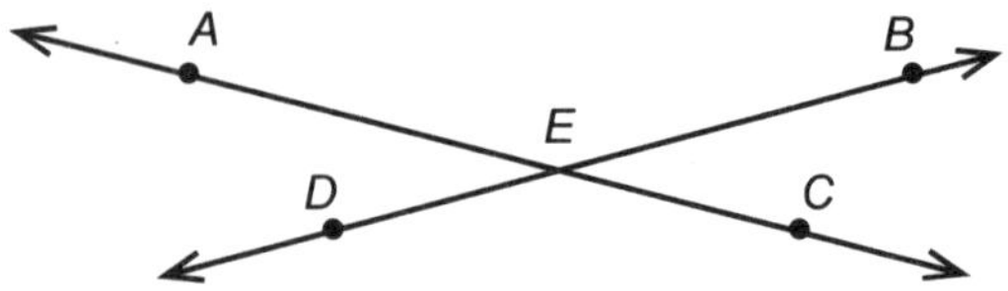

When there is no chance of confusion, you can name an angle with the vertex letter.

5. Circle the vertices of the angles you can name using only the vertex letter. Then name these angles.

a)
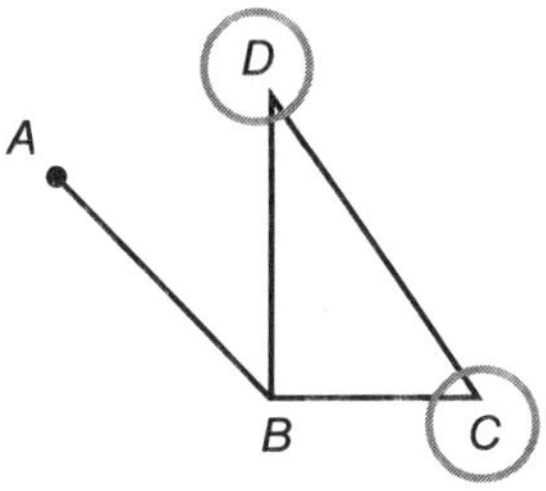

$\angle D$, $\angle C$

b)
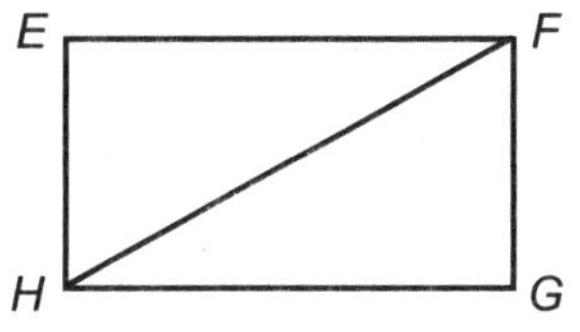

______

c)
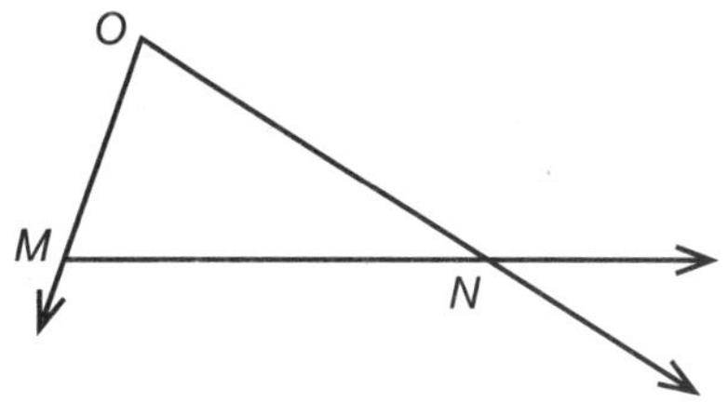

______

6. Name the sides of the triangle.

a)
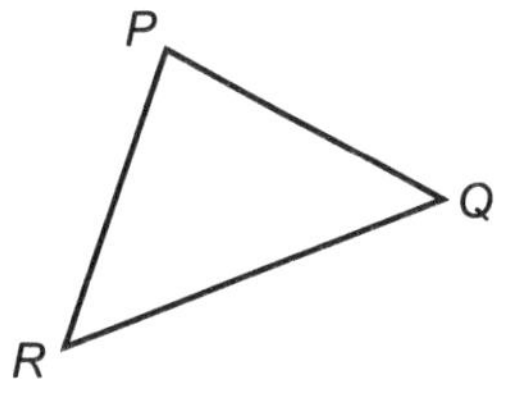

PQ, PR, RQ

b)
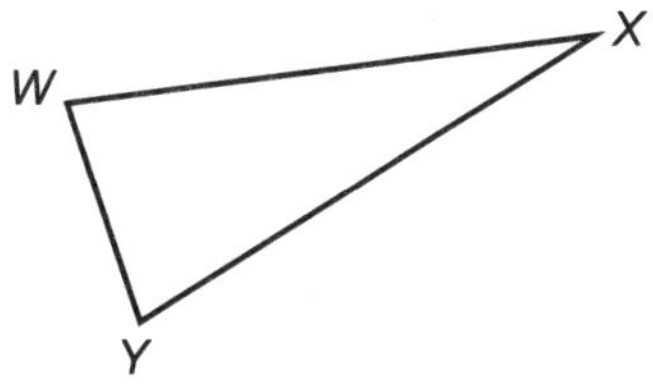

______

c)
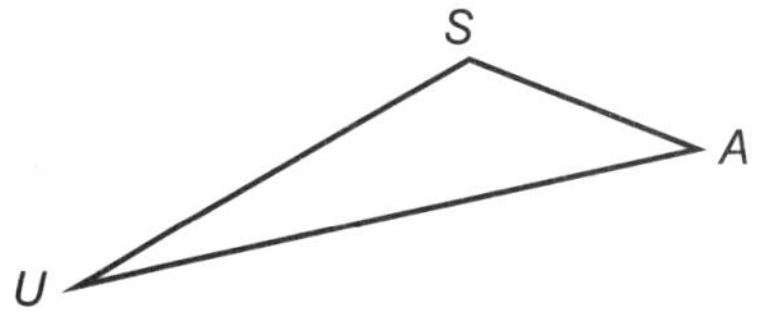

______

To name a polygon, write the names of the vertices in order (clockwise or counterclockwise). You can start at any vertex.

7. Name the polygon.

a)
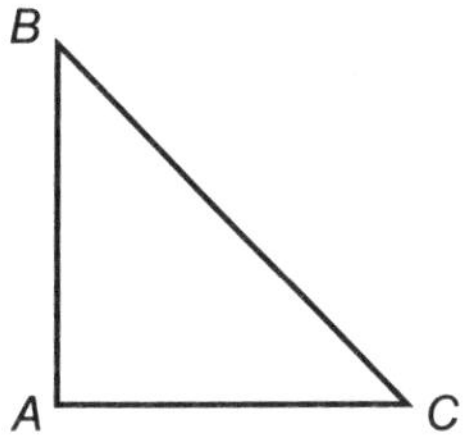

______

b)
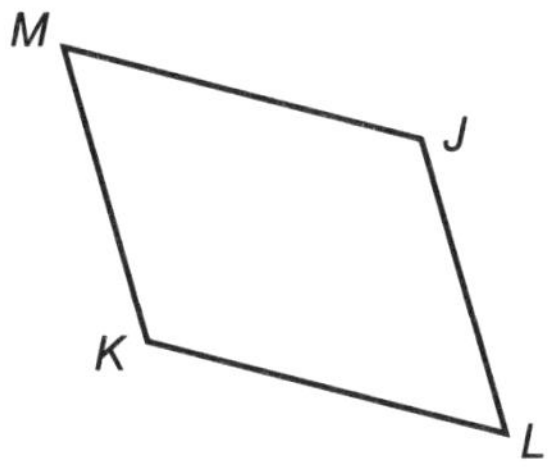

______

c)
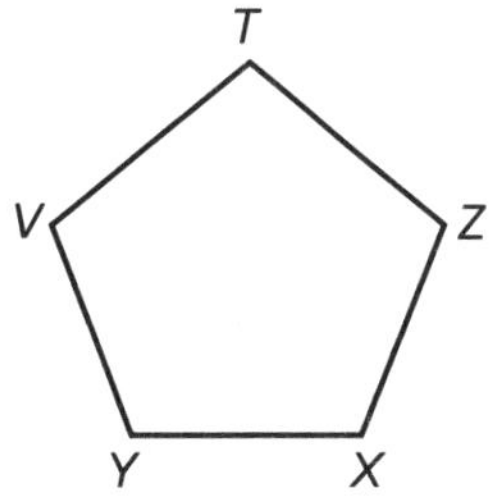

______

d)
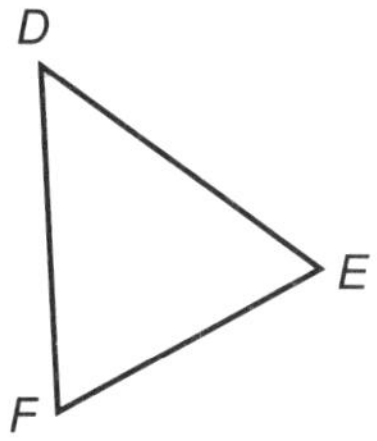

______

8. a) Circle the correct names for the polygon.

ABKLXY *ALYXBK* *BKALYX*

BKXAYL *XYLAKB* *LYBKAX*

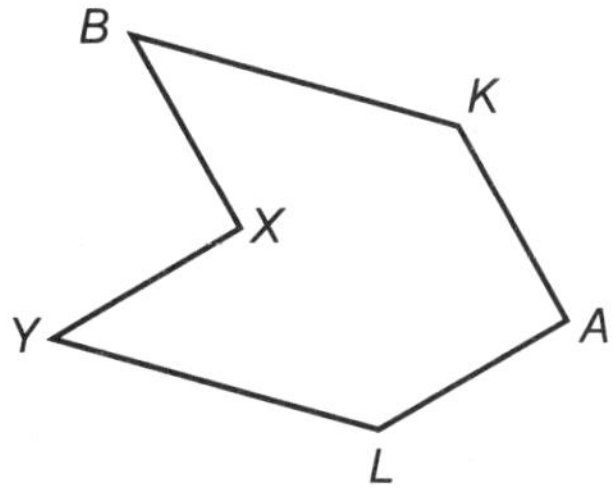

b) Write another correct name for the polygon. ______

Bonus ▶ Label the vertices, and then name the shape.

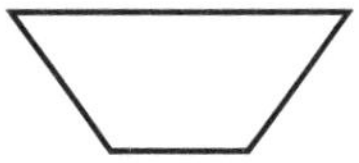

______

G8-3 Perpendicular and Parallel Lines

Perpendicular lines, rays, or line segments meet at a **right angle**. We mark right angles with a little square. The ⊥ symbol means "is perpendicular to."

EG ⊥ *FZ*

or

FZ ⊥ *EG*

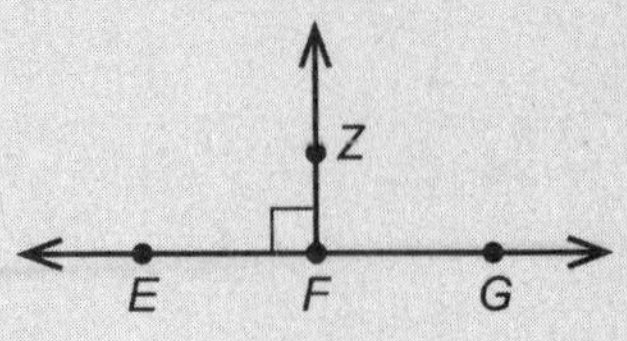

AB ⊥ *ST*

or

ST ⊥ *AB*

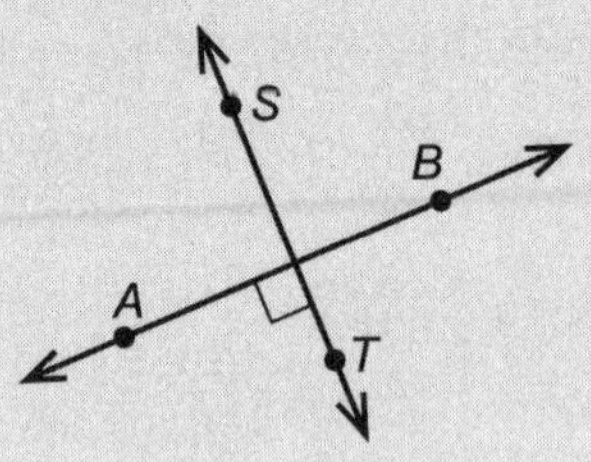

1. Name the perpendicular lines, rays, or line segments.

a) 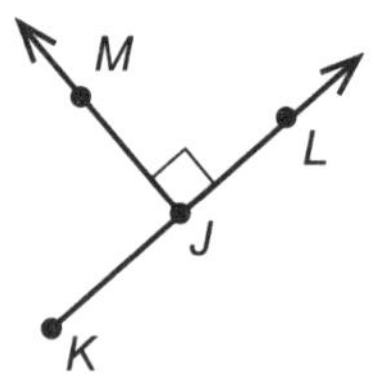

____

b) 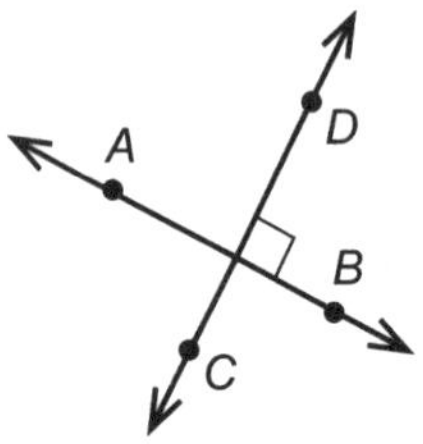

____

c) 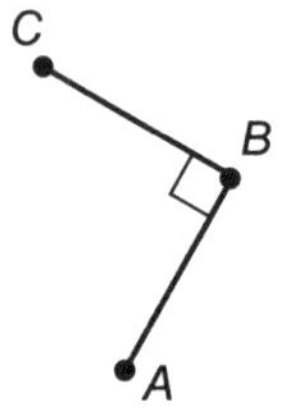

____

d) 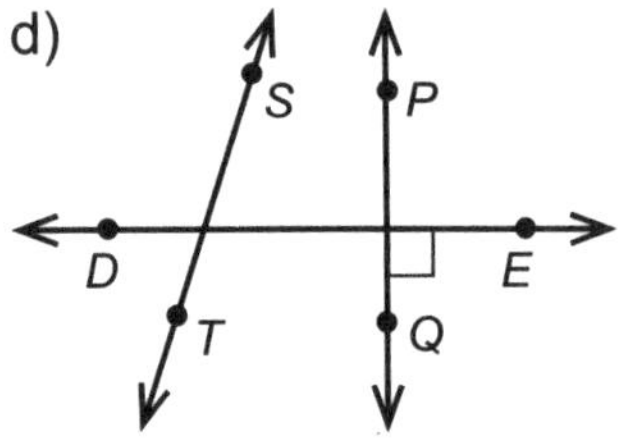

____

2. Use a square corner to find the right angles. Mark all the right angles with a square.

a) 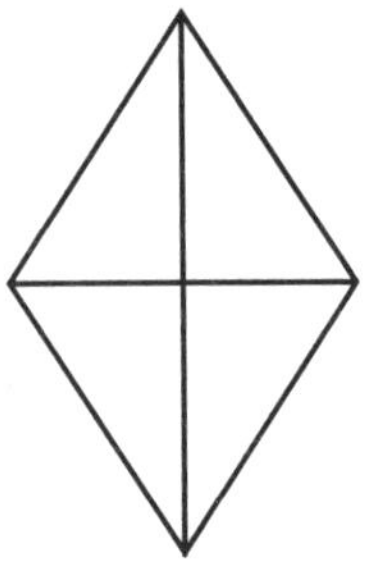

b) 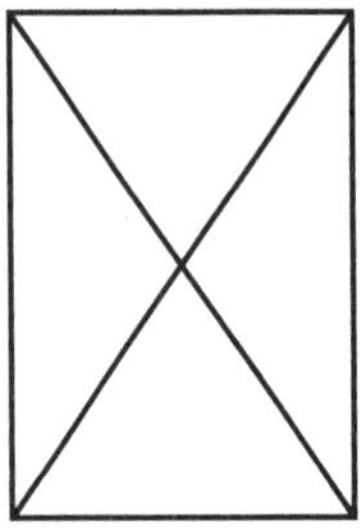

c) 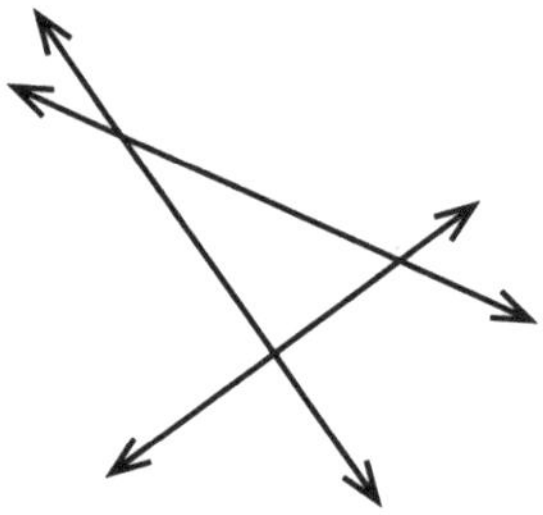

d) 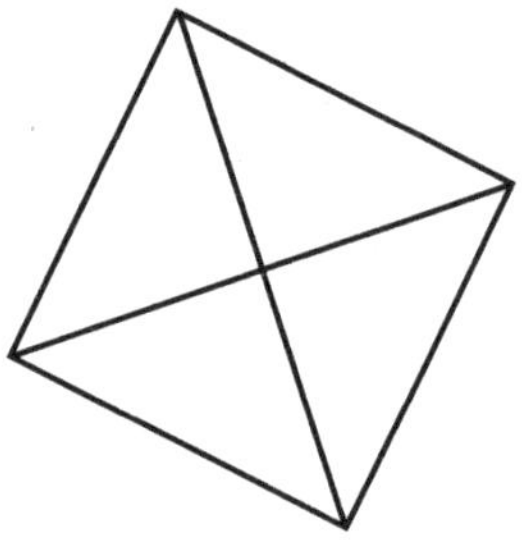

3. Match the diagram to the correct description.

A. 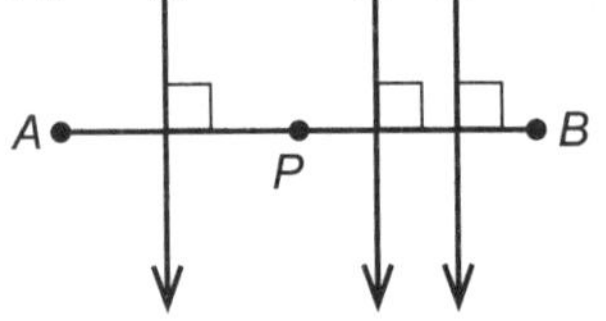

B. 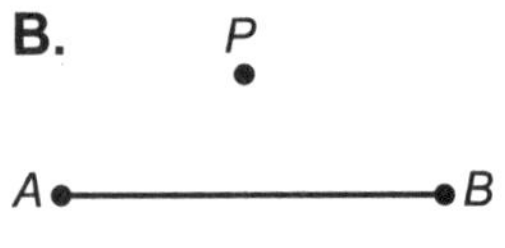

C. 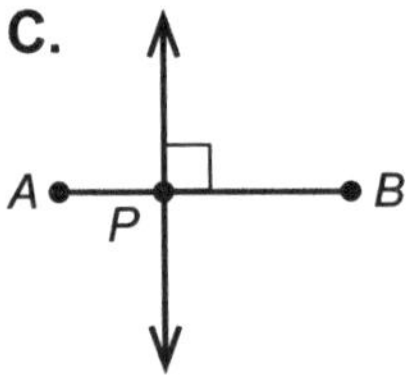

D. 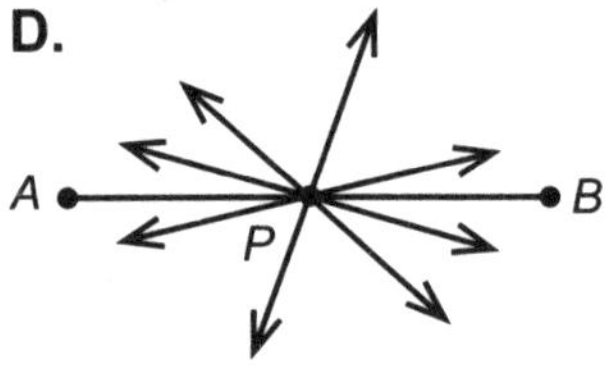

a) Point *P* is not on line segment *AB*. ______

b) Lines pass through point *P* on *AB*. ______

c) Lines are perpendicular to line segment *AB*. ______

d) The line perpendicular to *AB* passes through point *P*. ______

Parallel lines never intersect, no matter how far they are extended in either direction.

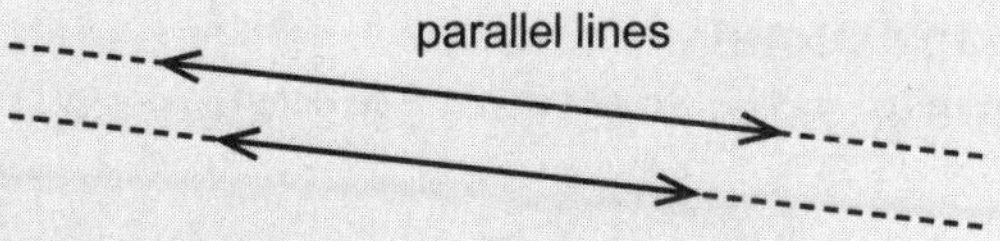

4. Use a ruler to extend both lines. Then circle parallel lines.

a) 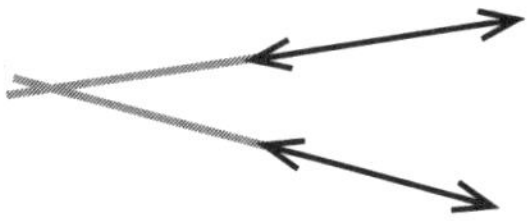

b) 

c) 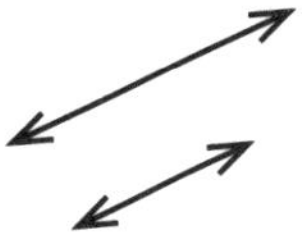

5. Match the diagram to the correct description.

A. 

B. 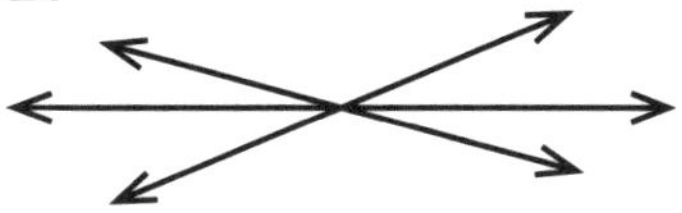

C. 

a) The lines intersect. ______

b) If the lines are extended far enough, they intersect. ______

c) The lines are parallel. ______

6. Give two examples of parallel lines in the world around you.

____

We mark parallel lines, rays, or line segments using matching arrow symbols (>, ≫).

The || symbol means "is parallel to." Examples: *AB* || *CD* and *BC* || *DA*.

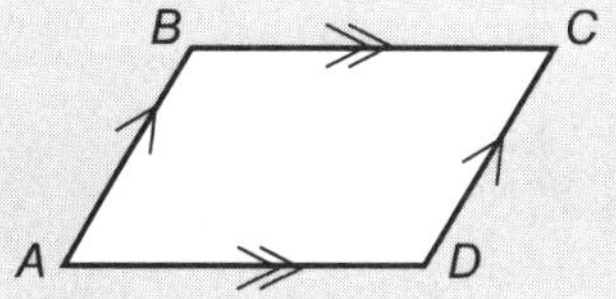

7. Use arrow symbols to mark the sides of the shape that look like they are parallel.

a) 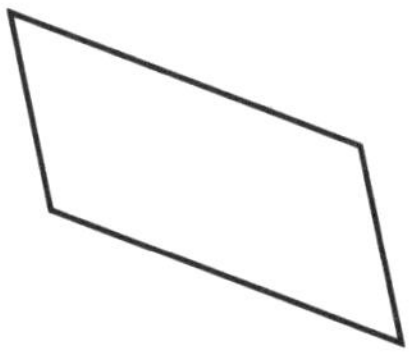

b) 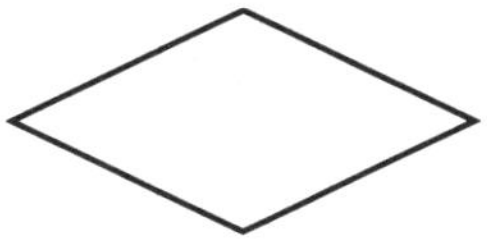

c) 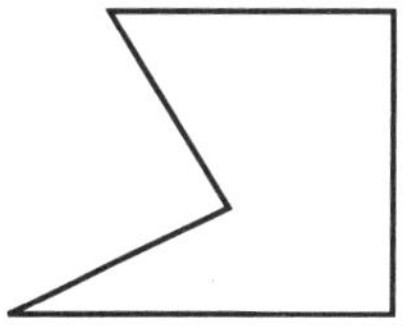

8. State which lines are parallel.

a) 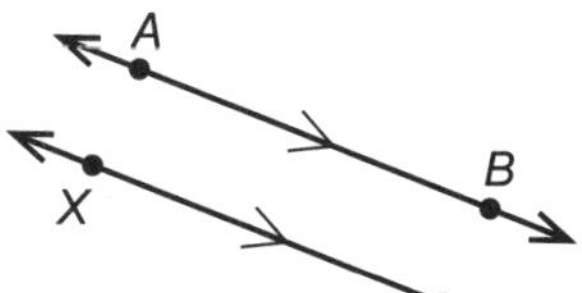

AB || ______

b) 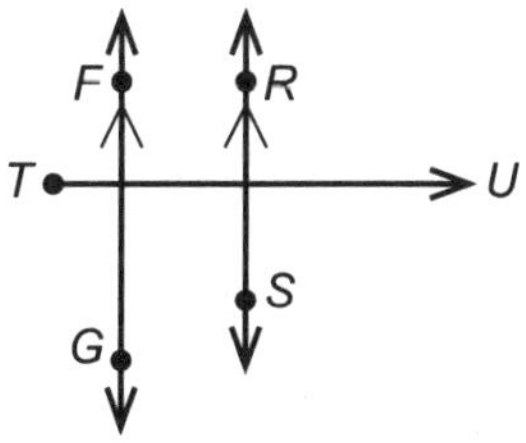

______ || ______

c) 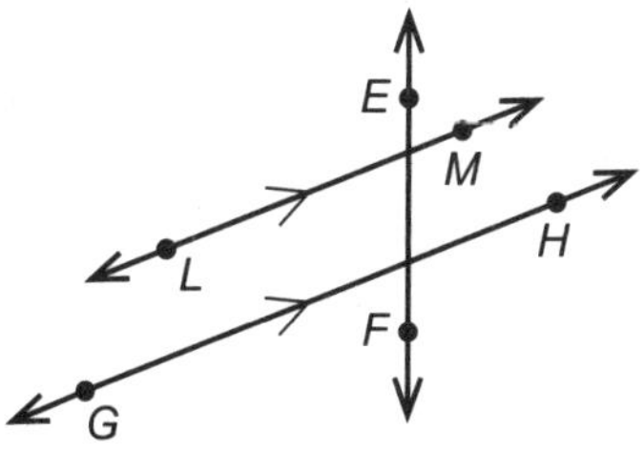

______ || ______

A **quadrilateral** with exactly 1 pair of parallel sides is called a **trapezoid**. A quadrilateral with 2 pairs of parallel sides is called a **parallelogram**.

Trapezoids

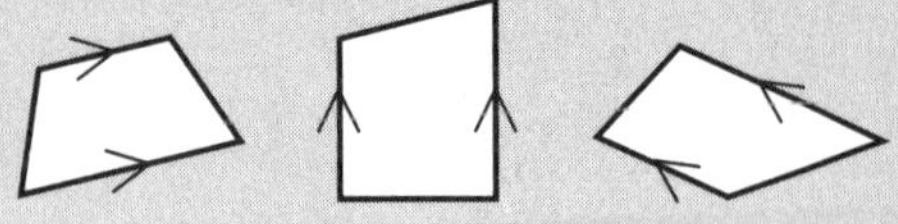

Parallelograms

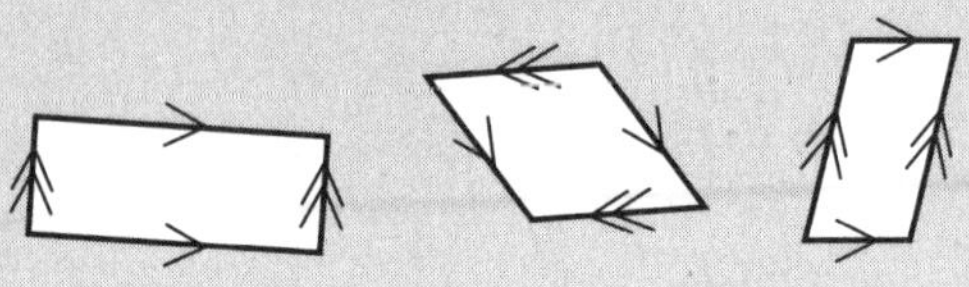

9. Mark the parallel sides with arrows. Then identify the type of quadrilateral.

a) 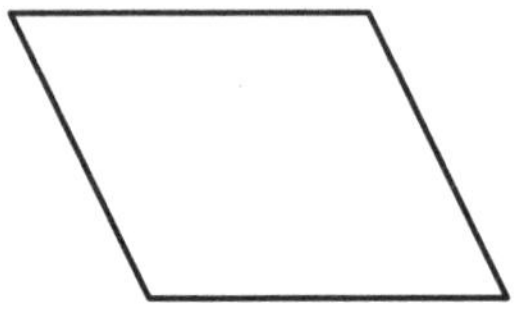

b) 

c) 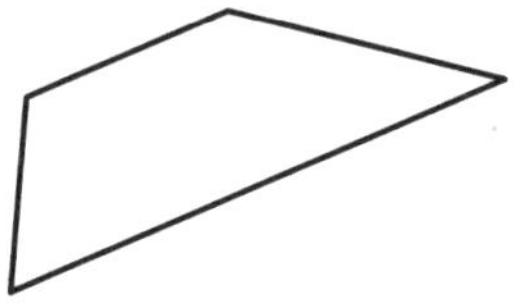

d) 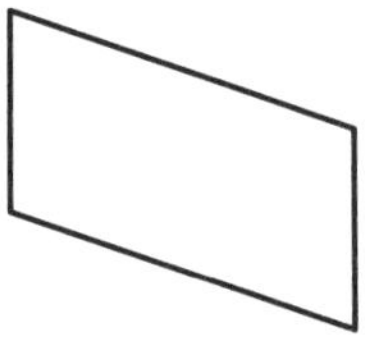

a) ____________________ b) ____________________ c) ____________________ d) ____________________

We use matching **hash marks** to show equal line segments.

This triangle has 2 equal sides.

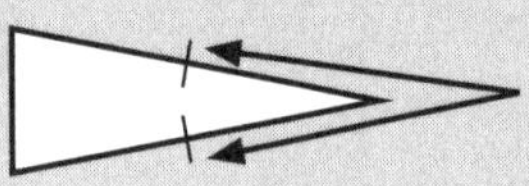

In a parallelogram, opposite sides are equal.

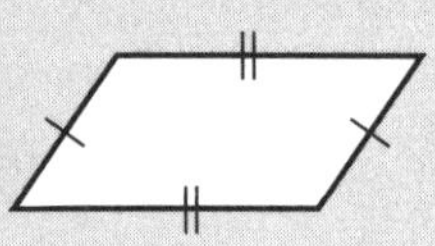

10. Measure the sides of the polygon to the closest millimeter. Mark equal sides with hash marks.

a)

_____ mm

_____ mm 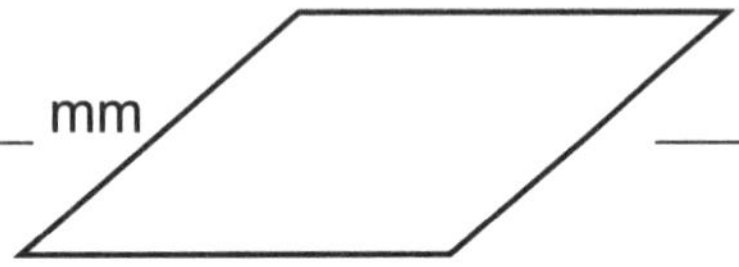 _____ mm

_____ mm

b)

_____ mm

_____ mm 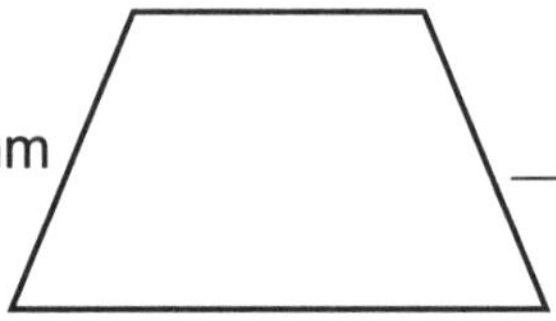 _____ mm

_____ mm

A **rhombus** is a parallelogram with all 4 sides the same length.

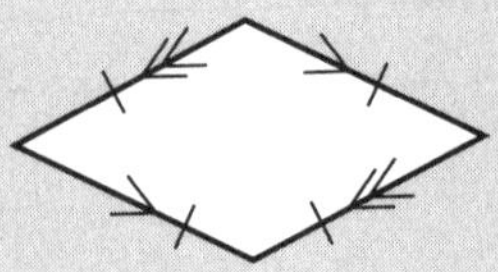

A **rectangle** is a parallelogram with 4 right angles.

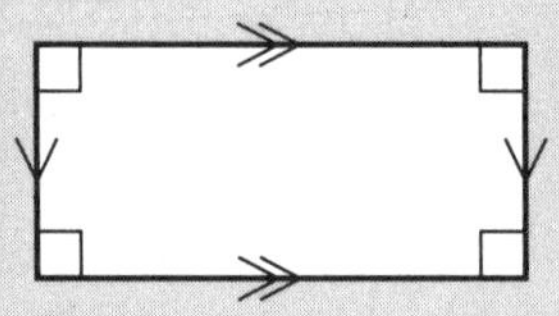

A **square** is a rectangle with all 4 sides the same length.

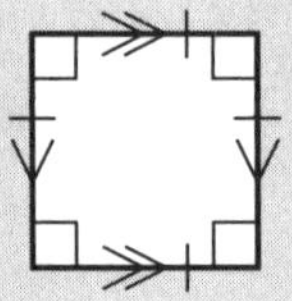

11. Name the polygon. Use the best name that fits.

a) 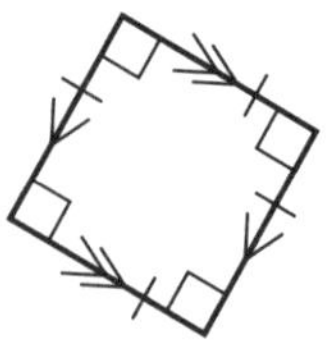

b) 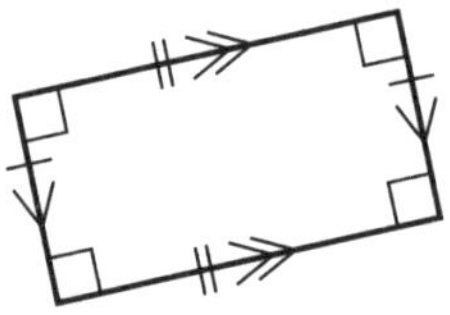

c) 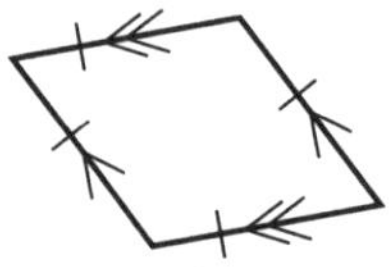

d) 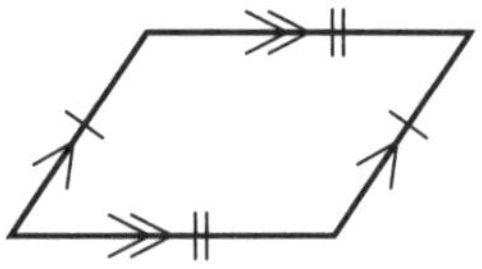

____________________ ____________________ ____________________ ____________________

G8-4 Measuring and Drawing Angles

We measure angles in degrees. The angle below measures 1 degree.

We use a small raised circle after the number instead of the word "degree": 1 degree = 1°.
A right angle measures 90°.

1. Identify the angle as less than 90° (< 90°) or more than 90° (> 90°).

a) 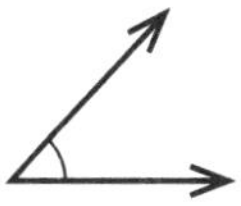

< 90°

b) 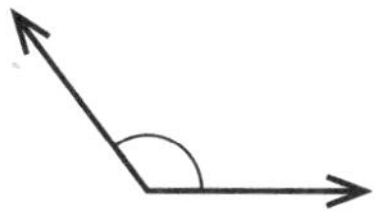

____

c) 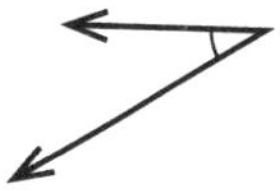

____

d) 

____

Acute angles are less than a right angle. They measure between 0° and 90°.
Obtuse angles are greater than a right angle. They measure between 90° and 180°.

2. Identify the angle as acute or obtuse.

a) 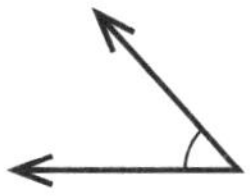

acute

b) 

____

c) 

____

d) 

____

To measure an angle, we use a **protractor**.

A protractor has 180 subdivisions of 1° around its curved side.
It has two scales to measure angles clockwise or counterclockwise.

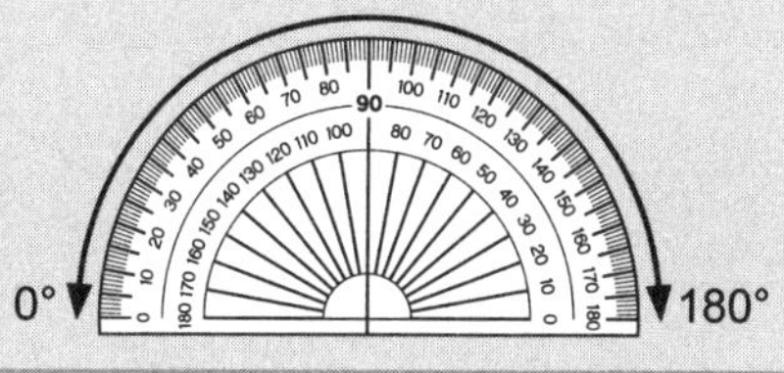

3. a) Use the scale that has a zero on one arm of the angle you measure. Write the measure of the angle.

i) 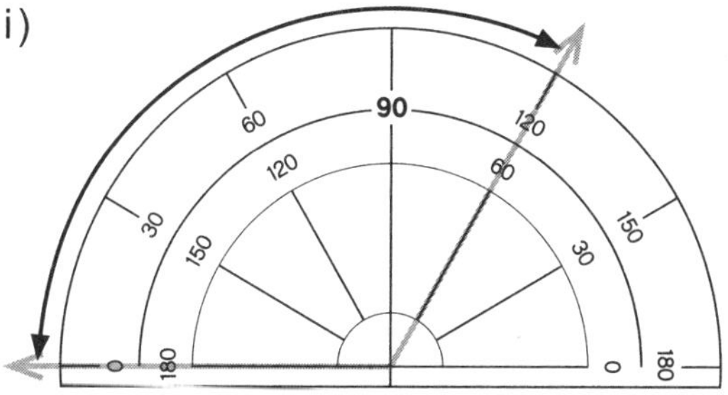

The angle measures ________.

ii) 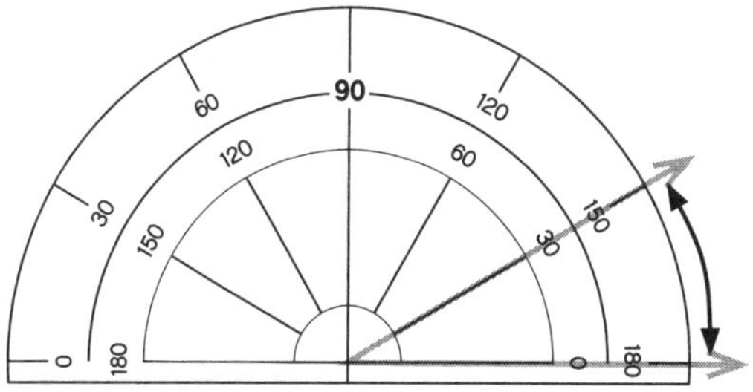

The angle measures ________.

b) Decide if each angle above is acute or obtuse. Does the measure you found in part a) fit your answer?

i) The angle is ____________.

ii) The angle is ____________.

4. Identify the angle as acute or obtuse. Then write the measure of the angle.

a)

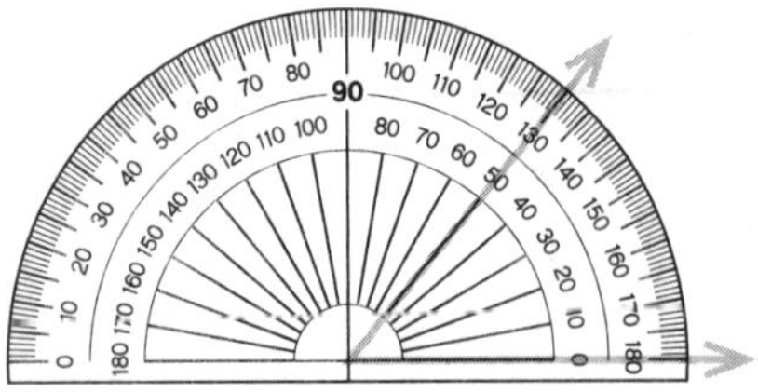

____

b)

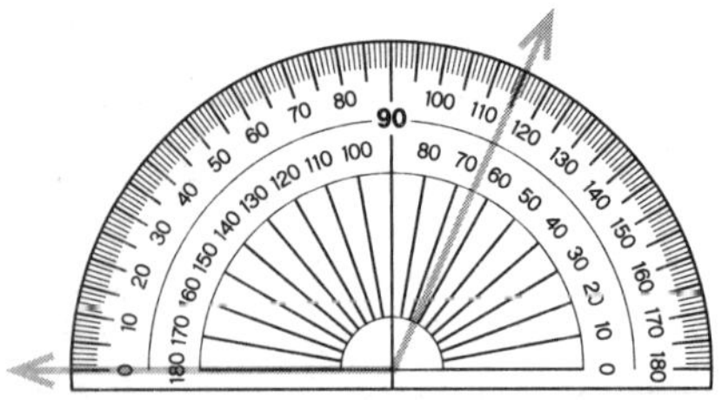

____

c)

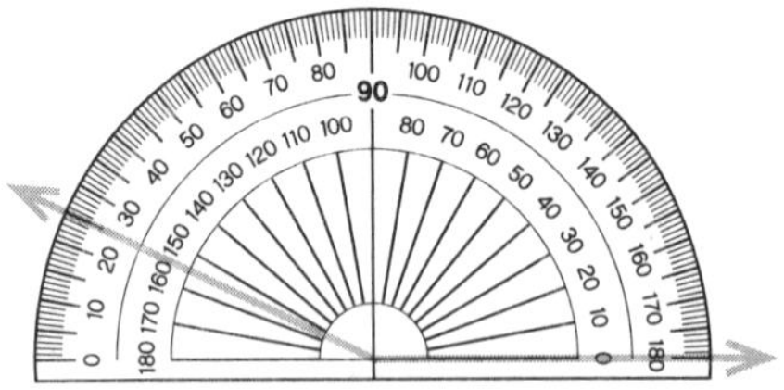

____

d)

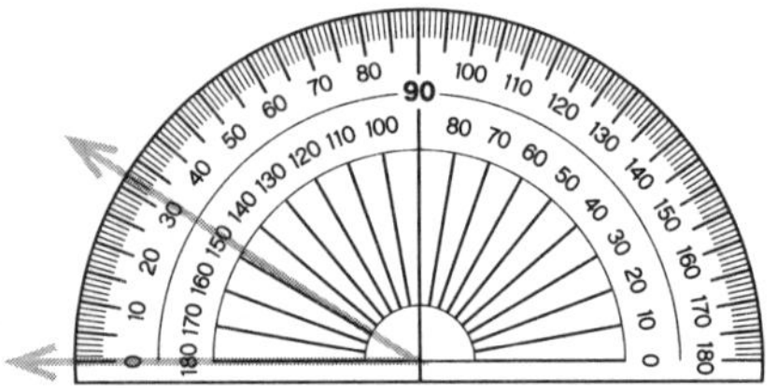

____

Each protractor has a **base line** and an **origin**.

To measure an angle, line up the base line of the protractor with one arm of the angle.

Place the origin of the protractor on the vertex of the angle.

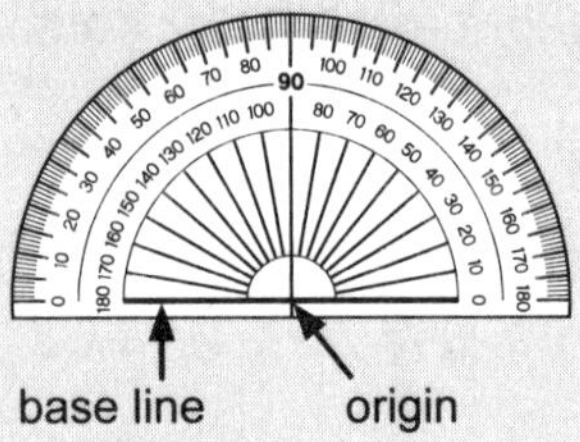

5. Measure the angle using a protractor.

a)

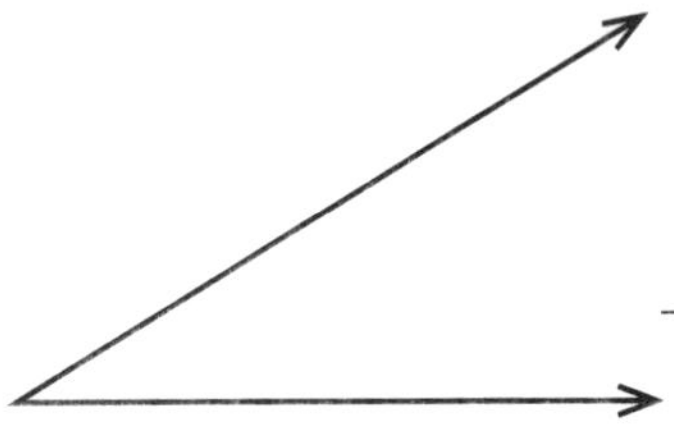

______

b)

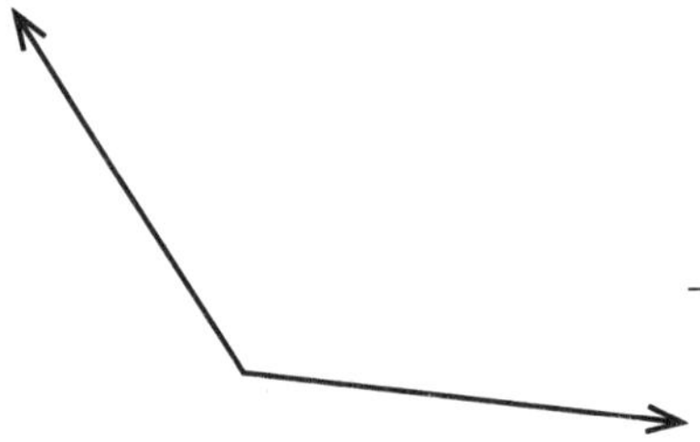

______

6. a) Measure the angles in the parallelogram. You might need to extend the arms as shown in angle *A* in part i).

i)

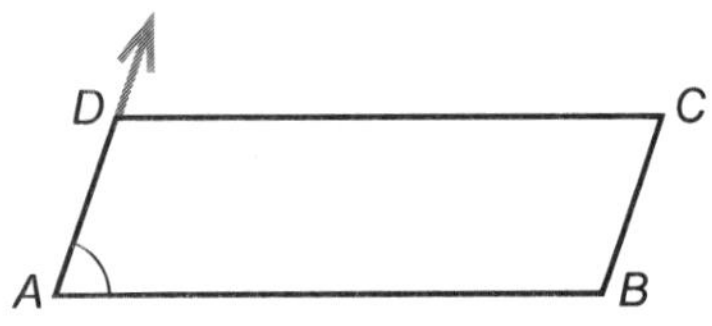

$\angle A =$ ______, $\angle B =$ ______

$\angle C =$ ______, $\angle D =$ ______

ii)

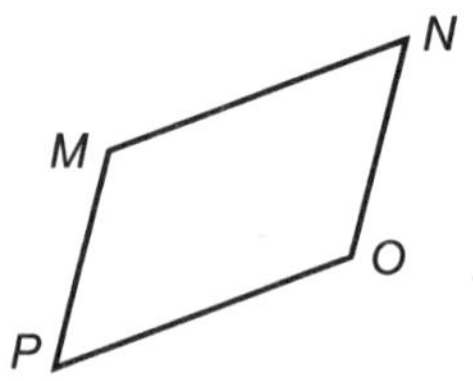

$\angle M =$ ______, $\angle N =$ ______

$\angle O =$ ______, $\angle P =$ ______

b) What do you notice about the opposite angles in a parallelogram?

Step 1: To draw a 60° angle, start with a ray.

Step 2: Place the protractor on the ray, as shown.

Step 3: Measure 60° and mark it.

Step 4: Use a ruler to draw a ray from the endpoint to the mark.

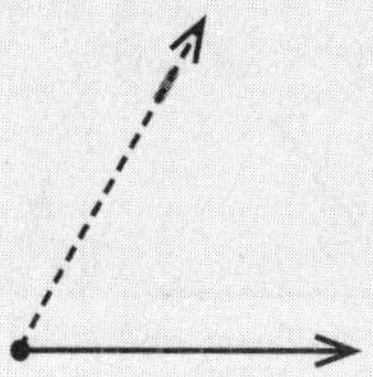

7. Finish drawing the angle.

a) 140°

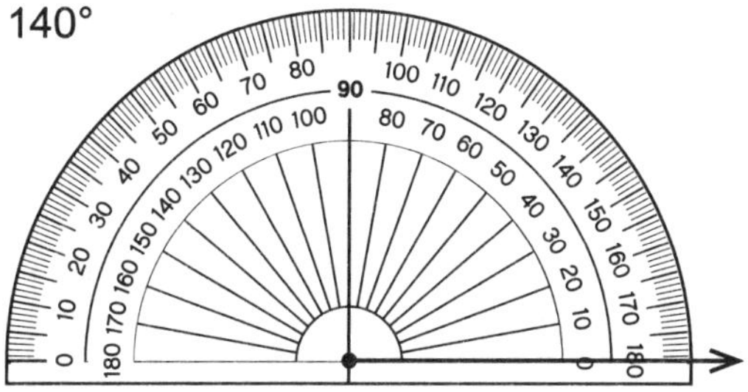

b) 65°

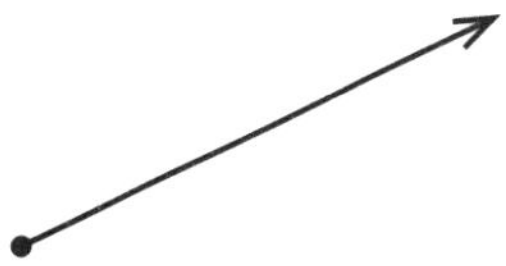

8. Use a protractor to draw the angle.

a) 25° b) 105° c) 82° d) 136°

To draw a line perpendicular to the line *AB* through point *P*, place the protractor so that ...

- its straight side touches *P*, and
- line *AB* passes through the origin and the 90° mark.

Then, use the straight side of the protractor to draw the line.

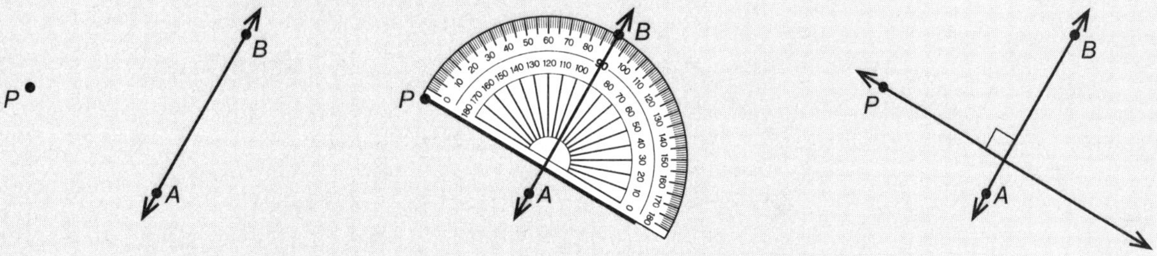

9. a) Draw a line *CD* so that it is not vertical and not horizontal.

b) Mark point *Q* away from the line, not on *CD*. Draw a line perpendicular to *CD* through *Q*.

c) Mark point *R* anywhere on *CD*. Draw a line perpendicular to *CD* through *R*.

Bonus ▶ What do you notice about the lines you drew in parts b) and c)?

G8-5 Sum of the Angles in a Triangle

1. Add the measures of the angles in each triangle.

a) 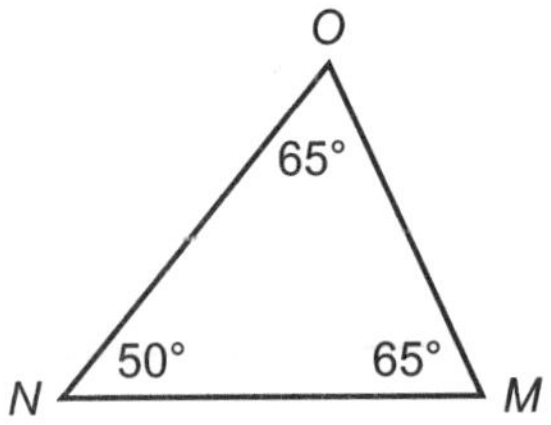

$\angle M + \angle N + \angle O$

= ____________________

= ______

b) 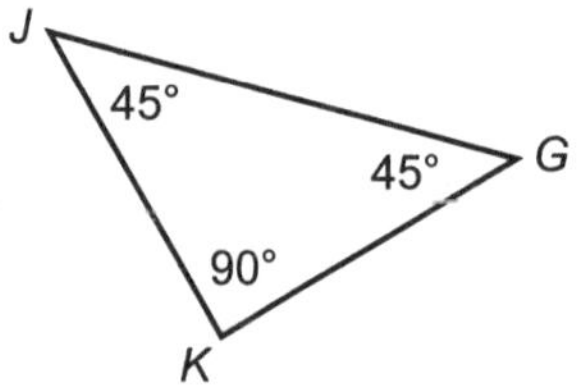

$\angle G + \angle J + \angle K$

= ____________________

= ______

c) 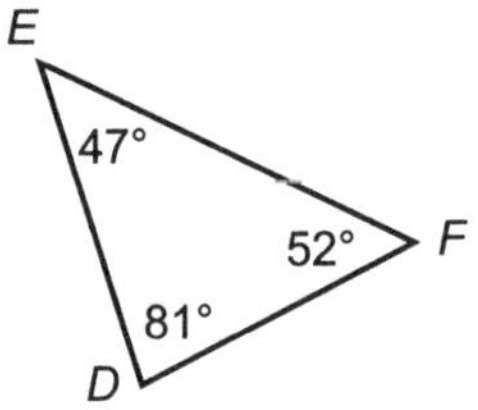

$\angle D + \angle E + \angle F$

= ____________________

= ______

d) 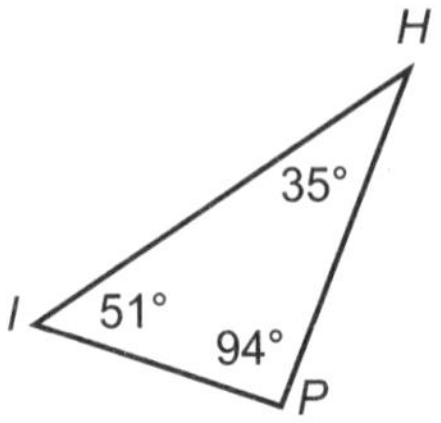

$\angle I + \angle P + \angle H$

= ____________________

= ______

e) 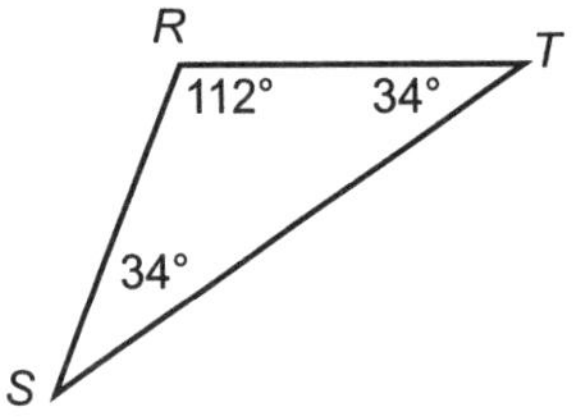

$\angle S + \angle R + \angle T$

= ____________________

= ______

Bonus ▶ 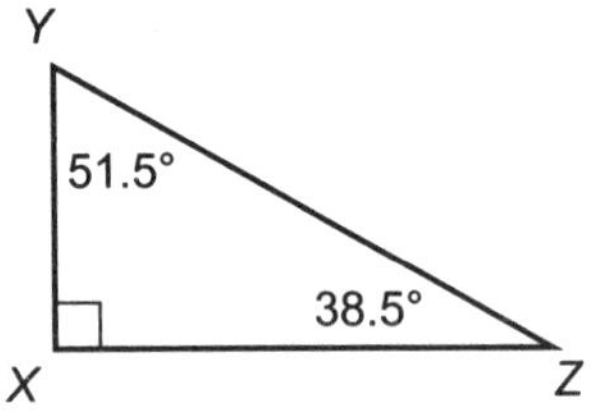

$\angle Z + \angle Y + \angle X$

= ____________________

= ______

2. Measure the angles in the triangle. Then add the angles.

a) 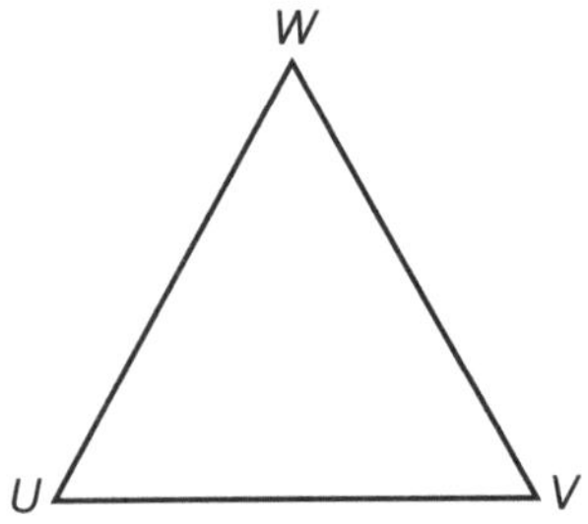

$\angle U =$ ______

$\angle V =$ ______

$\angle W =$ ______

$\angle U + \angle V + \angle W =$ ______

b) 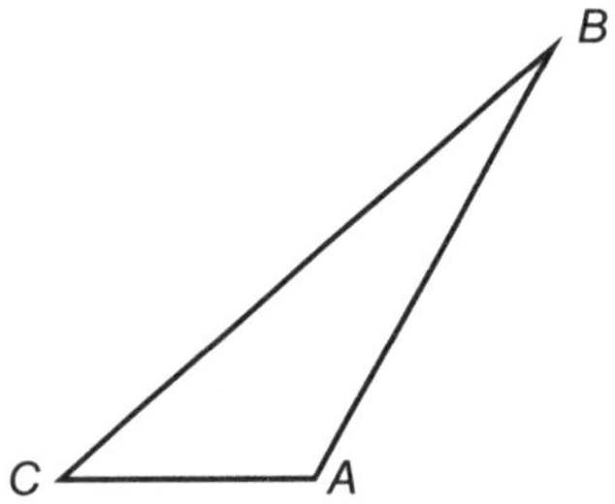

$\angle A =$ ______

$\angle B =$ ______

$\angle C =$ ______

$\angle A + \angle B + \angle C =$ ______

c) 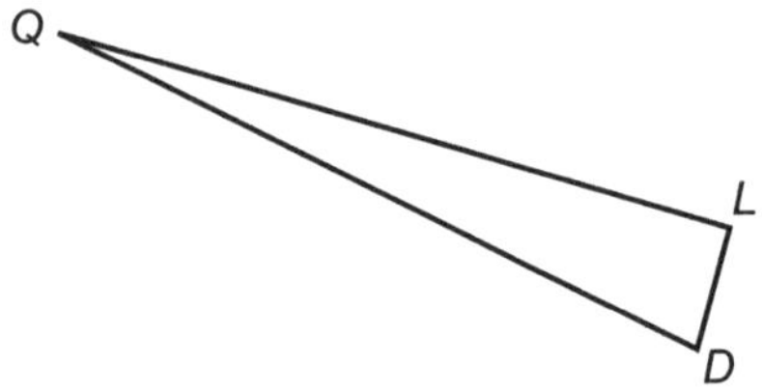

$\angle D =$ ______

$\angle L =$ ______

$\angle Q =$ ______

$\angle D + \angle L + \angle Q =$ ______

3. Look at the sum of the angles in each triangle in Questions 1 and 2. What do you notice?

____

The sum of the angles in a triangle is 180°.

$\angle A + \angle B + \angle C = 180°$

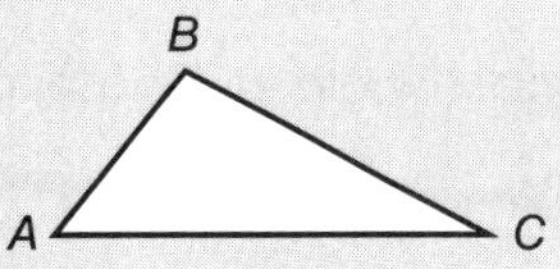

4. Use the sum of the angles in the triangle to find the measure of $\angle A$.

a)
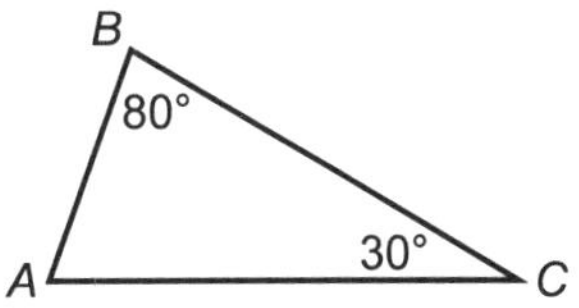

$\angle A =$ *180° − (80° + 30°)*

$=$ *180° − 110°*

$=$ *70°*

b)
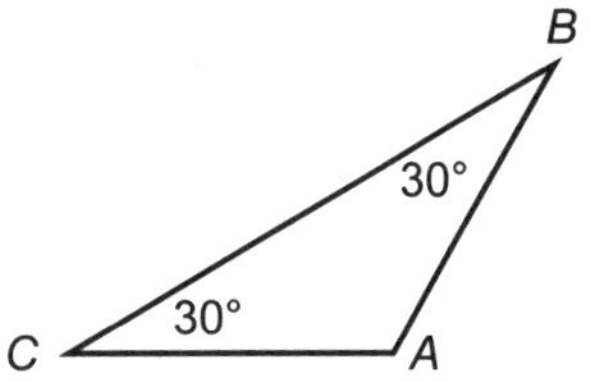

$\angle A =$ ______________

$=$ ______________

$=$ ______

c)
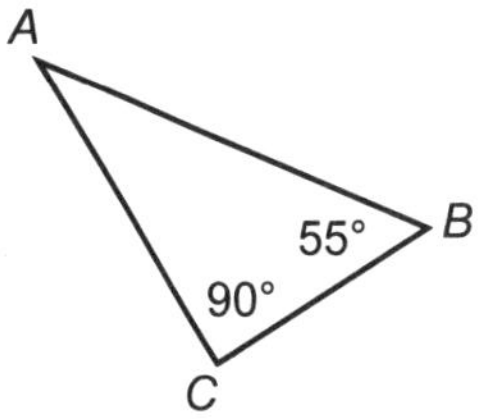

$\angle A =$ ______________

$=$ ______________

$=$ ______

To show that angles are equal, we mark them with arcs or double arcs.
Remember: To show right angles, we use small squares.

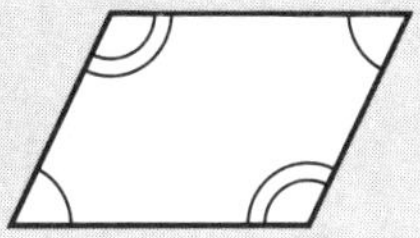

5. Find the measure of the missing angle.

a)
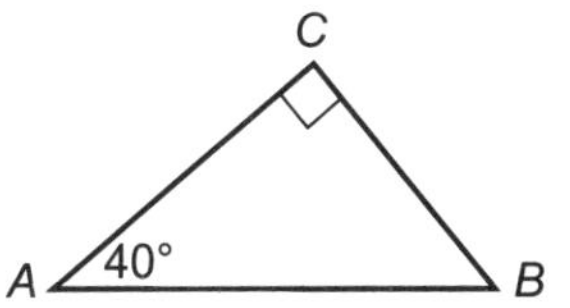

$\angle B =$ *180° − (90° + 40°)*

$=$ *180° − 130°*

$=$ *50°*

b)
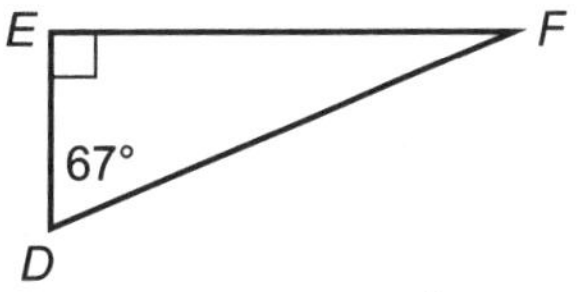

$\angle F =$ ______________

$=$ ______________

$=$ ______

c)
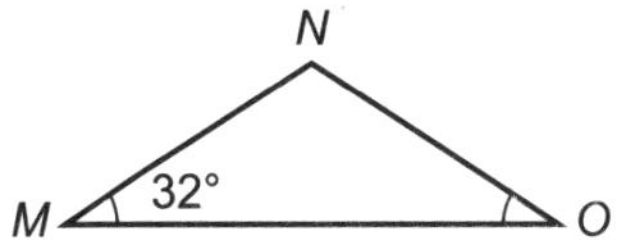

$\angle N =$ ______________

$=$ ______________

$=$ ______

6. a) A triangle has an angle that measures 30° and an angle that measures 60°. What is the measure of the third angle in the triangle?

b) A triangle has two angles of 45°. What is the measure of the third angle in the triangle?

c) A triangle has all angles equal. What is the measure of each angle?

7. a) Could a triangle ever have more than one obtuse angle? Use a sketch to explain.

b) Could a triangle ever have more than one right angle? Use a sketch to explain.

8. Use the picture to explain why the angles in a quadrilateral always add to 360°.

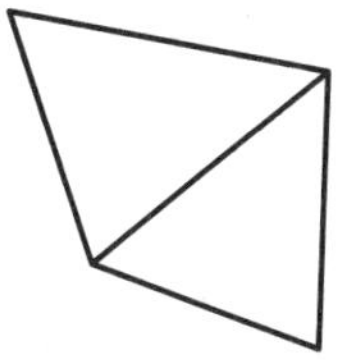

G8-6 Triangles

1. Mark the largest angle in the triangle with an arc.

a) 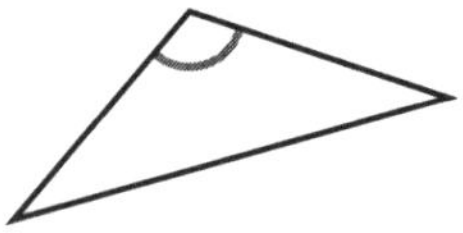

b) 

c) 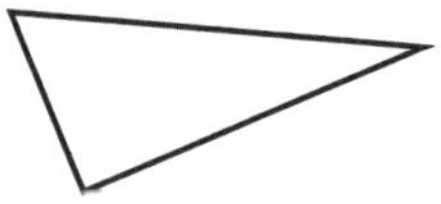

d) 

You can classify triangles by the size of the largest angle.

acute-angled or **acute** triangle

The largest angle is acute. 

right-angled or **right** triangle

The largest angle is right. 

obtuse-angled or **obtuse** triangle

The largest angle is obtuse. 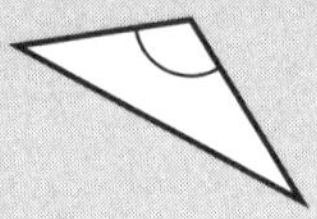

2. Mark the largest angle in the triangle with an arc. Use a protractor to check if the angle is acute, right angle, or obtuse. Then classify the triangle.

a) 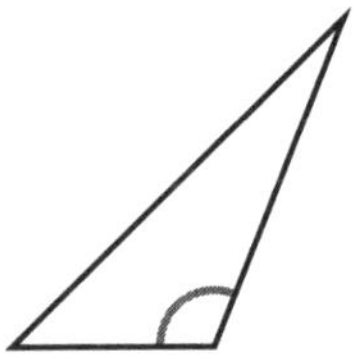

obtuse triangle

b) 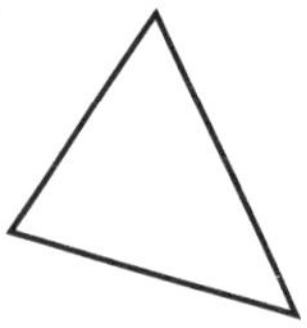

____

c) 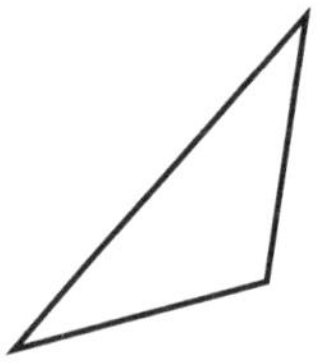

____

d) 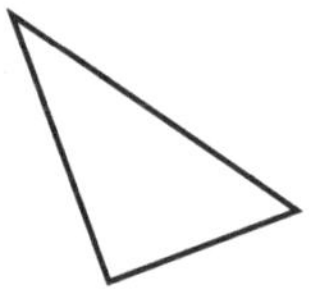

____

3. Classify the triangle.

a) 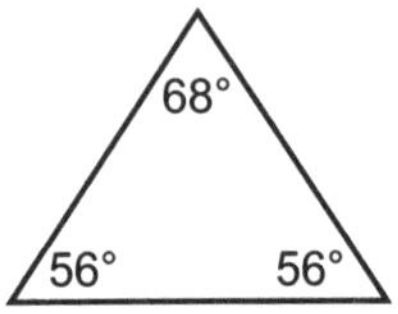

____

b) 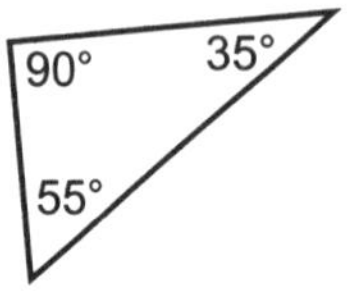

____

c) 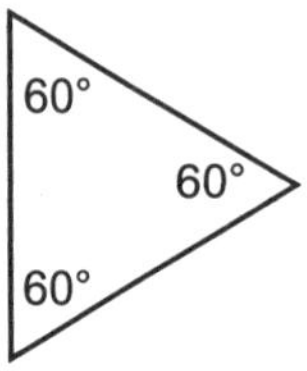

____

d) 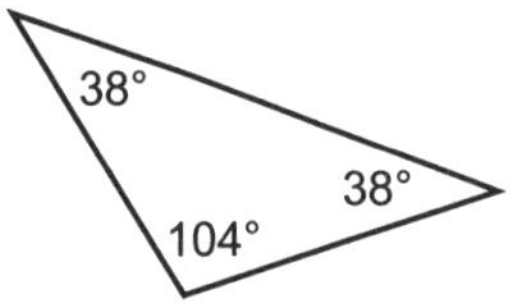

____

4. Remember: angles in a triangle add to 180°. Find the measure of the third angle in the triangle *ABC*. Then classify the triangle using the largest angle.

a) $\angle A = \angle B = 30°$

$\angle C = 180° - (\underline{\ 30°\ } + \underline{\ 30°\ }) = \_\_\_\_\_°$

The triangle is ________________.

b) $\angle A = 50°$ and $\angle B = 40°$

$\angle C = 180° - (\_\_\_\_ + \_\_\_\_) = \_\_\_\_\_°$

The triangle is ________________.

c) $\angle C = 75°$ and $\angle B = 25°$

$\angle A = 180° - (\_\_\_\_ + \_\_\_\_) = \_\_\_\_\_°$

The triangle is ________________.

d) $\angle A = 46°$ and $\angle C = 24°$

$\angle B = 180° - (\_\_\_\_ + \_\_\_\_) = \_\_\_\_\_°$

The triangle is ________________.

Bonus ▶ $\angle A = 90°$, $\angle C = 21°$, $\angle B =$ _____°. The triangle is ________________.

You can classify triangles by the number of *equal* sides.

Isosceles triangles have at least 2 equal sides.

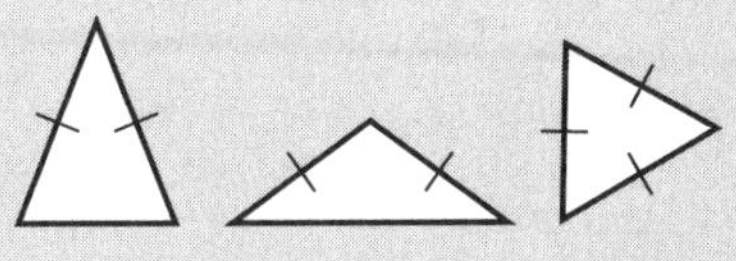

Scalene triangles have no equal sides.

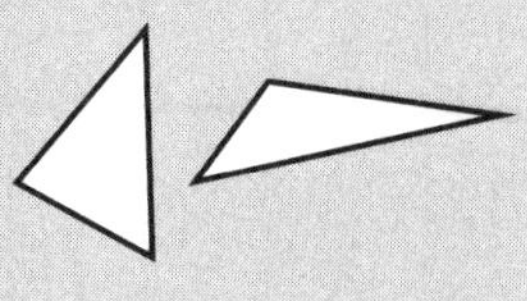

Isosceles triangles with *3 equal sides* are called **equilateral** triangles.

5. Classify the triangle by the number of equal sides.

a) b) c) d)

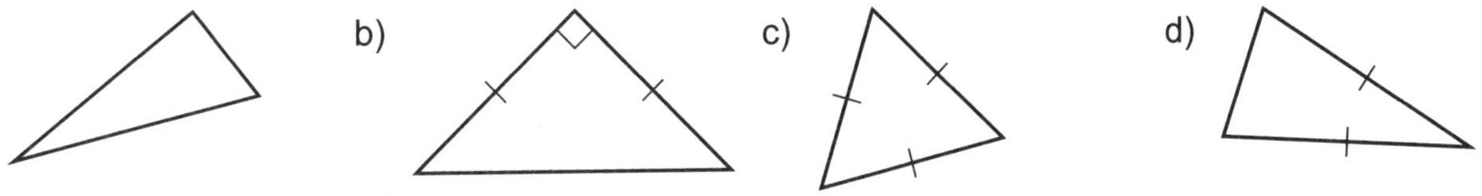

6. a) Mark the triangles for any equal sides, equal angles, and right angles. Do not measure all sides and angles; check only the angles and sides that look equal. Use a ruler and protractor to check as needed.

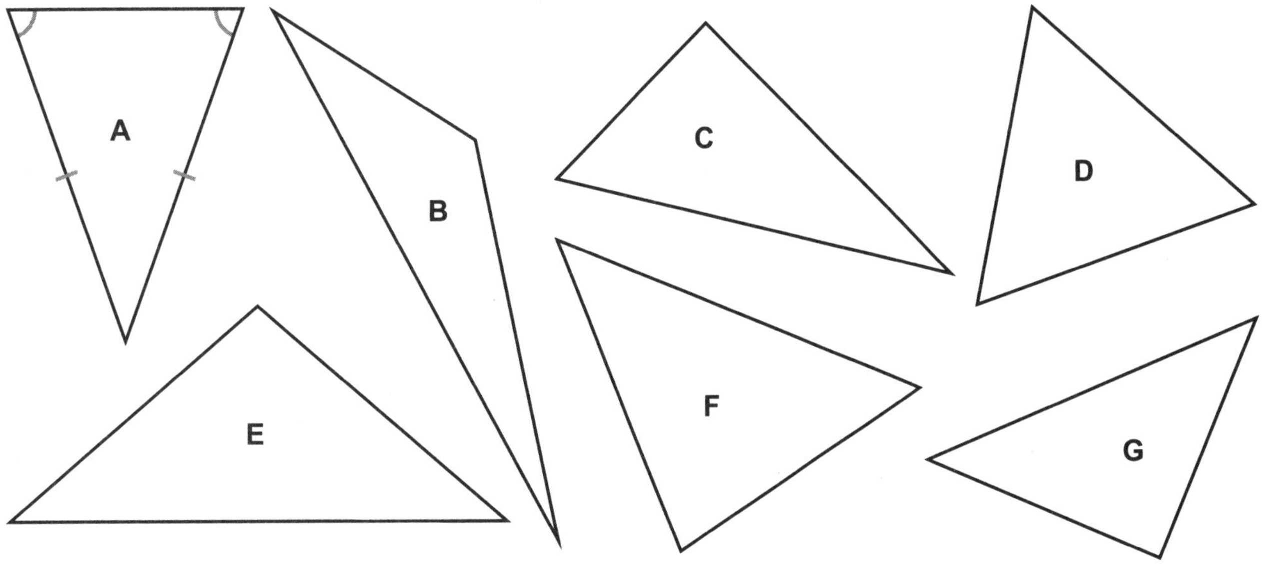

b) Classify the triangles in the tables below.

Acute-angled	*A,*
Right-angled	
Obtuse-angled	

Scalene	
Isosceles	*A,*

c) Look at the angles in the isosceles triangles. What do you notice?

d) Which triangle is equilateral? How many equal angles does it have?

7. An isosceles triangle has two equal angles and a third angle given below. Find the equal angles.

a) 80° b) 90° c) 126° d) 55°

G8-7 Making a Geometric Sketch

Work quickly—a sketch is not supposed to be perfect.

1. Sketch the figure described.

a) a rectangle divided into 2 triangles

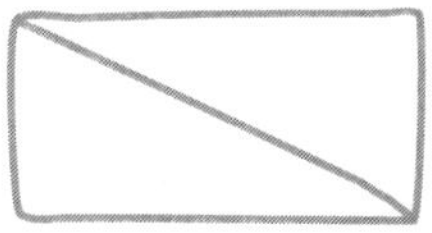

b) a line segment *AB* intersecting line *CD*

c) a parallelogram

d) a triangle *KLM*

Draw sides and angles roughly to scale. For example, a side marked 10 m should look twice the length of a side marked 5 m.

2. In the pair, circle the sketch that is roughly to scale.

a)

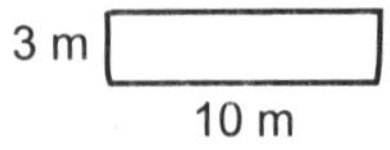

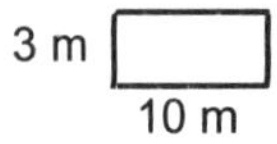

b)

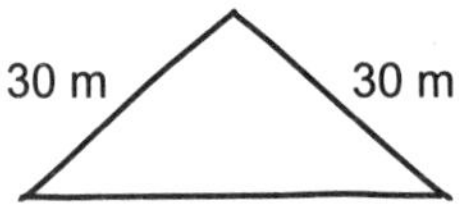

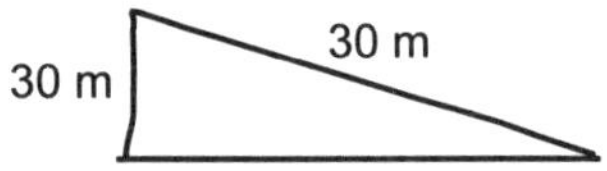

3. Read the description and circle the sketch that looks more like the description.

a) a 90° angle

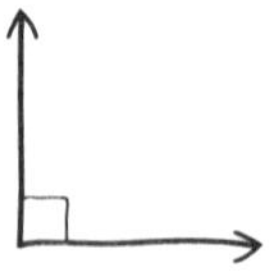

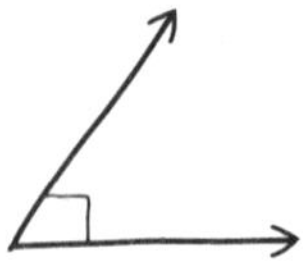

b) a 45° angle

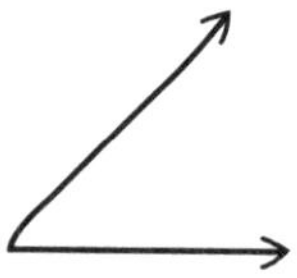

c) an equilateral triangle

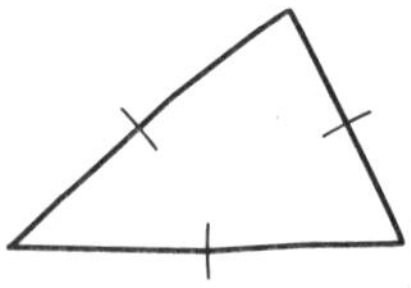

d) an obtuse isosceles triangle

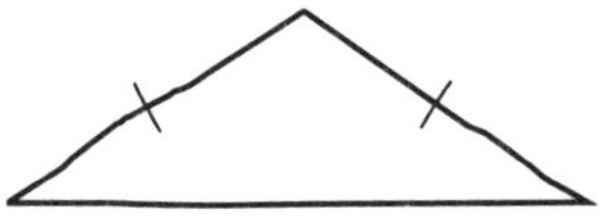

4. Make a better sketch.

a)

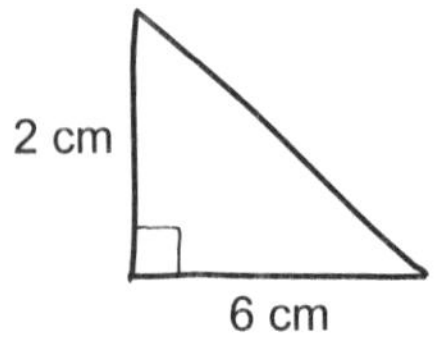

b)

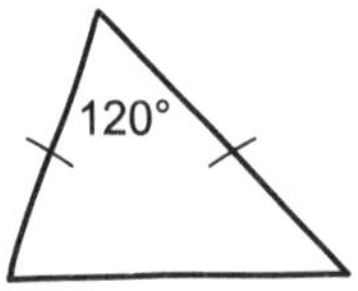

5. Sketch the figures. Add all necessary labels and markings for sides or angles.

a) $\triangle ABC$ has all sides equal. Line *AD* is parallel to *BC*.

b) $\triangle PQR$ is a right triangle with two 45° angles.

Include all the important information you have been given on the sketch.

6. Circle the sketch that includes all the important information given.

a) *ABC* has all sides equal.

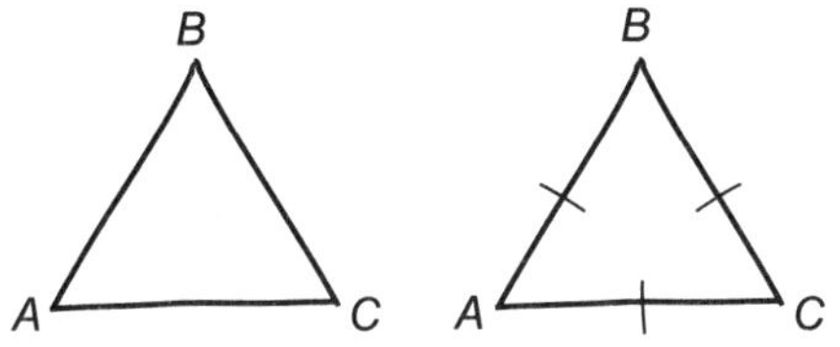

b) *TUV* is an isosceles triangle.

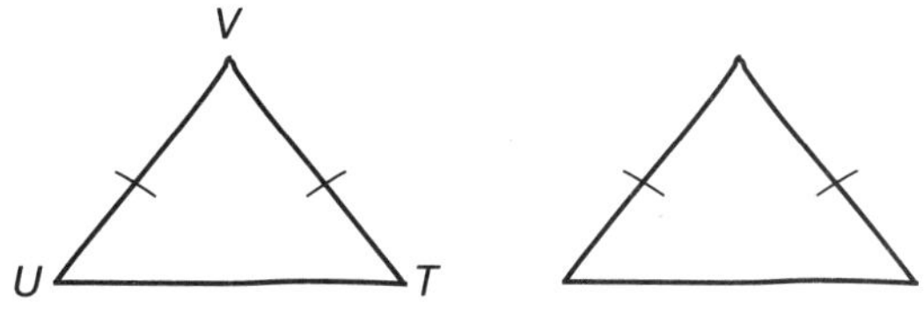

Do not accidentally add any information you do not know for sure.

7. Circle the sketch that adds more information than is in the description.

a) A quadrilateral has an 8 cm side.

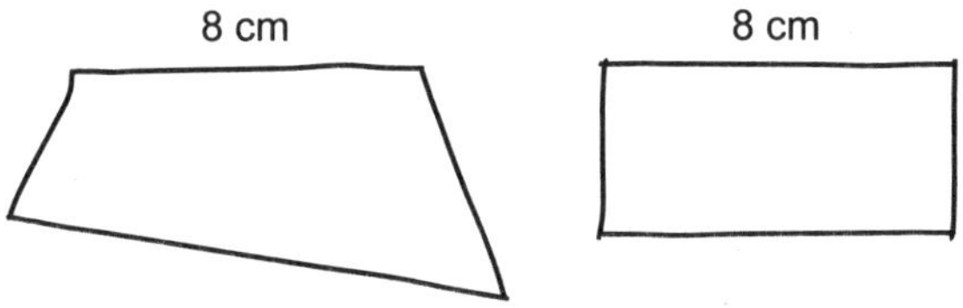

b) One angle of a triangle is 45°.

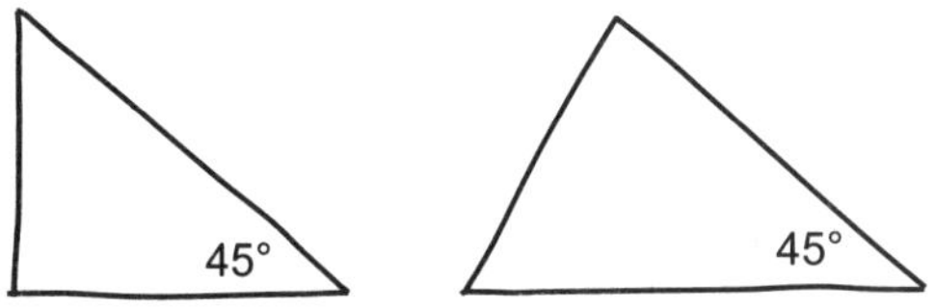

Sometimes you need to make a few sketches to see the problem in different ways.

8. One side of an isosceles triangle is 3 cm. The perimeter of the triangle is 11 cm. What are the lengths of the sides of the triangle?

Make two sketches to show the different options for placing the 3 cm side. Solve the problem.

In an isosceles triangle, the equal sides make equal angles with the third side.

9. Sketch an isosceles triangle of the given type. Mark all the equal sides and angles.

a) Acute isosceles triangle

b) Obtuse isosceles triangle

c) Right isosceles triangle

10. One angle of an isosceles triangle is 40°. Find the measures of the other two angles.

Make two sketches to show the different options for placing the 40° angle. Then solve the problem.

Use symbols instead of words to keep your sketch clear and uncluttered.

11. Circle the better sketch.

a) 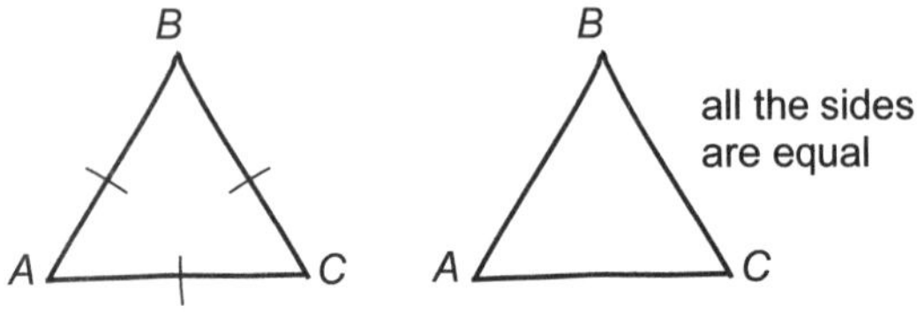

b) 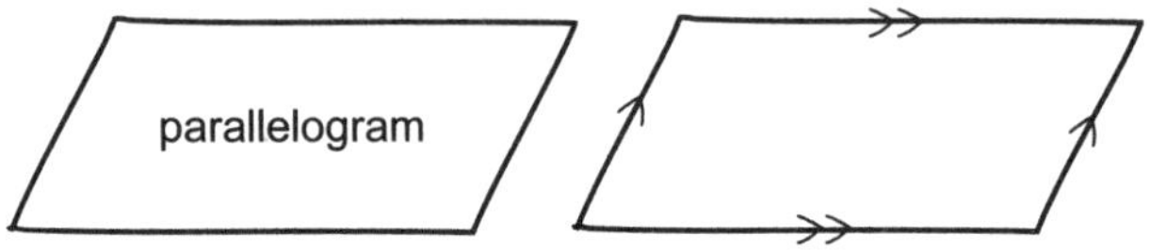

12. Sketch two quadrilaterals of different shapes that match the given description. Add all necessary labels, and side and angle markings.

a) *ABCD* has all equal sides.

b) *JKLM* has exactly 2 right angles.

c) *PQRS* has exactly 2 equal sides.

d) *UVWX* has no equal sides.

Add other information you can figure out.

13. These sketches show the information given in a problem. What other information can you figure out? Mark this additional information on the sketch.

a) Hint: What is the sum of the angles in a triangle?

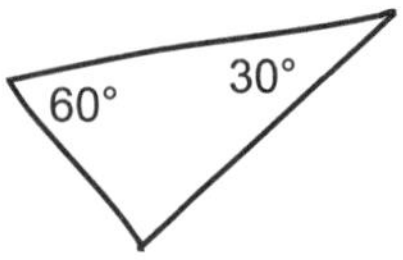

b) Hint: Which type of triangle is this? What do you know about the angles in this type of triangle?

c) Hint: What do you know about the opposite angles in a parallelogram?

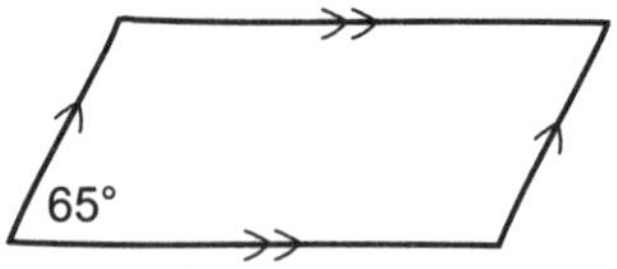

Bonus ▶ Find all the angles in the parallelogram.

Leave out any information you are sure you do not need.

14. Cross out any information you do *not* need to solve the problem. Then make a sketch for the problem.

	Problem	Sketch
a)	A support for a bridge ~~over a highway~~ is shaped like a triangle with two equal sides. The angle between them is 70°. What are the other two angles?	
b)	A rectangular gift box is 15 cm long and 10 cm wide. It has a transparent lid decorated with a paper flower 5 cm wide. What is the area of the bottom of the box?	

Bonus ▶ Solve the problems.

15. Answer the questions about the problem below. Then solve the problem.

The base of a ladder is 2 m from a vertical wall. The top of the ladder is 2 m up the wall. What angle does the ladder form with the ground if the ground is horizontal?

A.

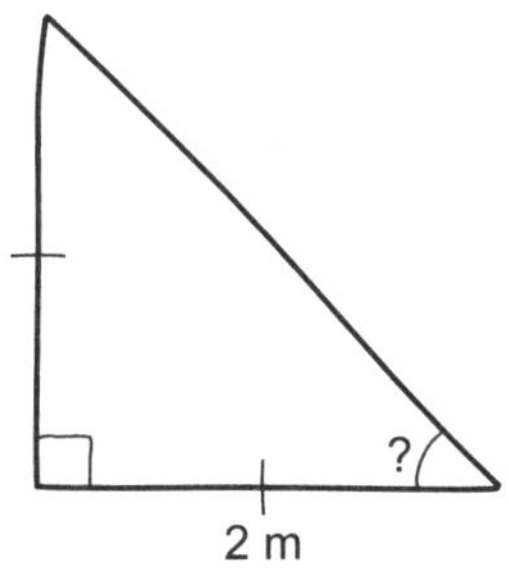

B.

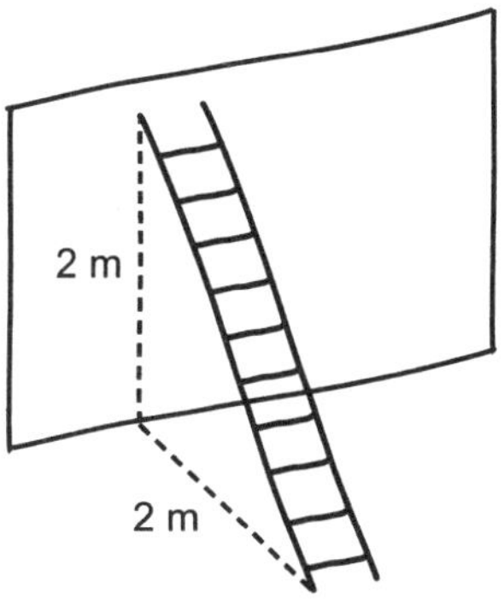

a) Do both of these sketches include all the important information given in the problem? Explain.

b) Does Sketch B tell you anything more than Sketch A does?

c) How does Sketch A make it easier to see that the shape formed by the ladder against the wall is an isosceles triangle?

d) Sketch A shows that the angle between the two equal sides of the triangle is a right angle. How did the student who drew the sketch know that the angle is a right angle?

e) Which sketch tells what the problem is asking you to find?

f) Which sketch will help the most to solve the problem?

G8-8 Counterexamples

1. Circle the picture that shows the statement is not true.

a) All circles are white.

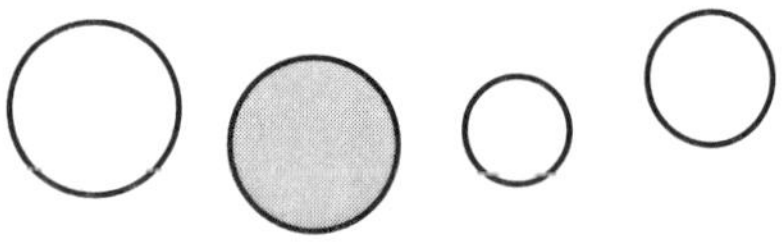

b) All squares are shaded.

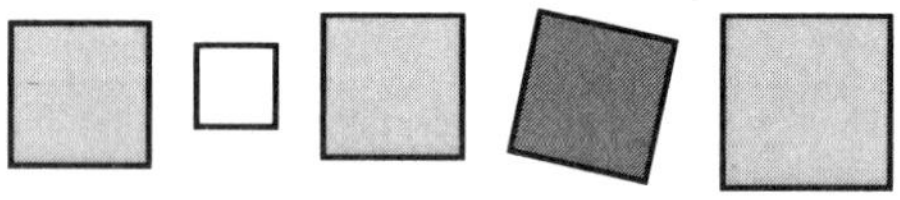

2. Which picture shows that the statement is not true?

a) All rectangles are shaded. ______

b) All rectangles have a horizontal side. ______

3. Which letter in the list shows the statement is not true?

A R U i E O

a) All letters are vowels. ______

b) All letters are capital letters. ______

An example that shows a statement is not true is called a **counterexample**. To show that a statement is not true, you need only one counterexample.

4. Circle the *first* counterexample when reading from left to right.

a) All words have the letter "o."
boat, oak, buy, globe, stair

b) All names have six letters.
Blanca, Sharon, Jayden, Sam, Peter

Example: "*All circles* are shaded."

Any counterexample *must* be a circle, not any other shape.

5. Circle the counterexample.

a) All triangles are shaded.

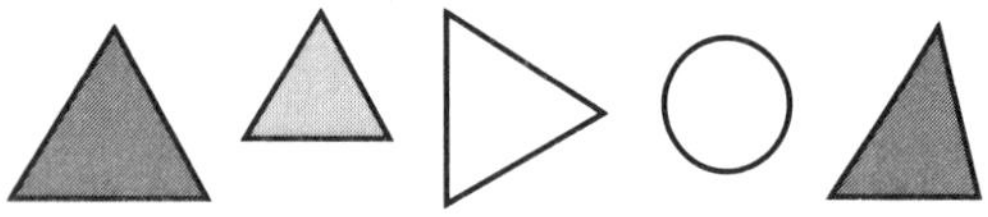

b) All rectangles are squares.

c) All triangles are isosceles.

d) All triangles are equilateral.

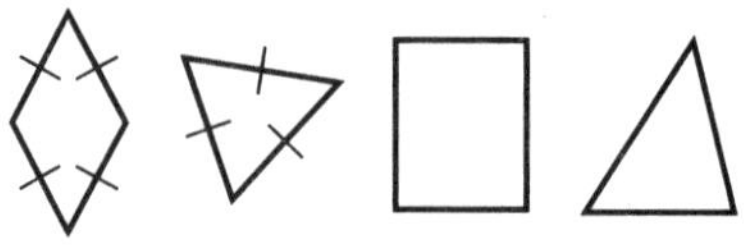

Bonus ▶ Draw an additional counterexample for one of the statements in Question 5.

6. Circle the counterexamples. Some statements will have more than one counterexample.

a) All vehicles have four wheels.

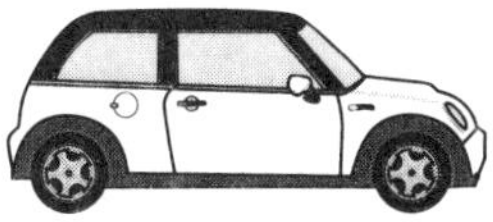

b) All English words have an "e."

triangle eagle men man apfh hrkesdl

c) All English sentences end with a period.

I am Helen. What's your name? Impossible! ¿Cual es tu nombre?

7. In Question 6.a), why are the bananas not a counterexample?

____

Remember: A counterexample must show a specific statement is false. For "All black shapes are circles," you need a *black* shape that is *not a circle*. A white shape will not be a counterexample.

8. a) Write "F" in the box if the picture shows the statement is false.

		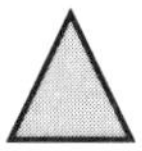		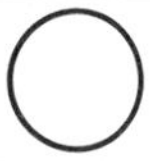		
All gray shapes are triangles.					*F*	*F*
All circles are white.						
All gray shapes are circles.						
All squares are gray.						

b) Check your answers in part a). There should be 6 Fs in total.

9. If the statement is true, write "T." If the statement is false, name a counterexample.

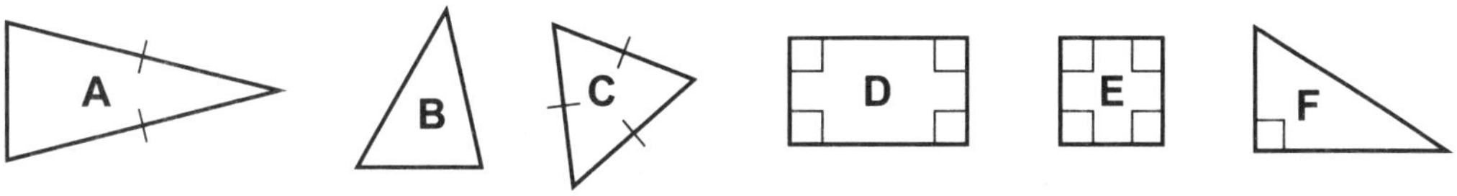

a) All squares are rectangles. ______

b) All rectangles are squares. ______

c) All triangles have three acute angles. ______

d) All triangles have some equal sides. ______

e) All triangles have at least two acute angles. ______

Bonus ▶ Draw another counterexample for each false statement in Question 9.

Example: "If a number is larger than 10, it has 2 digits."

This statement is about numbers larger than 10. A number less than 10 cannot be a counterexample for this. You need a number larger than 10 but not with 2 digits to show the statement is false.

10. Circle the counterexamples.

a) If a shape has a straight side, it is a polygon.

b) If a shape is gray, it is a circle.

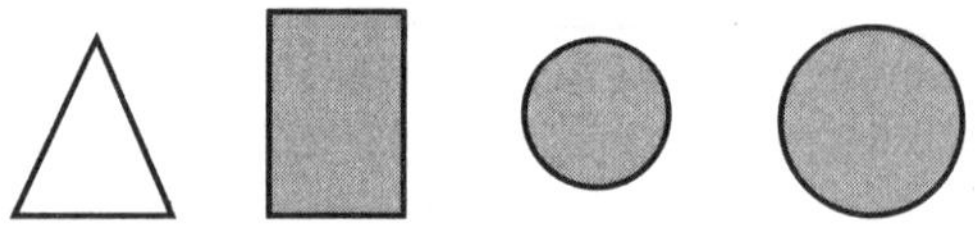

c) If a number is less than 10, it has 1 digit.

8, 12, 345, 10, −35

d) If a word is in English, it has an "e."

ear, cat, gato, hombre, hope

e) All angles are equal in isosceles triangles.

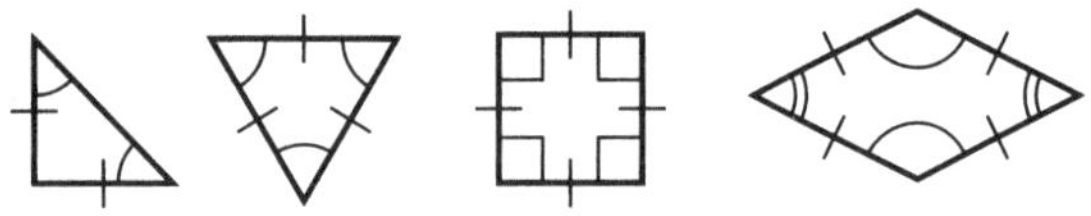

f) If a polygon is equilateral, it is a square.

11. For the statement, say what a counterexample should be.

a) If a triangle is acute, it has two equal angles.

an acute triangle with three different angles

b) If a triangle is acute, it has all sides the same length.

____

c) If a quadrilateral has two equal opposite sides, it is a trapezoid.

____

d) In all trapezoids, opposite sides are equal.

____

e) All numbers are either even or odd.

____

12. If the statement is true, write "T." If the statement is false, give a counterexample.

a) All angles in a triangle add to 180°.

b) If a triangle is obtuse, it has two acute angles.

c) All fractions are smaller than 1.

d) If a number is negative, it is smaller than −1.

e) If you multiply a number by itself, you get a larger number.

f) If a triangle is a right triangle, it has two equal angles.

G8-9 Congruence

Two shapes are **congruent** if they have the same size and shape. If you placed one shape on top of the other and lined them up, they would match exactly.

Congruent shapes:

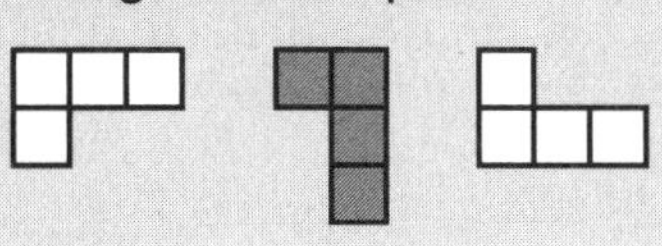

Non-congruent shapes:

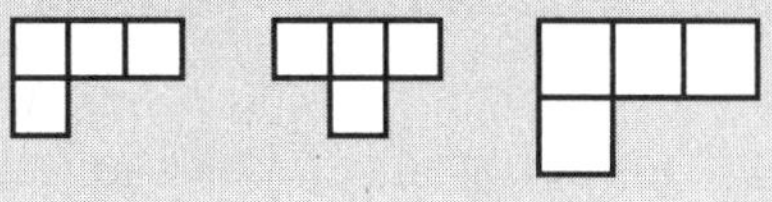

1. Circle the two congruent shapes.

a) 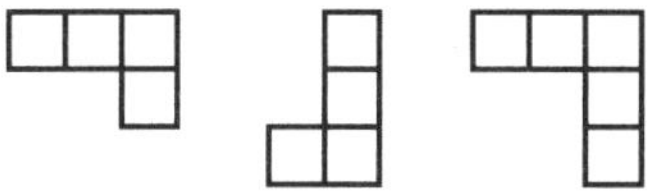

b) 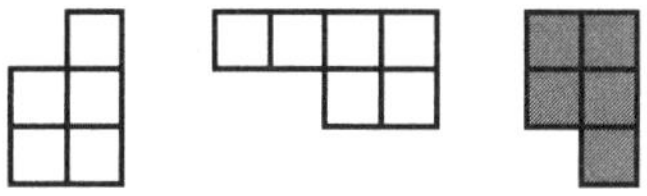

c) 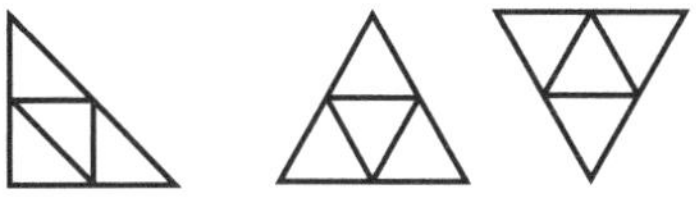

d) 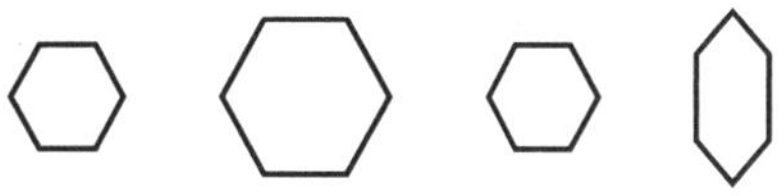

Congruent triangles have sides of the same length.

Example: Triangles A and B are congruent. Triangles B and C are not congruent.

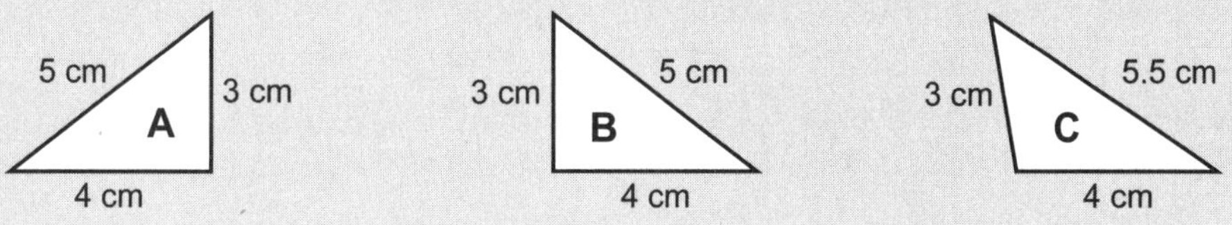

2. The two triangles shown are congruent. Mark the equal sides with hash marks. One pair of sides in part a) is marked for you.

a) 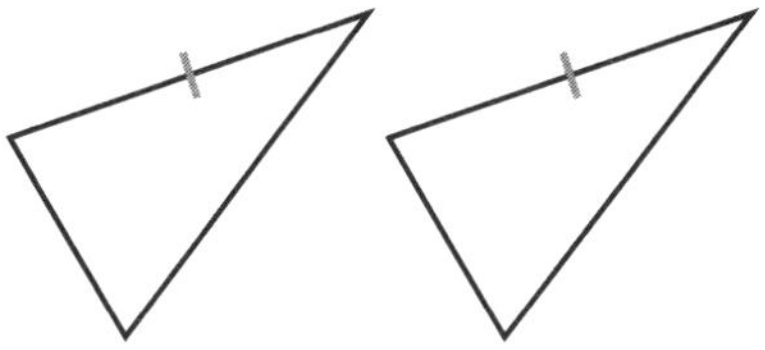

b) 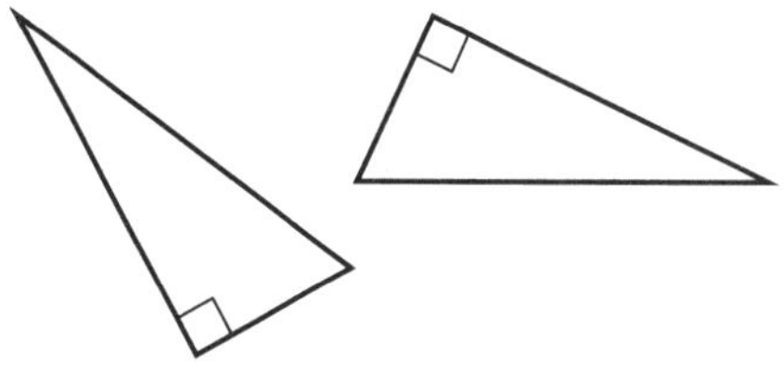

3. Triangles *ABC* and *DEF* are congruent. Which side in $\triangle ABC$ is equal to the given side of $\triangle DEF$?

a) 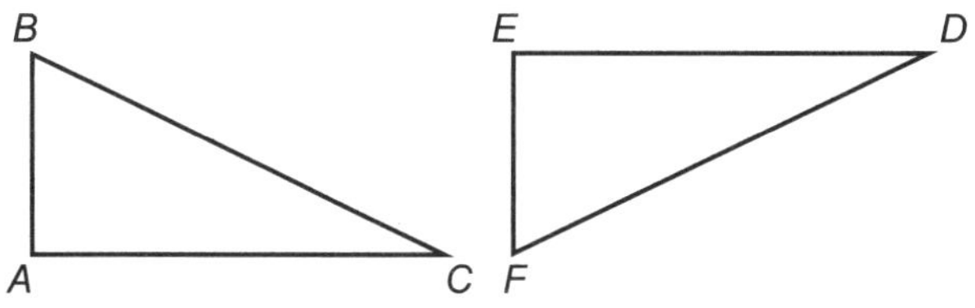

$DE =$ <u>AC</u>, $EF =$ ______, $DF =$ ______

b) 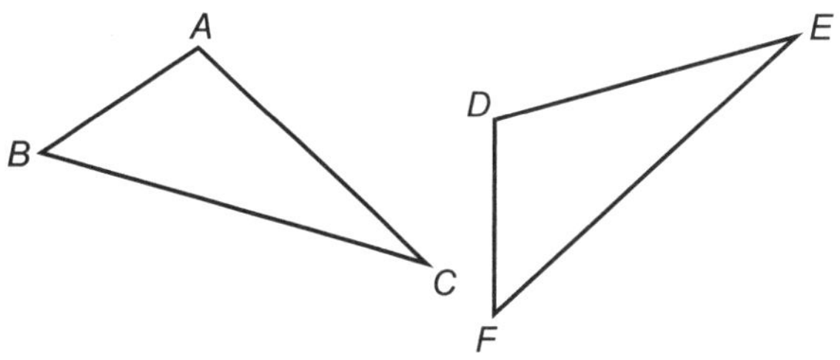

$DE =$ ______, $EF =$ ______, $DF =$ ______

If two triangles are congruent, they have angles of the same size.

Example: Triangles A and B are congruent, so they have angles of the same size. Triangles B and C have angles of different sizes. They are not congruent.

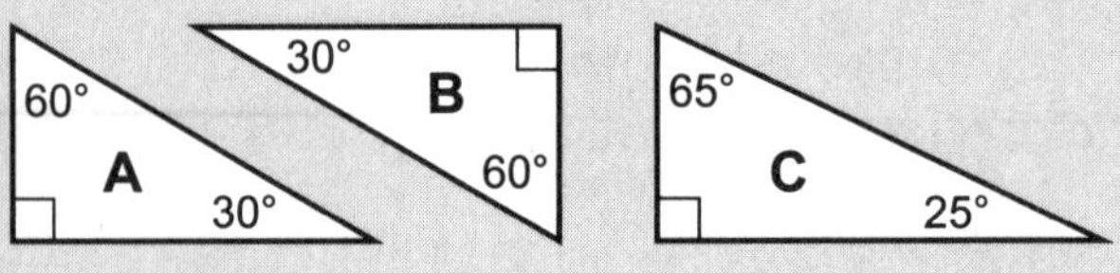

4. The triangles shown are congruent. Mark the equal angles with the same number of arcs. One pair of angles is marked for you.

a) 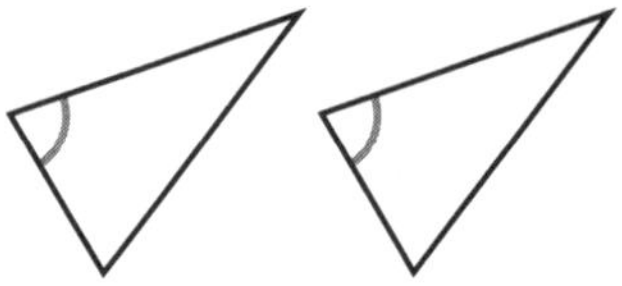

b) 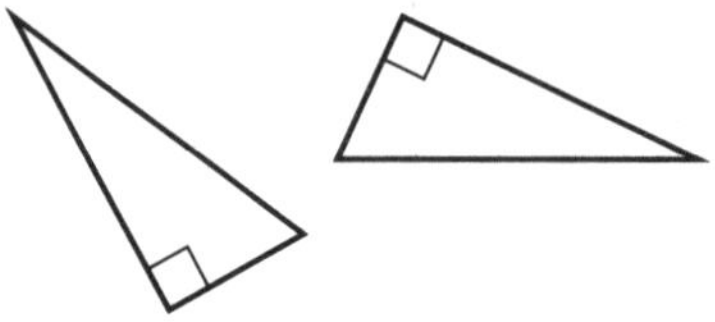

5. Triangles *ABC* and *DEF* are congruent. Which angle in $\triangle ABC$ is equal to the given angle of $\triangle DEF$?

a) 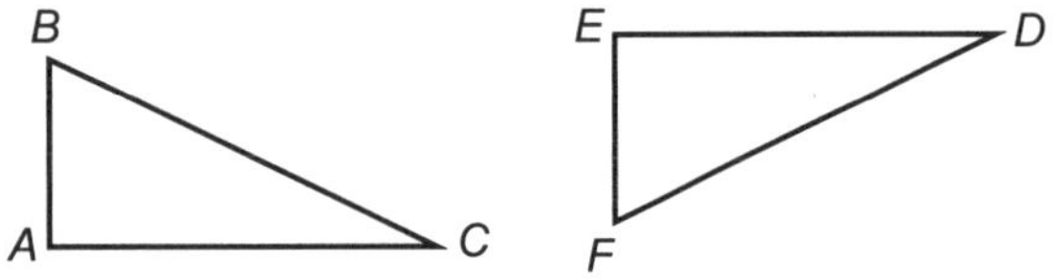

$\angle D =$ $\underline{\angle C}$, $\angle E =$ ______, $\angle F =$ ______

b) 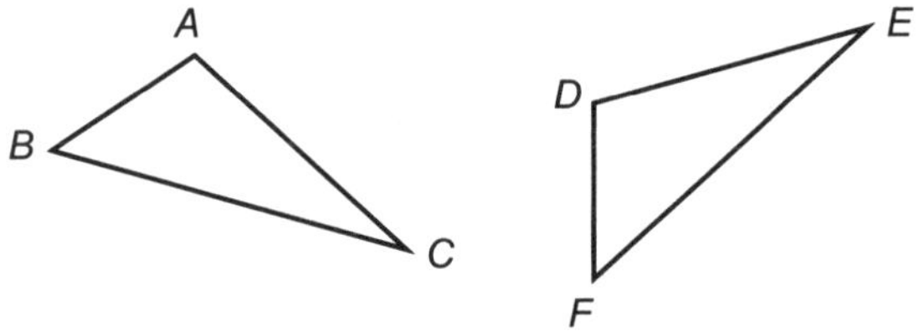

$\angle D =$ ______, $\angle E =$ ______, $\angle F =$ ______

6. These triangles are congruent. Identify the equal sides and equal angles.

a) 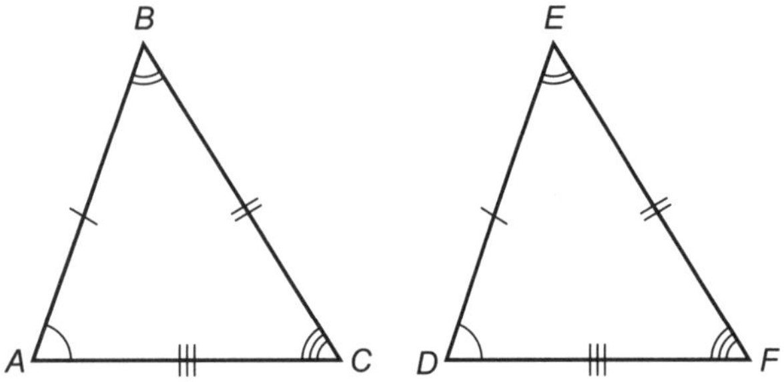

$AB = DE$ ______ $\angle A = \angle D$ ______

______ ______

______ ______

b) 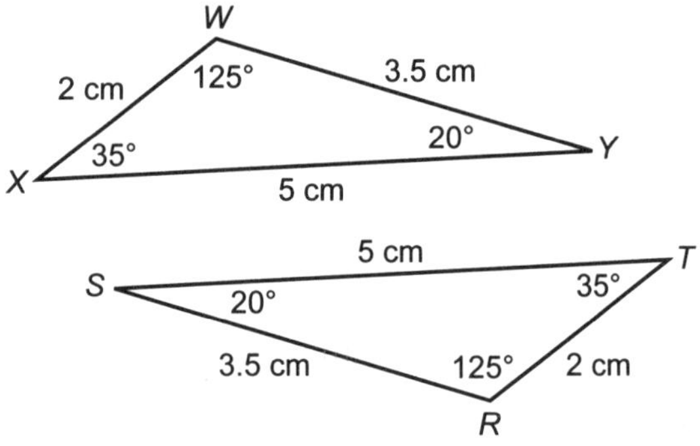

______ ______

______ ______

______ ______

7. Karen thinks that the triangles are congruent. Is she correct? Explain.

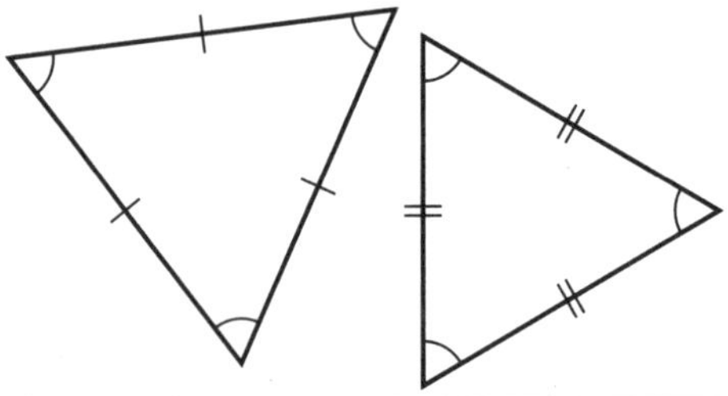

______

______

To check if two triangles are congruent, imagine placing them one on top of the other, trying to make them match exactly.

Compare the angles that are placed one on top of the other: $\angle A = \angle G$, $\angle B = \angle F$, $\angle C = \angle E$.

Compare the lengths of the sides placed one on top of the other: $AB = GF$, $BC = FE$, $CA = EG$.

If all pairs of angles and all pairs of sides are equal, the triangles are congruent.

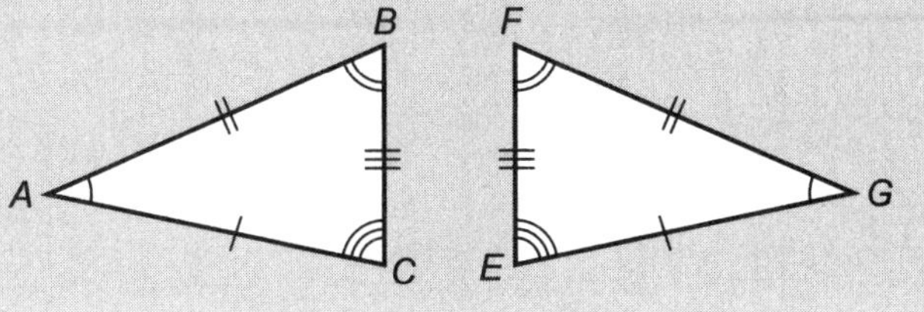

8. Are the triangles congruent? Use a ruler and a protractor to check. If yes, write the pairs of matching equal sides and matching equal angles.

a) 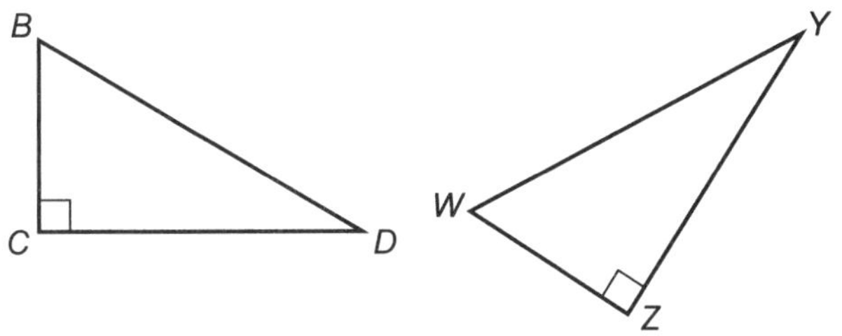

b) 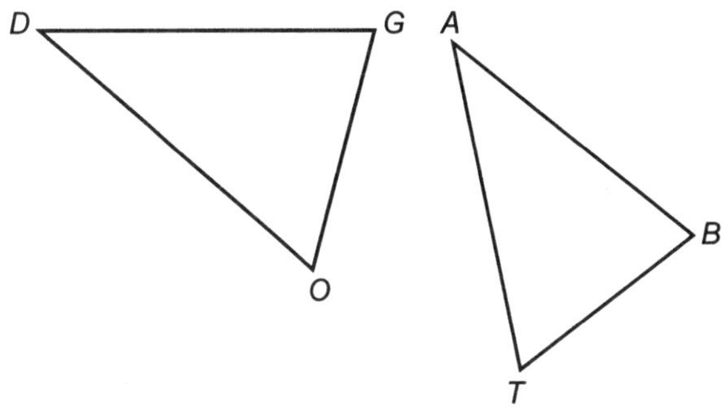

The triangles in the box above are congruent. We write a **congruence statement**: $\triangle ABC \cong \triangle GFE$. The order of the letters shows the match between the vertices.

9. Write the congruence statement for the pair of congruent triangles in Question 8.

10. These two triangles are congruent. Tom wrote a congruence statement: $\triangle VWX \cong \triangle ABC$. He used his congruence statement to list the equal sides and angles:

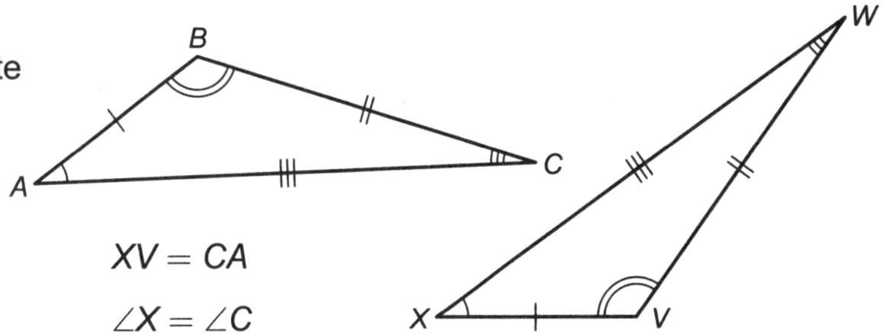

$VW = AB$ $\quad$ $WX = BC$ $\quad$ $XV = CA$

$\angle V = \angle A$ $\quad$ $\angle W = \angle B$ $\quad$ $\angle X = \angle C$

Is Tom's list correct? Explain and rewrite the congruence statement.

11. These two triangles are congruent.

a) Why do you not have to mark the third pair of angles to know that they are equal? Hint: Use the sum of the angles in a triangle.

b) Write the congruence statement for the triangles.

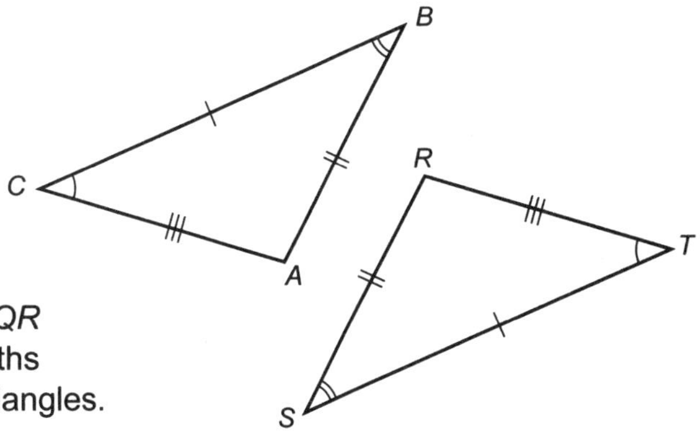

12. Use the congruence statement $\triangle ABC \cong \triangle XYZ \cong \triangle PQR$ and $AB = 5$ cm, $YZ = 6$ cm, $RP = 7$ cm. Find the lengths of all the sides in all three triangles. Hint: Sketch the triangles.

G8-10 Supplementary and Vertical Angles

Two angles are **supplementary angles** if they add to 180°.

Example: $\angle A = 60°$ and $\angle B = 120°$

$\angle A + \angle B = 60° + 120° = 180°$

$\angle A$ and $\angle B$ are supplementary angles.

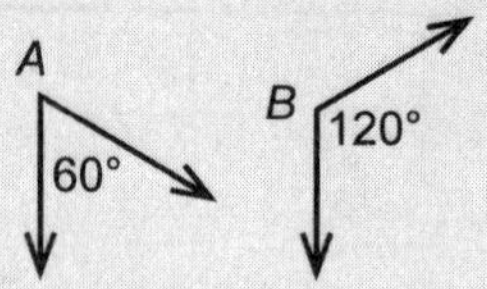

1. Are the two angles supplementary? Circle "yes" or "no."

a)

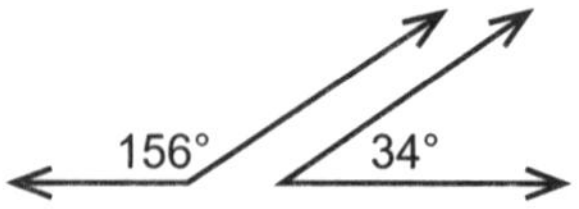

yes no

b)

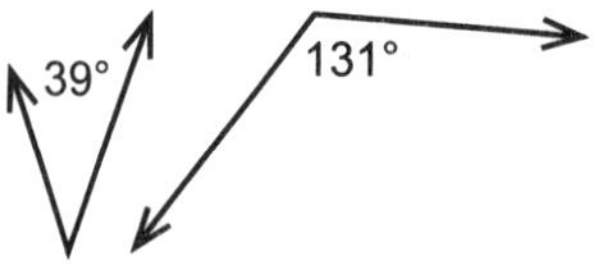

yes no

c)

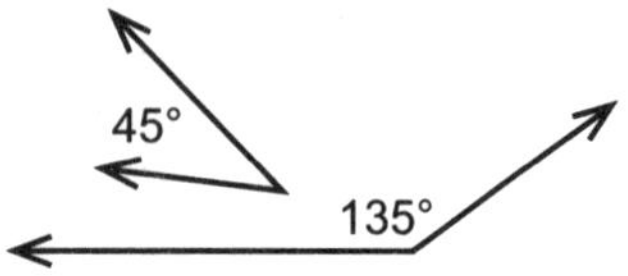

yes no

A **straight angle** measures 180°.

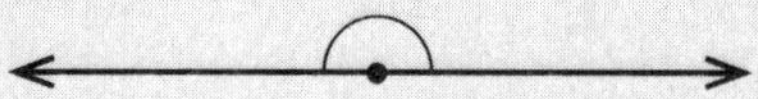

Two angles that combine to make a straight angle are supplementary. Examples:

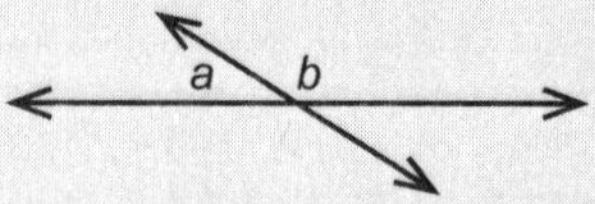

$\angle a + \angle b = 180°$

$\angle ABD + \angle CBD = \angle ABC = 180°$

2. Find the supplementary angles in each diagram.

a)

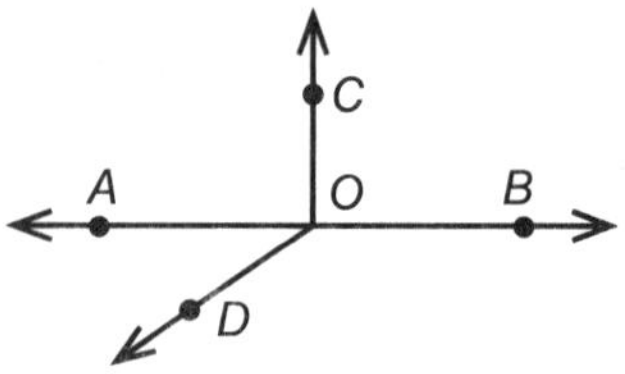

$\angle AOC +$ _______ $= 180°$

$\angle AOD +$ _______ $= 180°$

b)

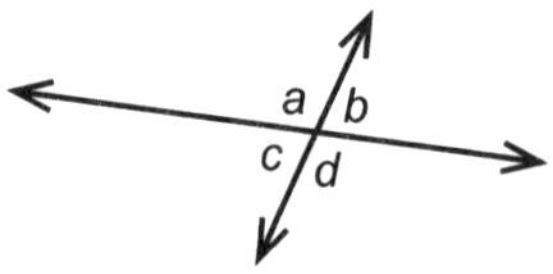

$\angle a +$ _____ $= 180°$

$\angle a +$ _____ $= 180°$

$\angle d +$ _____ $= 180°$

$\angle d +$ _____ $= 180°$

c)

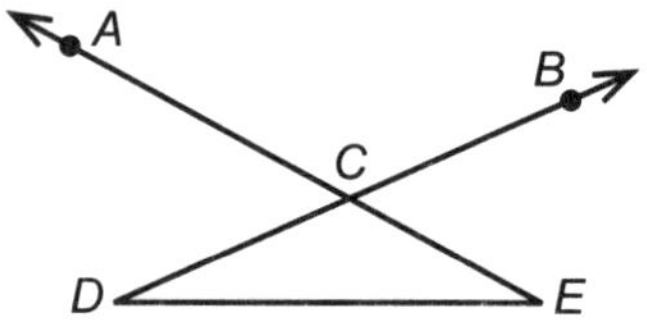

$\angle ACD +$ _______ $= 180°$

_______ $+$ _______ $= 180°$

_______ $+$ _______ $= 180°$

_______ $+$ _______ $= 180°$

3. Use the measure of the supplementary angle to find the measure of $\angle x$.

a)

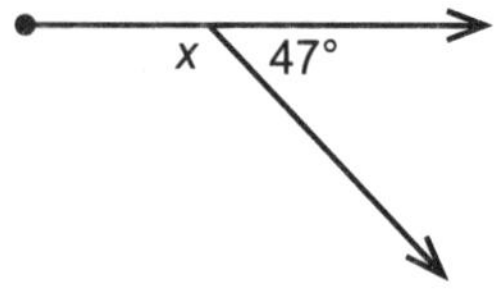

$\angle x =$ *180° − 47°*

$=$ *133°*

b)

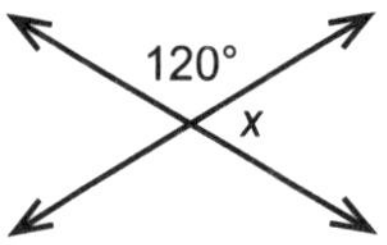

$\angle x =$ _______________

$=$ _______

c)

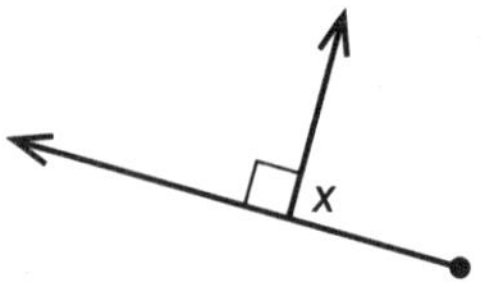

$\angle x =$ _______________

$=$ _______

4. Find ∠*x* and ∠*y*.

a)

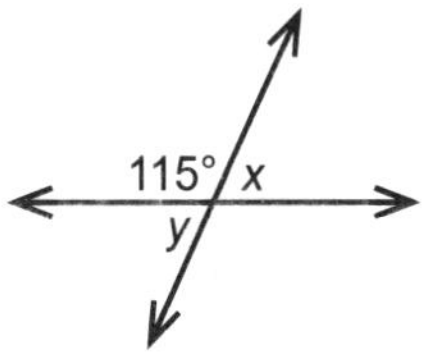

∠*x* = ______, ∠*y* = ______

b)

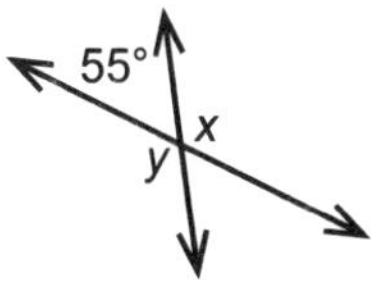

∠*x* = ______, ∠*y* = ______

c)

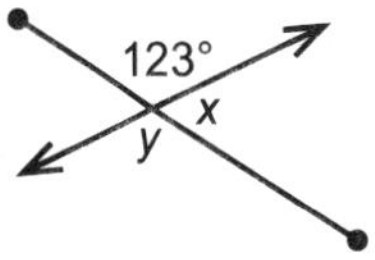

∠*x* = ______, ∠*y* = ______

Adjacent angles are beside each other. They share a vertex and an arm.

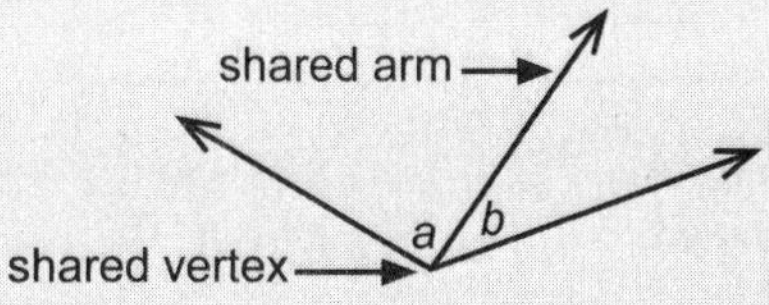

∠*a* and ∠*b* are adjacent angles.

Vertical angles are not adjacent and are formed by two intersecting lines.

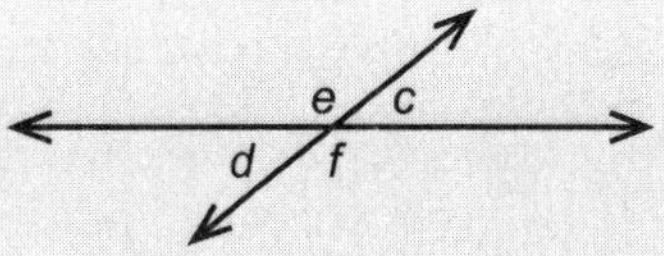

∠*c* and ∠*d* are vertical angles.
∠*e* and ∠*f* are also vertical angles.

5. List the pairs of vertical angles.

a)

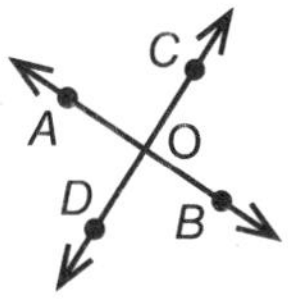

∠*AOC* and ∠______

∠*AOD* and ∠______

b)

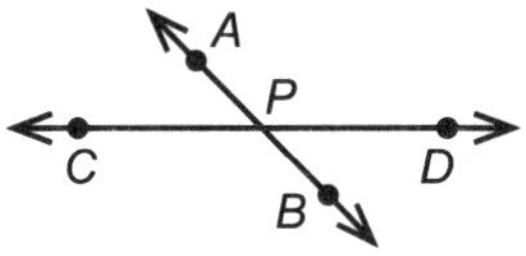

______ and ______

______ and ______

c)

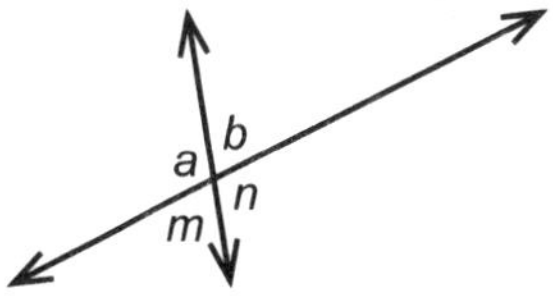

______ and ______

______ and ______

6. a) Measure the angles.

i)

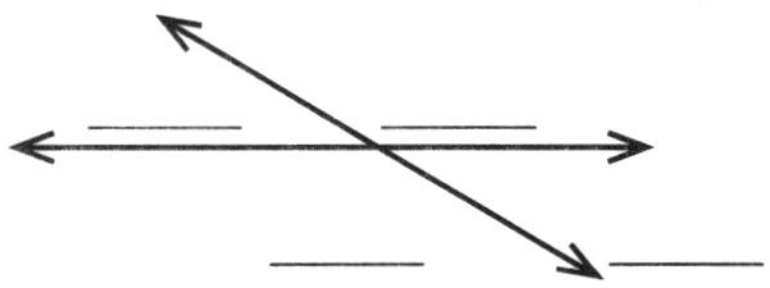

ii)

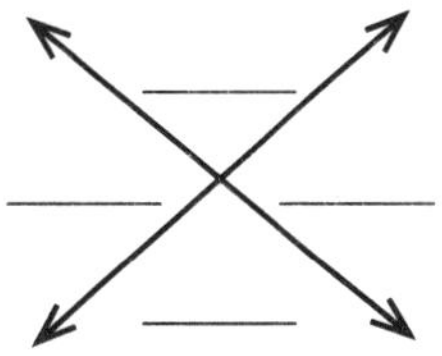

iii)

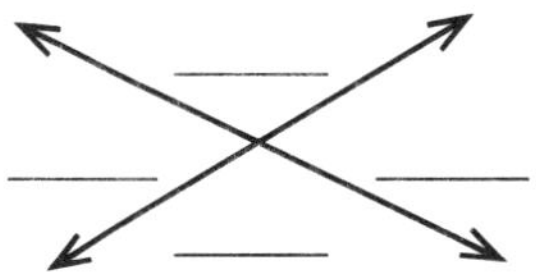

b) Compare the measures of the vertical angles. What do you notice? ________________

7. a) Which angles in this picture are supplementary angles?

There are four different pairs. ____________________

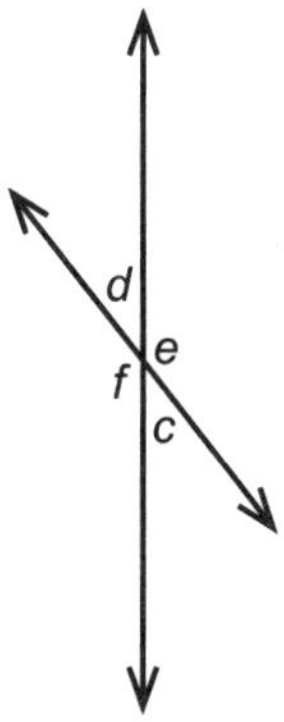

b) ∠*e* + ∠*c* = ______°, so ∠*c* = ______

∠*e* + ∠*d* = ______°, so ∠*d* = ______

c) What can you say about vertical angles ∠*c* and ∠*d*?

d) Explain why ∠*e* = ∠*f*.

Vertical angles are equal.

8. List the pairs of vertical (and equal) angles.

a)

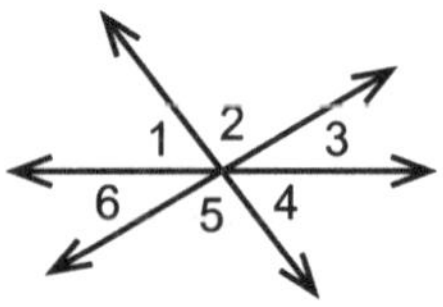

$\angle 1$ = $\angle 4$

_____ = _____

_____ = _____

b)

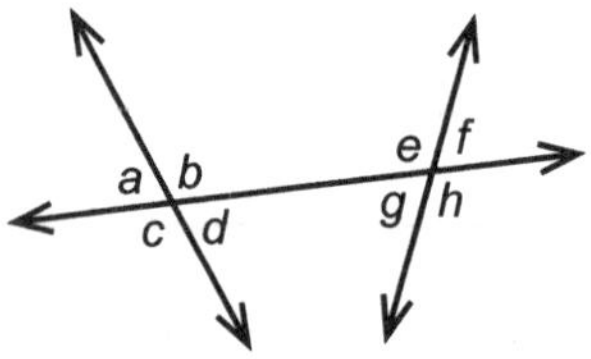

_____ = _____

_____ = _____

_____ = _____

_____ = _____

c)

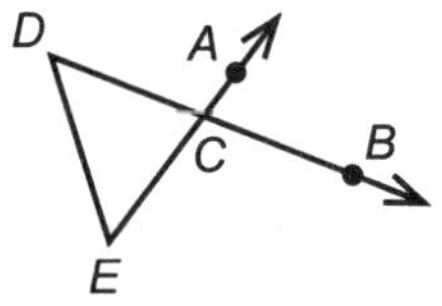

$\angle DCA$ = _____

_____ = _____

REMINDER: Angles in a triangle add to 180°. Angles that combine to make a straight line add to 180°.

9. Find the missing vertical angles.

a)

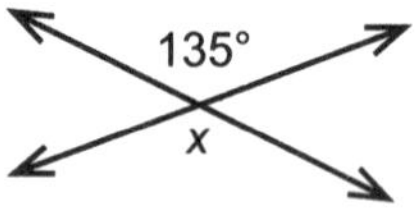

$\angle x =$ _____

b)

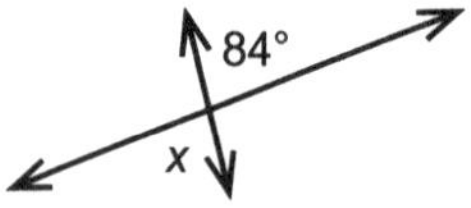

$\angle x =$ _____

c)

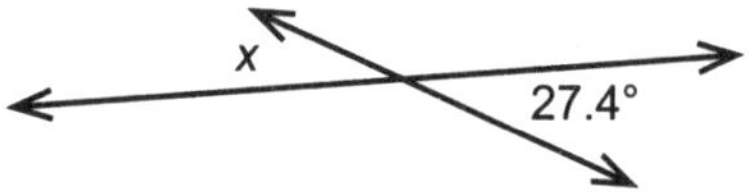

$\angle x =$ _____

d)

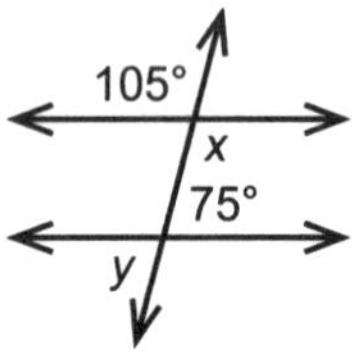

$\angle x =$ _____, $\angle y =$ _____

e)

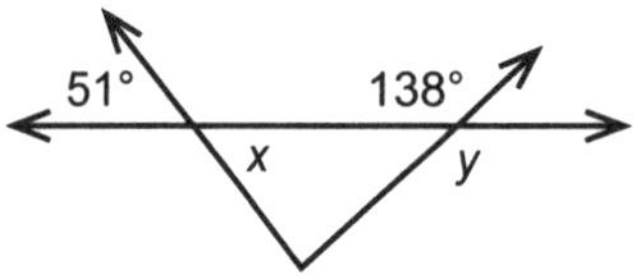

$\angle x =$ _____, $\angle y =$ _____

f)

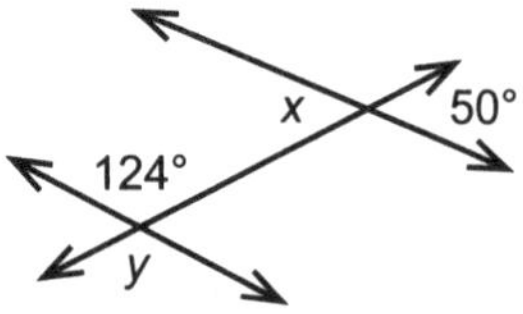

$\angle x =$ _____, $\angle y =$ _____

10. Find the missing vertical angles and supplementary angles.

a)

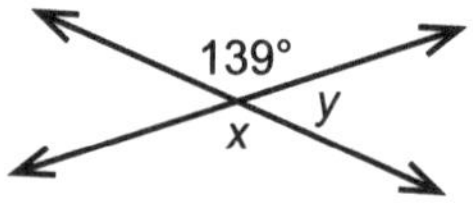

$\angle x =$ _____, $\angle y =$ _____

b)

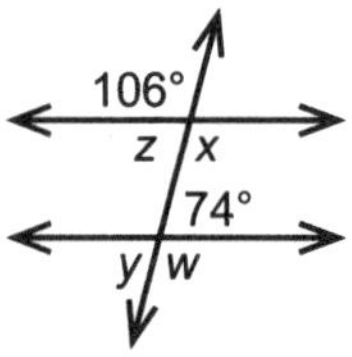

$\angle w =$ _____, $\angle x =$ _____

$\angle y =$ _____, $\angle z =$ _____

c)

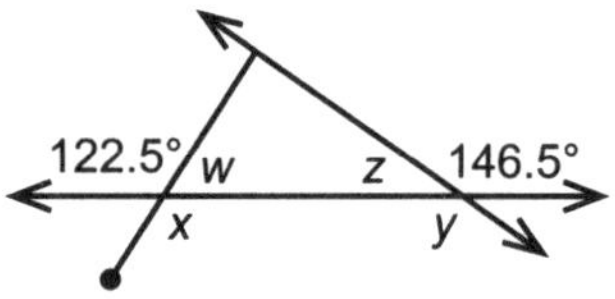

$\angle w =$ _____, $\angle x =$ _____

$\angle y =$ _____, $\angle z =$ _____

11. Find the missing angles. Hint: Use alphabetical order.

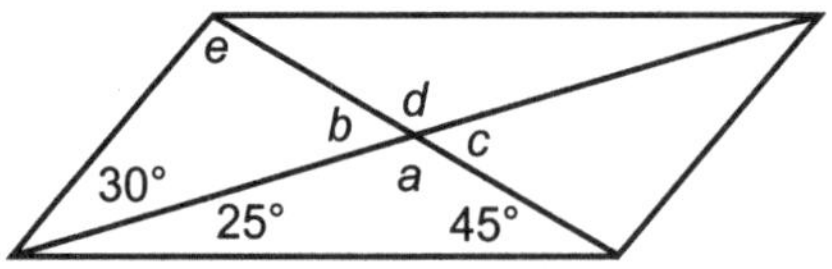

G8-11 Congruence Rules

If two polygons are congruent, you can place them one on top of the other so that they match exactly.
The vertices that match are called **corresponding vertices**.
The angles that match are called **corresponding angles**.
The sides that match are called **corresponding sides**.

1. The two triangles are congruent. Are the two thick sides corresponding sides? Explain.

a) 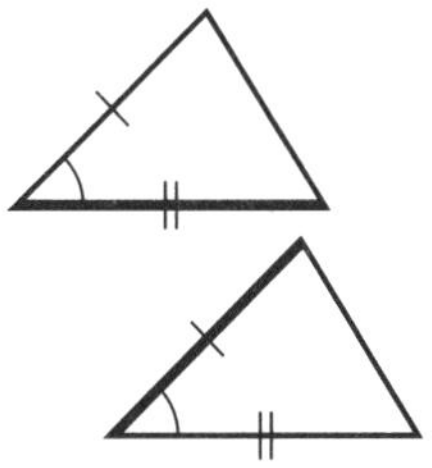

b) 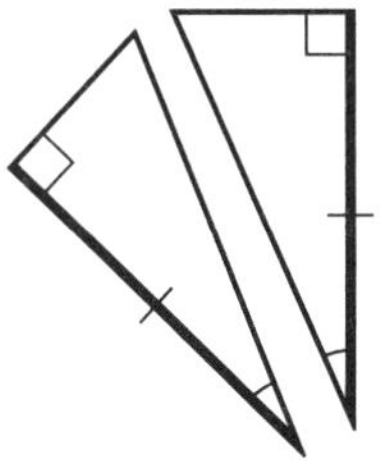

c) 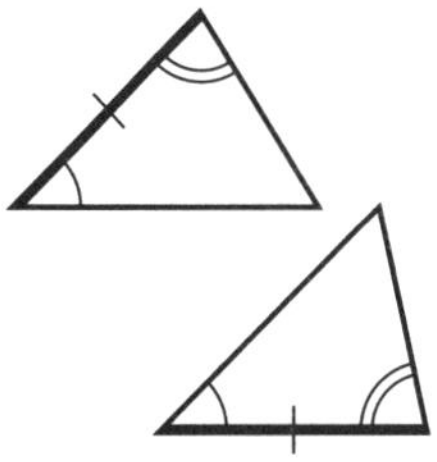

Congruence Rules for Triangles

SSS (side-side-side)

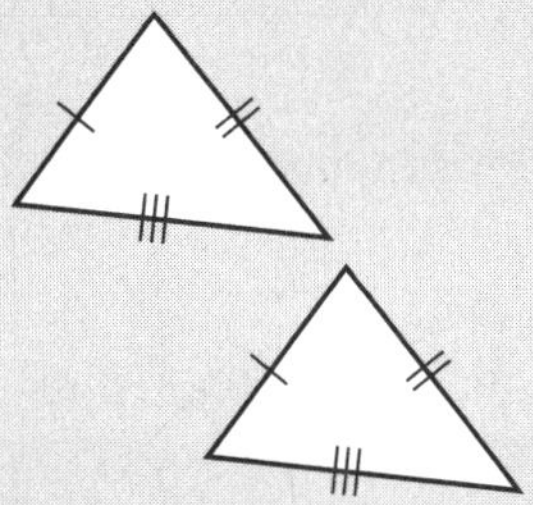

SAS (side-angle-side)

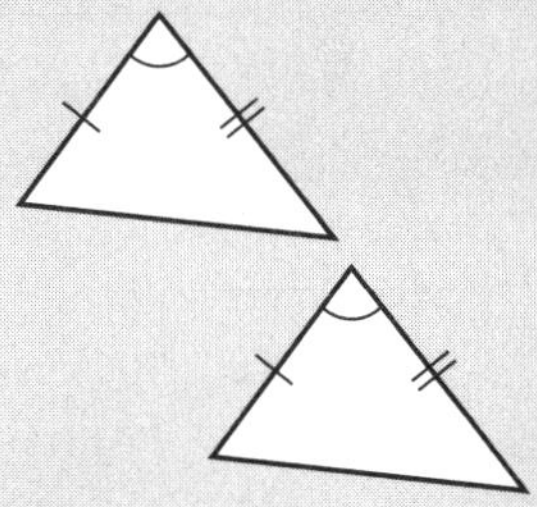

ASA (angle-side-angle)

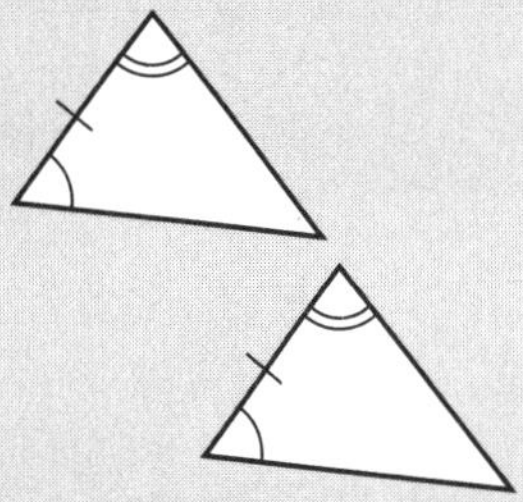

Two triangles are congruent if they have …

- three pairs of equal corresponding sides
- two pairs of equal corresponding sides and a pair of equal corresponding angles between these sides
- two pairs of equal corresponding angles and a pair of equal corresponding sides between these angles

2. Identify the congruence rule that tells you that each pair of triangles is congruent.
Write the congruence statement.

a) 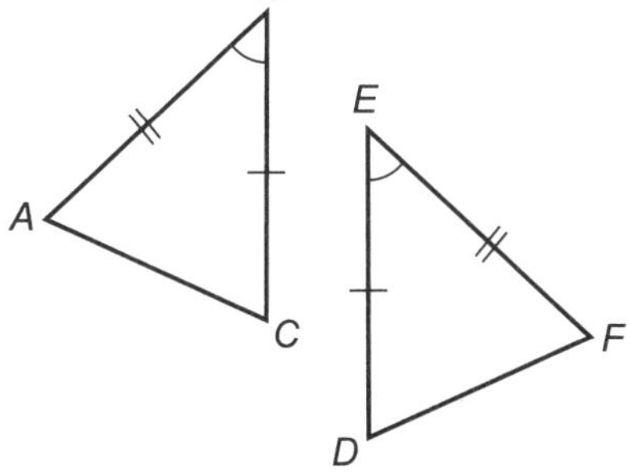

Congruence rule: ________

Δ *ABC* $\cong \Delta$ ________

b) 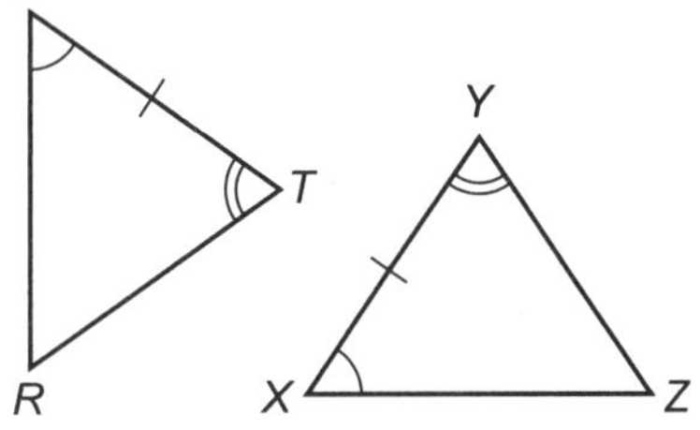

Congruence rule: ________

Δ ________ $\cong \Delta$ ________

c) 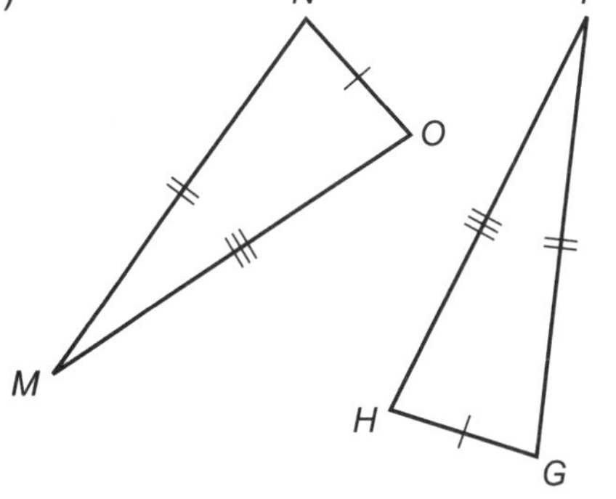

Congruence rule: ________

Δ ________ $\cong \Delta$ ________

3. In the triangles in the picture, $\angle A = \angle D = 20°$, $\angle B = \angle E = 35°$, and $BC = EF$.

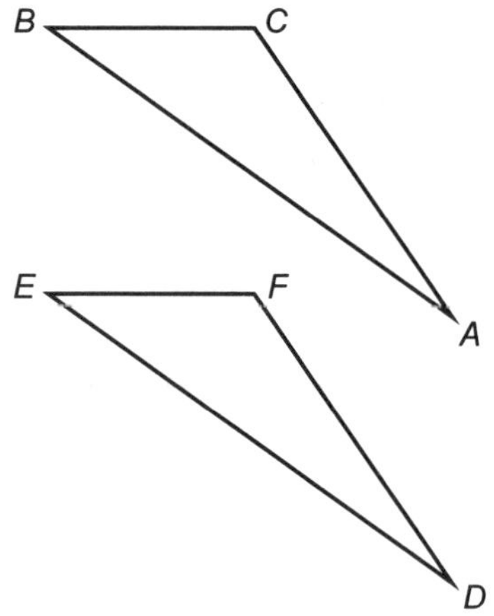

a) Mark the equal sides and angles on the picture.

b) Do the given equations of sides and angles

fit any congruence rule? ______

c) The sum of the angles in a triangle is ______.

$\angle C =$ ______ − ($\angle$______ + $\angle$______) = ______

$\angle F =$ ______ − ($\angle$______ + $\angle$______) = ______

d) Which congruence rule can you apply now? ______

Write the equations for the sides and angles that the congruence rule requires.

______ = ______, ______ = ______, ______ = ______

4. Nina thinks that she can apply the same method as in Question 3 to the two triangles shown.

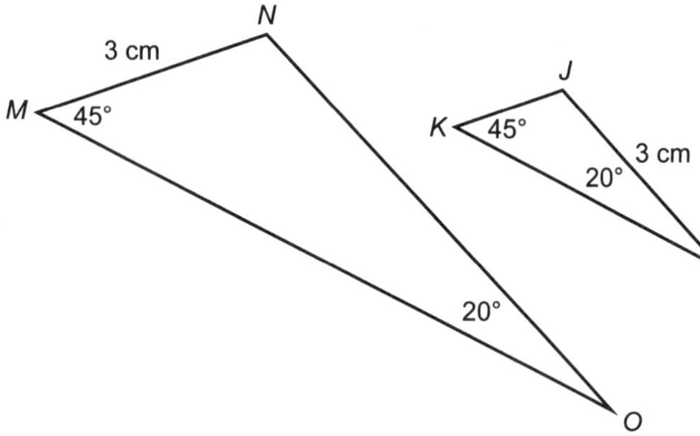

a) Are the triangles congruent? ______

b) $\angle N =$ ______ − $\angle$______ − $\angle$______ = ______

$\angle J =$ ______ − $\angle$______ − $\angle$______ = ______

c) Explain why the ASA congruence rule does not work for ΔJKL and ΔNOM.

____

____

5. a) Measure the angles and the sides of these triangles. Write the measurements on the diagram.

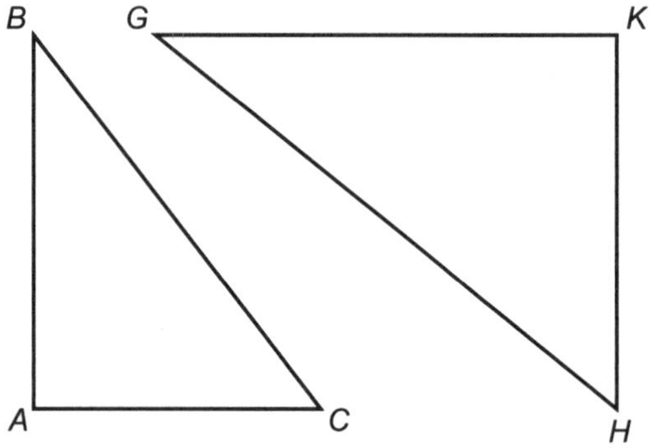

b) Which angles are equal?

____

c) Which sides are equal?

____

d) Are the triangles congruent? Explain why the congruence rules do not apply here.

Angle-angle-angle (**AAA**) is not a congruence rule.

6. Draw a counterexample for this statement:

All triangles that have three pairs of corresponding equal angles are congruent.

7. a) What sides and angles in $\triangle ABC$ and $\triangle DEF$ are equal?

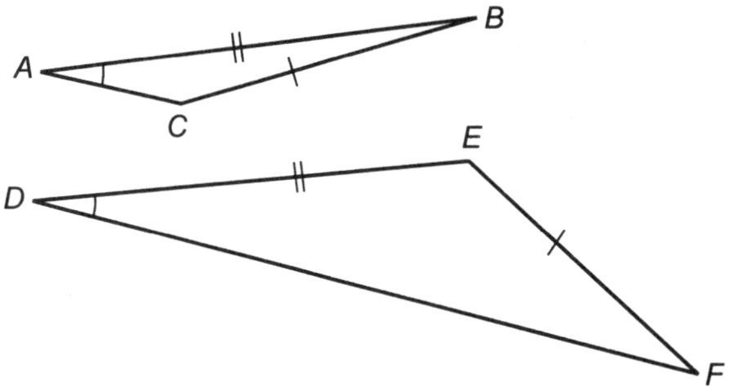

____

b) Can you use the SAS congruence rule? Why or why not? ______________________

____

c) Do triangles $\triangle ABC$ and $\triangle DEF$ look congruent? ______

d) Is side-side-angle a congruence rule? Is angle-side-side a congruence rule? Explain.

8. Scientists want to measure the distance across a crater on Mars. They send a rover along the path *AOCDOB*.

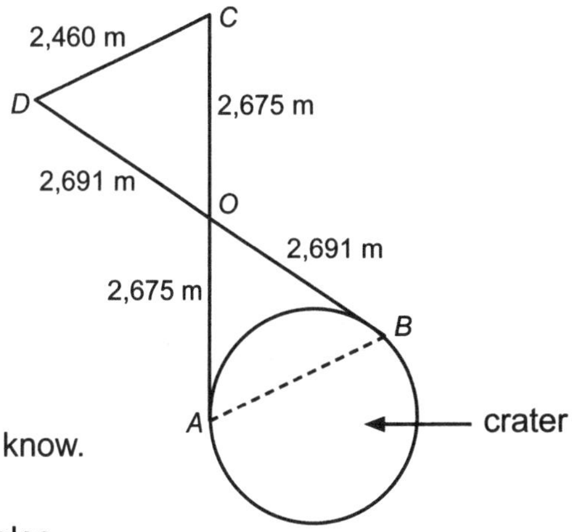

a) What are the equal sides and angles in triangles $\triangle ABO$ and $\triangle OCD$?

________ = ________ ________ = ________

________ = ________

b) What congruence rule can you use? ______

c) What is the distance *AB* across the crater? Explain how you know.

9. Draw two triangles that are not congruent. Explain why the triangles are not congruent.

10. Sketch a counterexample to show why this statement is false.

If two triangles have two pairs of corresponding sides that are equal, the triangles are congruent.

11. $\triangle PQR$ and $\triangle XYZ$ have $PQ = XY = 5$ cm and $QR = YZ = 7$ cm. Sketch the triangles. Does the statement given ensure that $\triangle PQR \cong \triangle XYZ$? If so, note the congruence rule.

a) $\angle P = \angle Y$ b) $\angle Q = \angle Y$ c) $\angle P = \angle X$ d) $PR = XZ$

12. $\triangle BCD$ and $\triangle FGH$ have $\angle C = \angle G$ and $\angle D = \angle H$. Sketch the triangles. Does the statement given ensure that $\triangle BCD \cong \triangle FGH$? If so, note the congruence rule.

a) $\angle B = \angle F$ b) $CD = GH$ c) $BD = FH$ d) $BC = GH$

G8-12 Congruence (Advanced)

REMINDER: Congruence Rules for Triangles

SAS (side-angle-side)

If in $\triangle ABC$ and $\triangle EFD$, $AB = EF$, $\angle B = \angle F$, and $BC = FD$, then $\triangle ABC \cong \triangle EFD$.

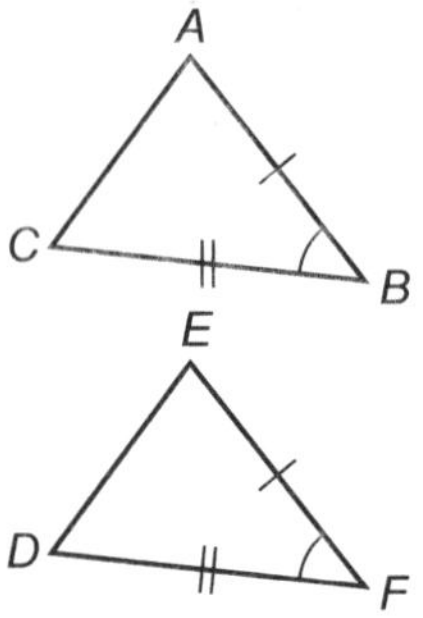

ASA (angle-side-angle)

If in $\triangle ABC$ and $\triangle EFD$, $\angle A = \angle E$, $AB = EF$, and $\angle B = \angle F$, then $\triangle ABC \cong \triangle EFD$.

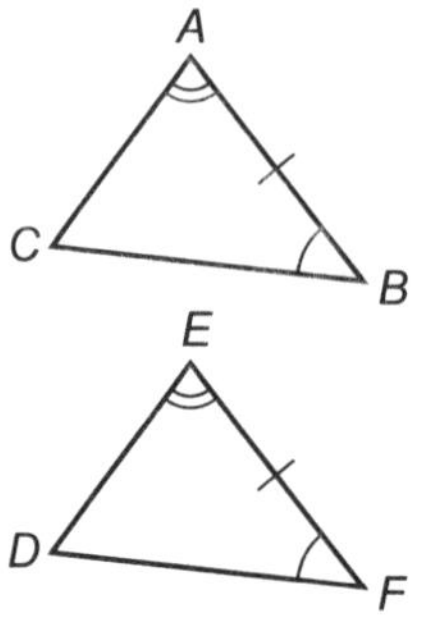

SSS (side-side-side)

If in $\triangle ABC$ and $\triangle EFD$, $AB = EF$, $AC = ED$, and $BC = FD$, then $\triangle ABC \cong \triangle EFD$.

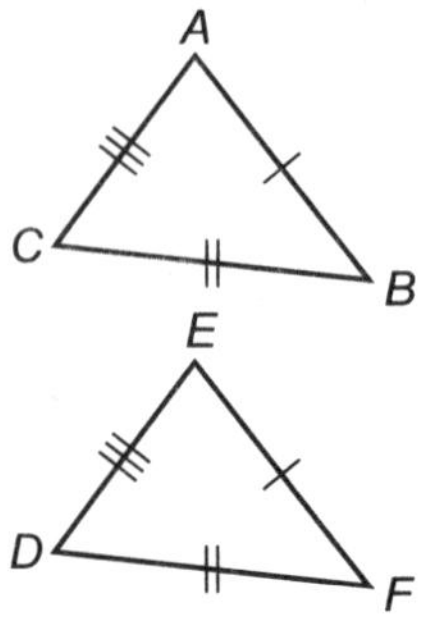

1. In the diagram, $CM = 7$ cm. Fill in the blanks to find the length of DM.

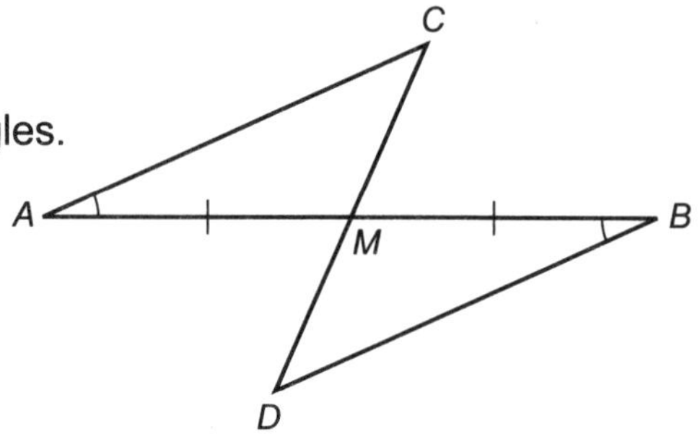

a) $AM =$ ______ and $\angle A =$ ______.

b) $\angle AMC =$ __________ because they are ________________ angles.

c) $\triangle AMC \cong \triangle$__________ by the __________ congruence rule.

This means $DM =$ ______ $=$ ______ cm.

2. In the diagram, $KL = MN = 42$ cm, and $KN = LM = 50$ cm. $\angle K = 20°$ and $\angle KNL = 50°$. Fill in the blanks to find $\angle M$ and $\angle MLN$.

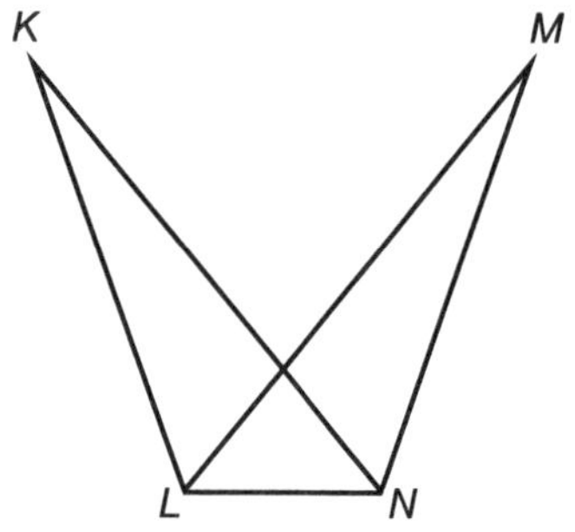

a) Which sides are equal in triangles KLN and LMN?

____

b) $\triangle KLN \cong \triangle$__________ by the __________ congruence rule.

So, $\angle M = \angle$__________ $=$ ______ and $\angle MLN = \angle$__________ $=$ ______.

3. A school wants to install a square rope climbing structure over a large circular sandbox. A contractor places a pole in the center O of the box and places rope anchors at the opposite sides of the pit in points W, X, Y, and Z.

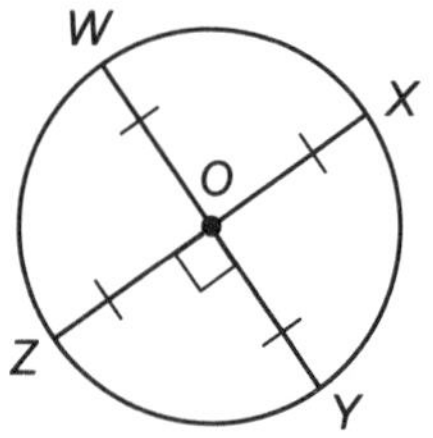

a) Draw the quadrilateral $WXYZ$.

b) The contractor claims that $WXYZ$ is a square. Is he correct? ______

c) Use congruent triangles to explain your answer in part b).

To prove that two polygons are congruent, imagine placing them one on top of the other, so that they match exactly. If the polygons have equal corresponding sides and equal corresponding angles, they are congruent. Example:

$\angle A = \angle G$, $\angle B = \angle F$, $\angle C = \angle E$, $\angle D = \angle H$

$AB = GF$, $BC = FE$, $CD = EH$, $DA = HG$

So $ABCD \cong GFEH$.

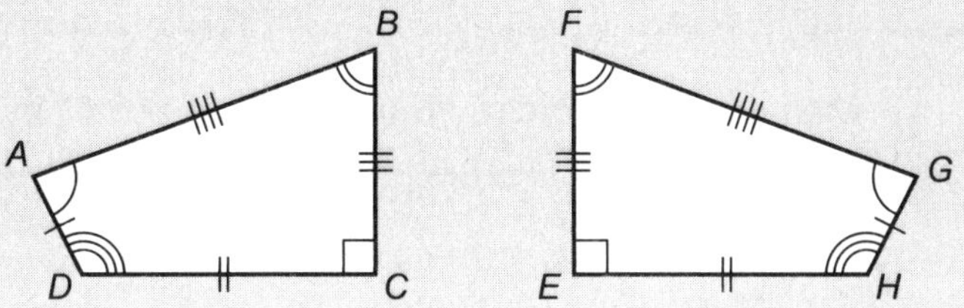

4. The equal sides are marked on the quadrilaterals *JKLM* and *NOPQ*. Also, $\angle J = \angle N$ and $\angle L = \angle P$.

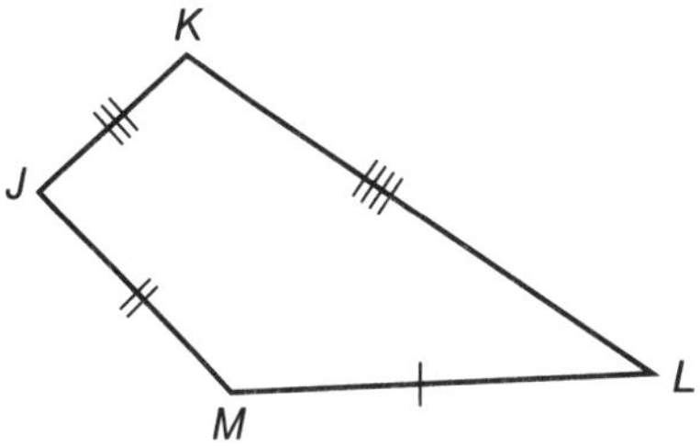

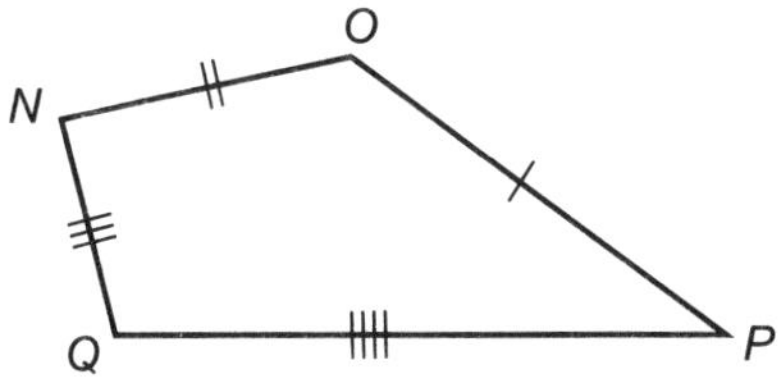

a) Mark the equal angles on the diagram.

b) Draw line segments *KM* and *OQ*.

c) $\Delta JKM \cong \Delta$______ by the ______ congruence rule.

This means $\angle JKM = \angle$______. Label both these angles *w*.

This also means $\angle JMK = \angle$______. Label both these angles *x*.

d) $\Delta KLM \cong \Delta$______ by the ______ congruence rule.

This means $\angle LKM = \angle$______. Label both these angles *y*.

This also means $\angle LMK = \angle$______. Label both these angles *z*.

e) Express the measure of $\angle JKL$ and the angle equal to it in *NOPQ* using *w*, *x*, *y*, *z*.

$\angle JKL = \angle$______ = ______________

f) Express the measure of $\angle JML$ and the angle equal to it in *NOPQ* using *w*, *x*, *y*, *z*.

$\angle JML = \angle$______ = ______________

g) Write the congruence statement for the quadrilaterals. ______________

5. Are the quadrilaterals congruent? Use a ruler and a protractor to check. If yes, write the pairs of corresponding equal sides and corresponding equal angles. Then write the congruence statement.

a)

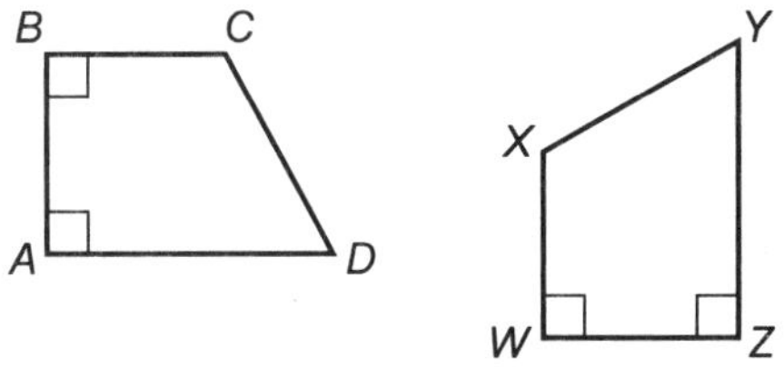

b)

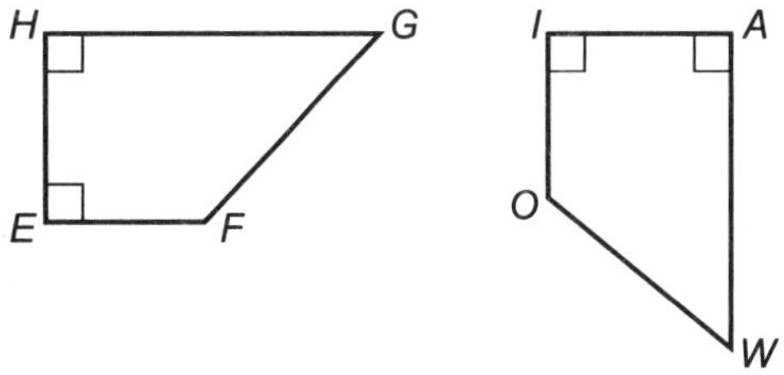

Bonus ▶ In parallelograms *ABCD* and *PQRS*, we have $AB = QR$, $BC = PQ$, and $\angle B = \angle Q$. Jake thinks the parallelograms are congruent. Is that correct? Explain.

G8-13 Exterior Angles of a Triangle

An **exterior angle** is formed by extending a side of a triangle.
Angle *x* is an exterior angle.

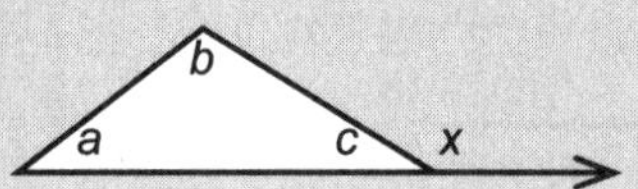

1. a) Measure the angles with a protractor and fill in the table.

	i) 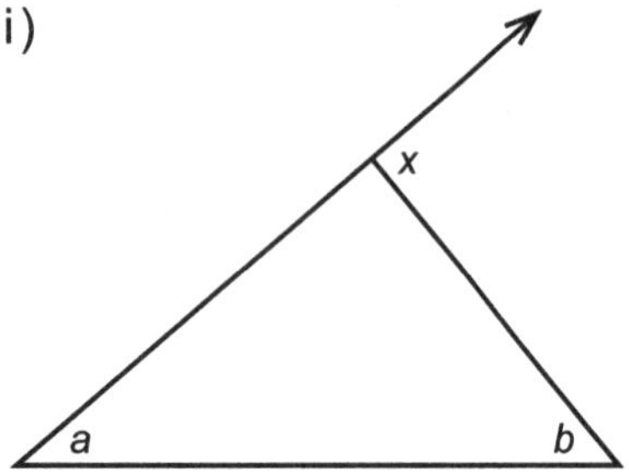	ii) 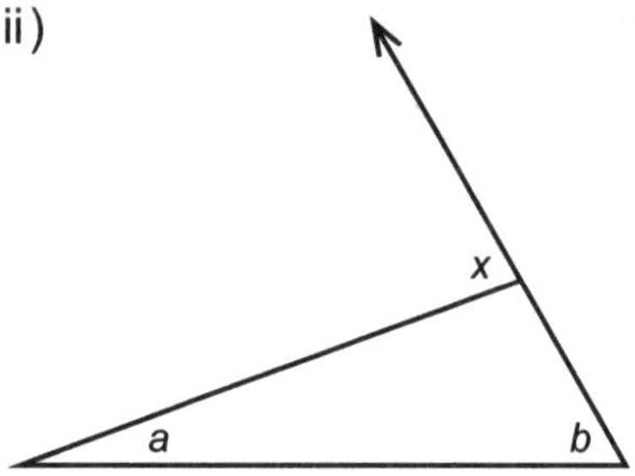	iii) 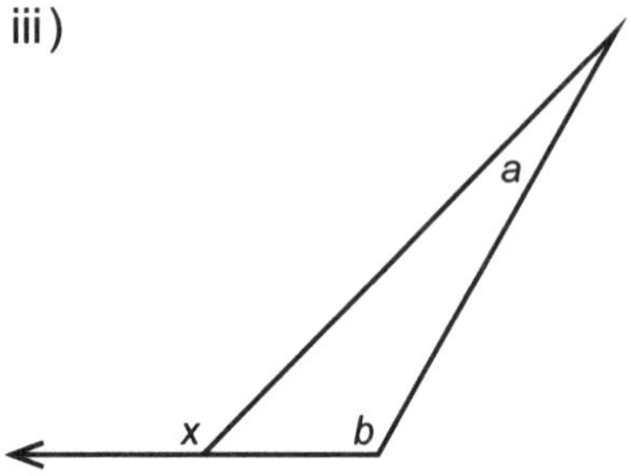
∠*a*			
∠*b*			
∠*x*			

b) Express the measure of ∠*x* using the measures of ∠*a* and ∠*b*. ____________________

An exterior angle of a triangle is equal to the sum of the two opposite angles in the triangle ($x = a + b$).

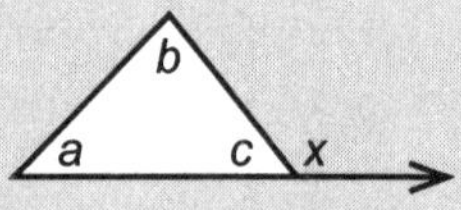

Examples:

$x = 88° + 45°$
$= 133°$

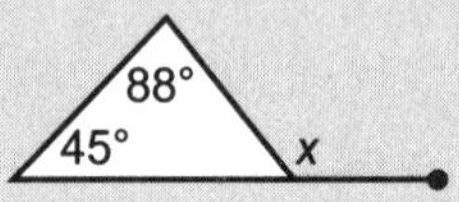

$a + 90° = 150°$
$a = 150° - 90° = 60°$

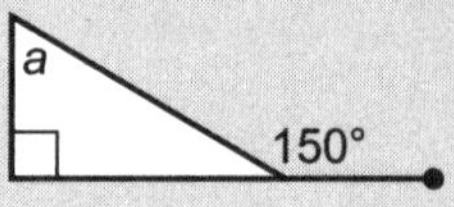

2. Find the missing angle. Show your work.

a)

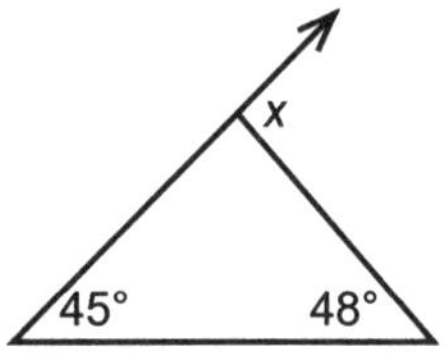

∠*x* = ______

b)

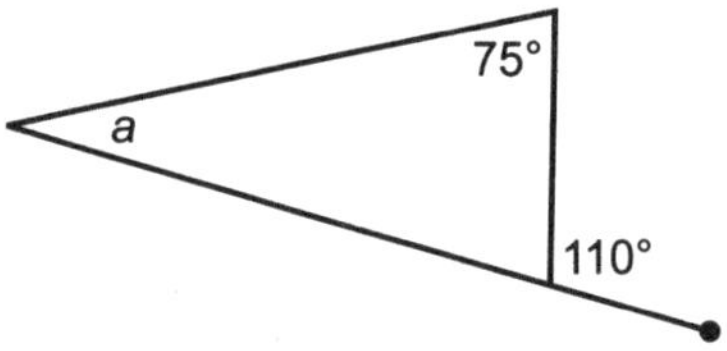

∠*a* = ______

c)

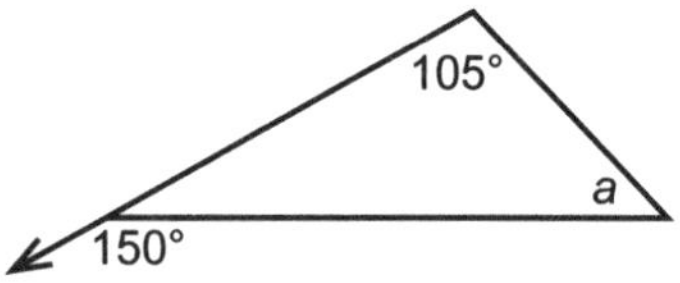

∠*a* = ______

d)

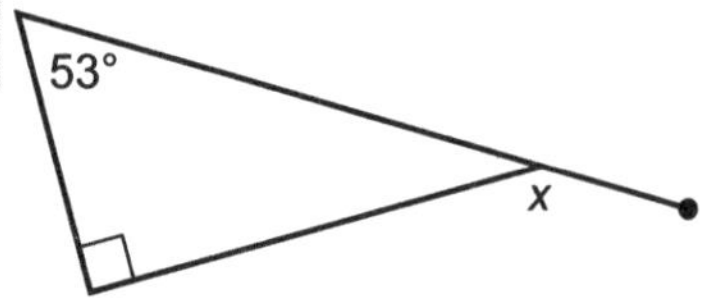

e)

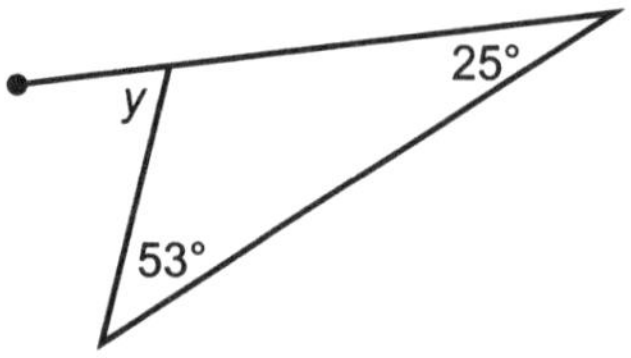

f)

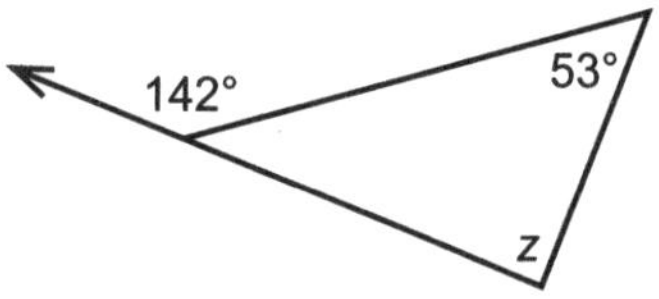

REMINDER: Angles in a triangle add to 180°.

Two angles that combine to make a straight line add to 180°. $a + b = 180°$.

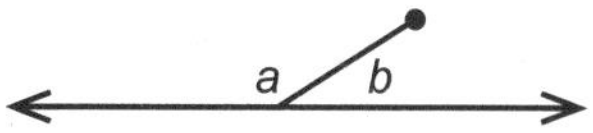

3. Find the missing angles. Show your work.

a)

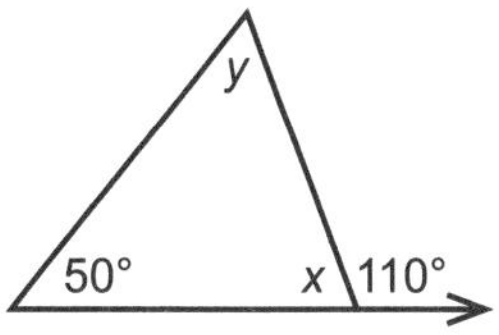

$\angle x =$ ______, $\angle y =$ ______

b)

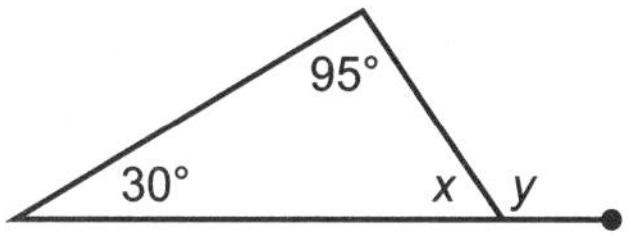

$\angle x =$ ______, $\angle y =$ ______

c)

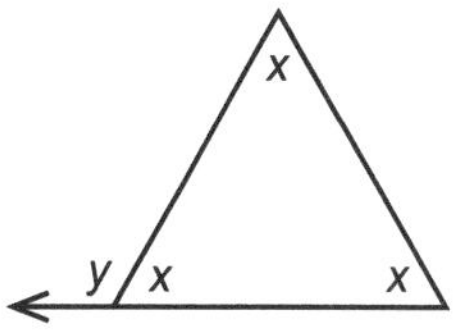

$\angle x =$ ______, $\angle y =$ ______

4. Find the missing angles.

a)

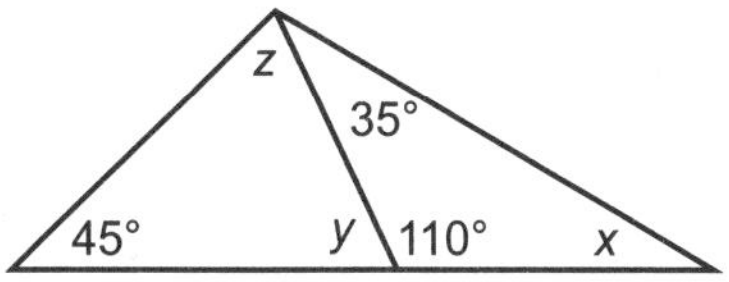

$\angle x =$ ______

$\angle y =$ ______

$\angle z =$ ______

b)

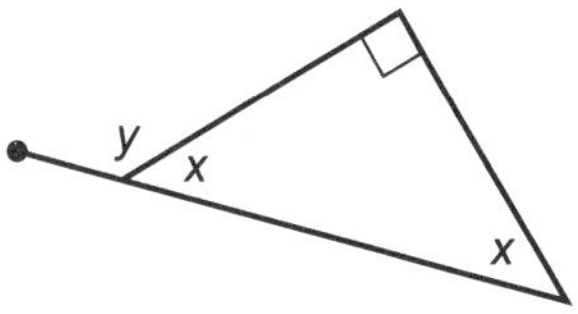

$\angle x =$ ______

$\angle y =$ ______

c)

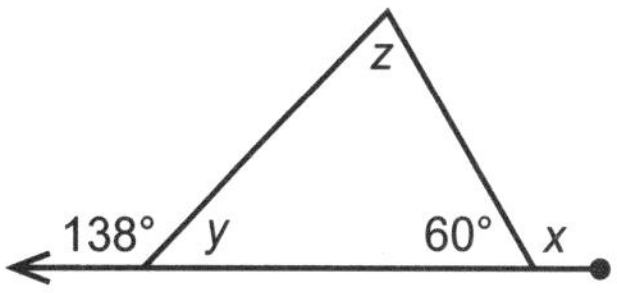

$\angle x =$ ______

$\angle y =$ ______

$\angle z =$ ______

d)

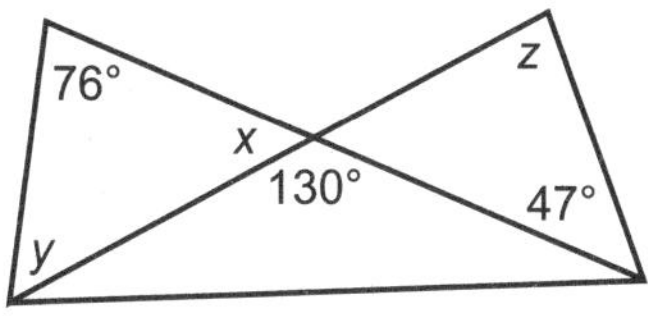

$\angle x =$ ______

$\angle y =$ ______

$\angle z =$ ______

e)

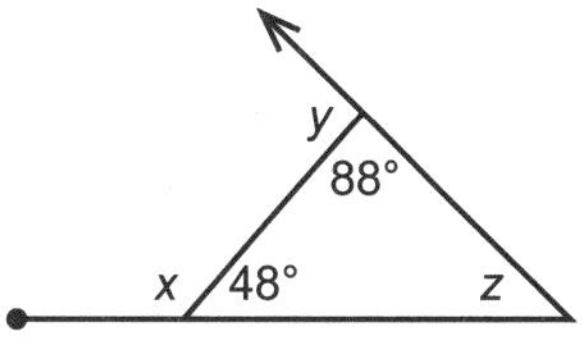

$\angle x =$ ______

$\angle y =$ ______

$\angle z =$ ______

f)

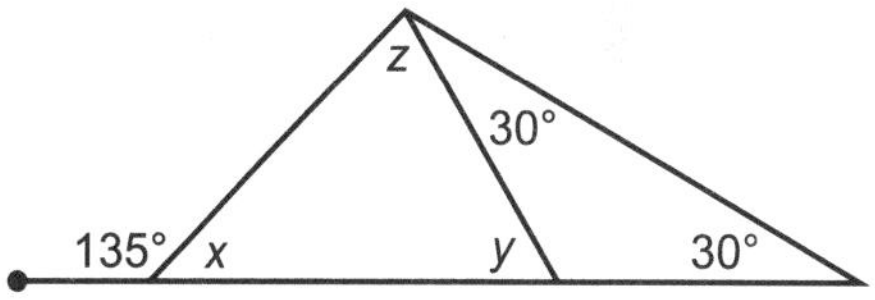

$\angle x =$ ______

$\angle y =$ ______

$\angle z =$ ______

5. Prove that $\angle x = \angle a + \angle b$ using the sum of the angles in a triangle and supplementary angles (angles that add to 180°).

a) What do you know about the measures of $\angle a$, $\angle b$, and $\angle c$? Explain.

b) What do you know about the measures of $\angle x$ and $\angle c$? Explain.

c) Write two expressions for the measure of $\angle c$ using your answers in parts a) and b).

d) Use the expressions in part c) to explain why $\angle x = \angle a + \angle b$.

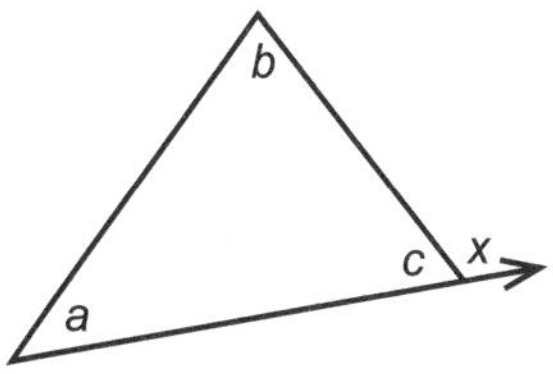

G8-14 Corresponding Angles and Parallel Lines

Corresponding angles create a pattern like in the letter F shown: 

These pairs of angles are corresponding angles for lines *m* and *n*:

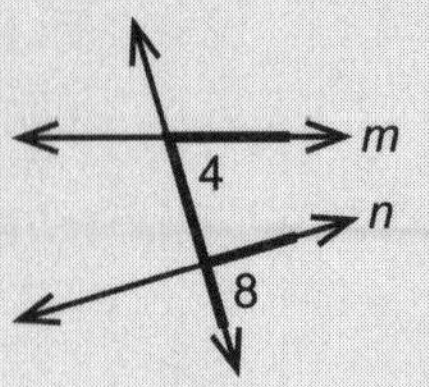

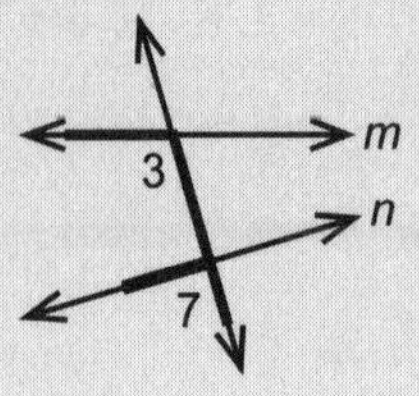

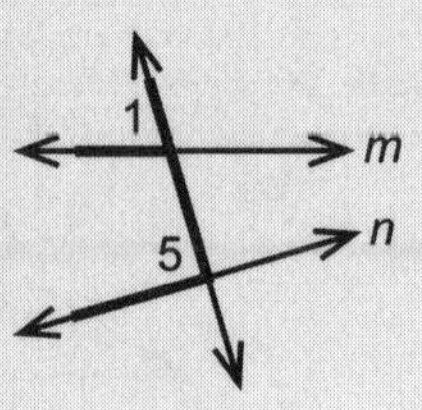

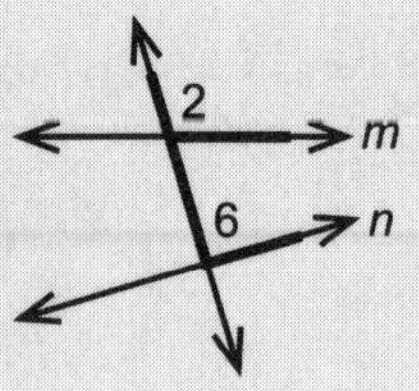

1. List the corresponding angles.

a)

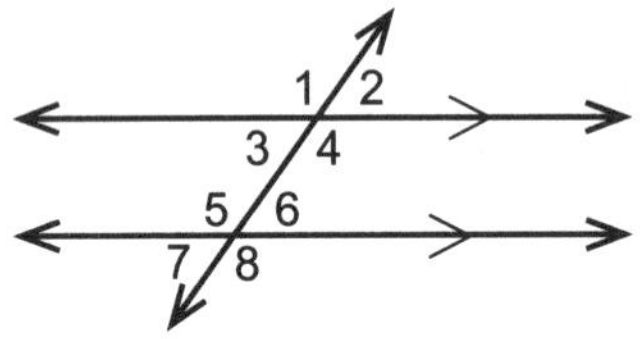

∠1 and ______, ∠2 and ______

∠3 and ______, ∠4 and ______

b)

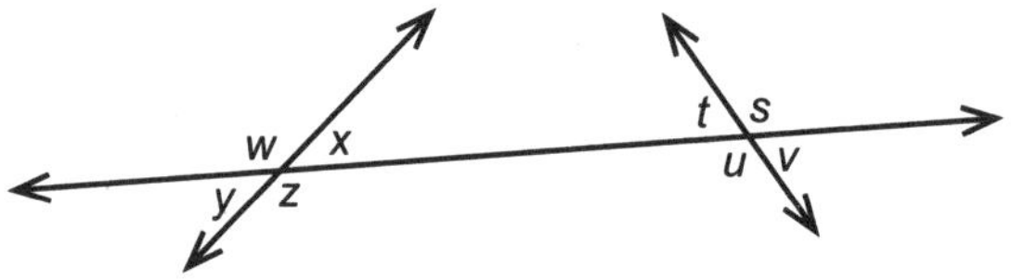

∠*w* and ______, ∠*x* and ______

∠*y* and ______, ∠*z* and ______

2. Measure the corresponding angles *a* and *b*. Are they equal or not equal?

a)

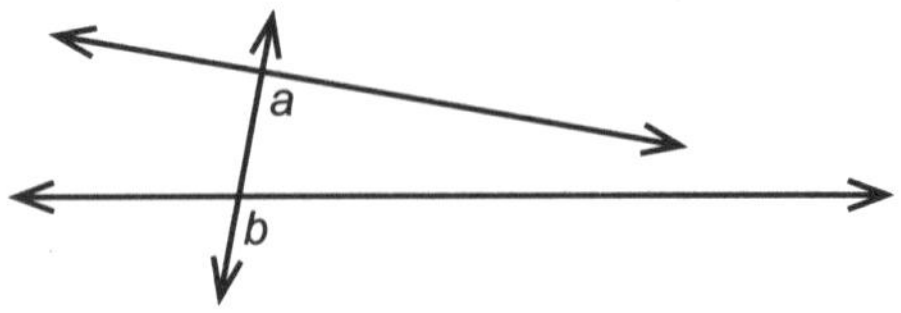

∠*a* = ______, ∠*b* = ______

The corresponding angles are ___________.

b)

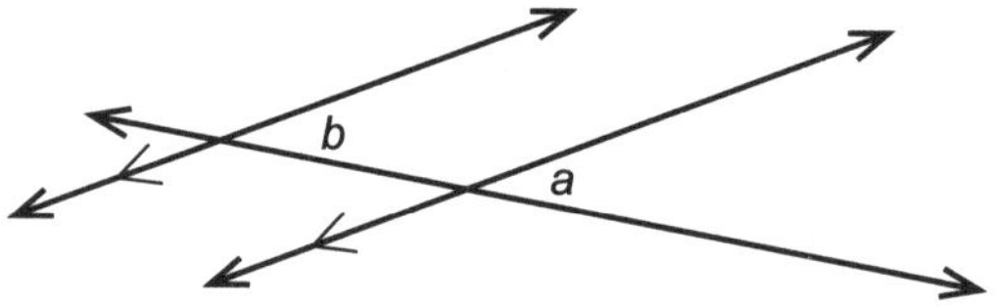

∠*a* = ______, ∠*b* = ______

The corresponding angles are ___________.

c)

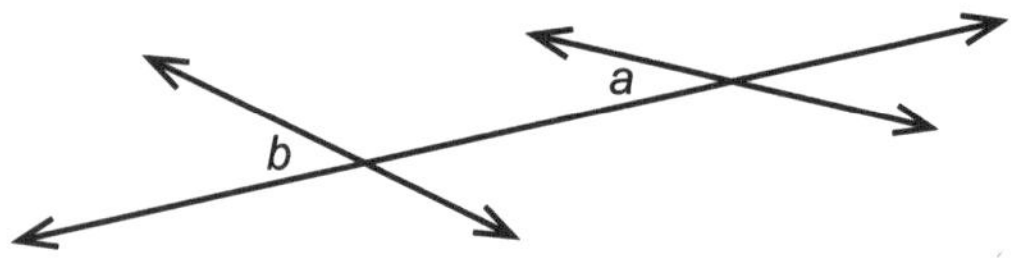

∠*a* = ______, ∠*b* = ______

The corresponding angles are ___________.

d)

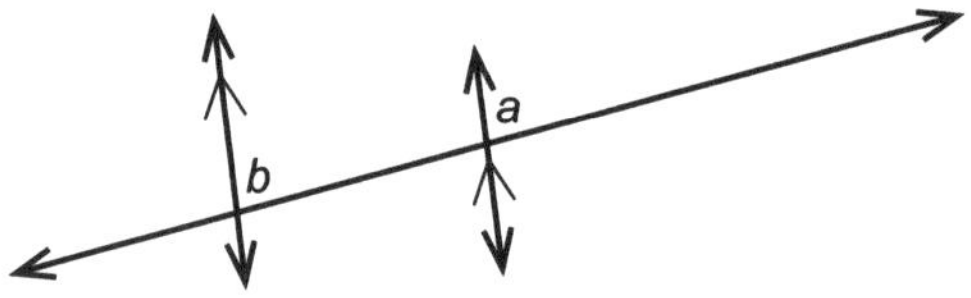

∠*a* = ______, ∠*b* = ______

The corresponding angles are ___________.

e)

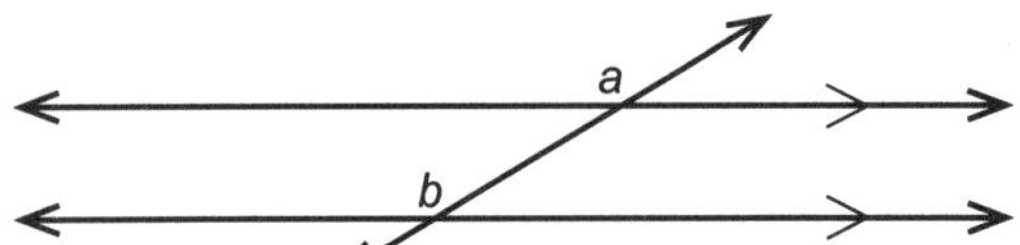

∠*a* = ______, ∠*b* = ______

The corresponding angles are ___________.

f)

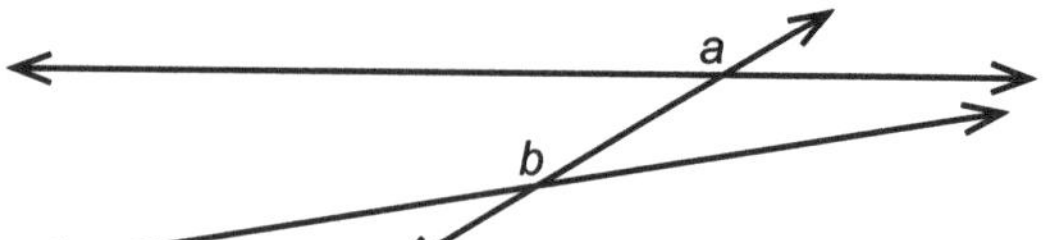

∠*a* = ______, ∠*b* = ______

The corresponding angles are ___________.

When the lines are parallel, corresponding angles are equal.

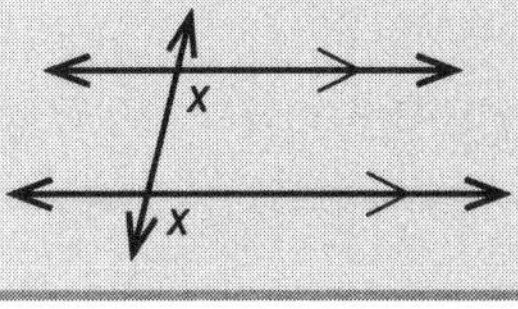

3. List the corresponding equal angles.

a)

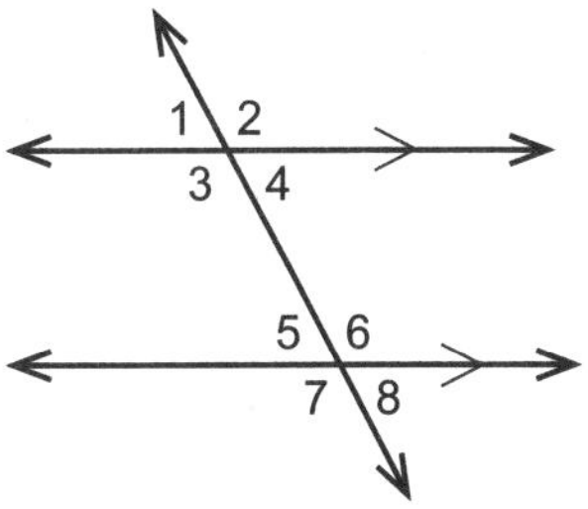

∠1 = __∠5__, ∠2 = ______

∠3 = ______, ∠4 = ______

b)

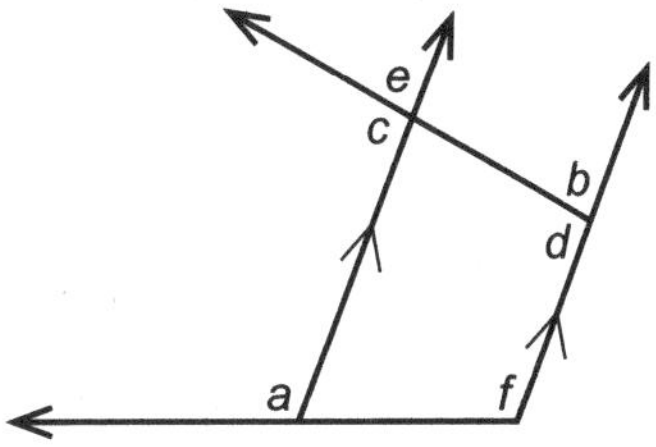

∠a = ______, ∠c = ______

∠e = ______

c)

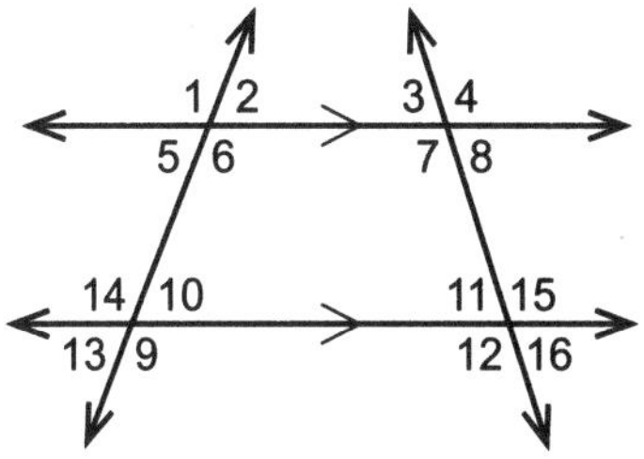

∠3 = ______, ∠4 = ______

∠5 = ______, ∠10 = ______

4. Give the measure of the corresponding angles.

a)

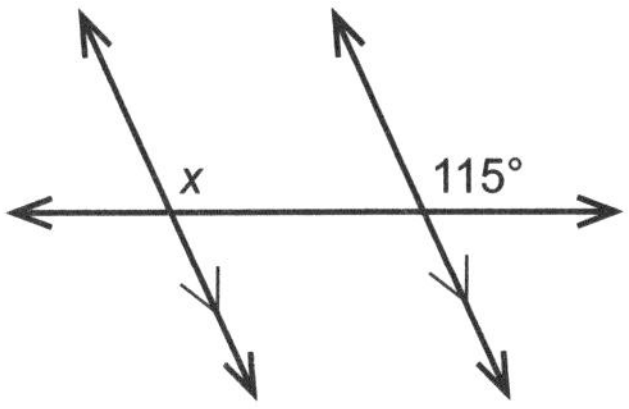

∠x = ______

b)

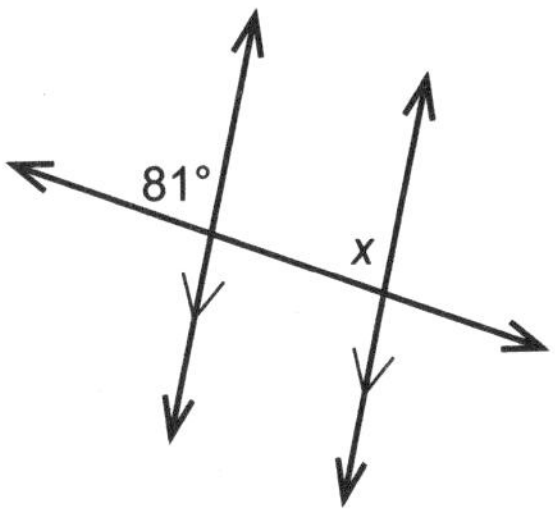

∠x = ______

c)

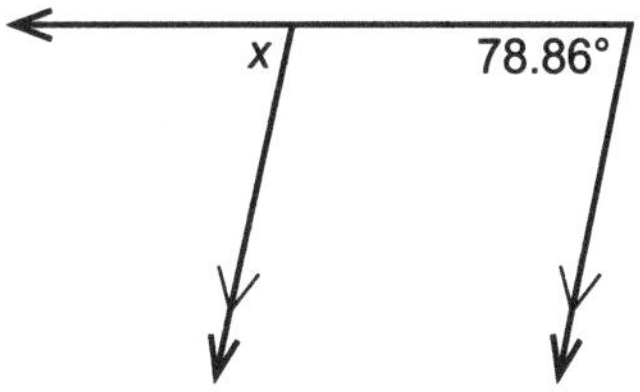

∠x = ______

d)

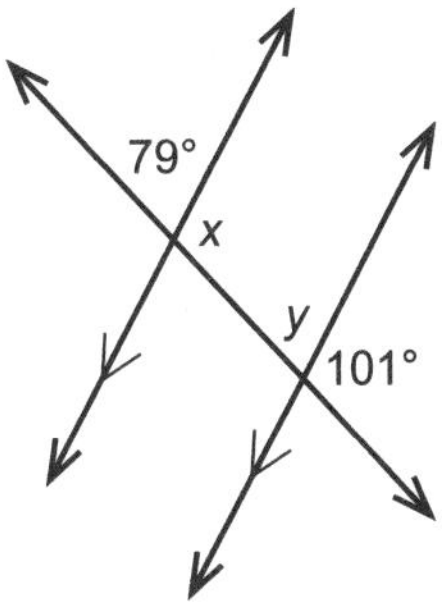

∠x = ______, ∠y = ______

e)

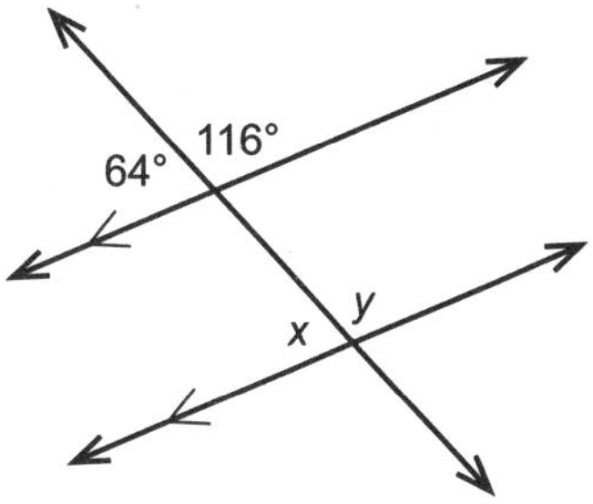

∠x = ______, ∠y = ______

f)

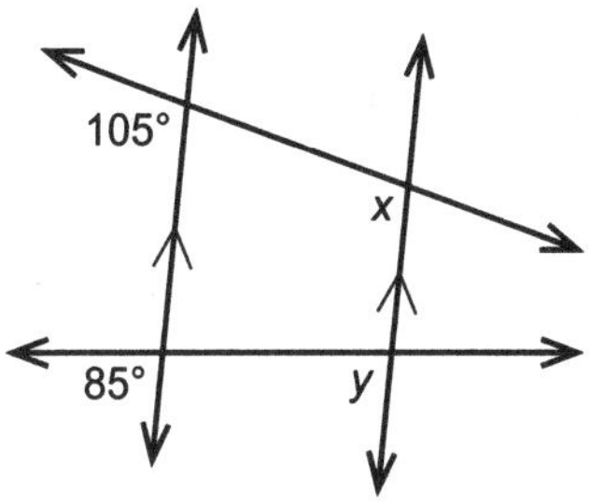

∠x = ______, ∠y = ______

When the corresponding angles are equal, the lines are parallel.

5. Find ∠x using supplementary angles. Circle the angle corresponding to ∠x. Then draw arrows to show if the lines are parallel.

a)

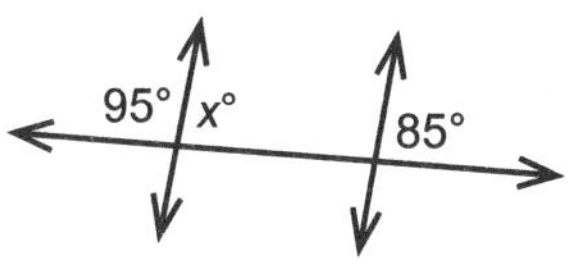

∠x = ______

b)

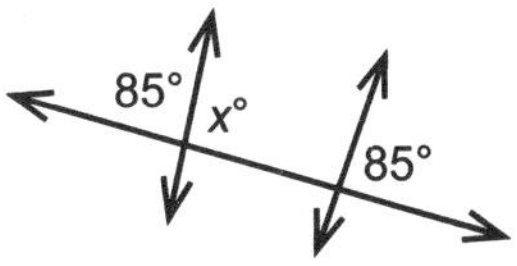

∠x = ______

c)

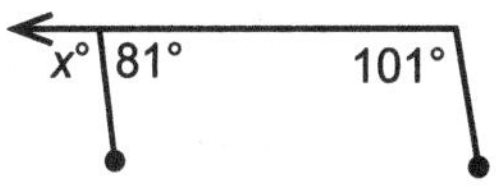

∠x = ______

REMINDER: Vertical angles are equal.

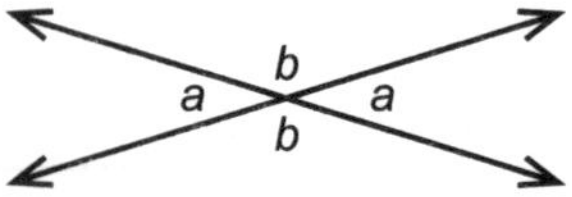

6. For each pair of lines that do not intersect in the picture …

- mark a pair of corresponding angles and find their measures.
- mark parallel lines.

a)

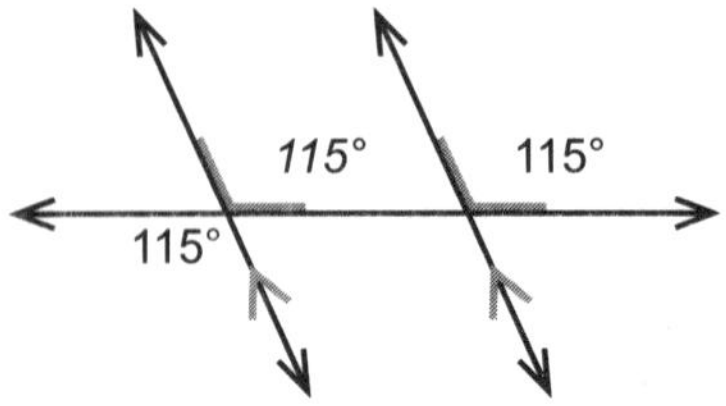

b)

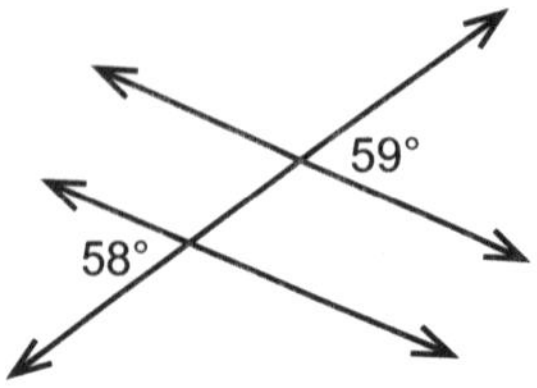

c)

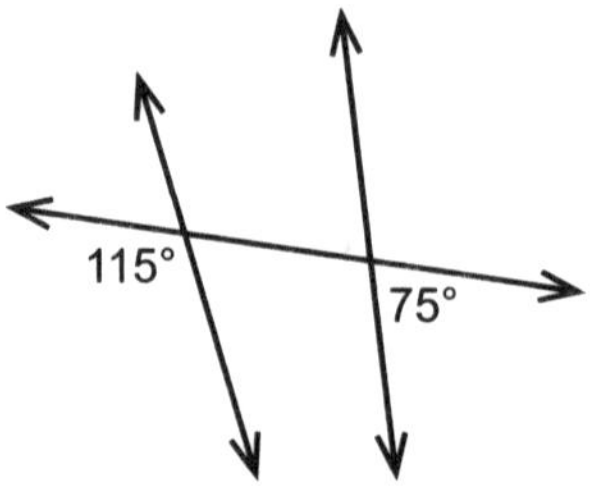

d)

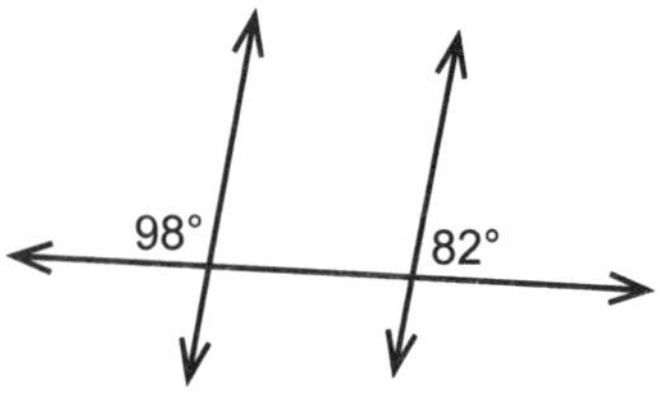

e)

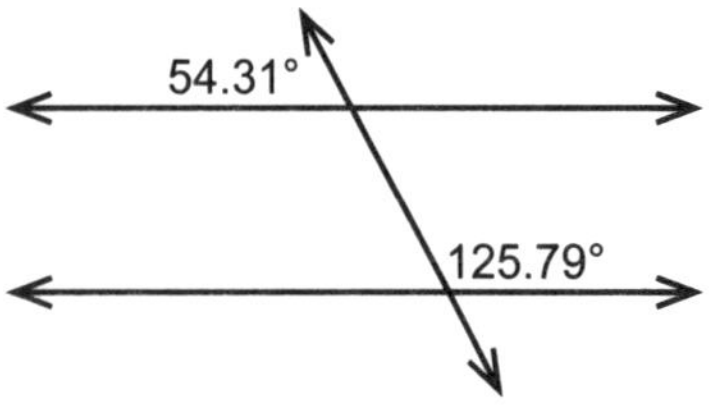

f)

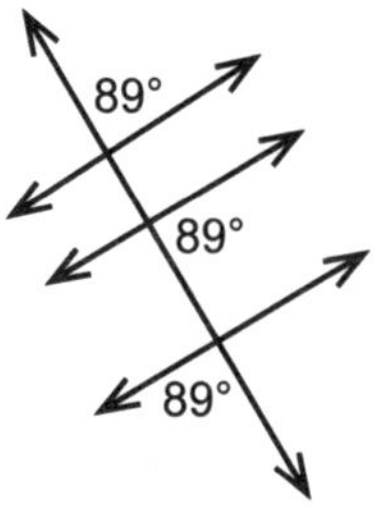

You can use small letters to label lines, too.

7. Lines ℓ and m are parallel. Use what you know about corresponding and vertical angles to explain why $\angle a + \angle b = 180°$.

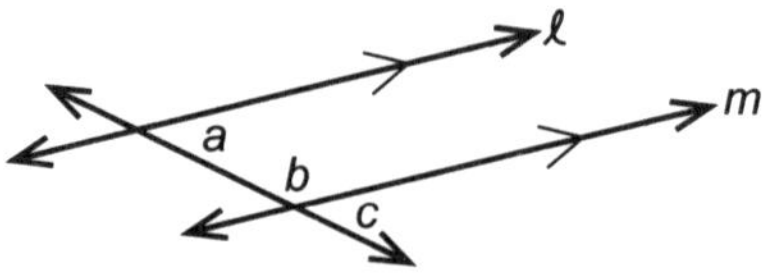

Co-interior angles create a pattern like in the letter "C": Angles 3 and 5, and angles 4 and 6, are co-interior angles.

These angles are sometimes called **same-side interior angles**.

If the lines a and b are parallel, co-interior angles add to 180°.

If the co-interior angles add to 180°, the lines are parallel.

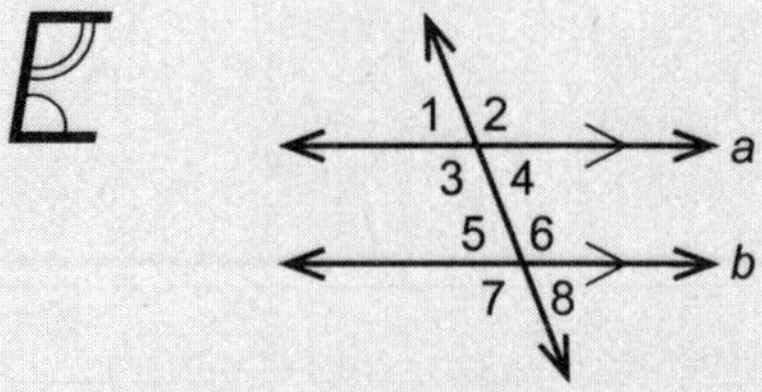

8. All angles in the quadrilateral $ABCD$ are right angles.

a) Identify a pair of co-interior angles for lines AB and CD.
Identify a pair of co-interior angles for lines AD and BC.

b) Use the angle measures of co-interior angles to explain that these pairs of sides are parallel.

c) I have just proven that a rectangle is a ________________.

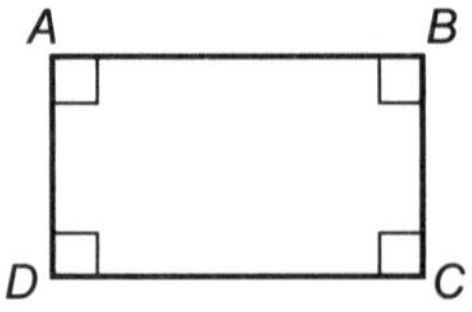

G8-15 Alternate Angles and Parallel Lines

Alternate angles or **alternate interior angles** make a pattern like the letter Z:

∠3 and ∠6 are alternate angles for parallel lines *m* and *n*.

∠4 and ∠5 are alternate angles for lines *p* and *r*.

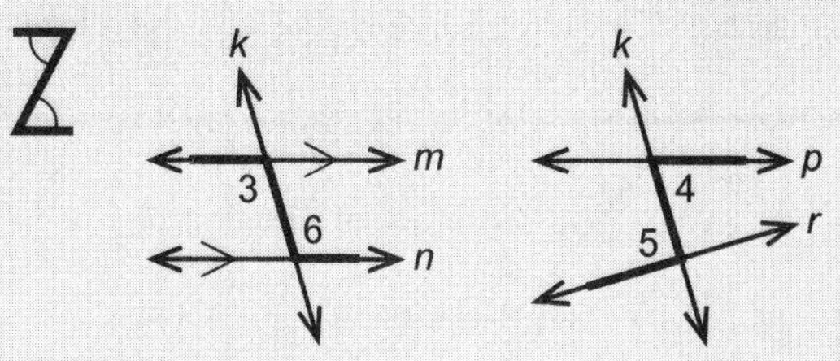

1. List the pairs of alternate angles.

a)

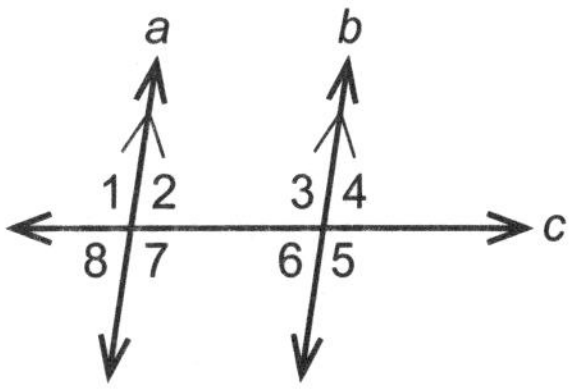

∠2 and ______

∠3 and ______

b)

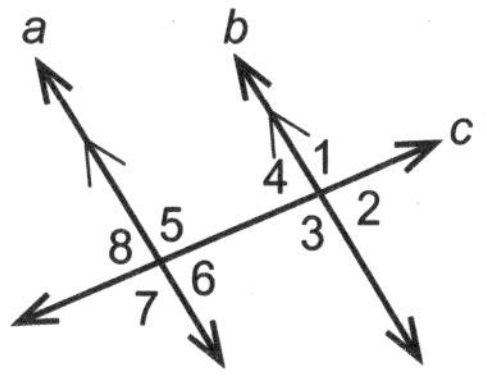

∠3 and ______

∠4 and ______

c)

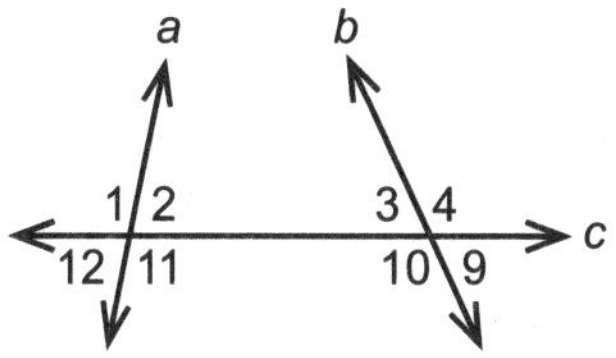

∠2 and ______

∠11 and ______

2. Measure the alternate angles *a* and *b*. Are they equal or not equal?

a)

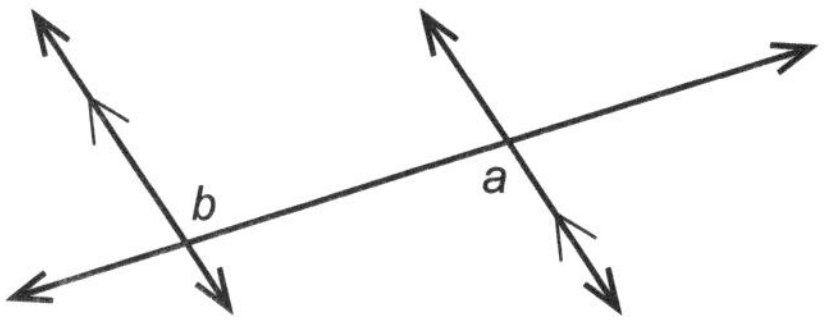

∠*a* = ______, ∠*b* = ______

The alternate angles are ________________.

b)

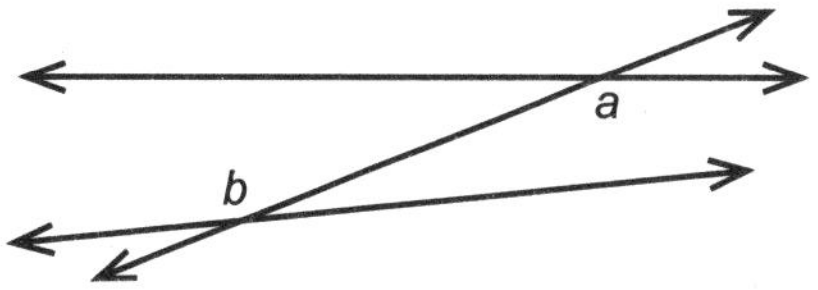

∠*a* = ______, ∠*b* = ______

The alternate angles are ________________.

c)

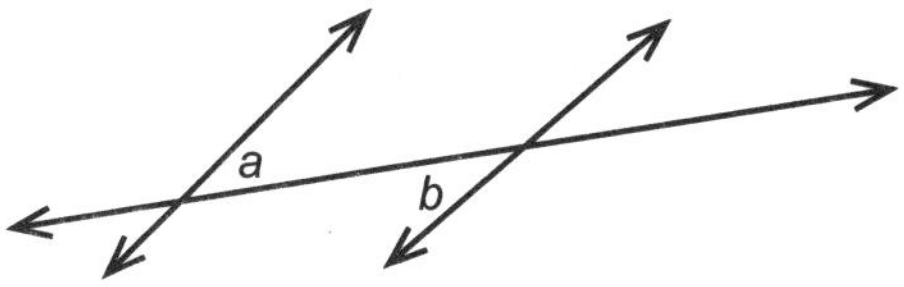

∠*a* = ______, ∠*b* = ______

The alternate angles are ________________.

d)

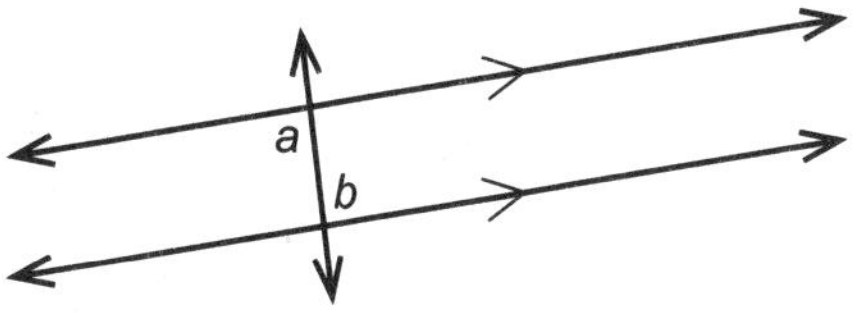

∠*a* = ______, ∠*b* = ______

The alternate angles are ________________.

3. Fill in the blanks to prove that alternate angles for parallel lines are equal.

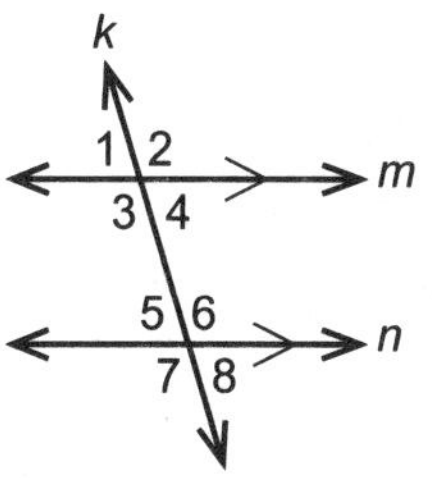

∠3 and ∠______ are alternate angles.

Lines *m* and *n* are ________________________.

∠3 and ∠7 are ________________________ angles, so ∠3 = ∠7.

∠6 and ∠7 are ________________________ angles, so ∠6 = ______.

This means ∠3 = ______.

4. Find the missing alternate angles.

a)

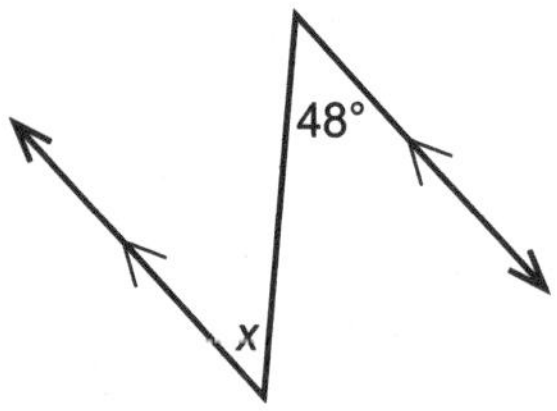

$\angle x =$ ______

b)

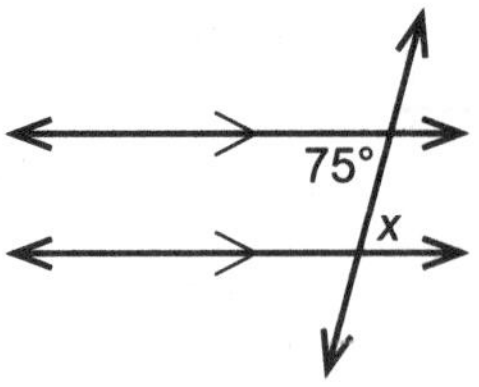

$\angle x =$ ______

c)

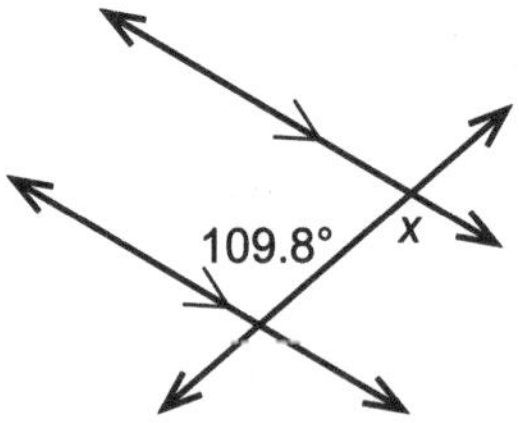

$\angle x =$ ______

d)

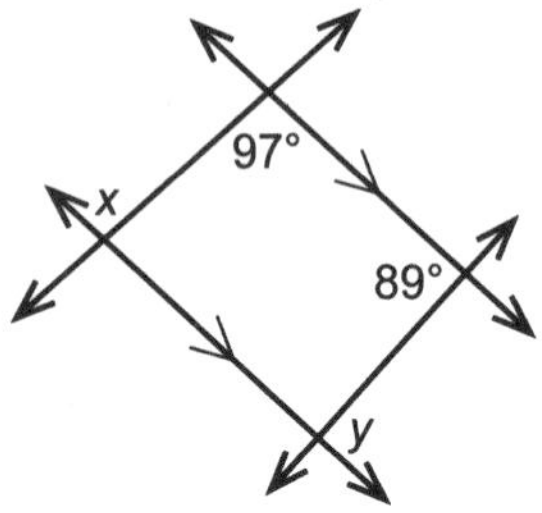

$\angle x =$ ______, $\angle y =$ ______

e)

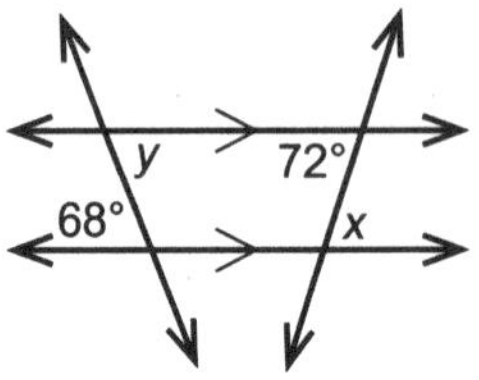

$\angle x =$ ______, $\angle y =$ ______

f)

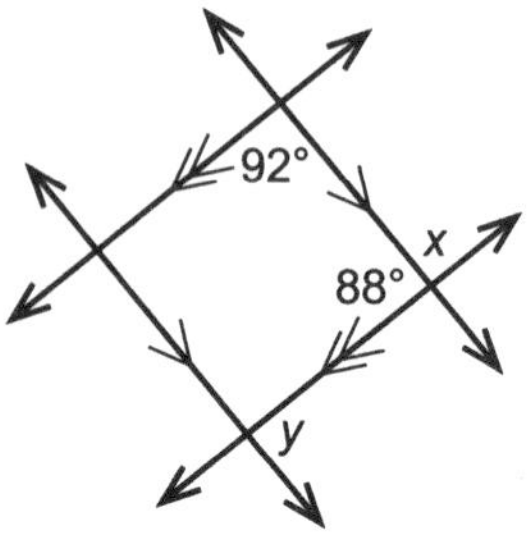

$\angle x =$ ______, $\angle y =$ ______

5. Find the missing alternate, corresponding, supplementary, or vertical angles.

a)

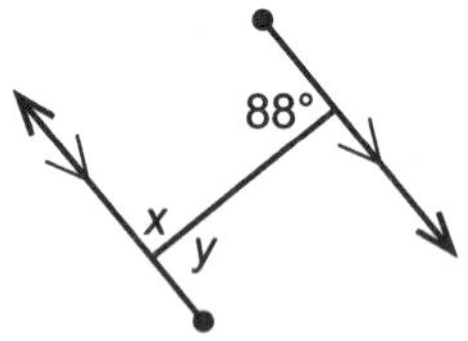

$\angle x =$ ______, $\angle y =$ ______

b)

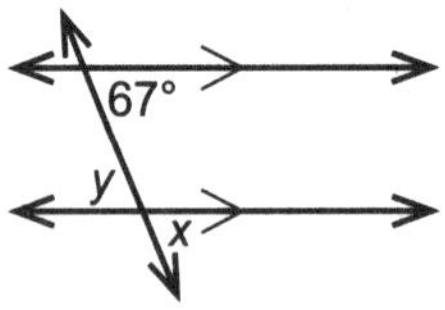

$\angle x =$ ______, $\angle y =$ ______

c)

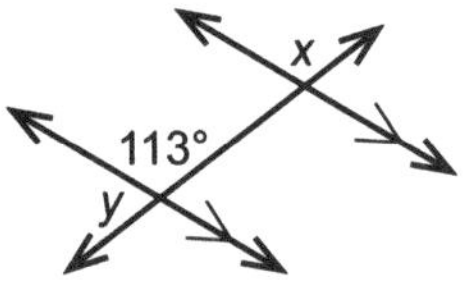

$\angle x =$ ______, $\angle y =$ ______

d)

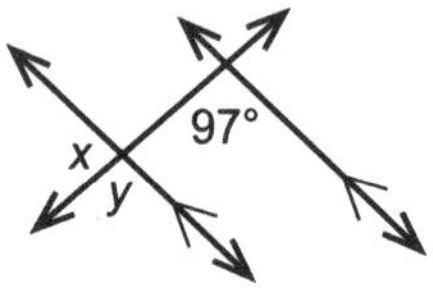

$\angle x =$ ______, $\angle y =$ ______

e)

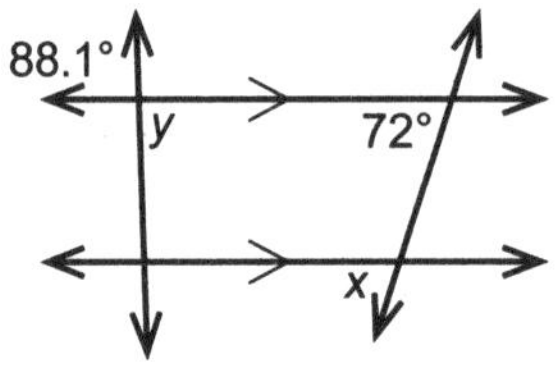

$\angle x =$ ______, $\angle y =$ ______

f)

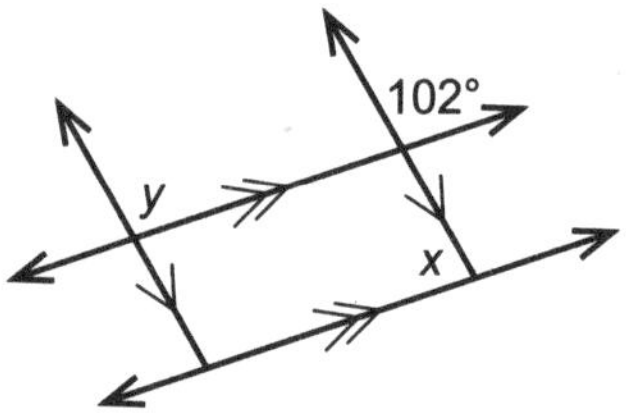

$\angle x =$ ______, $\angle y =$ ______

If the alternate angles are equal, the lines are parallel.

6. Find $\angle x$ using supplementary or vertical angles. Circle the angle that is alternate to $\angle x$. Then decide if the lines or rays are parallel.

a)

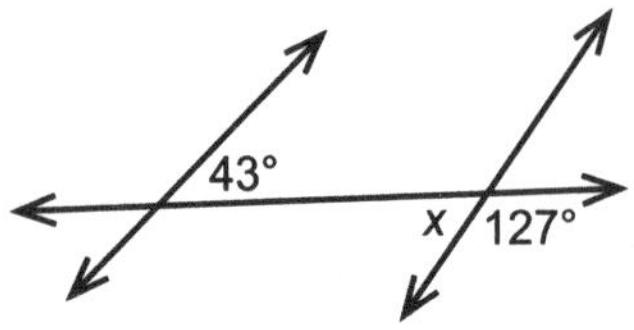

$\angle x =$ ______

parallel not parallel

b)

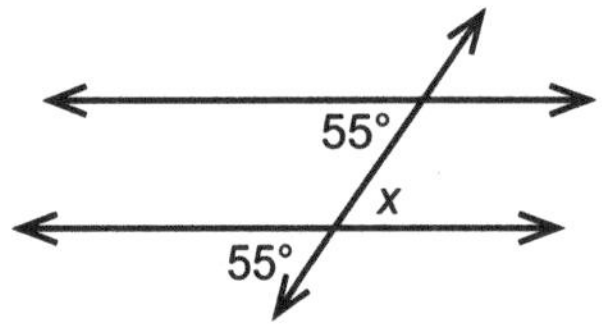

$\angle x =$ ______

parallel not parallel

c)

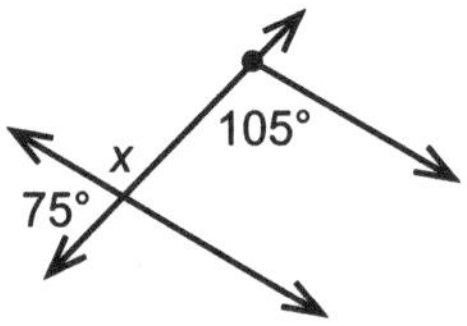

$\angle x =$ ______

parallel not parallel

7. Fill in the missing angles. Use arrows to mark parallel lines if they are not marked already.

a) 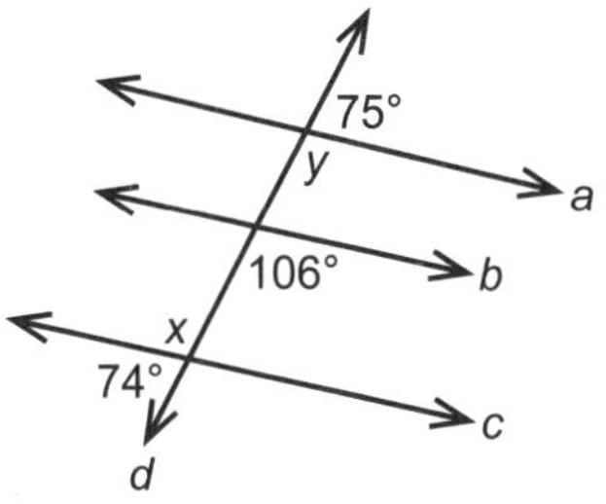

$\angle x =$ ______, $\angle y =$ ______

b) 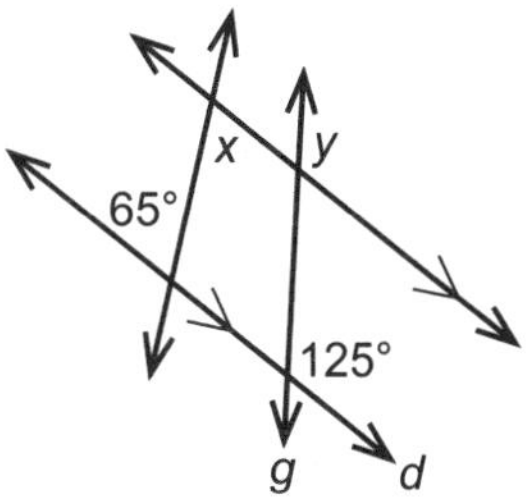

$\angle x =$ ______, $\angle y =$ ______

c) 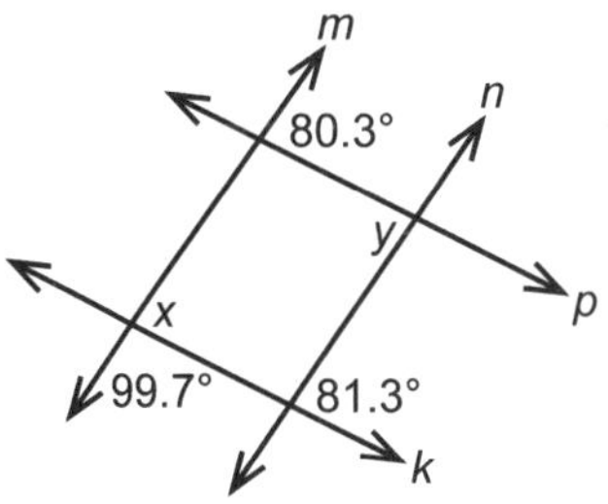

$\angle x =$ ______, $\angle y =$ ______

8. Fill in all the missing angles. Decide which lines or rays are parallel.

a) 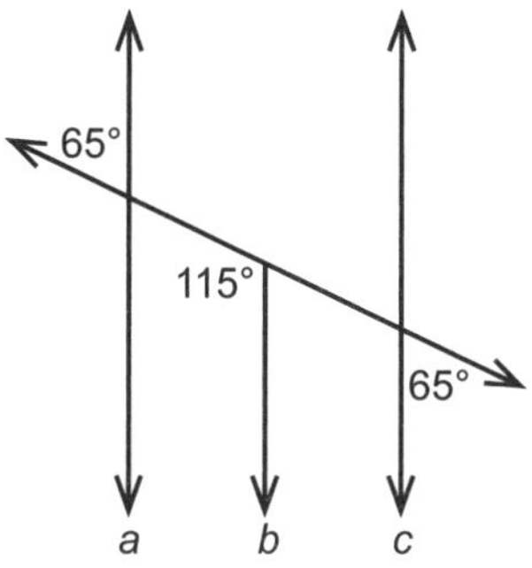

____

b) 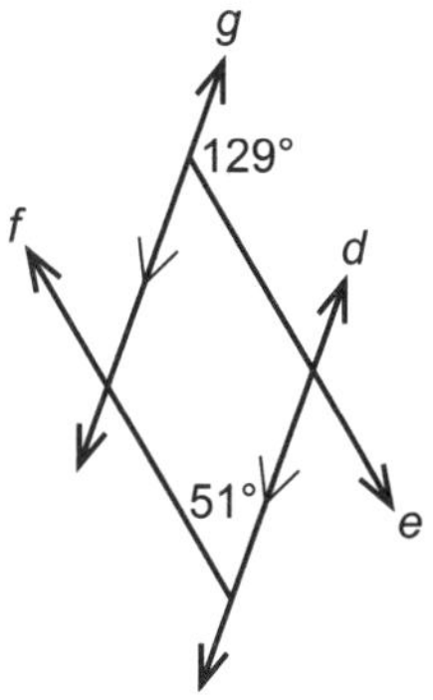

____

c) 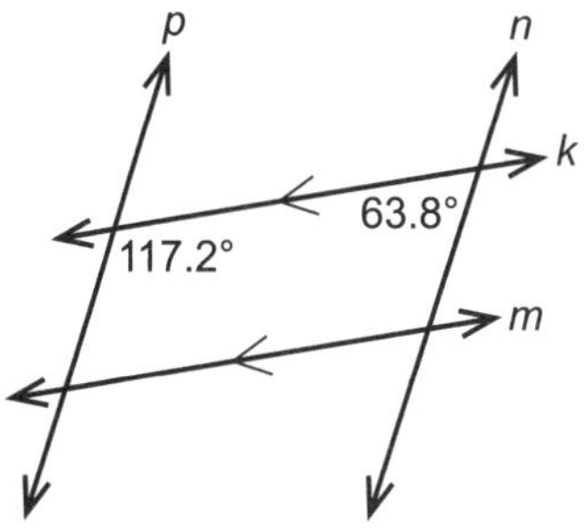

____

9. Sharon wants to prove (using logic) that the sum of the angles in a triangle is 180°.

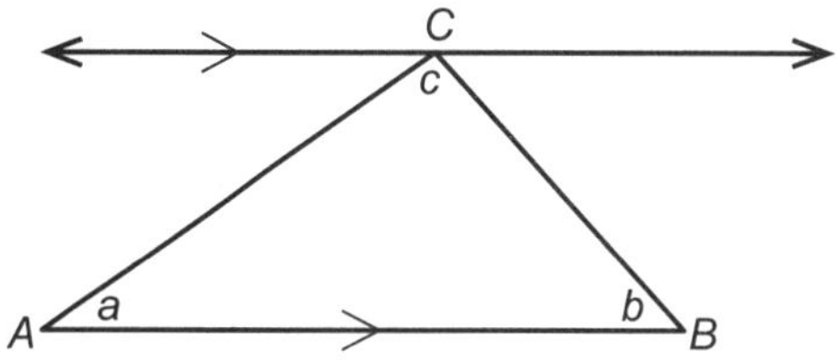

a) Sharon draws a triangle *ABC* and labeled the angle measures *a*, *b*, and *c*. Write an equation using *a*, *b*, *c* that she needs to prove. ______________________

b) Sharon draws a line parallel to *AB* through *C*. Label the alternate angles on the diagram with their measures.

c) Which angles on the diagram make a straight angle? What do their measures add to? Write an equation. ______________________

d) Did you prove what you needed to prove? ______________________

Bonus ▶

a) Find the measure of $\angle ECN$. Explain how you know.

b) If you extend the lines *ME* and *CN*, will they intersect? Explain.

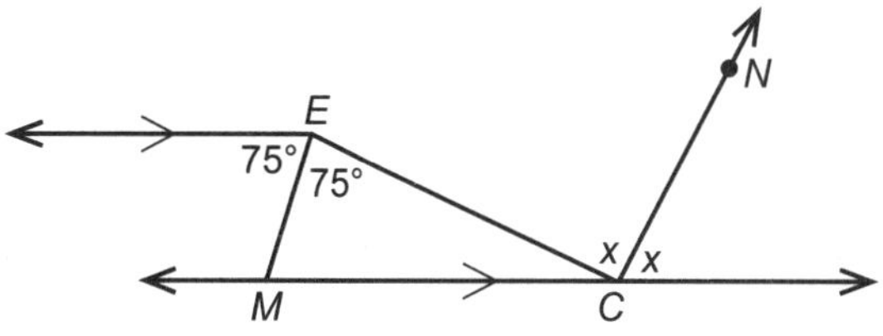

G8-16 Solving Problems Using Angle Properties

1. Match the diagrams to the statements about angles.

a) 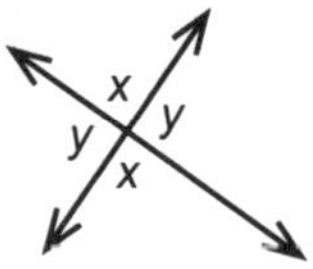

______

b) 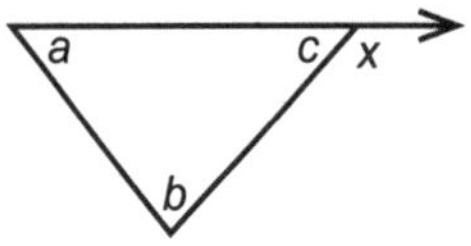

______

c) 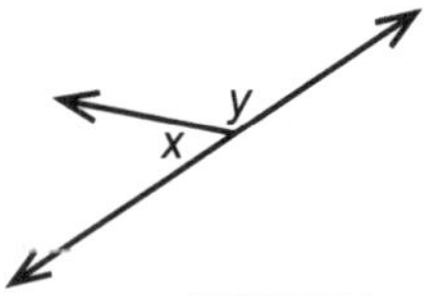

______

d) 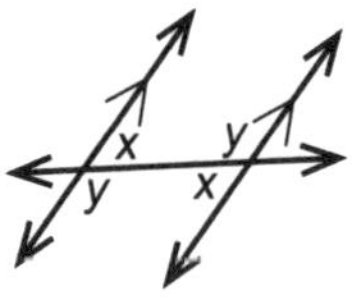

______

e) 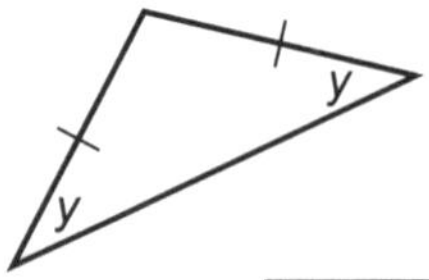

______

f) 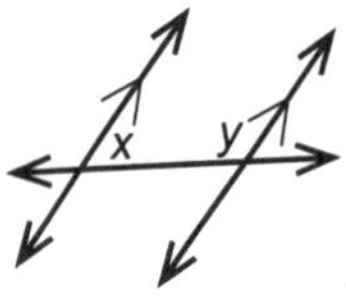

______

g) 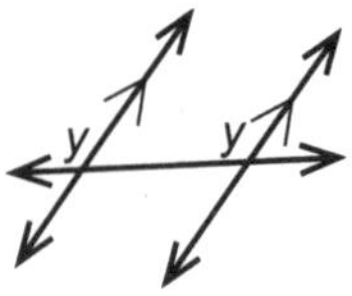

______

h) 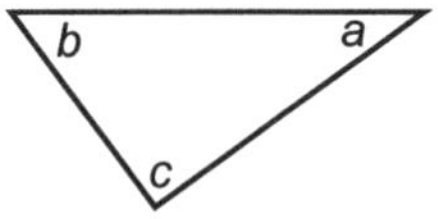

______

A. Angles that make a straight line are supplementary ($\angle x + \angle y = 180°$).

B. Vertical angles are equal.

C. Corresponding angles at parallel lines are equal.

D. Alternate angles at parallel lines are equal.

E. Co-interior angles at parallel lines add to 180°.

F. Angles in a triangle add to 180°.

G. The exterior angle of a triangle equals the sum of the two opposite angles.

H. The angles adjacent to the unequal side of an isosceles triangle are equal.

2. Find the missing angles. For each angle, list the statement you used from Question 1.

a) 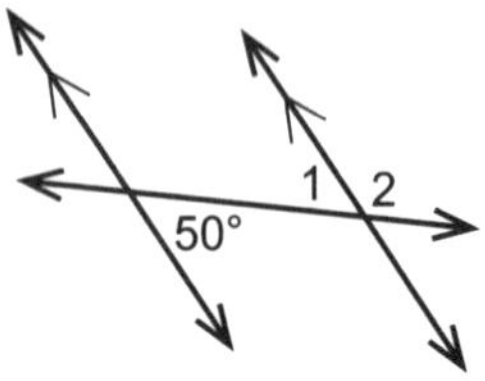

$\angle 1 =$ *50°(D)*

$\angle 2 =$ *130°(A)*

b) 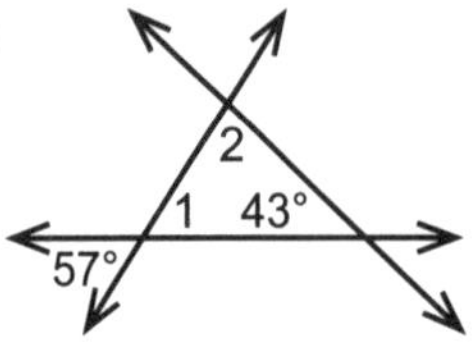

$\angle 1 =$ ______

$\angle 2 =$ ______

c) 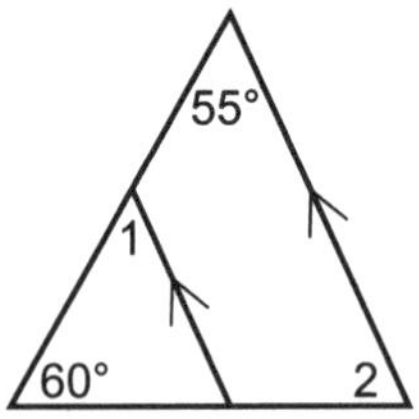

$\angle 1 =$ ______

$\angle 2 =$ ______

d) 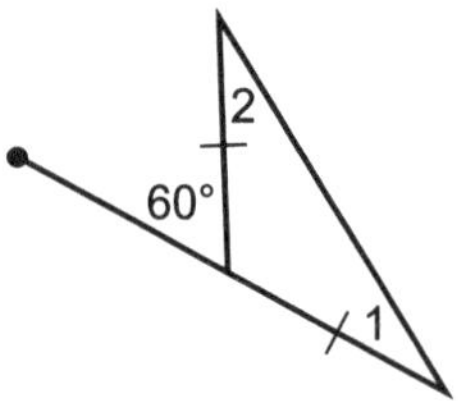

$\angle 1 =$ ______

$\angle 2 =$ ______

e) 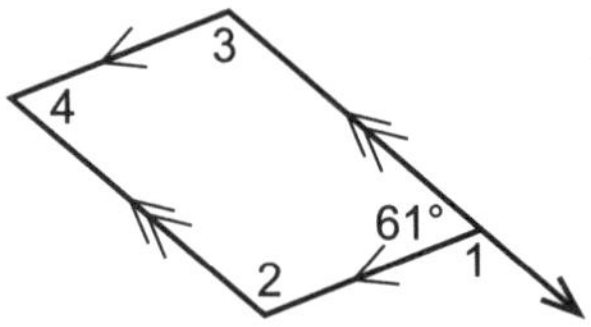

$\angle 1 =$ ______

$\angle 2 =$ ______

$\angle 3 =$ ______

$\angle 4 =$ ______

f) 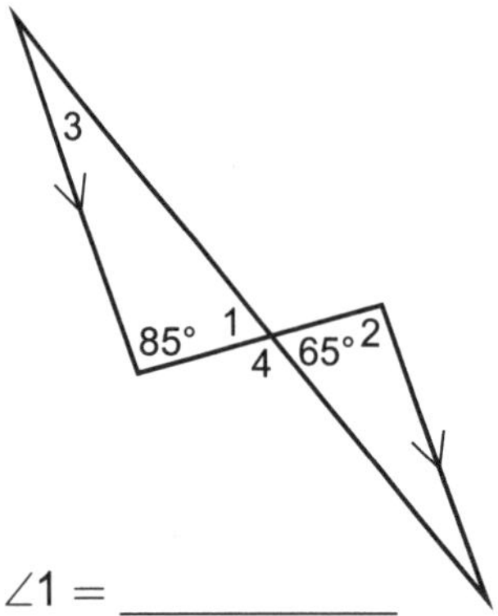

$\angle 1 =$ ______

$\angle 2 =$ ______

$\angle 3 =$ ______

$\angle 4 =$ ______

g) 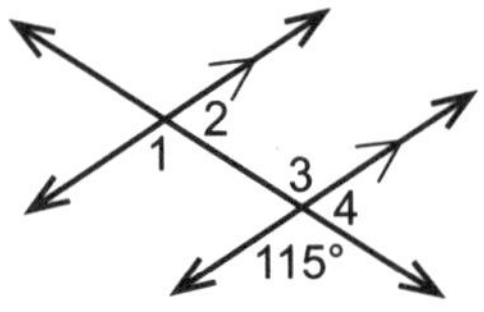

$\angle 1 =$ ______

$\angle 2 =$ ______

$\angle 3 =$ ______

$\angle 4 =$ ______

h) 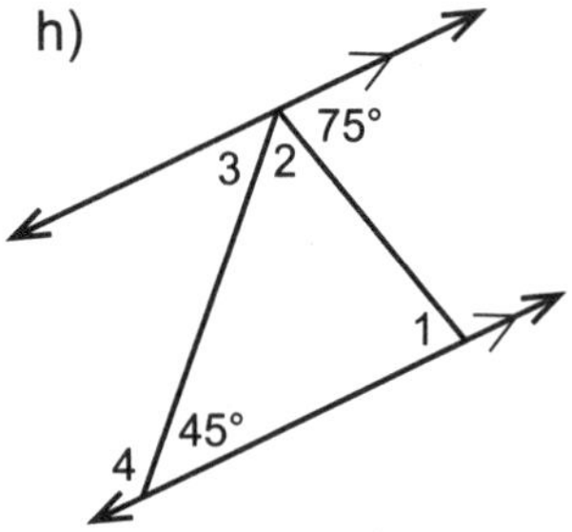

$\angle 1 =$ ______

$\angle 2 =$ ______

$\angle 3 =$ ______

$\angle 4 =$ ______

3. To find the missing angles, you need to find some angles that are not marked. Use numbers to label these angles on the diagrams. Explain how you found each angle.

a) 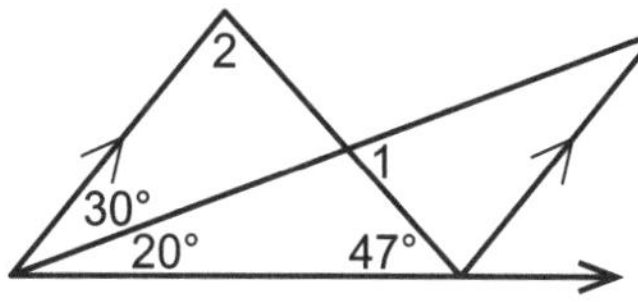

b) 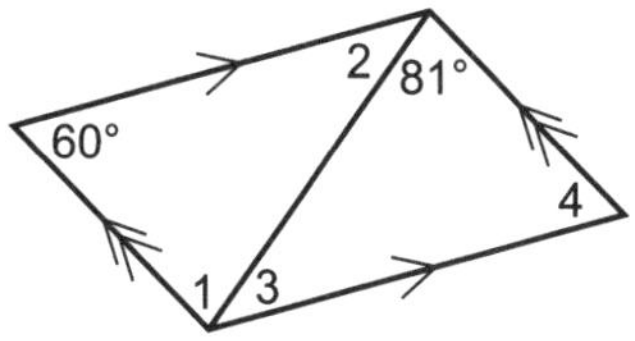

c) 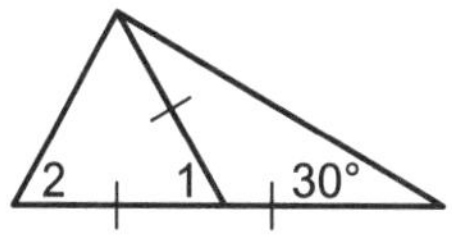

d) 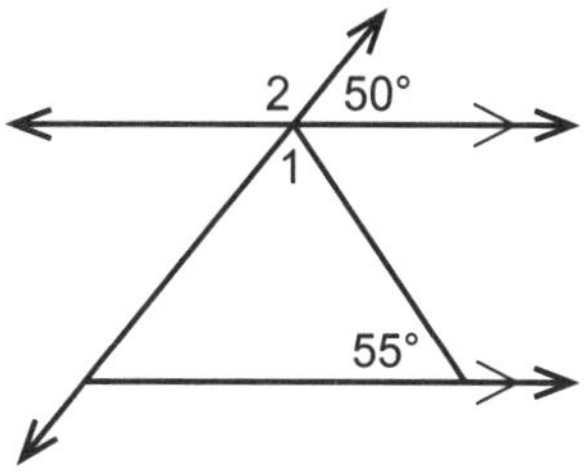

e) 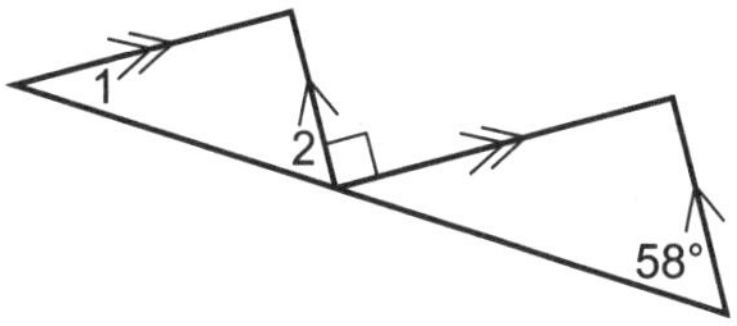

f) 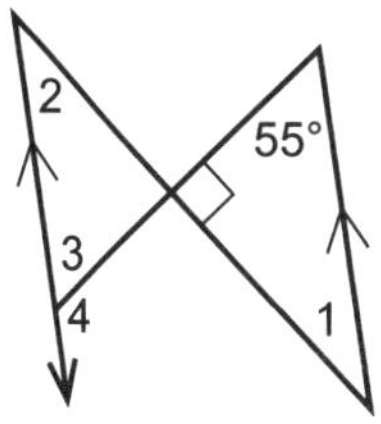

Two angles that share a side in a polygon are called **adjacent** angles.

4. Is the statement true or false? Explain why or draw a counterexample.

a) In any parallelogram, the sum of any pair of adjacent angles is 180°.

b) Any quadrilateral with two pairs of equal angles is a parallelogram.

c) In any trapezoid, the sum of any pair of adjacent angles is 180°.

d) If two angles in a quadrilateral add to 180°, the quadrilateral is either a trapezoid or a parallelogram.

REMINDER: SSS rule: Two triangles with three pairs of corresponding equal sides are congruent.

In a congruence statement, the order of the letters shows the corresponding angles and sides.

Example: $\Delta ABC \cong \Delta DEF$ means $\angle A = \angle D$, $\angle B = \angle E$, $\angle C = \angle F$, $AB = DE$, $BC = EF$, $AC = DF$.

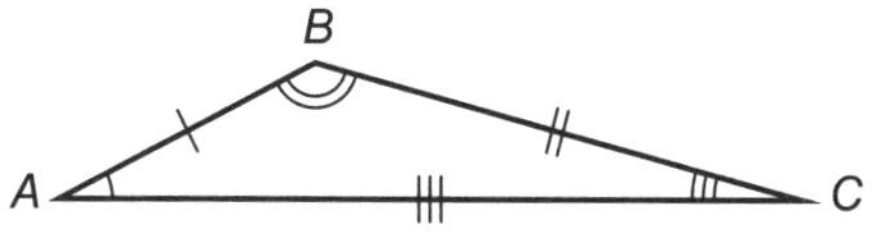

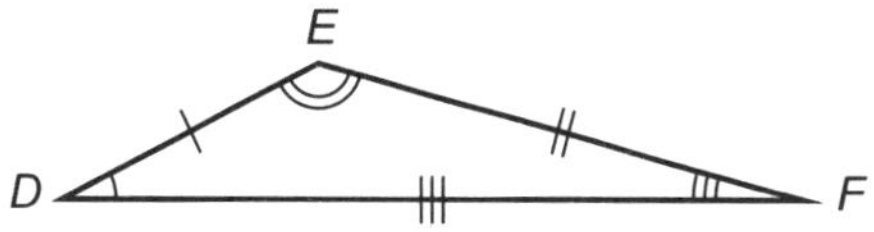

5. Use logic to prove that a quadrilateral with equal opposite sides is a parallelogram.

a) You need to prove that ______ || ______ and that ______ || ______.

b) The two triangles in the diagram are congruent by the SSS congruence rule. Write a congruence statement for them. ________________

c) Label the equal corresponding angles for angles *x* and *y*.

d) The two angles labeled with *x* are alternate angles at lines ______ and ______. This means the lines are ________________.

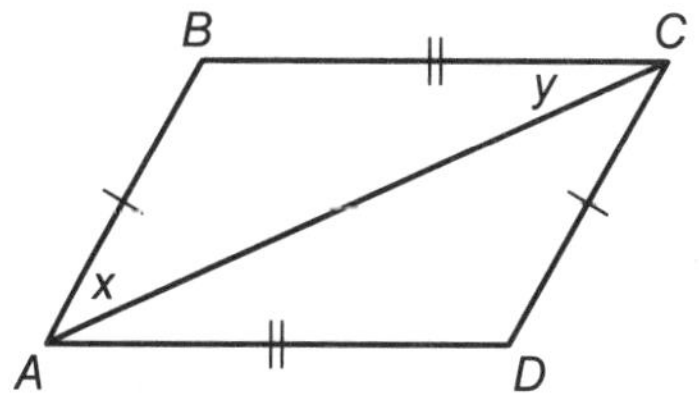

Bonus ▶ Explain why the other two sides of *ABCD* are parallel.

EE8-27 Variables and Expressions

1. Look at the picture on the right. Write an expression for the cost of renting the boat for …

Boat rental
$8 an hour

a) 2 hours: 8×2 b) 5 hours: ________   c) 6 hours: ________

A **variable** is a letter or symbol that represents a number (for example, x, n, or H).

An **algebraic expression** is a combination of one or more variables, operation signs, numbers, and sometimes brackets.

Examples: $x + 1$ $3 + 4 \times T$ $4.25 + (-3 - t) \times h$

2. Write an expression for the distance a car would travel at the given speed and in the given time.

a) Speed: 40 mi per hour
Time: 2 hours

Distance: 40×2 mi

b) Speed: 60 mi per hour
Time: 3 hours

Distance: ________ mi

c) Speed: 60 mi per hour
Time: h hours

Distance: ________ mi

In the product of a number and a variable, the multiplication sign is usually dropped.

Examples: $2 \times N$ can be written as $2N$ and $7 \times a$ can be written as $7a$

3. Look at the picture on the right. Write an algebraic expression for the cost of renting skis for …

Ski rental
$6 an hour

a) h hours: $6 \times h$ or $6h$ b) n hours: ________ or ______

c) t hours: ________ or ______   d) x hours: ________ or ______

When replacing a variable in an expression with a number, we use brackets.

Example: If we replace n with 7, $3n$ is $3(7)$, which is another way to write 3×7.

4. Evaluate the expression with $n = 2$.

a) $5n = 5(2)$
$= 10$

b) $7n = 7(2)$
$=$

c) $23n$

d) $30{,}000n$

5. Replace n with 3 and then evaluate.

a) $4n + 2$
$= 4(3) + 2$
$= 12 + 2$
$= 14$

b) $4n - 1$

c) $2n - 5$

d) $2n - 7$

e) $3n + 7$ f) $7 + 3n$ g) $11n - 11$ h) $11 \times (n - 1)$

6. Replace the variable with the given number and then evaluate.

a) $5h + 2$, $h = 3$
$= 5(3) + 2$
$= 15 + 2$
$= 17$

b) $6n - 4$, $n = 5$

c) $3x - 17$, $x = 7$

d) $12p + 6$, $p = 5$

e) $11 - 3w$, $w = 4$

f) $3 \times (c - 4)$, $c = 6$

In an expression, the **coefficient** of a variable is the number that is multiplied by that variable.

Examples: $5x + 2$ ⟵ the coefficient of x is 5
$w - 7 = 1w - 7$ ⟵ the coefficient of w is 1
$3 - 4x = 3 + (-4x)$ ⟵ the coefficient of x is -4

7. Write the coefficient.

a) $3a + 2$ ______
b) $m - 3$ ______
c) $3 - 8w$ ______
d) $2 + 6r$ ______
e) $9 + p$ ______
f) $-5s - 4$ ______

In an expression with two variables, we must name the variables.

Example: $3a - 7b + 5$ ⟵ the coefficient of a is 3
the coefficient of b is -7

8. Write the coefficient of x.

a) $3x + 4y + 7$ ______
b) $8x - y + 9$ ______
c) $2u + 4x - 5$ ______
d) $3u - 5x - 8$ ______
e) $9w + 3x + 8y$ ______
f) $-5 + 4w - 3x$ ______

In an expression, a number that is not multiplied by a variable is called a constant term.

Examples: $3x + 4$ ⟵ the constant term is 4
$5x = 5x + 0$ ⟵ the constant term is 0
$7x - 5$ ⟵ the constant term is -5

9. Write the constant term.

a) $2x - 4y + 9$ ______
b) $-5x + y + 3$ ______
c) $3u - 4v - 5$ ______
d) $3z + 7p - 4$ ______
e) $7w - x - 4$ ______

Bonus ▶ $2p + 3q - 7r$ ______

10. Is -3 the coefficient or the constant term?

a) $3 - 3x$ ______________
b) $3x - 3$ ______________
c) $-3 - x$ ______________

A **flat fee** is a fixed charge that does not depend on how long you rent an item.

Example: A company charges a flat fee of \$7 to rent a boat, plus \$3 for each hour the boat is used.

11. Write an expression for the cost to rent a boat for …

a) 4 hours
Flat fee: \$7
Hourly rate: \$5 per hour

$4 \times 5 + 7$

b) 4 hours
Flat fee: \$5
Hourly rate: \$6 per hour

____

c) 6 hours
Flat fee: \$7
Hourly rate: \$3 per hour

____

d) *h* hours
Flat fee: \$5
Hourly rate: \$7

$7h + 5$

e) *t* hours
Flat fee: \$9
Hourly rate: \$5

____

f) *w* hours
Flat fee: \$6
Hourly rate: \$4

____

12. Match the fee for renting a windsurfing board to the correct algebraic expression.

A. $12h + 5$ **B.** $5h + 12$ **C.** $12h$

a) \$12 flat fee and \$5 for each hour ______

b) \$12 for each hour, no flat fee ______

c) \$5 flat fee and \$12 for each hour ______

13. A taxi ride charges a flat fee of \$5 and \$2 for every mile traveled. The total is given by the expression $5 + 2m$. Find the cost of taking a taxi for …

a) 4 miles

$5 + 2(4)$

$= 5 + 8$

$= 13$

b) 2 miles

c) 5 miles

14. Gloves cost \$4 per pair. The cost of *n* pairs is $\$4n$. Anna says that the cost of 3 pairs is \$43 and the cost of 5 pairs is \$45. What mistake did Anna make?

____

____

15. An electrician's fee for an emergency call is a flat fee of \$90 plus \$20 for every 15 minutes spent on the job.

a) Write an expression to represent the electrician's fee.

b) What would you expect to pay for a 45-minute job?

c) Calculate how long the electrician was at the job if a fee of \$170 is charged.

EE8-28 Modeling and Solving Equations

1. Each bag contains the same unknown number of apples. Let x stand for the number of apples in one bag. Write an expression for the total number of apples.

a) 

$x + 2$ ______

b) 

______

c) 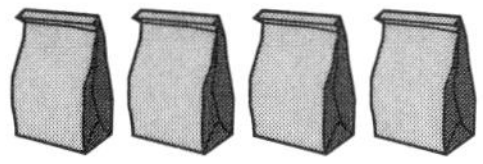

______

An **equation** is a statement that has two equal expressions separated by an equal sign.

Example: $x + 2 = 5$ is an equation. When x is 3, the equation $x + 2 = 5$ is true, because $3 + 2 = 5$.

2. Write an expression for the total number of apples. Then write an equation for the total number of apples.

a) There are 7 apples in total.

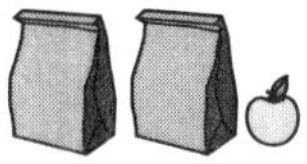

Expression $2x + 1$

Equation $2x + 1 = 7$

b) There are 11 apples in total.

Expression ______

Equation ______

c) There are 20 apples in total.

Expression ______

Equation ______

3. The scales are balanced because the sides are equal. Cross out the same number of apples on each side to find how many apples are in the bag.

a) 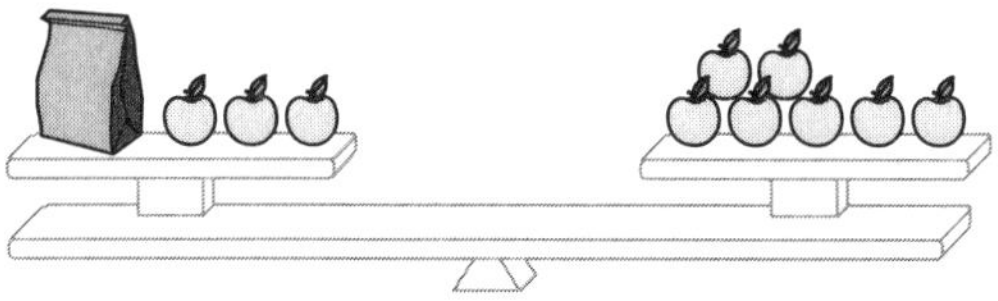

There are ______ apples in the bag.

b) 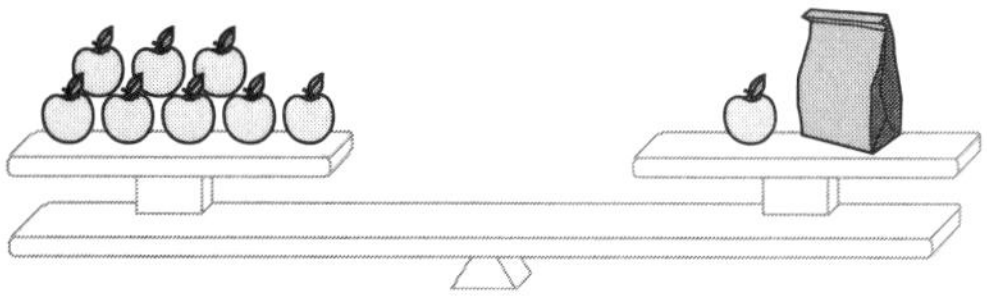

There are ______ apples in the bag.

An equation is like a set of balanced scales. An equal sign between the sides shows that they are equal.

Finding the value of a variable that makes an equation true is called **solving for the variable**.

To solve $x + 4 = 10$, subtract 4 from both sides of the equation.

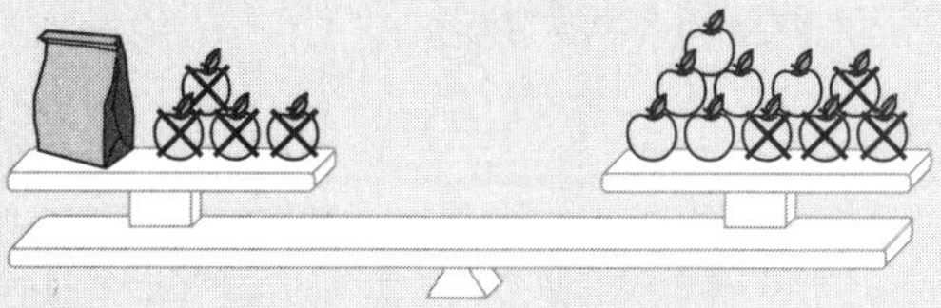

$$\begin{array}{rcr} x + 4 & = & 10 \\ -\,4 & & -\,4 \\ \hline x & = & 6 \end{array}$$

4. Subtract 3 from both sides of the equation.

a) $$\begin{array}{rcr} x + 3 & = & 11 \\ -\,3 & & -\,3 \\ \hline x & = & 8 \end{array}$$

b) $$\begin{array}{rcr} x + 3 & = & 8 \\ -\,3 & & -\,3 \\ \hline x & = & \end{array}$$

c) $$\begin{array}{rcr} 13 & = & x + 3 \\ -\,3 & & -\,3 \\ \hline & = & x \end{array}$$

d) $$\begin{array}{rcr} 54 & = & x + 3 \\ -\,3 & & -\,3 \\ \hline & = & x \end{array}$$

5. Which number will you subtract from both sides to solve for the variable? Subtract the number and solve the equation.

a) $x + 5 = 19$
$- 5 \quad -$ ____
$x =$

b) $x + 23 = 32$
$-$ ____ $\quad -$ ____
$x =$

c) $27 = x + 9$
$-$ ____ $\quad -$ ____
$= x$

d) $171 = x + 37$
$-$ ____ $\quad -$ ____
$= x$

6. Solve the equation by subtracting the same number from both sides.

a) $x + 15 = 33$
$-15 \quad -15$
$x = 18$

b) $x + 42 = 93$

c) $131 = x + 16$

d) $39 + x = 107$

7. The scales are balanced. All bags in the same picture have the same number of apples. How many apples are in each bag?

a)

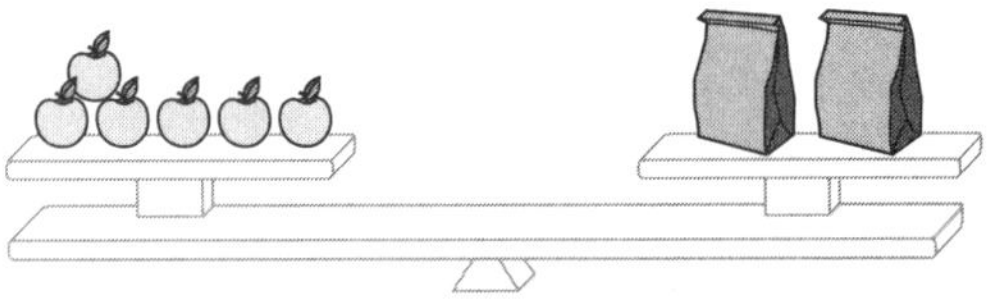

There are ______ apples in each bag.

b)

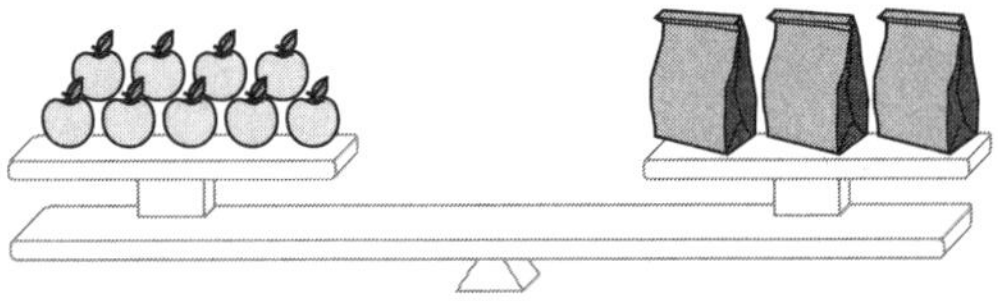

There are ______ apples in each bag.

8. Complete the picture and solve the equation.

a) $6 = 3 \times b$

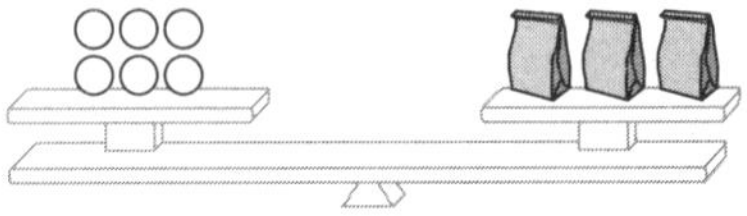

$b =$ ______

b) $2 \times b = 8$

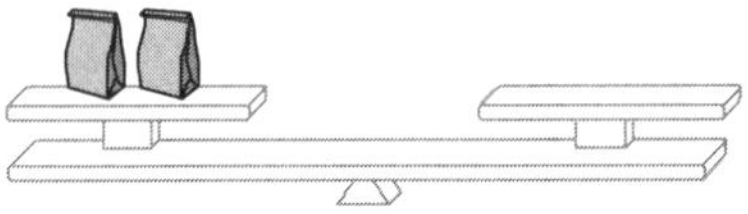

$b =$ ______

c) $4 \times b = 12$

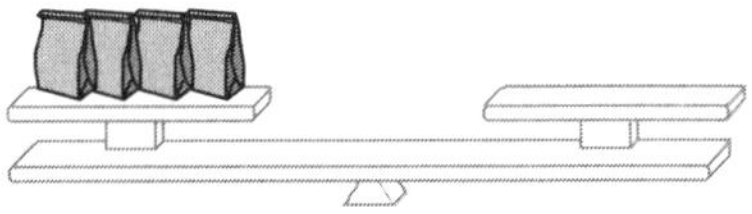

$b =$ ______

Remember: With multiplying and dividing, you can use the opposite operation to go back to the number you started with.

Example: $4 \times 3 = 12$, so $12 \div 3 = 4$ or $(4 \times 3) \div 3 = 4$

9. What number should you divide the expression by to get back to b?

a) $(b \times 2) \div$ ________ $= b$

b) $(b \times 3) \div$ ________ $= b$

c) $(b \times 7) \div$ ________ $= b$

10. Divide both sides by the same number to solve the equation.

a) $b \times 3 = 15$
$b \times 3 \div 3 = 15 \div 3$
$b = 5$

b) $5 \times b = 30$

c) $4b = 32$

11. Use the picture to explain why you can divide both sides by 3 to solve the equation $b \times 3 = 6$.

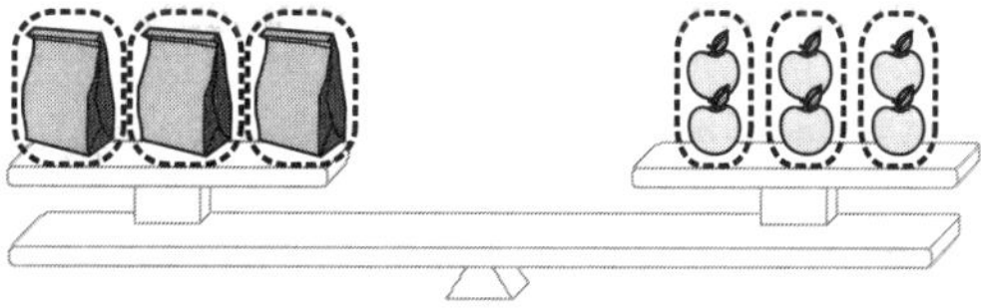

____

____

____

Majid uses a table to solve $2x + 1 = 7$.

x	$2x + 1$	Is the equation true?
1	3	✗
2	5	✗
3	7	✓

$x = 3$ makes the equation true.

12. Complete the table and then solve for x.

a) $3x + 2 = 14$

x	$3x + 2$	True?
1	*3(1) + 2 = 5*	✗
2	*3(2) + 2 = 8*	✗

$x =$ ______

b) $5x + 1 = 26$

x	$5x + 1$	True?
1	*5(1) + 1 = 6*	✗

$x =$ ______

c) $7x - 1 = 20$

x	$7x - 1$	True?

$x =$ ______

13. Replace n with 5 and say whether 5 is too high or too low. Then try a lower or higher number.

a) $2n + 3 = 15$

n	$2n + 3$	Answer
5	*2(5) + 3*	*13*

5 is *too low*.

b) $4n - 1 = 15$

n	$4n - 1$	Answer
5	*4(5) − 1*	*19*

5 is *too high*.

c) $5n - 5 = 15$

n	$5n - 5$	Answer
5		

5 is ______________.

d) $7n - 2 = 40$

e) $6n + 3 = 27$

f) $6n - 3 = 27$

14. Solve for n by guessing small values for n, checking, and revising.

a) $3n + 2 = 14$

b) $5n - 2 = 13$

c) $4n - 1 = 15$

d) $6n - 5 = 31$

e) $7n - 2 = 19$

f) $2n + 3 = 9$

EE8-29 Solving Equations—Preserving Equality

1. Write the number that makes the equation true.

a) $8 + 5 - \square = 8$ b) $8 \times 2 \div \square = 8$ c) $8 \div 4 \times \square = 8$ d) $8 - 5 + \square = 8$

e) $12 \div 3 \times \square = 12$ f) $17 - 9 + \square = 17$ g) $3 \times 5 \div \square = 3$ h) $48 + 3 - \square = 48$

2. Write the operation that makes the equation true.

a) $9 + 2 \bigcirc 2 = 9$ b) $7 \times 5 \bigcirc 5 = 7$ c) $12 \div 3 \bigcirc 3 = 12$ d) $15 - 4 \bigcirc 4 = 15$

e) $18 \div 6 \bigcirc 6 = 18$ f) $8 - 2 \bigcirc 2 = 8$ g) $5 \times 3 \bigcirc 3 = 5$ h) $17 + 4 \bigcirc 4 = 17$

3. Write the operation and number that make the equation true.

a) $17 + 3$ *− 3* $= 17$ b) $30 \div 5$ ______ $= 30$ c) 14×2 ______ $= 14$

d) $23 - 4$ ______ $= 23$ e) 4×4 ______ $= 4$ f) $15 + 2$ ______ $= 15$

4. How can you undo the action to get back to the number you started with?

a) Add 4 *Subtract 4* b) Multiply by 5 ____________

c) Divide by 3 ____________ d) Subtract 4 ____________

5. a) Start with the number 3. Do the operations in order and then undo them in reverse order.

Add 7	*10*	Subtract 7	______
Multiply by 2	*20*	Divide by 2	______
Subtract 5	______	Add 5	______
Divide by 3	______ →	Multiply by 3	______

Did you finish with the number you started with? ________

b) Start with the number −2. Do the operations in order and then undo them in reverse order.

Add 8	*6*	____________	______
Divide by 3	______	____________	______
Subtract 1	______	____________	______
Multiply by 4	______ →	*Divide by 4*	______

Did you finish with the number you started with? ________

Remember: The variable x represents a number, so you can treat it like a number. In word problems, read carefully for the operations.

Examples:			
Add 3 to x	$x + 3$	Multiply 3 by x	$3 \times x = 3x$
Add x to 3	$3 + x$	Multiply x by 3	$x \times 3 = 3x$
Subtract 3 from x	$x - 3$	Divide x by 3	$x \div 3$
Subtract x from 3	$3 - x$	Divide 3 by x	$3 \div x$

6. Write the algebraic expression.

a) Multiply x by 7 ___*7x*___ b) Add 4 to x ___*x + 4*___ c) Subtract 2 from x ________

d) Subtract x from 2 ________ e) Divide x by 5 ________ f) Divide 5 by x ________

g) Multiply 5 by x ________ h) Add x to 5 ________ **Bonus ▶** Add x to y ________

7. Write the operation and number that make the equation true.

a) $x + 4$ ___*− 4*___ $= x$ b) $x - 5$ ______ $= x$ c) $2x$ ______ $= x$

d) $x \div 3$ ______ $= x$ e) $x + 7$ ______ $= x$ f) $x \div 5$ ______ $= x$

g) $x + (-1)$ ______ $= x$ h) $x - (-3)$ ______ $= x$ i) $(-2) \times x$ ______ $= x$

8. Solve for x by doing the same thing to both sides of the equation. Then check your answer by replacing x with your answer.

a) $3x = 12$

$3x \div 3 = 12 \div 3$

$x = 4$

$3(4) = 12$ ✓

b) $x \div 7 = 3$

$x \div 7 \times 7 = 3 \times 7$

c) $x - 4 = 15$

d) $x \div 5 = 3$

e) $12 + x = -22$

f) $-44 = 4x$

g) $x - 17 = -25$

h) $31 = -19 + x$

i) $x + 26 = 17$

j) $22 = x \div 3$

k) $9x = -81$

Bonus ▶ $x + 9 = 9 - 45$

9. Start with 3. Multiply by 2. Then add 4.

Which sequence of operations will get you back where you started? ______

A. Divide your answer by 2 and subtract 4.

B. Subtract 4 from your answer and divide by 2.

EE8-30 Fractions, Decimals, and Integers in Expressions and Equations

REMINDER: $\frac{3}{8}\times 5=\frac{3\times 5}{8}=\frac{15}{8}=1\frac{7}{8}$

1. Replace the variable with the given fraction and evaluate. Write your answer as a mixed number or proper fraction.

a) $2x,\quad x=\frac{1}{3}$

$2x=2\left(\frac{1}{3}\right)=\frac{2}{3}$

b) $u+5,\quad u=\frac{5}{7}$

c) $3r,\quad r=\frac{2}{5}$

d) $s+6,\quad s=\frac{3}{5}$

e) $3x+2,\quad x=\frac{5}{8}$

f) $z-2,\quad z=\frac{13}{5}$

g) $5z-1,\quad z=\frac{3}{5}$

h) $3v-2,\quad v=\frac{4}{5}$

i) $2h-1,\quad h=\frac{2}{3}$

j) $4t+1,\quad t=\frac{3}{8}$

k) $5t-6,\quad t=\frac{7}{4}$

l) $3w-8,\quad w=2\frac{3}{4}$

2. Replace the variable with the given decimal and evaluate. Write your answer as a decimal.

a) $6x,\quad x=0.5$

$6x=6(0.5)$

$=3.0$

b) $z+4,\quad z=5.83$

c) $w-2,\quad w=3.7$

d) $9p,\quad p=4.2$

e) $4x+3,\quad x=1.3$

f) $3m-5,\quad m=4.75$

g) $3t-2,\quad t=0.8$

h) $4z-5,\quad z=2.31$

3. a) Which parts from Questions 1–2 have the same answer? ______ and ______

b) Why are these parts the same? ________________________________

4. A sandwich costs \$4.50 and a drink costs \$1.25. The cost of s sandwiches and d drinks is $4.50s+1.25d$. Find the cost of …

a) 5 sandwiches and 4 drinks

$4.50s+1.25d=4.50(5)+1.25(4)$

$=22.50+5.00$

$=27.50$

The cost is *\$27.50*.

b) 4 sandwiches and 6 drinks

The cost is ________.

c) 3 sandwiches and 2 drinks

The cost is ________.

5. Solve the equation by subtracting the same fraction from both sides.

a) $x + \frac{1}{5} = \frac{3}{5}$

$\quad -\frac{1}{5} \quad -\frac{1}{5}$

$\quad x = \frac{2}{5}$

b) $x + \frac{3}{7} = \frac{5}{7}$

c) $\frac{8}{10} = x + \frac{7}{10}$

Bonus ▶ $\frac{2}{3} + x = \frac{2}{3}$

6. Solve the equation by subtracting or adding the same fraction on both sides.

a) $x + 1\frac{1}{5} = 4\frac{3}{5}$

$\quad -1\frac{1}{5} \quad -1\frac{1}{5}$

$\quad x = 3\frac{2}{5}$

b) $x + 2\frac{3}{7} = 3\frac{5}{7}$

c) $\frac{3}{4} = x - \frac{1}{2}$

d) $-2\frac{1}{5} + x = 4\frac{2}{5}$

e) $x - 3\frac{1}{2} = 1\frac{1}{2}$

f) $x - 2\frac{3}{5} = -3\frac{1}{10}$

g) $-\frac{8}{6} = x - \frac{2}{3}$

h) $3\frac{2}{5} + x = 4\frac{3}{10}$

7. Solve the equation by subtracting or adding the same decimal on both sides.

a) $x + 2.1 = 3.6$

$\quad -2.1 \quad -2.1$

$\quad x = 1.5$

b) $x - 3.4 = 5.8$

c) $2.6 = x + 3.2$

d) $3.1 + x = 3.1$

e) $x - 1.5 = -1.3$

f) $x - 0.04 = 0.4$

g) $x - 3.4 = -5.8$

Bonus ▶ $x + 1.3 = 2\frac{1}{2}$

REMINDER: $+(+) = +$ $\quad +(-) = -$ $\quad -(+) = -$ $\quad -(-) = +$

8. Add or subtract.

a) $(-2) + 3 =$ ______

b) $-5 - 3 =$ ______

c) $-5 + 2 =$ ______

d) $4 - 9 =$ ______

e) $(-4) + (+6) =$ ______

f) $(-5) - (-13) =$ ______

g) $(-15) - (+2) =$ ______

h) $+14 + (-29) =$ ______

i) $(+42) + (-16) =$ ______

j) $5 - (-14) =$ ______

k) $(-1) - (+32) =$ ______

l) $(+61) + (-22) =$ ______

9. Multiply or divide.

a) $(-2) \times 3 =$ ______

b) $(-4) \times (+3) =$ ______

c) $-6 \times (-2) =$ ______

d) $7 \times (-9) =$ ______

e) $(-48) \div (+6) =$ ______

f) $(-15) \div (-3) =$ ______

g) $-18 \div (+3) =$ ______

h) $+28 \div (-14) =$ ______

i) $(-2) \times (-9) =$ ______

j) $-56 \div (-7) =$ ______

k) $(-11) \times 3 =$ ______

l) $(+63) \div (-9) =$ ______

10. Evaluate the expression.

a) $2x, \quad x = -3$

$2x = 2(-3)$

$= 2 \times (-3) = -6$

b) $u + 5, \quad u = -8$

c) $-3r, \quad r = -6$

d) $2n + 3, \quad n = -5$

$2n + 3 = 2(-5) + 3$

$= -10 + 3 = -7$

e) $-4t + 6, \quad t = -5$

f) $6 - 2n, \quad n = 4$

g) $3x + 2, \quad x = -7$

h) $-z - 2, \quad z = 12$

i) $-5z - 1, \quad z = -10$

j) $-4x + 3, \quad x = 3$

k) $3m - 5, \quad m = -7$

l) $2 + 3t, \quad t = -7$

m) $-3 + 3x, \quad x = -4$

n) $-3m + (-5), \quad m = -7$

o) $-3t - 12, \quad t = 2$

11. Evaluate the expression.

a) $-2x, \quad x = 3$

$-2(3) = (-2) \times 3$

$= -6$

b) $u \times (-5), \quad u = -7$

c) $-3(m - 5), \quad m = 7$

d) $\frac{x}{2}, \quad x = -6$

$\frac{(-6)}{2} = (-6) \div 2 = -3$

e) $\frac{w}{5}, \quad w = -10$

f) $\frac{q}{-4}, \quad q = 4$

g) $\frac{a}{2} + (-4), \quad a = -10$

h) $\frac{q}{-4} + (-2), \quad q = -16$

i) $\frac{u}{5} - (-3), \quad u = -40$

12. During the day, the average temperature on the surface of Mars rises 9°C per hour. The temperature on the surface of Mars at 9:00 a.m. is −60°C.

a) How much will the temperature rise in 2 hours? ______ In 3 hours?______ In *n* hours? ______

b) Write an expression to show the temperature *n* hours after 9:00 a.m. ________________

c) Use your expression from b) to find the temperature at 12:00 noon. ________________

d) What was the temperature at 6:00 a.m.? Hint: What value will you substitute for *n* in the expression from b)? ________________________

13. Zara had some money. She saved an additional $6 every week for 8 weeks. Now she has $61.

a) Write an expression for Zara's savings using *w* for the number of weeks.

b) Use your expression to find out how much money Zara started with 8 weeks ago.

EE8-31 Solving Equations—Two Operations

1. Jayden does some operations to an unknown number x. He gets 37 every time.
Perform Jayden's operations to write an equation and then work backward to find x.

a) Perform Jayden's operations:

Start with x	x
Multiply by 5	$5x$
Add 7	$5x + 7$
Get 37	$5x + 7 = 37$

Work backward to find x:

Write the equation again	$5x + 7 = 37$
Undo adding 7 by subtracting 7	$5x + 7 - 7 = 37 - 7$
Write the new equation	$5x = 30$
Undo multiplying by 5 by dividing by 5	$5x \div 5 = 30 \div 5$
Write the new equation You solved for x!	$x = 6$

Check your answer by doing the operations in order:

Start with your answer: 6 Multiply by 5: 30 Add 7: 37 Do you get 37? Yes

b) Perform Jayden's operations:

Start with x	x
Multiply by 8	______
Add 5	______
Get 37	______

Work backward to find x:

Write the equation again	______
Undo adding 5 by subtracting 5	______
Write the new equation	______
Undo multiplying by 8 by dividing by 8	______
Write the new equation You solved for x!	______

Check your answer by doing the operations in order:

Start with your answer: ______ Multiply by 8: ______ Add 5: ______ Do you get 37? ______

c) Perform Jayden's operations:

Start with x	x
Multiply by 4	______
Subtract 3	______
Get 37	______

Work backward to find x:

Write the equation again	______
Undo subtracting 3 by adding 3	______
Write the new equation	______
Undo multiplying by 4 by dividing by 4	______
Write the new equation You solved for x!	______

Check your answer by doing the operations in order:

Start with your answer: ______ Multiply by 4: ______ Subtract 3: ______ Do you get 37? ______

2. Solve for the variable by undoing one operation at a time in the equation.

a) $8x + 3 = 27$

$8x + 3 - 3 = \underline{\ 27\ } - \underline{\ 3\ }$

$8x = \underline{\qquad}$

$8x \div 8 = \underline{\qquad} \div \underline{\qquad}$

$x = \underline{\qquad}$

b) $2.5h - 3 = 18$

$2.5h - 3 + 3 = \underline{\ 18\ } + \underline{\qquad}$

$2.5h = \underline{\qquad}$

$2.5h \div 2.5 = \underline{\qquad} \div \underline{\qquad}$

$h = \underline{\qquad}$

c) $\frac{x}{3} + 2 = 9$

$\frac{x}{3} + 2 - 2 = \underline{\ 9\ } - \underline{\ 2\ }$

$\frac{x}{3} = \underline{\ 7\ }$

$\frac{x}{3}(3) = \underline{\ 7\ }(\underline{\ 3\ })$

$x = \underline{\ 21\ }$

d) $\frac{x}{2} + 3 = 9$

$\frac{x}{2} + 3 - 3 = \underline{\qquad} - \underline{\qquad}$

$\frac{x}{2} = \underline{\qquad}$

$\frac{x}{2}(2) = \underline{\qquad}(\underline{\qquad})$

$x = \underline{\qquad}$

e) $3s + 4 = -29$

f) $-1.5t + 2 = 9.5$

g) $\frac{x}{3} + 5 = 7$

Bonus ▶ $-\frac{x}{2} - 4 = 7$

Emma solves $7 - x = 5$ in two steps.

Step 1: She subtracts 7 from both sides:

$7 - x - 7 = 5 - 7$

$-x = -2$

Step 2: She divides both sides by (−1) to find x:

$(-x) \div (-1) = (-2) \div (-1)$

$x = 2$

Emma checks her answer. She replaces x in the equation with 2: $7 - 2 = 5$ ✓

3. Solve the equation in two steps. Check your answer by replacing x with your answer.

a) $12 - x = -6$

$12 - x - 12 = -6 - 12$

$-x = -18$

$(-x) \div (-1) = (-18) \div (-1)$

$x = 18$

$12 - 18 = -6$ ✓

b) $6 = 13 - x$

c) $9 - x = 20$

d) $3 = -x + 15$

e) $-x + 19 = 52$

f) $-13 = -x + 19$

g) $18 - x = -42$

h) $-x + 14 = 41$

i) $17 - x = 17$

4. Write an expression for the amount of money (in dollars) that each person earns.

a) Kate earns $1 for every 3 phone calls she makes. She makes x calls. $\frac{x}{3}$

b) Jin earns $3 for every call he makes. He makes m calls. ________

c) Tim earns $1 for every 5 people he serves. He serves p people. ________

d) Sandy earns $5 for every person she serves. She serves p people. ________

5. a) A store charges $2.50 each hour to rent a pair of inline skates. Write an expression (using h for hours) for the cost of renting the inline skates. ______________

b) Ravi rented inline skates for 4 hours. How much did he pay? __________

c) Sue paid $15 to rent inline skates. How many hours did she rent them for? __________

6. Kim has $20 in savings. Then she earns $1.50 for every 5 newspapers she delivers.

a) Write an expression for the total amount she will have after delivering x papers. __________________

b) How much will she have after delivering 100 newspapers? ______________

c) How many newspapers does she have to deliver to be able to buy a shirt for $65? ______________

7. a) For which part of Question 6 did you replace for x? ____________

b) For which part of Question 6 did you solve for x? ____________

8. Three boat companies charge to rent boats and require each person to rent a life jacket.

	Rental Fee		
Item	**Company X**	**Company Y**	**Company Z**
Boat	$100	$120	$70
A life jacket	$3	$5	$7

a) Write an expression for the rental cost for each company for one boat for n people.

b) Ivan's family chose Company Z and paid $126. How many people were in the boat?

c) How much would Ivan's family have paid with Companies X and Y?

d) Was Company Z the cheapest choice for Ivan's family? Why or why not?

EE8-32 Adding and Subtracting Expressions

REMINDER: 3×2 is short for $2 + 2 + 2$. Similarly, $3x$ is short for $x + x + x$.

1. Write the sum as a product of a number and a variable.

a) $x + x + x + x + x =$ _______ b) $t + t + t + t + t + t =$ _______

2. Write the product as a sum.

a) $5z =$ _____________________ b) $4w =$ _____________________

3. Add by writing how many x's there are altogether.

a) $2x + 3x$
$= x + x + x + x + x =$ $5x$

b) $3x + 4x$
$= x + x + x + x + x + x + x =$ ______

c) $x + 5x$
$=$ ________ $+$ __________________ $=$ ______

d) $4x + 3x$
$=$ ______________ $+$ ____________ $=$ ______

Two algebraic expressions are equivalent if they are the same for every value of the variable.
Example: $3 + x$ and $x + 3$ are equivalent expressions because both are the same for every value of x.

4. Write two equivalent expressions for $5x$.

$5x = x + x + x + x + x$
$=$ ________ $+$ ___________

$5x = x + x + x + x + x$
$=$ ______________ $+$ _____

Using the distributive property:
$2 \times 4 + 3 \times 4 = (2 + 3) \times 4$
$4 + 4 + 4 + 4 + 4 = 4 + 4 + 4 + 4 + 4$

The distributive property applies for any value of x.
$2x + 3x = (2 + 3)x$
$x + x + x + x + x = x + x + x + x + x$

5. Add.

a) $2x + 5x = (2 + 5)x =$ ______ b) $3x + 4x = (3 + 4)x =$ ______

c) $x + 6x = ($___________$)x =$ ______ d) $2x + 4x + x = ($___________$)x =$ ______

6. Evaluate both expressions for the given value. Are your answers the same? If not, find the mistake.

	$2x + 5x$	$7x$
a) $x = 2$	$2(2) + 5(2) = 4 + 10 = 14$	$7(2) = 14$
b) $x = 6$		
c) $x = \frac{2}{3}$		

We can think of subtraction of variables as taking away. $5x - 3x = 2x \rightarrow x + x(+ x + x + x)$

7. Subtract by taking away x's.

a) $7x - 2x =$ _________

$x + x + x + x + x(+ x + x)$

b) $6x - x =$ _________

$x + x + x + x + x + x$

c) $9x - 7x =$ _________

$x + x + x + x + x + x + x + x + x$

d) $8x - 7x =$ _________

$x + x + x + x + x + x + x + x$

8. Write x's and take some away to subtract.

a) $6x - 2x =$ __________________

b) $7x - 6x =$ __________________

9. Add and subtract. Hint: Circle the x's being added and evaluate those first.

a) $(7x) - 4x (+ 3x)(+ 2x) - x$

$= 12x - 5x = 7x$

b) $5x - 2x - x + 3x$

c) $-3x + x - 2x + 7x - x$

d) $4x - 3x + 2x - 5x - x$

REMINDER: $+(+) = +$ $\quad +(-) = -$ $\quad -(+) = -$ $\quad -(-) = +$

10. Add and subtract.

a) $3x + (-2x) - (-6x) - (+4x) + (+7x) - (-3x)$

$= 3x - 2x + 6x - 4x + 7x + 3x$

$= 19x - 6x$

$= 13x$

b) $5x + 2x - 4x - (-2x) + 3x$

c) $2x + (-4x) - (-5x) - x + (-2x)$

d) $-3x + x - (-4x) + (-4x)$

EE8-33 Like Terms

Terms with the same variable are called **like terms**. Constant terms are also like terms, because they do not have any variables.

To **simplify** an expression, you can combine like terms.

Example: $3x + 7 + 4x + 2 + 5x + x = 13x + 9$

$3x + 4x + 5x + x$ → $13x$ $7 + 2$ → 9

1. Combine like terms to simplify the expression.

a) $4x + 3 + x$ b) $5x + 3 - 2$ c) $7 + 4x - x + 2$

d) $5x - x + 4 - 2x$ e) $3 - 3x + 4 + x - 2$ f) $5x - 7 - 4x + 5 - 3x$

2. Find the perimeter. Then simplify the expression.

a) 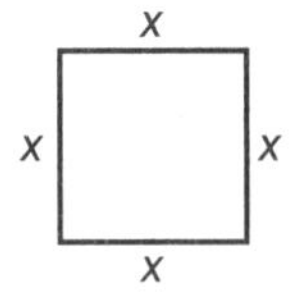

$x + x + x + x = 4x$

b) 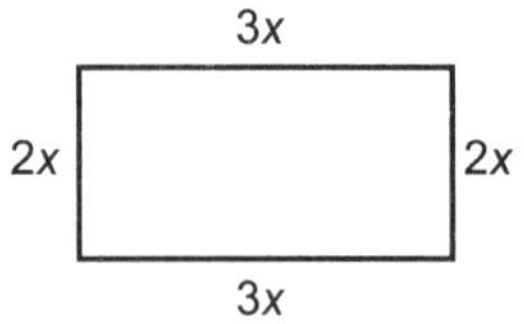

c) 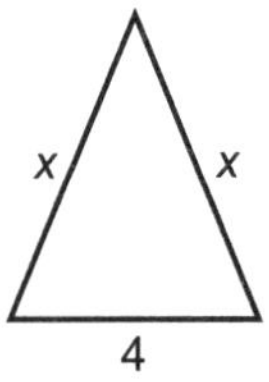

d) 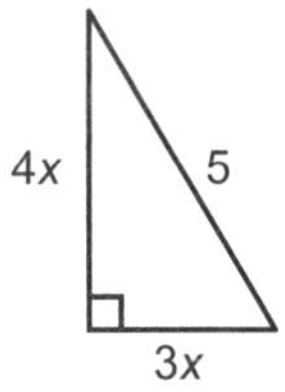

e) 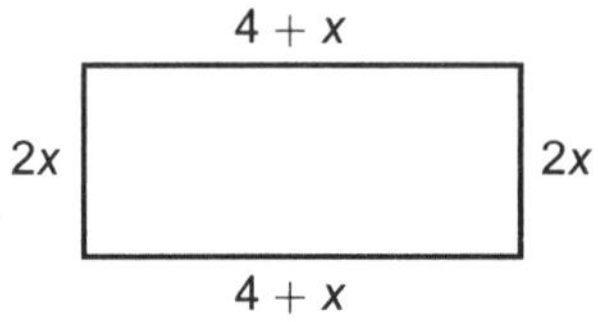

f) 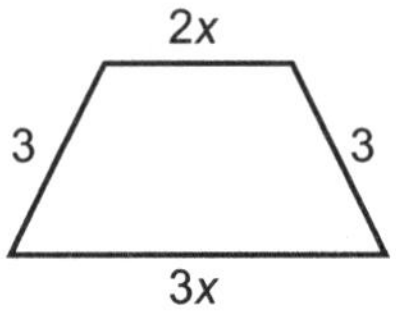

REMINDER: $+(+) = +$ $+(-) = -$ $-(+) = -$ $-(-) = +$

3. Combine like terms to simplify the expression with addition.

a) $(10x + 3) + (5x - 4)$

$= 10x + 3 + 5x - 4$

$= 10x + 5x + 3 - 4$

$= 15x - 1$

b) $(5 + 2x) + (3x - 1)$

c) $(-4x + 3) + (2x - 2)$

d) $(6 - 4x) + (x - 5)$

4. a) Fill in the table.

x	$-(x + 3)$	$-x + 3$	$-x - 3$
0	$-(0 + 3) = -3$	$-0 + 3 = 3$	$-0 - 3 = -3$
1	$-(1 + 3) =$		
2			
-1			

b) Is $-(x + 3)$ equivalent to $-x + 3$ or $-x - 3$? __________

Remember: $-(+) = -$ $\quad -(-) = +$

A negative sign before a bracket changes the sign of every term in the brackets.

Examples: $-(x + 3) = -x - 3$ and $-(x - 3) = -x + 3$

5. Combine like terms to simplify the expression with subtraction.

a) $(7x + 5) - (3x + 4)$

$= 7x + 5 - 3x - 4$

$= 7x - 3x + 5 - 4$

$= 4x + 1$

b) $(3x - 4) - (2x + 1)$

c) $(2x + 1) - (3x + 4)$

d) $(-x + 3) - (2x + 4)$

e) $(2x + 5) - (3 + 8x)$

f) $(2x + 5) - (3 - 3x)$

Bonus ▶ $(-4x + 7 - 3x + 5x) - (5 + 4x - 2x - 3)$

You can add or subtract like terms with decimal and fractional coefficients in a similar way.

Example: $2.5x + \frac{3}{5} + 1.3x - \frac{1}{5} = 3.8x + \frac{2}{5}$

$3.8x$ comes from $2.5x + 1.3x$; $\frac{2}{5}$ comes from $\frac{3}{5} - \frac{1}{5}$

6. Combine like terms to add or subtract.

a) $1.3x - (0.4x + 2)$

b) $3.4x + (1.9 - 4.1x)$

c) $\left(\frac{2}{3} + \frac{4}{5}x\right) + \left(-\frac{1}{3} - \frac{1}{5}x\right)$

d) $\left(\frac{4}{9}x - \frac{3}{11}\right) - \left(\frac{2}{11} + \frac{1}{9}x\right)$

e) $\left(\frac{4}{9}x - \frac{3}{10}x\right) + \left(\frac{1}{5} - \frac{4}{9}x\right)$

f) $\left(\frac{4}{9}x - \frac{3}{10}x\right) - \left(\frac{1}{5} - \frac{4}{9}x\right)$

EE8-34 The Distributive Property in Expressions

A triangle has a mass of t kg and a circle has a mass of 1 kg.

The mass of  is $2t$ kg and the mass of  is 3 kg.

1. Write the mass of the set.

a) 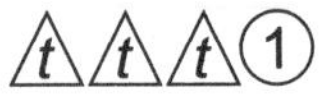
$\underline{3t + 1}$ kg

b) 
________ kg

c) 
________ kg

d) 
________ kg

2. a) Write the mass as an expression.

i)  has a mass of ________ kg

ii)  has a mass of ________ kg

b) Will the two pictures always have the same mass for the same value of t? ________

Are the expressions $t + 3$ and $3 + t$ equivalent? ________

c) Evaluate the expressions $t + 3$ and $3 + t$ when ...

i) $t = 1$ _____   ii) $t = 2$ _____   iii) $t = 1.5$ _____   iv) $t = \frac{1}{2}$ _____

d) The expressions $t + 3$ and $3 + t$ are equivalent. Circle the property that this shows.

A. associative   **B.** commutative

3. a) Draw a picture beside each expression using circles and triangles to show the mass.

$3 + 2t$ $2t + 3$

b) Are $3 + 2t$ and $2t + 3$ equivalent? _____ How do you know? ____________________

____

c) Evaluate the expressions from part a) when ...

i) $t = 1$ _____   ii) $t = 2$ _____   iii) $t = 2.1$ _____   iv) $t = \frac{1}{2}$ _____

4. a) Draw a picture to show the masses of $2(3t)$ and $(2 \times 3)t$.

b) Are the expressions equivalent? How do you know?

c) Evaluate the expressions $2(3t)$ and $(2 \times 3)t$ when ...

i) $t = 1$ ii) $t = 2$ iii) $t = 0.5$ **Bonus ▶** $t = -1$

d) The expressions $3(4t)$ and $(3 \times 4)t$ are equivalent. Circle the property that this shows.

A. associative   **B.** commutative   **C.** distributive

Using the associative property, $3(5w) = (3 \times 5)w = 15w$ and $-2(3m) = (-2 \times 3)m = -6m$

5. Multiply.

a) $2(5t)$ $= \_\_\_\_\_\_$ b) $4(6w)$ $= \_\_\_\_\_\_$ c) $-2(3z)$ $= \_\_\_\_\_\_$ d) $7(-5u)$ $= \_\_\_\_\_\_$

6. Draw triangles and circles to show each mass in kg.

a) $x + 3$ ⟶ $2(x + 3)$

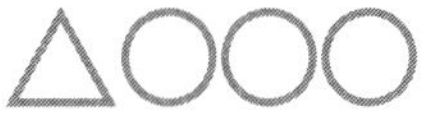

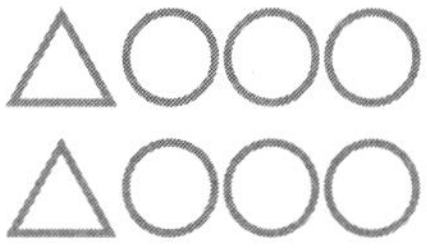

b) $2x + 1$ ⟶ $3(2x + 1)$

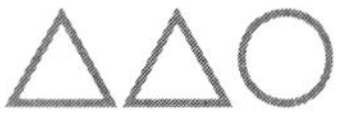

c) $3x + 2$ ⟶ $2(3x + 2)$

d) $4x + 2$ ⟶ $3(4x + 2)$

7. Draw a picture for the expression. Write a new equivalent expression without brackets.

a) $2(x + 4)$

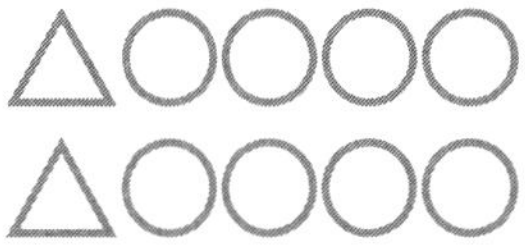

$2x + 8$

b) $3(2x + 3)$ ______

c) $2(3x + 1)$ ______

d) $2(3x + 3)$ ______

e) $2(4x + 3)$ f) $3(x + 5)$ g) $5(2x + 3)$ h) $4(3x + 1)$

Using the distributive property, $3(2w + 5) = 3(2w) + 3(5)$
$= 6w + 15$

8. To multiply an expression by 5, multiply each term by 5.

a) $5(x + 1)$ *$5x + 5$*   b) $5(x + 3)$ ______   c) $5(3 + x)$ ______   d) $5(3x + 1)$ ______

e) $5(-x + 1)$ ______   f) $5(-x - 1)$ ______   g) $5(4 - 2x)$ ______   h) $5(-5x - 5)$ ______

i) $(x - 1)5$ ______   j) $(2 - 3x)5$ ______   k) $(-x - 4)5$ ______   l) $(-50 + 50x)5$ ______

EE8-35 Solving Equations Using the Distributive Property

You can rewrite an addition or subtraction expression without brackets and then simplify.

$$\begin{aligned} 7 - 2(3x + 4) &= 7 - (6x + 8) \\ &= 7 - 6x - 8 \\ &= -1 - 6x \end{aligned}$$

1. Write the expression without brackets and then simplify.

a) $9x - 3(x + 4)$

$= 9x - (3x + 12)$

$=$

b) $9x - (3x + 4)$

c) $9 - 3(2x + 4)$

d) $9 - 3(2x - 4)$

e) $7 - 2(3 - 8x)$

f) $8x - 3(4 - 5x)$

g) $2 - 4(3 - 2x)$

h) $4x - 3(-7 + 3x)$

i) $(8x + 2) - 4(3 - 2x) + (3x - 5)$

j) $(5 + 4x) + (9 - 4x) - 3(-7 + 3x)$

Bonus ▶ $2(x + 2) + 3(x + 7) - 5(2x - 4)$

2. Ben tries three ways to solve $2(x + 3) = 14$:

Method 1	**Method 2**	**Method 3**
$2(x + 3) = 14$	$2(x + 3) = 14$	$2(x + 3) = 14$
$2x + 6 = 14$	$2(x + 3) \div 2 = 14 \div 2$	$2x + 3 = 14$
$2x + 6 - 6 = 14 - 6$	$x + 3 = 7$	$2x + 3 - 3 = 14 - 3$
$2x = 8$	$x + 3 - 3 = 7 - 3$	$2x = 11$
$2x \div 2 = 8 \div 2$	$x = 4$	$2x \div 2 = 11 \div 2$
$x = 4$		$x = \frac{11}{2}$

a) Do Ben's three ways give the same answer? __________

b) Substitute $x = 4$ into the expression $2(x + 3)$. Do you get 14? __________

Substitute $x = \frac{11}{2}$ into the expression $2(x + 3)$. Do you get 14? __________

What is the correct answer? __________

c) Describe in words each step in Methods 1, 2, and 3. Where did Ben make a mistake in Method 3?

3. Decide whether each solution is correct by substituting the answer into the original expression. For each incorrect solution, describe the mistake. Mark the correct solution with a checkmark.

a)

$$\begin{aligned} 3(x-1) &= 15 \\ 3x - 1 &= 15 \\ 3x - 1 + 1 &= 15 + 1 \\ 3x &= 16 \\ 3x \div 3 &= 16 \div 3 \\ x &= \frac{16}{3} \end{aligned}$$

$$\begin{aligned} 3(x-1) &= 15 \\ 3x - 3 &= 15 \\ 3x - 3 + 3 &= 15 + 3 \\ 3x &= 18 \\ 3x \div 3 &= 18 \div 3 \\ x &= 6 \end{aligned}$$

b)

$$\begin{aligned} 5(x+2) &= 30 \\ 5(x+2) \div 5 &= 30 \div 5 \\ x + 2 &= 4 \\ x + 2 - 2 &= 4 - 2 \\ x &= 2 \end{aligned}$$

$$\begin{aligned} 5(x+2) &= 30 \\ 5x + 10 &= 30 \\ 5x + 10 - 10 &= 30 - 10 \\ 5x &= 20 \\ 5x \div 5 &= 20 \div 5 \\ x &= 4 \end{aligned}$$

c)

$$\begin{aligned} 3x + 6 &= 21 \\ 3(x+6) &= 21 \\ x + 6 &= 7 \\ x + 6 - 6 &= 7 - 6 \\ x &= 1 \end{aligned}$$

$$\begin{aligned} 3x + 6 &= 21 \\ 3(x+2) &= 21 \\ x + 2 &= 21 \\ x + 2 - 2 &= 21 - 2 \\ x &= 19 \end{aligned}$$

$$\begin{aligned} 3x + 6 &= 21 \\ 3(x+2) &= 21 \\ x + 2 &= 7 \\ x + 2 - 2 &= 7 - 2 \\ x &= 5 \end{aligned}$$

$$\begin{aligned} 3x + 6 &= 21 \\ 3x + 6 - 6 &= 21 + 6 \\ 3x &= 27 \\ 3x \div 3 &= 27 \div 3 \\ x &= 9 \end{aligned}$$

Remember: an equation is like a set of balanced scales. You can add or subtract the same value on both sides. Example: May solves $8 - x = 3x$ in two steps:

Step 1: She treats x as a number and adds x to both sides. $8 - x + x = 3x + x$, $8 = 4x$

Step 2: She divides both sides by 4 to find x. $8 \div 4 = 4x \div 4$, $2 = x$

May checks her answer. She replaces x in the equation with 2: $8 - 2 = 6$, and $3(2) = 6$ ✓

4. Solve the equation. Remember to group like terms.

a)

$$\begin{aligned} 3x &= 15 - 2x \\ 3x + 2x &= 15 - 2x + 2x \\ 5x &= 15 \\ 5x \div 5 &= 15 \div 5 \\ x &= 3 \end{aligned}$$

b) $6x = 8 + 4x$

c) $4x - 3x + 4 = 9 - 2x$

d) $4x - 3x + 4 = -6$

e) $5x - 9x + 3 = 4 - (-5)$

f) $3x - 5 - 4x = 17 - 3x - 2$

g) $32 + 2x = 5x + 17$

h) $2x - 4 - 5 = 21 - 13x$

i) $1 - 5x = -6 - 2 - 7 + 4 - x$

In an equation, a term may be moved to the other side of the equal sign, but only if the sign (+ or −) of the term is changed to the opposite sign. Examples:

If $7 = 5 + 2$	If $x - 2 = 8$	If $x + 2 = 5$	If $2 + 3 = -4 + x$	If $3x = 15 - 2x$
Then $7 - 2 = 5$	Then $x = 8 + 2$	Then $x = 5 - 2$	Then $2 + 3 + 4 = x$	Then $3x + 2x = 15$

5. Move all variable terms to the same side of the equal sign. Hint: a term with x is a variable term.

a) $4x = 2x + 8$

$4x$ ___$-2x$___ $= 8$

b) $5x = 3x + 6$

$5x$ ________ $= 6$

c) $2x = 12 - 4x$

$2x$ ________ $= 12$

d) $-2x = 4x - 8$

$-2x$ ________ $= -8$

e) $14 - 3x = 4x$

$14 = 4x$ ________

f) $7 - 2x = 5x$

$7 = 5x$ ________

To solve an equation:

Step 1: If there are brackets, rewrite the equation without them.

Step 2: Move all the variable terms to one side of the equal sign and all the constant terms to the other side.

Step 3: Simplify both sides of the equation.

Step 4: Divide by the coefficient of x.

You just solved for x!

Example:

$3(2x - 3) + 4 = -2(x + 4) - 5$

$6x - 9 + 4 = -2x - 8 - 5$

$6x + 2x = 9 - 4 - 8 - 5$

$8x = -8$

$x = -1$

6. Solve the equation.

a) $-x - 3 = x - 9$

$-3 + 9 = x + x$

$6 = 2x$

$3 = x$

b) $3x - 17 = 5x - 9$

c) $3(x + 5) = x + 7$

d) $3(5 - x) = 2(4 - 5x)$

e) $6 + \frac{2}{3}x = 11 - x$

f) $\frac{3}{5} + 5x = \frac{7}{5} - 3x$

g) $3(x + 4) + 4(5 - x) = 2(x - 2)$

h) $2(3x + 7) = 5(9 - 2x) + 1$

i) $2(3x - 5) + 3(7 - 4x) = 2x + 3$

7. Check your answers to Question 6 by replacing x in the original equation with your answer. Check your answers for parts d) to i) in your notebook.

a) $-3 - 3 = 3 - 9$

$-6 = -6$ ✓

b)

c)

EE8-36 Advanced Algebra

1. Solve the equation by first moving all variable terms to the same side of the equal sign.

a) $2x = -3x + 15$

$2x + 3x = 15$

$5x = 15$

$x = 15 \div 5$

$x = 3$

b) $5x = 2x + 9$

c) $8x = 3x + 20$

2. Move all variable terms to one side of the equal sign and all constant terms to the other side.

a) $-2x + 5 = -4x + 2$

$-2x + 4x = 2 - 5$

b) $5x - 3 = 2x + 9$

c) $2x + 3 = -x + 21$

d) $-\frac{3}{5}x + 5 = \frac{1}{5}x + 2$

$-\frac{3}{5}x - \frac{1}{5}x = 2 - 5$

e) $\frac{5}{7}x - \frac{4}{9} = \frac{2}{7}x + \frac{1}{9}$

f) $\frac{2}{5} - \frac{3}{5}x = \frac{1}{5} + \frac{2}{5}x$

3. Solve the equation. Hint: Group like terms first, if necessary.

a) $\frac{3}{5}x + 3 = -\frac{1}{5}x + 11$

$\frac{3}{5}x + \frac{1}{5}x = 11 - 3$

$\frac{4}{5}x = 8$

$\frac{4}{5}x \div \frac{4}{5} = 8 \div \frac{4}{5} = 8 \times \frac{5}{4}$

$x = 10$

b) $\frac{2}{3}x + 5 = \frac{1}{3}x + 6$

c) $\frac{3}{5}x - \frac{2}{7} = -\frac{2}{5}x + \frac{5}{7}$

d) $\frac{5}{9} + 3x = 2x + \frac{4}{9}$

e) $\frac{1}{3}(2x - 2) = \frac{2}{3}(3 - x)$

Bonus ▸ $\frac{3}{5}(5x - 3) = x - 2$

4. A box contains some red and yellow beads. Let x represent the number of red beads in the box. Write the number of yellow beads in terms of x.

a) 4 more yellow beads than red beads

red: x

yellow: $x + 4$

b) 3 fewer yellow beads than red beads

red: ____________

yellow: ____________

c) 5 more red beads than yellow beads

d) 4 times as many yellow beads as red beads

e) 2 fewer red beads than yellow beads

f) 4 times as many red beads as yellow beads

5. A box contains 20 red and yellow beads. Find the numbers of red and yellow beads if ...

a) there are 4 more red beads than yellow beads.

red: $\underline{\ x\ }$

yellow: $\underline{\ x - 4\ }$

equation: $x + \underline{\ x - 4\ } = 20$

$$x + x - 4 = 20$$
$$2x = 20 + 4$$
$$2x = 24$$
$$2x \div 2 = 24 \div 2$$
$$x = 12$$

There are 12 red beads and $12 - 4 = 8$ yellow beads.

b) there are 10 more yellow beads than red beads.

c) there are 3 times as many yellow beads as red beads.

d) there are 2 more red beads than yellow beads.

e) there are 4 times as many red beads as yellow beads.

6. Write expressions for the numbers of red, green, and yellow beads in a box.
Hint: Underline the color that appears in both sentences. Let x represent that color.

a) There are 3 more yellow beads than green beads. There are 4 times as many red beads as green beads

red: ______

green: $\underline{\ x\ }$

yellow: ______

b) There are 4 fewer yellow beads than red beads. There are 5 times as many green beads as yellow beads

red: ______

green: ______

yellow: ______

c) There are 2 fewer red beads than green beads. There are 3 more yellow beads than green beads.

d) There are 2 more red beads than green beads. There are 2 times as many yellow beads as green beads.

7. There are 5 more red beads than green beads in a box. There are 3 times as many yellow beads as red beads. The number of red and green beads is 12 less than the number of yellow beads. How many beads are in the box?

8. Liz and Amit went windsurfing together. Liz paid $7 to rent her windsurfing board, plus $3 for each hour she surfed. Amit paid $10 for his windsurfing board, plus $2 for each hour he surfed. Liz and Amit paid the same amount. How many hours did they windsurf together?

9. The boxes have the same perimeter. Find the perimeter of each box.

EE8-37 How Many Solutions?

A number that makes an equation true is called the **solution** of the equation.

Example: $x = 2$ is the solution of $3x - 1 = 5$, because $3 \times 2 - 1 = 5$.

1. a) $7 \times 0 = 0 + 0 + 0 + 0 + 0 + 0 + 0 =$ ________

b) $5 \times 0 = 0 + 0 + 0 + 0 + 0 =$ ________

c) What is 974×0? ________

d) What answer will ☐ $\times$ 0 always have? ________

e) Can you find a number that makes ☐ $\times 0 = 7$? ________

There are no numbers that can make the equation $n \times 0 = 7$, so the equation $n \times 0 = 7$ has no solution.

2. Complete the table to find 0 × the number.

a)

n	*n* × 5
4	*20*
3	*15*
2	
1	
0	

(−5 between each row)

b)

n	*n* × 7
4	*28*
3	
2	
1	
0	

(−7 between each row)

3. Calculate the product.

a) $0 \times 3 =$ _____ b) $0 \times 2 =$ _____ c) $0 \times 0 =$ _____ d) $0 \times 1 =$ _____

4. What is $0 \times 34{,}716$? How do you know? ________________________________

____

5. Write the solution in the box or X if there is no answer.

a) ☐ $\times 7 = 7$ b) $0 \times 1 =$ ☐ c) $0 \times$ ☐ $= 1$ d) $0 \div 8 =$ ☐

e) $7 \div$ ☐ $= 1$ f) $8 \div 8 =$ ☐ g) $1 \times 0 =$ ☐ h) ☐ $\times 0 = 9$

i) $8 \times$ ☐ $= 0$ j) $8 \div 0 =$ ☐ k) $0 \times 0 =$ ☐ l) $0 \div 0 =$ ☐

With a multiplication statement, the terms can be moved to write the statement as division.

Example: Start with 2 and multiply by 4 to get 8: $2 \times 4 = 8$. Divide by 4 to get back to 2: $8 \div 4 = 2$.

6. Write the multiplication statement as division.

a) Since $1 \times 0 = 0$, then $0 \div 0 =$ ______.

b) Since $2 \times 0 = 0$, then $0 \div 0 =$ ______.

c) Since $3 \times 0 = 0$, then $0 \div 0 =$ ______.

d) Since $4 \times 0 = 0$, then $0 \div 0 =$ ______.

7. a) What answer will ☐ $\times 0$ always have? ______

b) Can you find a number that makes ☐ $\times 0 = 7$? ______

c) Does $7 \div 0$ have an answer? Explain. ______________________

____

For $0x = 0$, any number can be the solution because any number makes the equation true.

The equation $0x = 0$ has an **infinite** number of solutions, so $0 \div 0$ can have many answers. Since the result of an operation needs to be exactly one number (for example, $15 \div 3 = 5$), mathematicians have decided not to define $0 \div 0$ at all.

8. Write "no answer" or "too many answers."

a) $0 \div 0$ does not make sense because it has ______________________.

b) $9 \div 0$ does not make sense because it has ______________________.

9. Either write the one, unique solution or explain why you cannot write a solution.

a) $5 \times$ *0* $= 0$

b) $0 \times$ _____ $= 5$
no solution

c) $0 \times$ _____ $= 0$
too many solutions

d) $0 \times 5 =$ _____

e) $5 \times$ _____ $= 5$

f) $3 \div 0 =$ _____

g) $x + 1 = x$

h) $0 \div 0 =$ _______

i) $2(x + 1) = 2x + 2$

j) $3(x + 1) = x - 2 + 2x$

k) _______ $\times 0 = 10$

l) $4(x + 2) = 2x - 1 + x$

EE8-38 Applications of Linear Equations

To solve word problems, you turn the words into algebraic expressions. Words such as the following give clues to the operations you need to use:

Add	**Subtract**	**Multiply**	**Divide**
increased by	less than	product	divided by
sum	difference	times	divided into
more than	decreased by	twice as many	
	reduced by		

1. Match each description with the correct algebraic expression.

   a) **A.** $4x$ **B.** $x - 2$ **C.** $x + 2$ **D.** $x - 3$ **E.** $x \div 3$ **F.** $3 \div x$

   i) 2 more than a number ______
   ii) A number divided by 3 ______
   iii) 2 less than a number ______
   iv) 3 divided by a number ______
   v) A number decreased by 3 ______
   vi) The product of a number and 4 ______

   b) **A.** $3x$ **B.** $x \div 2$ **C.** $x + 3$ **D.** $x - 4$ **E.** $2x$ **F.** $2 \div x$

   i) 2 divided into a number ______
   ii) A number reduced by 4 ______
   iii) 2 divided by a number ______
   iv) Twice as many as a number ______
   v) A number increased by 3 ______
   vi) A number times 3 ______

2. Write an algebraic expression for the description.

   a) Four more than a number
   b) A number decreased by 10
   c) The product of 7 and a number
   d) A number divided by 8
   e) Two less than a number
   f) The sum of a number and 7
   g) Five times a number
   h) Six divided into a number
   i) The product of a number and 3
   j) Five more than a number, then three times the answer
   k) A number reduced by 4, then multiplied by 2
   l) Twice as many as 3 less than a number

In word problems, "is" often means "equals" or =.
Example: "Two more than a number is seven" can be written $x + 2 = 7$.

3. Solve the problem by first writing an equation.

   a) Four more than a number is thirty-two.
   b) Five less than a number is 19.
   c) Five times a number is thirty.
   d) A number divided by four is seven.
   e) Six divided into a number is four.
   f) The product of a number and 5 is forty.
   g) A number multiplied by two then decreased by five is thirty-five.
   h) A number divided by three then increased by four is seventeen.
   i) 3 divided into a number is 2 less than 8.
   j) 3 less than a number is 5 times smaller than 20.
   k) Three times two more than a number is 17.
   l) Three times a number is 14 more than 5.

Two numbers are **consecutive** if one is the next number after the other.

Examples: 6 and 7 are consecutive numbers because 7 is the next number after 6.

6 and 8 are consecutive even numbers because 8 is the next even number after 6.

4. Fill in the blanks.

a) 36, 37, 38, and ______ are consecutive numbers.

b) 4, 6, 8, and ______ are consecutive even numbers.

c) 7 and ______ are consecutive odd numbers.

d) 7 and ______ are consecutive prime numbers.

e) x, $x + 1$, and ______ are consecutive numbers.

f) x is even. x, ______, and ______ are consecutive even numbers.

g) x is odd. x, ______, and ______ are consecutive odd numbers.

5. The sum of three consecutive numbers is 18. What are the numbers?
Solve the problem in two ways.

a) Use a table to list all possible consecutive numbers in order and then find the sums. Stop when the sum reaches 18.

Three Consecutive Numbers	**Their Sum**
1, 2, 3	$1 + 2 + 3 = 6$
2, 3, 4	$2 + 3 + 4 = 9$
3, 4, 5	
4, 5, 6	

b) Use algebra.

i) If the smallest of the consecutive numbers is x, write an expression for each of the other numbers.

Smallest number $= x$

Middle number $=$ __________

Largest number $=$ __________

ii) Write an equation to express the statement above: The sum of the three consecutive numbers is 18.

____________________________________ $= 18$

iii) Solve your equation. What is the smallest number? What are the three numbers?

____

6. The sum of three consecutive even numbers is 42. What are the three numbers?

a) Let the smallest number be x and solve the problem.

b) Let the middle number be x and solve the problem.

c) Let the largest number be x and solve the problem.

d) Did you get the same answer all three ways?

7. a) Answer Question 6 using tables.

b) Did you get the same answer using a table as you did using algebra?

c) Which method do you like better: a table or algebra? Explain.

REMINDER: The area of a rectangle is length multiplied by width, or $A = \ell \times w$ (or $A = \ell w$).

8. a) Evaluate the expression for the area of a rectangle with …

i) $\ell = 2, \quad w = 7$ ii) $\ell = 3\frac{1}{5}, \quad w = \frac{1}{2}$ iii) $\ell = 3.7, \quad w = 10$

b) A rectangle has an area of $5\frac{2}{3}$ and length of $3\frac{1}{2}$. Write an equation for the width w and solve it.

9. a) Write an expression for the perimeter. x stands for the length of one or more unknown sides.

i)

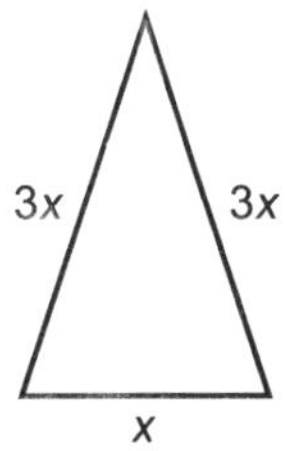

ii)

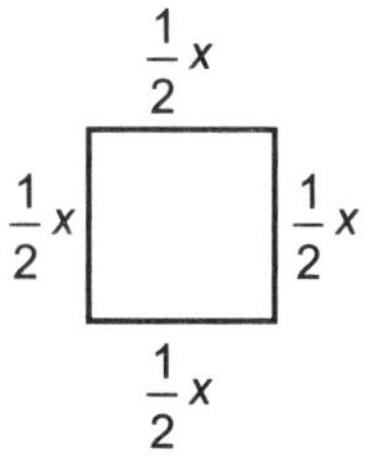

iii)

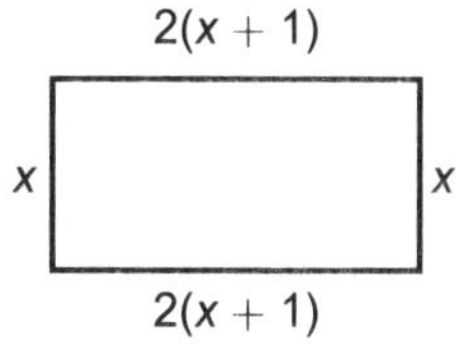

iv)

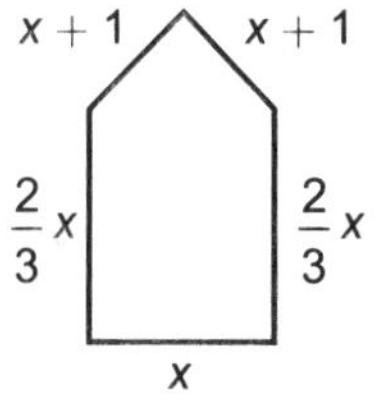

b) The perimeter of each shape in part a) is 28. Find the unknown side lengths.

i) ii) iii) iv)

10. Mark's dad is three times older than Mark. Mark's sister is 2 years younger than Mark. The sum of all three ages is 48. How old is Mark?

Bonus ▶ Randi's sister is half as old as Randi. Randi's mother is $2\frac{1}{2}$ times Randi's age.

Randi's father is 4 years older than Randi's mother. The sum of all four ages is 95. How old was Randi's father when Randi was born?

EE8-39 Ratios and Fractions

A fraction compares a part to a whole. A **ratio** can compare a part to a part, or a part to a whole.

Example: 

The **part-to-part ratio** of circles to squares is 3 to 2 or 3 : 2.

The **part-to-whole ratio** of circles to shapes is 3 to 5 or 3 : 5.

1. 

a) The ratio of moons to stars is _____ : _____.

b) The ratio of squares to moons is _____ : _____.

c) The ratio of stars to circles is _____ : _____.

d) The ratio of triangles to shapes is _____ : _____.

2. a) Write the ratio of vowels (a, e, i, o, u) to consonants (other letters) in the word.

i) star _____ : _____

ii) moon _____ : _____

iii) oak _____ : _____

iv) America _____ : _____

v) Seattle _____ : _____

vi) Jefferson _____ : _____

b) Are the ratios you found in part a) part-to-part ratios or part-to-whole ratios?

____

3. Classify the ratio. Circle if it is a part-to-whole ratio. Underline if it is a part-to-part ratio.

a) vowels in "Maine" : letters in "Maine"

b) vowels in "Oregon" : consonants in "Oregon"

c) school days in a week to days of the week

d) days in May to days in June

You can think of a part-to-whole ratio as a fraction.

Example: 

The ratio of circles to shapes is 2 to 5 or 2 : 5, so $\frac{2}{5}$ of the shapes are circles.

4. Write a ratio and a fraction.

a) 

circles to shapes = _____ : _____

_______ of the shapes are circles.

b) 

circles to shapes = _____ : _____

_______ of the shapes are circles.

When there are only two parts, you can change a part-to-part ratio to a fraction.

Example: There are 3 circles for every 5 triangles in a set of circles and triangles.

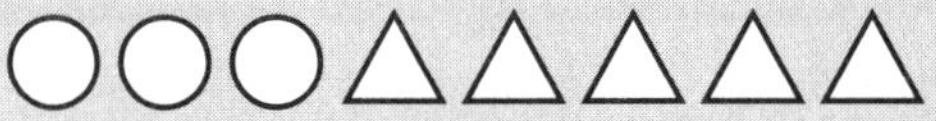

So there are 3 circles for every total of 8 shapes. $\frac{3}{8}$ of the shapes are circles.

5. Write the number of boys (b), girls (g), and students (s) in each class.

a) There are 7 boys and 5 girls in a class. b: *7* g: *5* s: *12*

b) There are 11 girls in a class of 20 students. b: ______ g: ______ s: ______

c) There are 6 boys in a class of 11 students. b: ______ g: ______ s: ______

6. Write the fraction of students in the class who are boys and the fraction who are girls.

a) There are 7 boys and 8 girls in the class. b: $\frac{7}{15}$ g: ☐

b) The ratio of boys to girls in the class is 5 to 6. b: ☐ g: ☐

c) The ratio of girls to boys in the class is 8 : 7. b: ☐ g: ☐

7. In Class A, $\frac{2}{5}$ of the students are girls. In Class B, $\frac{5}{8}$ of the students are girls.

a) What is the ratio of girls to boys in each class? A. ______ : ______ B. ______ : ______

b) Which class has more girls than boys? How can you tell from the fraction? How can you tell from the ratio?

In the picture, there are 3 circles for every 2 squares.

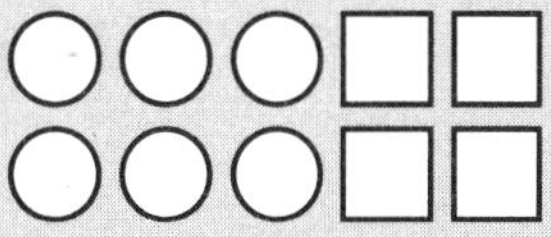

There are also 6 circles for every 4 squares.

The ratios 3 : 2 and 6 : 4 are **equivalent ratios** because they both compare circles to squares in the same set.

8. Find two equivalent ratios for the picture.

a) 

circles to squares = 1 : ______ = 2 : ______

b) 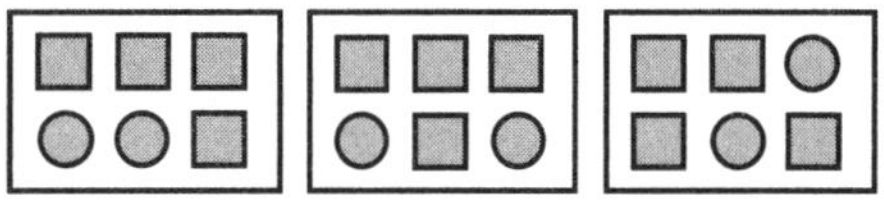

circles to squares = 2 : ______ = 6 : ______

9. Skip count to write a sequence of three equivalent ratios.

a) 3 : 2

= 6 : 4

= 9 : 6

= ____ : ____

b) 3 : 5

= ____ : ____

= ____ : ____

= ____ : ____

c) 5 : 8

= ____ : ____

= ____ : ____

= ____ : ____

d) 3 : 10

= ____ : ____

= ____ : ____

= ____ : ____

There are 5 girls for every 2 boys in the class.
There are 20 girls in the class.

To find out how many boys are in the class, write a sequence of equivalent ratios.

Stop when there are 20 girls. → 20 : 8 ← There are 8 boys in the class.

Girls		Boys
5	:	2
10	:	4
15	:	6
20	:	8

10. Write a sequence of equivalent ratios to solve the problem.

a) There are 5 boys for every 4 girls in a class with 20 boys. How many girls are in the class?

Boys **Girls**

b) There are 7 red beads for every 3 blue beads in a bracelet. The bracelet has 21 red beads. How many blue beads are there?

Red **Blue**

c) A recipe for soup calls for 2 cups of carrots for every 1 cup of lentils. How many cups of carrots are needed for 5 cups of lentils?

Carrots **Lentils**

d) A car travels 100 km on 6 L of gas. The tank holds 36 L. How many kilometers can the car travel on a full tank of gas?

Distance (km) **Gas (L)**

e) To make liquid plant food, you mix 3 ounces of fertilizer with 2 gallons of water. How much water do you need for 12 ounces of fertilizer?

There are 3 boys for every 2 girls in a class of 20 students.

To find out how many boys are in the class, write a sequence of equivalent ratios.

Stop when the parts add to 20.

12 boys + 8 girls = 20 students, so there are 12 boys in the class.

Boys		Girls	Total
3	:	2	5
6	:	4	10
9	:	6	15
12	:	8	20

11. Write a sequence of equivalent ratios to solve the problem.

a) There are 5 boys for every 6 girls in a class of 33 students. How many girls are in the class?

Boys **Girls** **Total**

b) A recipe for lentil stew calls for 1 cup of lentils for 3 cups of rice. How much rice do you need for 12 cups of lentil stew?

Lentils **Rice** **Total**

c) A chain of music stores knows that for every 97 good keyboards received, there will be 3 defective ones. How many defective keyboards are in a shipment of 500 keyboards?

Good **Defective** **Total**

d) 28 people voted in an election with 2 candidates. There were 2 votes for Helen for every 5 votes for Will. How many people voted for Will?

Helen **Will** **Total**

e) A company spends $7,000 on TV advertising for every $4,000 spent on radio advertising. The company budget for TV and radio advertising is $77,000. How much of the budget is spent on each type of advertising?

12. In Class A, the ratio of boys to girls is 3 : 4. There are 35 students in total. In Class B, $\frac{5}{9}$ of the students are girls. There are 36 students in total. Which class has more boys?

EE8-40 Ratio Tables

The numbers in a ratio are called **terms**. To create an equivalent ratio, multiply each term in the ratio by the same number.

Example: There are 2 circles and 1 square. Draw them four times.

Multiply each term by 4.

So the ratio of circles to squares is:

2 : 1
× 4 ↓ ↓ × 4
8 : 4

1. What number are both terms multiplied by to make the second ratio?

a) 1 : 3 (× *4*, × ___) → 4 : 12

b) 2 : 7 (× ___, × ___) → 6 : 21

c) 5 : 3 (× ___, × ___) → 25 : 15

d) 3 : 2 (× ___, × ___) → 30 : 20

2. Multiply both terms by the same number to make an equivalent ratio.

a) 1 : 4 (× 3, × 3) → ___ : ___

b) 5 : 7 (× 5, × 5) → ___ : ___

c) 5 : 3 (× 10, × 10) → ___ : ___

d) 8 : 2 (× 2, × 2) → ___ : ___

3. What is the first term multiplied by? Multiply the second term by the same number.

a) 2 : 3 (× *5*, × *5*) → 10 : *15*

b) 7 : 3 (× ___, × ___) → 28 : ___

c) 11 : 12 (× ___, × ___) → 77 : ___

d) 4 : 10 (× ___, × ___) → 48 : ___

A **ratio table** has equivalent ratios in every row.
To make a ratio table, make a list of equivalent ratios.

You can find each row from the first row by multiplying both terms in the ratio by the same number.

	First Term	Second Term	
	3	5	
×2	6	10	×2
×3	9	15	×3
×4	12	20	×4

4. Multiply to complete the ratio table.

a) 5 : 1

First row	5	1
First row × 2	*10*	*2*
First row × 3	*15*	*3*
First row × 4	*20*	*4*

b) 2 : 5

First row	2	5
First row × 2		
First row × 3		
First row × 4		

c) 7 : 3

First row	7	3
First row × 2		
First row × 3		
First row × 4		

5. Complete a ratio table for the ratio. Multiply the first row by 2 and then by 3.

a) 3 : 2

3	2	
6	*4*	×2
9	*6*	×3

b) 1 : 5

1	5

c) 6 : 5

6	5

d) 4 : 7

4	7

6. Find the missing number(s) in the ratio table.

a) 3 : 7

3	7
6	14
9	

b) 5 : 2

5	2
10	
	6

c) 1 : 10

1	10
	20
3	

d) 6 : ____

6	
12	20
18	

Sometimes a ratio table has only two rows. The rows show equivalent ratios.

7. What number do you multiply the first row by to get the second row? Find the missing number in the ratio table.

a) × *2*

4	3
8	*6*

b) × ____

3	20
9	

c) × ____

4	1
22	

d) × ____

2	5
	24

8. Solve the problem by making a ratio table.

a) Five bus tickets cost $13. How much will 20 tickets cost?

Tickets	Cost ($)
5	*13*

b) A box can hold 20 lb. How many boxes are needed to ship 100 lb of goods?

Boxes	Weight (lb)
1	*20*

c) Mike earns $155 in 2 weeks. How much money will he earn in 8 weeks?

Weeks	Earnings ($)

d) A 10 ft long wall is made of 525 bricks. How many bricks are needed for a wall 50 ft long?

Length (ft)	Bricks

Bonus ▶ A car uses 3.1 gal of fuel for 100 miles. The fuel tank can hold 12.4 gal of fuel. How far can you drive the car if the tank is half full?

Graphing Ratios

We use a pair of numbers in brackets to give the position of a point on a coordinate grid. The numbers are called **coordinates** of the point.

A (3, 1) — **x-coordinate**, **y-coordinate**

B (1, 3) — *x*-coordinate, *y*-coordinate

The *x*-coordinate is always written first. The pair of numbers is also called an **ordered pair**.

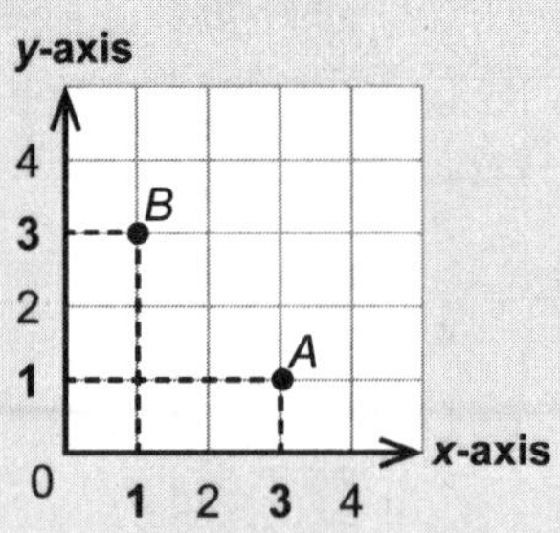

1. Find the coordinates of the points.

A (1 , 3)　　*B* (_____, _____)

C (_____, _____)　　*D* (_____, _____)

E (_____, _____)　　*F* (_____, _____)

G (_____, _____)　　*H* (_____, _____)

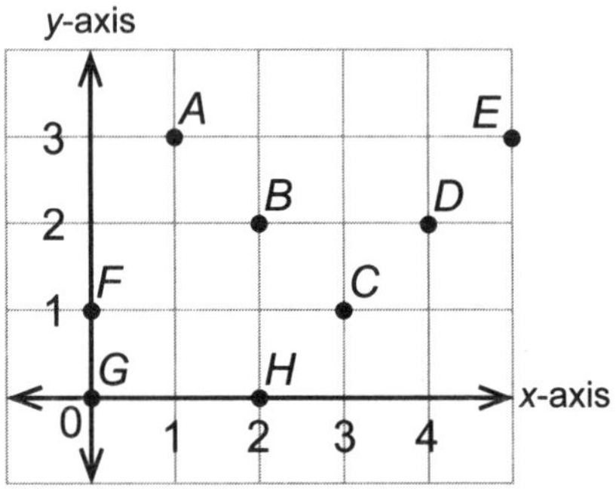

We use number lines to mark the grid lines.

The number lines are called **axes**. One number line is called an **axis**.

The axes meet at the point (0, 0), called the **origin**.

Axes can have positive and negative numbers, fractions, and decimals. You can label axes using skip counting.

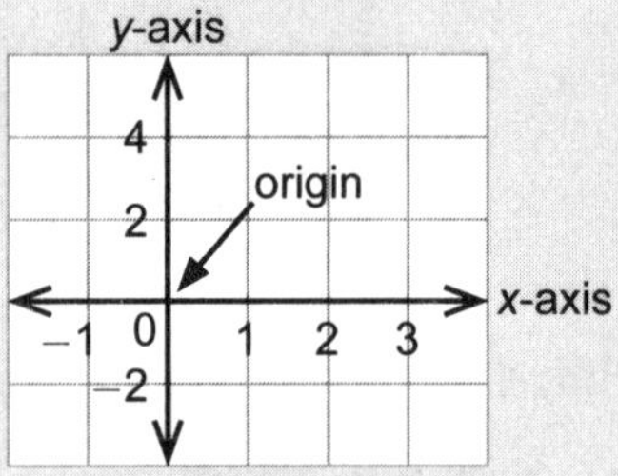

2. Plot and label the points on the coordinate grid. After you plot a point, cross out the coordinates.

a) *A* ~~$\left(2.5, 3\frac{1}{4}\right)$~~　*B* (3, 2)　*C* (3.5, 1)

$D\left(1, 1\frac{3}{4}\right)$　$E\left(1\frac{1}{2}, 0\right)$　$F\left(0, \frac{1}{2}\right)$

b) *A* (3, −1)　*B* (2, 2)　*C* (4, 1)

D (1, −2)　*E* (1, 0)　*F* (2, −3)

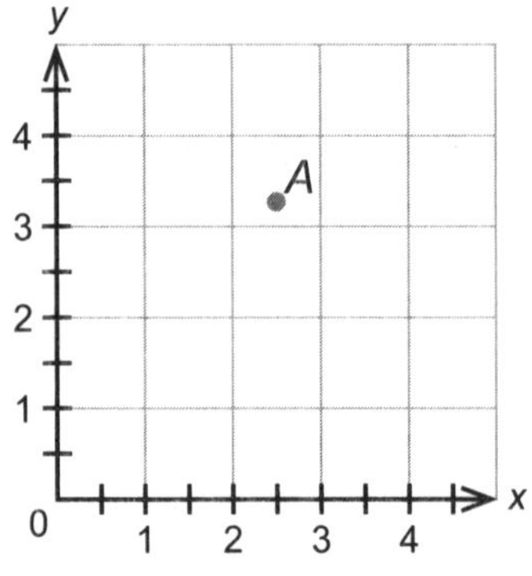

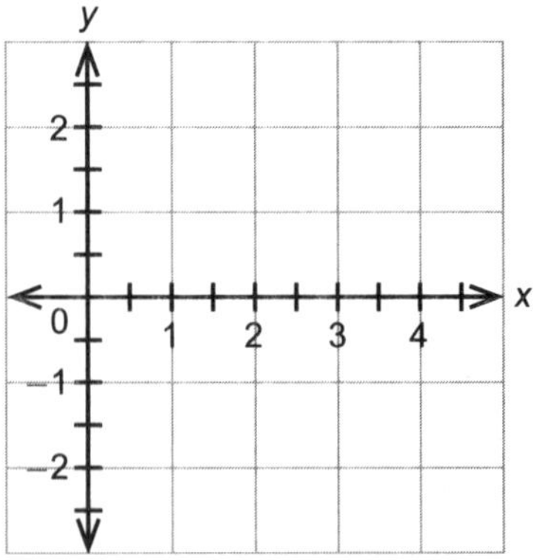

3. a) All the coordinates are whole numbers. Write the coordinates of the points.

i)

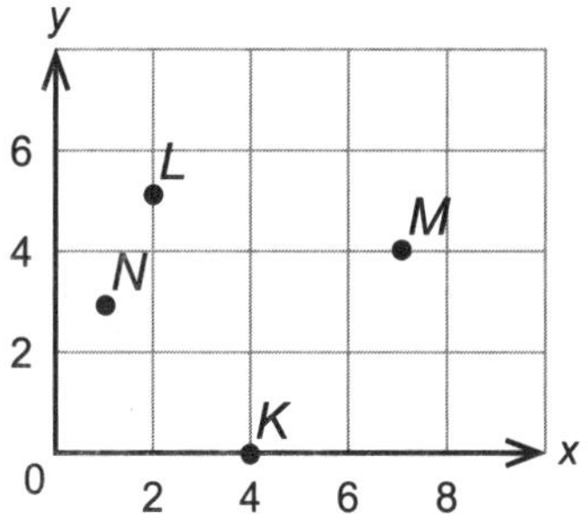

ii)

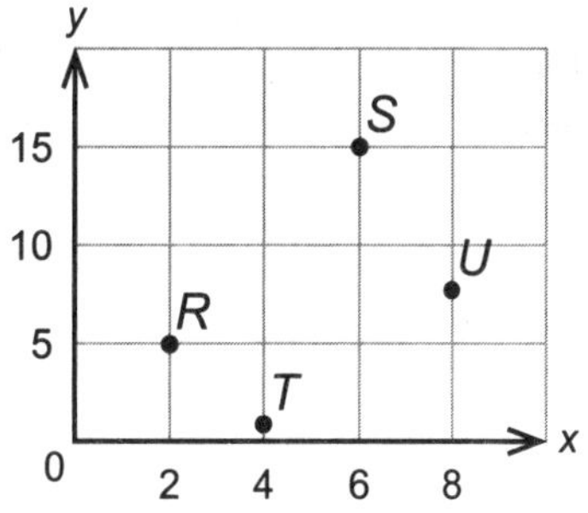

K (______, ______), *L* (______, ______),

M (______, ______), *N* (______, ______)

R (______, ______), *S* (______, ______),

T (______, ______), *U* (______, ______)

b) Plot the points on the grid above. Cross out the coordinates as you go.

i) *O* (5, 6), *P* (0, 7), *Q* (9, 1)

ii) *V* (0, 12), *W* (5, 0), **Bonus ▶** *Z* (1.5, 14)

4. a) Make a ratio table for the ratio. Write an ordered pair for each row of the table.

i) 1 : 2

1	2	*(1, 2)*
2	*4*	*(2, 4)*
3	*6*	*(3, 6)*
4	*8*	*(4, 8)*

ii) 1 : 1

1	1	

iii) 2 : 3

2	3	

b) Plot the ordered pairs from part a) on the grid and connect the points.

i)

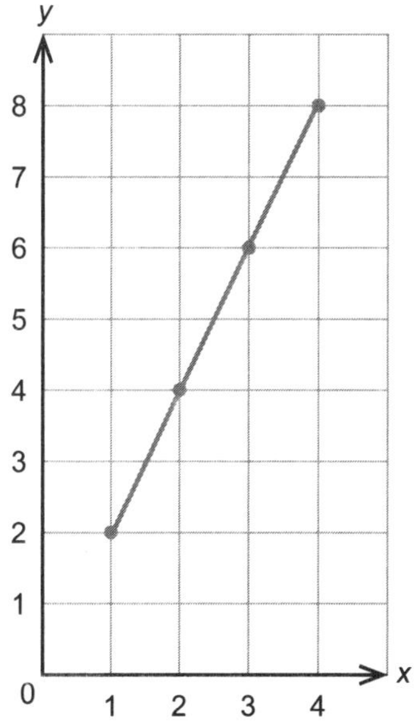

ii)

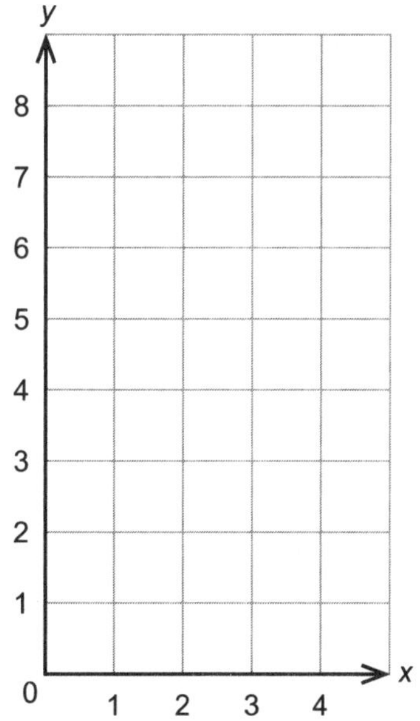

iii)

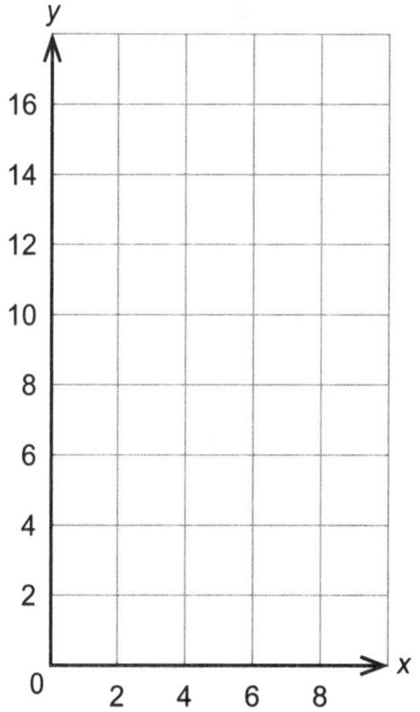

c) Extend the line to intersect the axes. What do you notice about the intersection points?

To graph a ratio:

Step 1: Make a ratio table.

Step 2: Write an ordered pair for each row of the table.

Step 3: Plot the ordered pairs and join the points with a line. If extended, the line should pass through (0, 0).

5. Graph the ratio.

a) 3 : 2 b) 2 : 5 c) 1 : 4 d) 4 : 1 e) 5 : 3 f) 7 : 6

6. A plane flies 1,000 km every hour.

a) Complete the ratio table for the situation.

Time (h)	Distance (km)	Ordered pair
1	*1,000*	
2		

b) Graph the ratio.

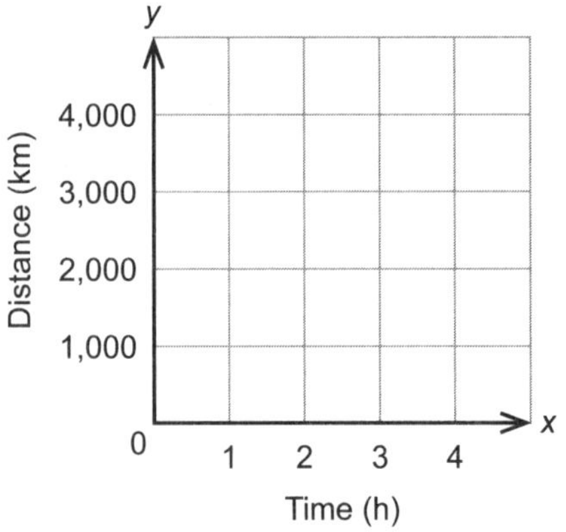

c) Use the graph to tell how far the plane flew in 2.5 hours. ________________

7. A train travels 50 miles every hour.

a) Make a ratio table for the situation.

b) Graph the ratio.

c) Extend the line to tell how far the train travels in 6 hours. ____________

d) A car drives 75 miles every 2 hours. Graph this ratio on the same grid as part b).

e) How far does each vehicle go in 3 hours?

Train: _________ Car: _________

Which travels farther in 3 hours, the train or the car? ____________

f) What travels faster, the car or the train? How do you know?

g) How can you find the answers to parts e) and f) from the graph?

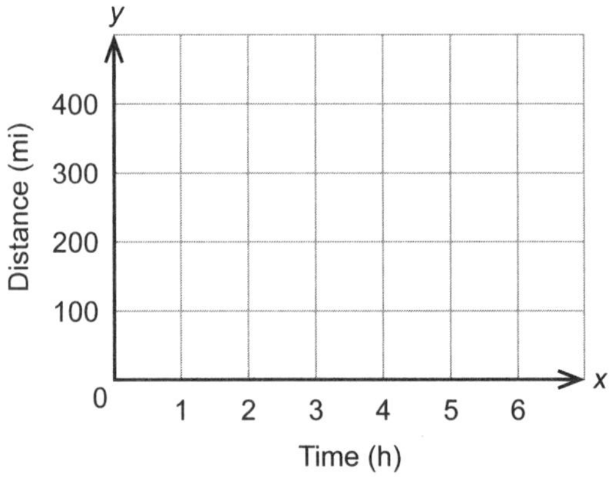

EE8-42 Proportional Relationships

1. Circle the ratio tables.

2	5
4	10

3	8
12	2

2	5
4	7

6	8
12	16

3	5
6	15

4	9
12	27

Two quantities are **proportional** if the table comparing their values is a ratio table.

2. a) Is the distance traveled by the car proportional to the time? Write "yes" or "no."

i)

Time (h)	Distance (km)
1	50
2	100
3	150

ii)

Time (h)	Distance (m)
1	20
2	35
3	50

iii)

Time (h)	Distance (mi)
1	40
2	80
3	120

__________ __________ __________

b) Graph the relationships in part a). Use the given number to skip count on the y-axis.

i) 50 km ii) 20 m iii) 40 mi

c) Join the points on each graph in order.

d) Predict which lines will pass through the origin if extended. Explain your prediction.

e) Extend the line on each graph until it intersects the y-axis. Which lines pass through the origin? Was your prediction in part c) correct?

A **formula** is an equation that shows how to calculate one quantity from another.

Example: There are 3 triangles for every 1 square.

Formula: number of triangles = 3 × number of squares

We can use variables such as t for the number of triangles and s for the number of squares to shorten the formula: $t = 3 \times s$ or $t = 3s$.

3. Complete the table for the formula. Then circle the table if s and t are proportional.

a)

s	$4 \times s = t$	t
1	$4 \times 1 = 4$	4
2	$4 \times 2 = 8$	8
3	$4 \times 3 = 12$	12

b)

s	$2 \times s = t$	t
1		
2		
3		

c)

s	$3 \times s = t$	t
3		
5		
7		

4. Complete the table for the formula. Then circle the table if *s* and *t* are proportional.

a)

s	$s + 4 = t$	**t**
1	$1 + 4 = 5$	5
2		
3		
4		

b)

s	$s + 2 = t$	**t**
1		
2		
3		
4		

c)

s	$s - 1 = t$	**t**
3		
6		
10		
4		

5. Predict which formulas show a proportional relationship based on your answers to Questions 3 and 4. Check your answers to parts a) and c) using a table.

a) $s = 3t$ b) $5 \times t = s$ c) $2 + s = t$

d) $y = 7x$ e) $y = x - 7$ f) $a = b \times 6$

6. Complete the table for the formula. Then circle the table if *s* and *t* are proportional.

a)

s	$4 \times s - 3 = t$	**t**
1	$4 \times 1 - 3 = 4 - 3 = 1$	1
2		
3		
4		

b)

s	$2 \times s + 6 = t$	**t**
1		
2		
3		
4		

c)

s	$2 \times s - 1 = t$	**t**
1		
2		
3		
4		

d)

s	$3 \times s + 3 = t$	**t**
1		
2		
3		
4		

An equation shows a proportional relationship if you get one quantity by *multiplying* the other quantity by a constant (a number). This number is called the **constant of proportionality**.

Example: In the equation $t = 3 \times s$, the constant of proportionality is 3.

7. Find the constant of proportionality.

a) $s = 3t$ ________ b) $5 \times t = s$ ________ c) $9 \times s = t$ ________

d) $y = 60x$ ________ e) $y = 0.7x$ ________ f) $a = b$ ________

8. a) Fill in the table. Then write a formula for the number of blocks in the figures.

i)

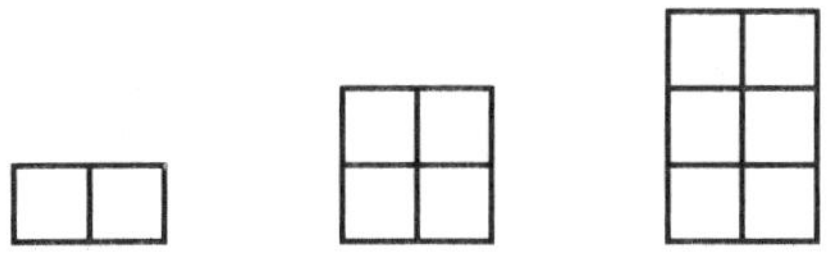

Figure 1 Figure 2 Figure 3

Figure Number (n)	Number of Blocks (b)
1	*2*
2	*4*
3	*6*

Formula: $b = 2 \times n$ or $2n$

ii)

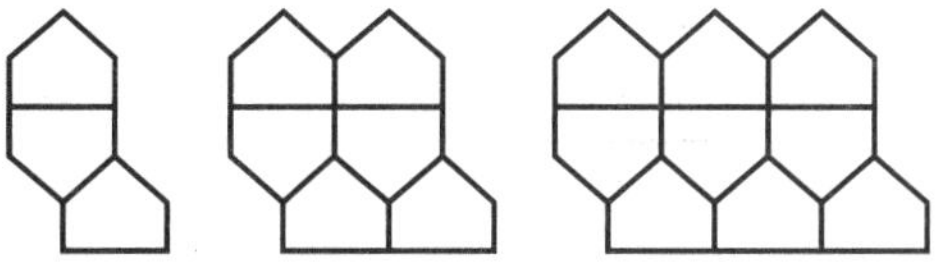

Figure 1 Figure 2 Figure 3

Figure Number (n)	Number of Blocks (b)
1	
2	
3	

Formula: ________________

iii)

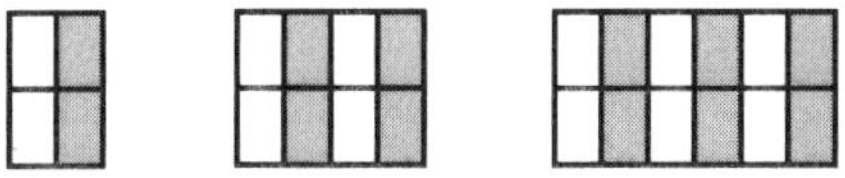

Figure 1 Figure 2 Figure 3

Figure Number (n)	Number of Blocks (b)
1	*4*
2	
3	

Formula: ________________

iv)

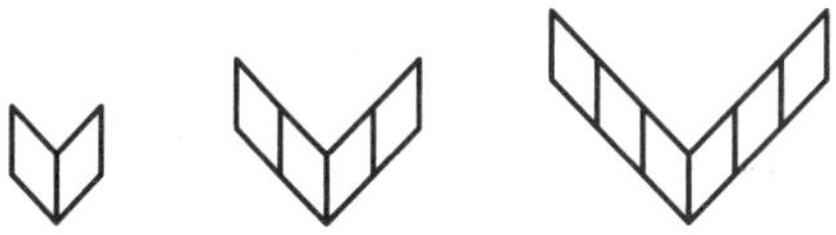

Figure 1 Figure 2 Figure 3

Figure Number (n)	Number of Blocks (b)
1	
2	
3	

Formula: ________________

b) Are the numbers of blocks and the figure numbers proportional in each table? __________

c) Use the formula to find the number of blocks in Figure 100.

i) $b =$ $2 \times n$ ii) $b =$ __________ iii) $b =$ __________ iv) $b =$ __________

$=$ __________ $=$ __________ $=$ __________ $=$ __________

d) Which pattern will have the largest number of blocks in Figure 100? __________

Which pattern has the largest constant of proportionality? __________

e) Why should your answers in part d) be the same?

Bonus ▶ Which will be larger, the number of blocks in the 100th figure in the pattern $b = 2 \times n$, or the number of blocks in the 50th figure in the pattern $b = 4 \times n$? Explain.

9. a) Use the figure number (n) to write a formula for the number of shaded blocks (s), and a formula for the total number of blocks (b).

i)

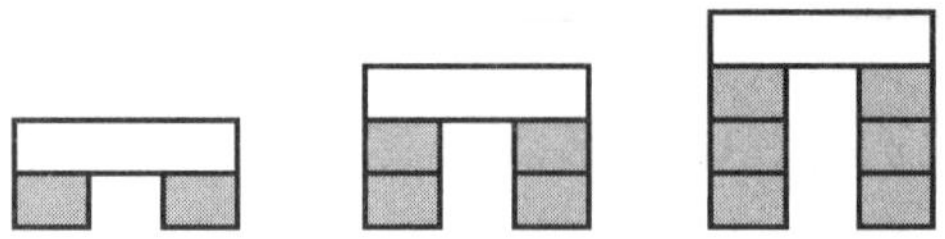

Figure 1 Figure 2 Figure 3

Number of shaded blocks: $s =$ <u>2n</u>

Total number of blocks: $b =$ <u>2n + 1</u>

ii)

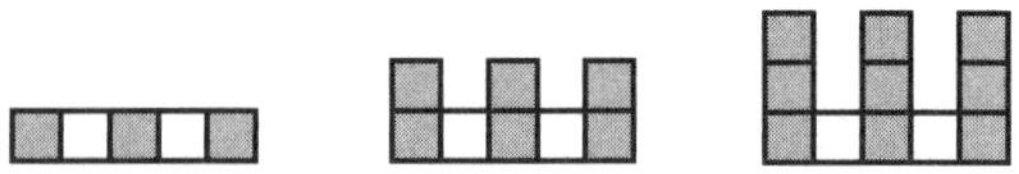

Figure 1 Figure 2 Figure 3

Number of shaded blocks: $s =$ ____________

Total number of blocks: $b =$ ____________

iii)

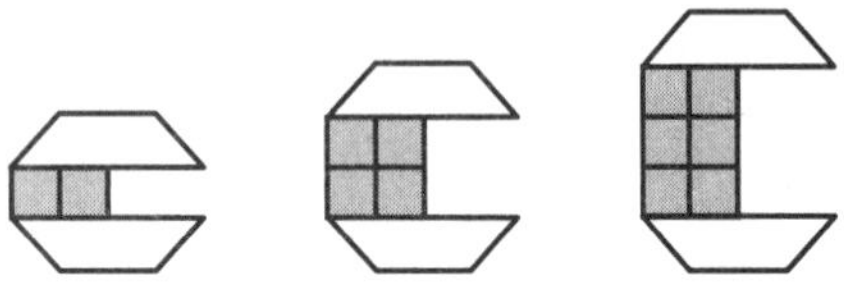

Figure 1 Figure 2 Figure 3

Number of shaded blocks: $s =$ ____________

Total number of blocks: $b =$ ____________

iv)

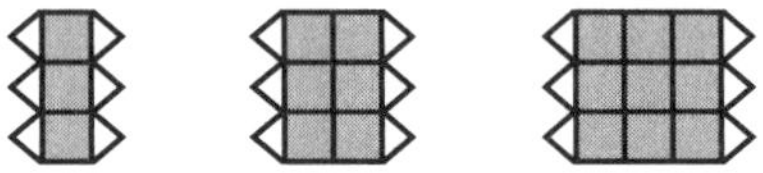

Figure 1 Figure 2 Figure 3

Number of shaded blocks: $s =$ ____________

Total number of blocks: $b =$ ____________

b) Look at the two formulas you wrote for each pattern in part a). Which quantity is proportional to the figure number (n): the number of shaded blocks (s)

or the total number of blocks (b)? ____________________

c) Which operations are involved in the formulas that show proportional relationships? Which operations are involved in the formulas that do not show proportional relationships?

10. Circle the part that is proportional to n in the expression.

a) $2 \times n + 3$ b) $3n - 1$ c) $5 \times n$ d) $4 + 2.5 \times n - 3$

REMINDER: If a company charges a flat fee of $25 to rent a boat and an hourly rate of $30, the total cost of renting the boat for h hours is $30h + 25$ dollars.

11. a) Write a formula for the cost C to rent a boat for h hours.

i) hourly rate: $10
flat fee: $20

cost: ____________

ii) hourly rate: $20
flat fee: $10

cost: ____________

iii) hourly rate: $0
flat fee: $25

cost: ____________

iv) hourly rate: $12.50
flat fee: $0

cost: ____________

b) Circle the formula that shows a proportional relationship.

c) For the cost to be proportional to the hourly rate, what should the flat fee be? Explain.

EE8-43 Proportional Relationships and Graphs

To graph an equation:

Step 1: Make a table of values.

Step 2: Write an ordered pair for each row of the table.

Step 3: Plot the points.

1. a) Graph the formula, paying attention to the scale on the axes. Join the points in order.

i) $y = 2x - 1$

x	Calculating y	y	Ordered Pair
1	$y = 2(1) - 1 = 1$	1	(1, 1)
2			
3			
4			

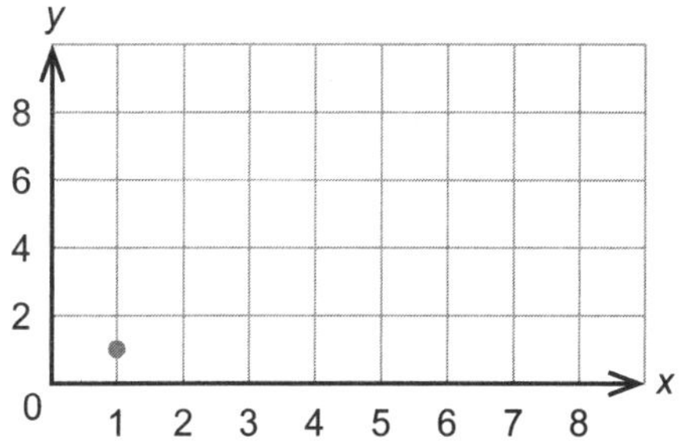

ii) $y = x + 1$

x	Calculating y	y	Ordered Pair
1			
2			
3			
4			

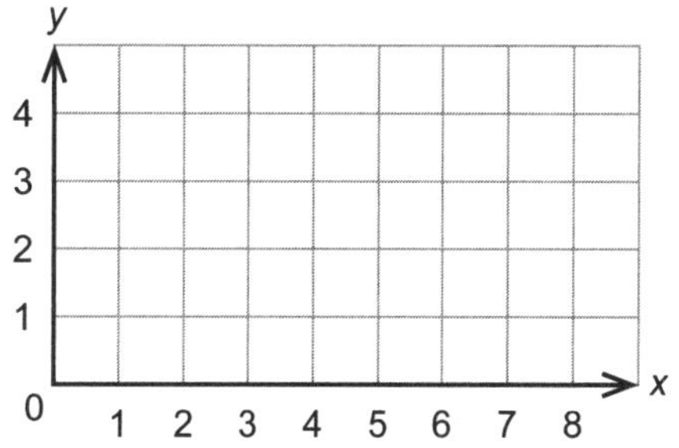

iii) $y = 0.5x$

x	Calculating y	y	Ordered Pair
2			
4			
6			

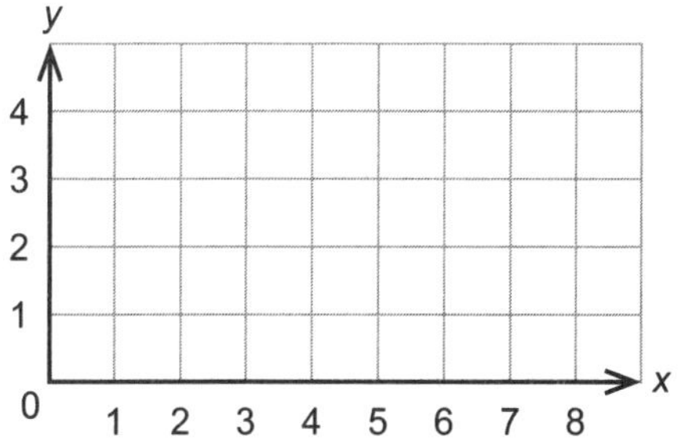

iv) $y = 3x$

x	Calculating y	y	Ordered Pair
1			
2			
3			

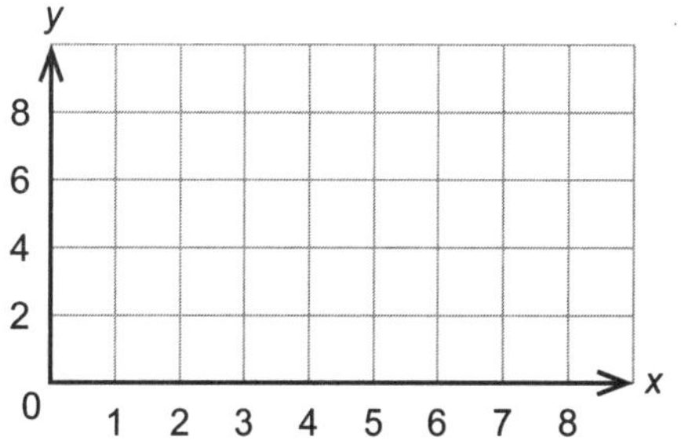

b) Which equations from part a) show proportional relationships? ________________

c) Extend each graph in part a) so that it intersects at least one axis.

d) How are the graphs of the proportional relationships different from the other graphs?

2. a) Fill in the table.

Equation	$y = 2x$	$5x = y$	$y = 10x$	$y = 0.6x$
Is this a proportional relationship?	*yes*			
If $x = 0$, $y =$?	$y = 2(0) = 0$			
(x, y)	$(0, 0)$			

b) Explain why the graph of a proportional relationship always passes through the origin.

____

____

____

3. a) Make a table for each equation.

A. $y = 2x$

x	y	(x, y)
0	*0*	*(0, 0)*
1	*2*	*(1, 2)*
2	*4*	
3	*6*	

B. $y = 3x$

x	y	(x, y)
0		
1		
2		
3		

C. $y = 4x$

x	y	(x, y)

b) Plot the points and join them in order. Label the lines A, B, and C.

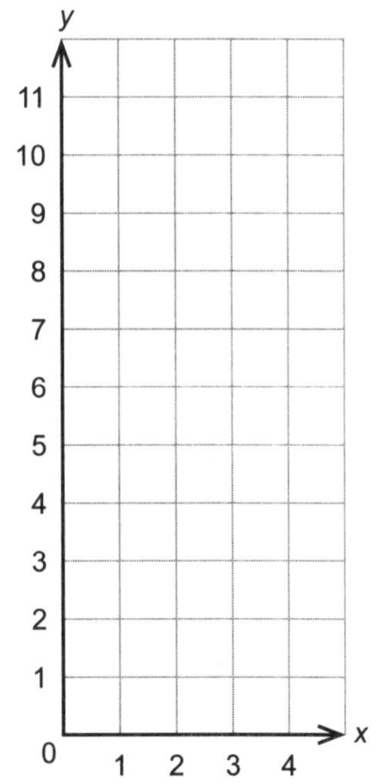

c) Which equation has the largest constant of proportionality? ________

d) Which line is the steepest? ________

e) Predict: The line for the equation $y = 2.5x$ will be steeper than line ________ but less steep than line ________.

f) Make a table for $y = 2.5x$ and plot the points.

x	y	(x, y)
2		
4		

g) Was your prediction from part e) correct? ________

4. a) Two tickets cost \$3.

i) Write a ratio for this situation. ___________

ii) Make a ratio table. Plot the ordered pairs.
Join the points in order.

Number of Tickets	Cost (\$)	Ordered Pair
2		
4		
6		

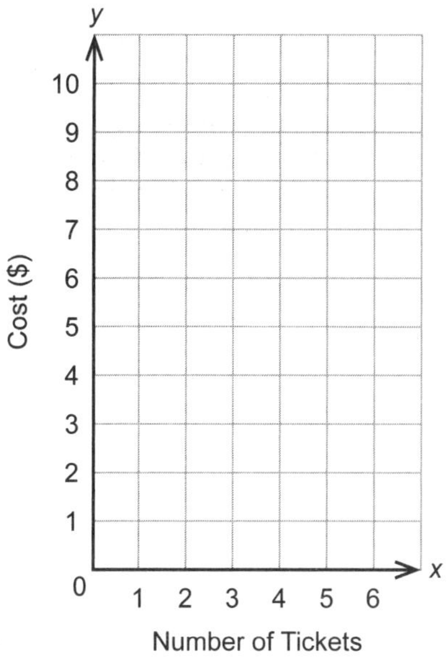

iii) Plot the point that shows the price of 1 ticket.
Label the point *A*.

How much does 1 ticket cost? ___________

b) A rocket flies 3 miles in 2 seconds.

i) Write a ratio for this situation. ___________

ii) Make a ratio table. Plot the ordered pairs.
Join the points in order.

Time (s)	Distance (mi)	Ordered Pair

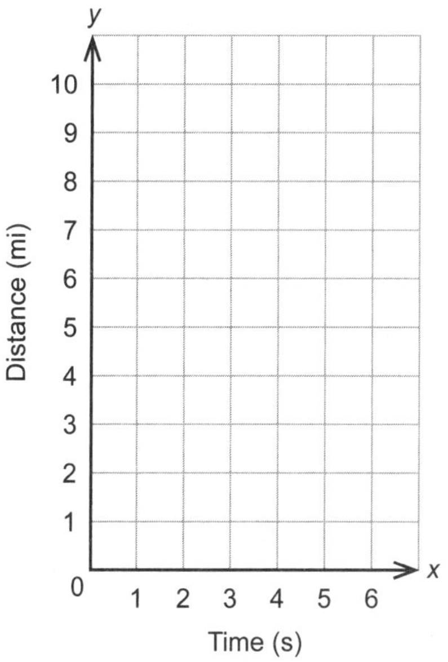

iii) Plot the point that shows the distance the rocket traveled
in 1 second. Label it *B*.

How far did the rocket travel? ___________

c) Plot the point (4.5, 6.75) on the graph in part a). Label it *C*.

d) Plot the point (4.5, 6.75) on the graph in part b). Label it *D*.

e) One point, *C* or *D*, has no meaning on the graph. Which one? Explain.

____

____

5. Draw a graph for the situation. Then answer the questions.

a) Kathy runs 2 km in 10 minutes. At the same speed, how far will she run in 25 minutes?
In 1 minute? How long will it take her to run 3 km?

b) Carlos earns \$15 in 2 hours. How much will he earn in 30 minutes? In 5 hours?
How long will it take him to earn \$52.50?

EE8-44 Unit Rates

A **unit rate** is a ratio where one quantity is equal to 1. Unit rates are easy to work with because 1 is easy to multiply and divide by.

Example: Each apple costs 25¢, so the unit rate of apples to cents is 1 : 25.

1. Multiply to find the missing information.

a) 1 book costs $6

4 books cost *$24*

b) 30 miles in 1 hour

_______ miles in 5 hours

c) 1 melon costs $2

5 melons cost _______

2. Divide to find the missing information.

a) 3 notebooks cost $18

1 notebook costs _______

b) 2 jackets cost $200

1 jacket costs _______

c) 5 scarves cost $20

1 scarf costs _______

3. Find the unit rate for each deal. Then circle the best deal.

a) 8 baseball hats for $24 or 5 baseball hats for $20 or 6 baseball hats for $21

1 baseball hat for _______ 1 baseball hat for _______ 1 baseball hat for _______

b) 5 songs for $7.50 or 8 songs for $10.00 or 10 songs for $11.50

1 song for _______ 1 song for _______ 1 song for _______

Bonus ▶ Hint: Which deal is better than 1 T-shirt for $10?

8 T-shirts for $95 28 T-shirts for $275 35 T-shirts for $355

In a ratio table, all the rows are equivalent ratios so every row has the same unit rate.

4. Find the unit rate for each row. Circle the table if it is a ratio table.

a)

8	40	*1 : 5*
5	25	*1 : 5*
10	50	*1 : 5*

b)

5	15	_______
2	6	_______
7	21	_______

c)

6	12	_______
12	36	_______
10	40	_______

d)

7	42	_______
5	30	_______
10	60	_______

e)

2	10	_______
10	50	_______
50	250	_______

f)

6	42	_______
7	56	_______
12	84	_______

5. Find the unit rate. Write a rule and a formula for getting the second column from the first column.

a)

x	*y*
2	6
6	18
8	24

1 : 3

Multiply by 3

$y = 3x$

b)

x	*y*
4	16
5	20
8	32

_____ : _____

____

____

c)

x	*y*
5	35
8	56
10	70

_____ : _____

____

____

d)

x	*y*
9	45
12	60
100	500

_____ : _____

____

____

REMINDER: Two quantities are proportional if the table comparing their values is a ratio table.

A formula shows a proportional relationship between two quantities if quantity 1 × the constant of proportionality = quantity 2.

6. Where does the constant of proportionality appear in a unit rate? Circle the constant of proportionality in each unit rate in Question 5.

7. Find the constant of proportionality. It can be a whole number, a fraction, or a decimal. Then find the missing number in the ratio table.

a) *× 0.3*

2	0.6
5	*1.5*

× 0.3

b) __________

1	$\frac{1}{2}$
2	

____

c) __________

2	$\frac{2}{3}$
3	

____

d) __________

2	0.2
10	

____

8. a) Make a table to show the *x* and *y* coordinates for each point.

i)

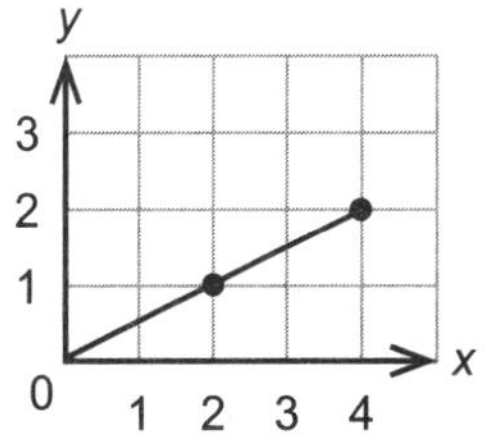

ii)

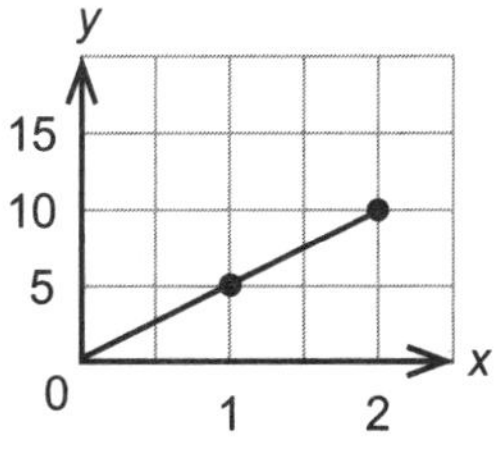

iii)

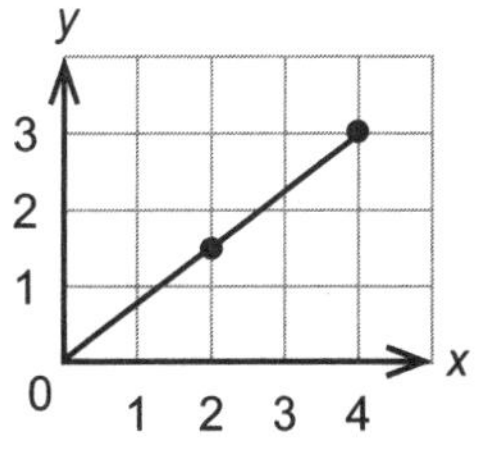

iv)

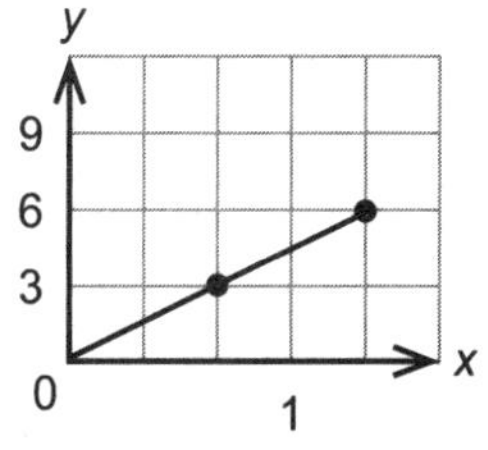

b) Find the unit rate and the constant of proportionality for each table from part a).

c) Write an equation for each table.

In a ratio table, the rows are equivalent ratios. You can divide or multiply by the same number to get from one row to the other.

9. a) Complete the ratio table.

i)

4	12
1	
5	

÷ *4*

× *5*

ii)

3	7
1	
8	

÷ ____

× ____

iii)

5	2
	1
	3

÷ ____

× ____

b) Which row of the tables in part a) shows the unit rate? ______________________

c) Complete the ratio table by finding the unit rate.

i)

4	5
1	
5	

ii)

3	5
1	
8	

iii)

3	0.6
1	
4	

If the second term in a unit rate is 1, the 1 is often left out. Example: 50 mi per 1 hour is 50 mi/h.

10. Density is the ratio of mass to volume measured in grams per cubic centimeter (g/cm^3).
Remember: 1,000 cm^3 = 1 L = 1,000 mL.

a) Write the density as a unit rate with both units.

i) gold 19.3 g/cm^3 ______________

ii) olive oil 0.8 g/cm^3 ______________

iii) iron 7.87 g/cm^3 ______________

b) Make a ratio table to find the mass of 500 cm^3 of each material in part a).

i)

Mass (g)	**Volume (cm^3)**
19.3	*1*
9,650	*500*

ii)

Mass (g)	**Volume (cm^3)**

iii)

Mass (g)	**Volume (cm^3)**

c) 500 cm^3 of human blood has a mass of 503 g. What is the density of human blood?

d) One liter of milk has a mass of 1.003 kg. Is milk more dense than human blood?

e) The density of gasoline for a car is 0.737 g/cm^3. Which has more mass: 500 mL of gasoline or 400 mL of milk?

f) Order the materials in this question from the greatest mass to the least mass per 1 cm^3.

EE8-45 Percentages

A **percent** is a ratio that compares a number to 100. The word percent means “for every 100” or “out of 100.” You can write a percentage as a fraction with the denominator 100 or as a decimal.

Example: $84\% = \frac{84}{100} = 0.84$. On a test, 84% means 84 out of 100.

1. Fill in the table. Write decimals to 2 decimal places and fractions with the denominator 100.

Percent	25%			30%			100%			105%	
Fraction		$\frac{6}{100}$			$\frac{20}{100}$			$\frac{13}{100}$			$\frac{123}{100}$
Decimal			0.34			0.03			0.70		

2. Write the fraction as a percentage by first changing the denominator to 100.

a) $\frac{2 \times 20}{5 \times 20} = \frac{40}{100} = 40\%$ b) $\frac{1}{5}$ c) $\frac{1}{10}$

d) $\frac{1}{2}$ e) $\frac{7}{20}$ f) $\frac{9}{50}$

g) $\frac{3}{4}$ h) $\frac{17}{25}$ i) $\frac{3}{5}$

3. Reduce the fraction to lowest terms. Then change it to a percentage.

a) $\frac{9 \div 3}{15 \div 3} = \frac{3 \times 20}{5 \times 20} = \frac{60}{100} = 60\%$ b) $\frac{3}{15}$ c) $\frac{3}{12}$

d) $\frac{11}{22}$ e) $\frac{75}{125}$ f) $\frac{9}{30}$

4. Convert to fractions with the denominator 100. Then compare using >, <, or =.

a) $\frac{50 \times 1}{50 \times 2}$ 43% b) $\frac{3}{5}$ 65% c) 75% $\frac{3}{4}$

$\frac{50}{100} > \frac{43}{100}$

d) $\frac{2}{5}$, 10% e) 25%, 0.2 f) 0.1, 10% g) 73%, $\frac{16}{25}$ h) 19%, $\frac{6}{30}$ i) 0.125, 12%

$60\% = \frac{60}{100}$, so 60% of 20 is $\frac{60}{100} \times 20 = (60 \times 20) \div 100 = 1{,}200 \div 100 = 12$

5. Use a fraction to find the percentage of a number.

a) 25% of 44 b) 30% of 50 c) 27% of 40 d) 6% of 25

You can write 35% as 0.35. To find 35% of 27, multiply 0.35×27.

6. a) Use decimals to solve the problems in Question 5.

b) Compare the two methods of finding a percentage of a number. How are they the same?

7. a) Mike wants to leave a 15% tip on a meal that cost $40. How much money should he leave for the tip? How much will he pay altogether?

b) Yu wants to save 20% of her earnings and spend the rest. If she earns $255 a month, how much can she spend each month?

When you pay a tax of 6% on a price, you pay full price + tax = 100% + 6%

= 106% of the price

= $1.06 \times$ original price

8. a) The tax is 8%. The total price = ________ × original price.

b) The tax is 15%. The total price = ________ × original price.

c) The tax is 20%. The total price = ________ × original price.

9. The sales tax in Irvine, CA, is 8%. Find the total cost for the sale price.

a) sofa: $200

= *1.08* × $200

= ________

b) coat: $120

= ________ × $120

= ________

c) book: $11

= ________ × $11

= ________

d) soccer ball: $12.95

= ________ × $12.95

= ________

10. A restaurant suggests a tip of 20% on each meal.

a) Make a graph to show the cost of the meal with the tip. Skip count by $5 on both axes.

b) Use the graph to find the cost of the meal with the tip from the given cost.

i) $5 ii) $10 iii) $12.50 iv) $18.75

c) Check your answers to part b) by calculation. Which method do you prefer? Explain.

11. a) A room in a hotel costs $129.00 per night. The tax is 14%. How much will you pay for the room per night?

b) A taxi ride costs $12.50. Karen wants to give a tip of 15%. How much will she pay?

12. Ron's meal at a restaurant cost $18 before taxes. The tax is 15%. Ron also wants to leave a tip of 20% of the cost of the meal before taxes. How much will he pay in total?

EE8-46 Cross Multiplication

REMINDER: In a ratio table, the rows are equivalent ratios.

There are 2 ways to find the missing number:

1. Multiply the other number in the row by the constant of proportionality.
2. Multiply both numbers in one row by the same number to get the other row.

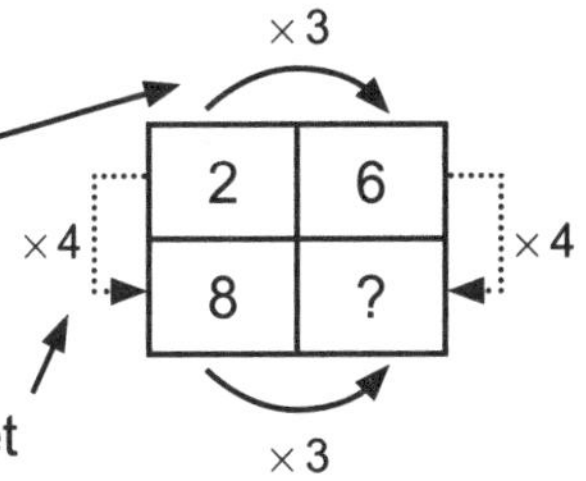

1. Find the number that makes the table a ratio table.

a)

2	5
10	

b)

2	5
8	

c)

2	5
9	

d)

2	5
1.5	

2. a) Check that the table is a ratio table.

i)

25	100
1	4

ii)

35	5
14	2

iii)

2	3
6	9

iv)

4	0.5
12	1.5

b) Multiply the numbers that are diagonally opposite in each ratio table in part a).

i) *$25 \times 4 = 100$* ii) ______________ iii) ______________ iv) ______________

$1 \times 100 = 100$ ______________ ______________ ______________

c) What do you notice about the products in part b)? ______________________________

d) Write the equivalent ratios for each table in part a) as fractions.

i) $\frac{25}{100} = \frac{1}{4}$ ii) iii) iv)

e) Multiply the numerator and the denominator of each fraction from part d) by the denominator of the other fraction.

i) $\frac{4 \times 25}{4 \times 100} = \frac{1 \times 100}{4 \times 100}$ ii) iii) iv)

f) Where in part e) do you see the products you found in part b)? Circle them.

g) Explain why the numbers that are diagonally opposite in a ratio table multiply to the same number, as in part b).

3. Solve the equation.

a) $25x = 100$ b) $4x = 10$ c) $3 = 4(x - 2)$ d) $4 = 3(x - 1)$

$x = 100 \div 25$

$= 4$

The numbers in the **diagonal cells** of a 2 by 2 ratio table multiply to the same number.

You can find a missing number in a ratio table by multiplying the numbers in the diagonal cells. This is called **cross multiplying**.

$x \times 10 = 5 \times 4$

$10x = 20$

x	5
4	10

4. Cross multiply to write an equation for x. Do not solve the equation.

a)

7	3
5	x

$7x = 3 \times 5$

b)

x	2
8	5

____

c)

5	11
2	x

____

d)

4	x
9	3

____

5. Cross multiply to write an equation for x. Then solve the equation.

a)

4	3
6	x

$4x = 3 \times 6$

$= 18$

$x = 18 \div 4 = 4.5$

b)

x	2
9	5

c)

5	11
2	x

d)

4	x
9	3

The equation $\frac{x}{2} = \frac{5}{3}$ shows equality between two fractions or ratios. You can cross multiply to solve it.

6. Cross multiply to solve the equation.

a) $\frac{x}{2} = \frac{5}{3}$

$3x = 10$

$x = 10 \div 3 = \frac{10}{3}$

b) $\frac{6}{5} = \frac{x}{3}$

$18 = 5x$

c) $\frac{x}{2} = \frac{15}{4}$

d) $\frac{7}{2} = \frac{x}{5}$

e) $\frac{\frac{2}{3}x+3}{2} = \frac{12}{5}$

$5\left(\frac{2}{3}x+3\right) = 12 \times 2$

$\frac{10}{3}x + 15 = 24$

$\frac{10}{3}x = 24 - 15 = 9$

$x = 9 \div \frac{10}{3}$

$= \frac{27}{10} = 2.7$

f) $\frac{\frac{x}{2}-1}{7} = \frac{4}{3}$

g) $\frac{\frac{3}{8}x-2}{7} = \frac{21}{4}$

h) $\frac{7}{3} = \frac{0.2x+1}{2.1}$

EE8-47 Applications of Ratios

1. What are you comparing in the ratio? Show with underlines. When you make a ratio table for the question, what will the headings of the table be?

a) There are 8 fluid ounces in a cup. How many cups are in 25 fl oz?

fl oz ________ *cups* ________

b) Ed buys 12 lb of meat for $15.48. How much will 7 lb of the same meat cost?

________ ________

c) There are 5 miles in 8 km. How many kilometers are in 15 miles?

________ ________

d) A car uses 1.4 gallons of gas for 100 km. How much gas is needed to drive 900 km?

________ ________

2. Find the missing number in the ratio table using three different methods.

a) Multiply each number in the row by the same number.

i) (× 2 on each column)

4	6
8	

ii)

5	15
2	

iii)

4	
7	3

b) Multiply by the constant of proportionality.

i) (× 1.5 across each row)

4	6
8	

ii)

5	15
2	

iii)

4	
7	3

c) Write *x* for the missing number, cross multiply, and solve the equation.

d) Compare the methods. Which method is better for which question?

3. Make a ratio table to solve the problem. Use any method to find the missing number in the ratio table.

a) A family saves $85 every 2 weeks. How much will the family save in 6 weeks?

Weeks	Savings ($)
2	85
6	$85 \times 3 = 255$

(× 3 on each column)

b) Bo saves $75 every 2 weeks. He needs to save $1,200. How many weeks of saving is that?

Weeks	Savings ($)

c) Five miles are about 8 km. How many miles are in 24 km? The speed limit on a road is 80 km/h. About how many miles per hour is the speed limit?

d) A car uses 2.3 gallons of gas for 100 miles. How much gas is needed to drive 520 miles? The gas tank of the car can hold 14.2 gallons of gas. Is this enough for the trip?

Percentage problems compare part and whole. 100% is the whole.

Example: 54 is 60% of what number?

Part	Whole
60	100
54	x

4. Fill in the blanks.

a)

Part	Whole
5	?
30	100

_5_ is _30%_ of _?_

b)

Part	Whole
?	18
15	100

_____ is _______ of _____

c)

Part	Whole
25	38
?	100

_____ is _______ of _____

d)

Part	Whole
5	140
?	100

_____ is _______ of _____

e)

Part	Whole
35	?
25.4	100

_____ is _______ of _____

f)

Part	Whole
?	0.9
2.7	100

_____ is _______ of _____

5. Fill in the ratio table.

a) 6 is 30% of x

Part	Whole
6	x
30	*100*

b) x is 50% of 0.78

Part	Whole
	100

c) 4 is 3.5% of x

Part	Whole

d) 4 is x% of 70

Part	Whole

e) 67 is x% of 15

Part	Whole

f) x is 3% of 12.5

Part	Whole

6. Make a ratio table for the problem. Do not solve the problem.

a) If 3 is 12%, what number is 100%?

Part	Whole
3	*?*
12	*100*

b) What percent of 90 is 4?

Part	Whole

c) If 3 is 5%, what number is 100%?

Part	Whole

d) What is 25% of 75?

e) 7 is 21% of what number?

f) What percent of 75 is 12?

You can solve percentage problems by making a ratio table with a variable, and then cross multiplying.

Examples:

What percent of 12 is 3?

Part	Whole
x	100
3	12

$12x = 300$

$x = 300 \div 12 = 25$

3 is 25% of 12.

9 is 2% of what number?

Part	Whole
9	x
2	100

$900 = 2x$

$x = 900 \div 2 = 450$

9 is 2% of 450.

7. Solve the problem by making a ratio table with a variable, and then cross multiplying.

a) What is 90% of 6?

b) 9 is 3% of what number?

c) What percent of 8 is 5?

d) What percent of 25 is $31\frac{1}{4}$?

8. Solve the problem by making a ratio table. Hint: The price is the whole.

a) \$12 is 80% of the price. What is the price?

b) An 8% tax adds \$15 to the price. What is the price?

c) The price is \$12. A tax of 6.25% is added to the price. How much is the tax?

9. a) Tasha pays \$45 for a pair of pants on sale. This is 75% of the original price. What was the original price for the pants?

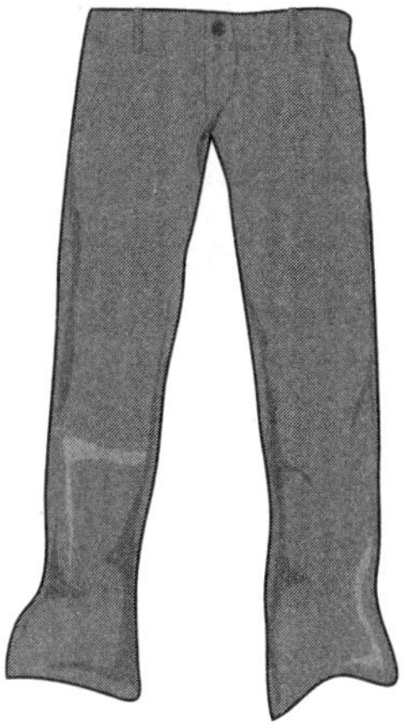

b) Ron buys a coat on sale for \$70. That is 60% of the original price. What was the original price?

c) Alexa gets a 25% discount for a pair of shoes. She pays \$30 less than the original price. What was the initial price of the shoes?

d) Camille pays \$24 for a book with an original price of \$30. What percent of the original price did she pay?

10. A train ticket costs \$8.90.

a) Students get a 10% discount. What percent of the price will a student pay?

b) How much will a student pay for a ticket?

11. Tina buys a shirt with a 30% discount. She pays \$35.70. What was the original price? Hint: What percent of that price did she pay?

12. A night in a hotel costs \$120. Kyle gets a 20% discount. There is 14.5% tax on the price after the discount. How much will Kyle pay?

EE8-48 Comparing Proportional Relationships

1. a) A car travels at a constant speed. Fill in the table to show how far it travels during different time periods.

Time (h)	1	2	3	4
Distance (mi)		110		

b) How far does the car travel in 3 hours? ______

c) The graph shows how far a bus travels in the given time.

How far does the bus travel in 3 hours? ______

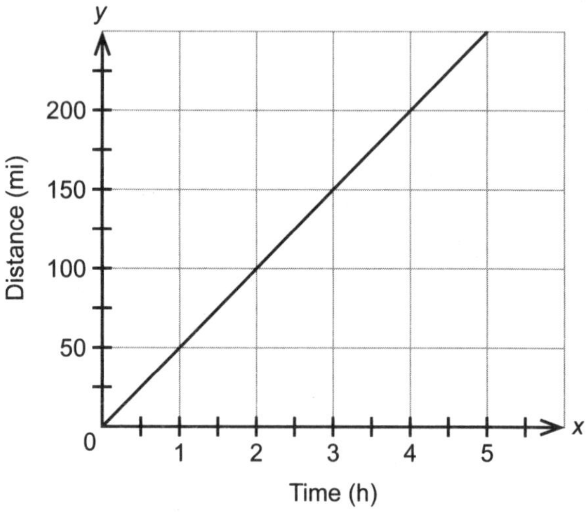

d) Which travels faster: the car or the bus? Explain.

____

____

e) A train travels at a speed of 57 mi/h.

How far does the train travel in 3 hours? ______

f) Order the three means of transportation from the slowest to the fastest. Explain how you did it.

g) How far will the car, the bus, and the train each travel in 5 hours? How do you know?

Bonus ▶ A boat travels d miles in t hours. The equation for the boat's movement is $d = 44t$. Add the boat to your list in part f). Explain your reasoning.

2. a) A carton contains 7 fl oz of Fruity Punch. There are 25 g of sugar in it. Fill in the table.

Volume (fl oz)	Sugar (g)	Ordered Pair

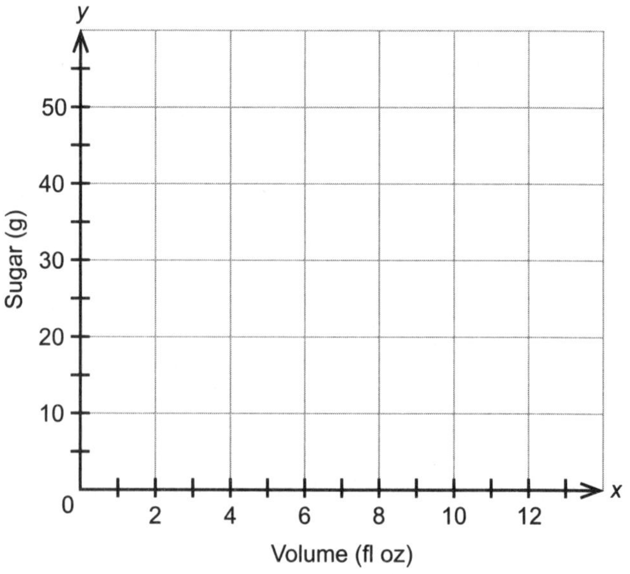

b) Plot the ordered pairs and join the points with a line.

c) There are 19 g of sugar in a 6 fl oz pouch of Tropical Drink. Plot this relationship on the same grid.

d) Which drink has more sugar? How do you know?

e) A doctor recommends limiting the sugar intake of teens to 40 g a day. Is it a good idea to drink two servings of either drink in part a) or part c)? Explain.

3. The graph shows the cost of orange juice.

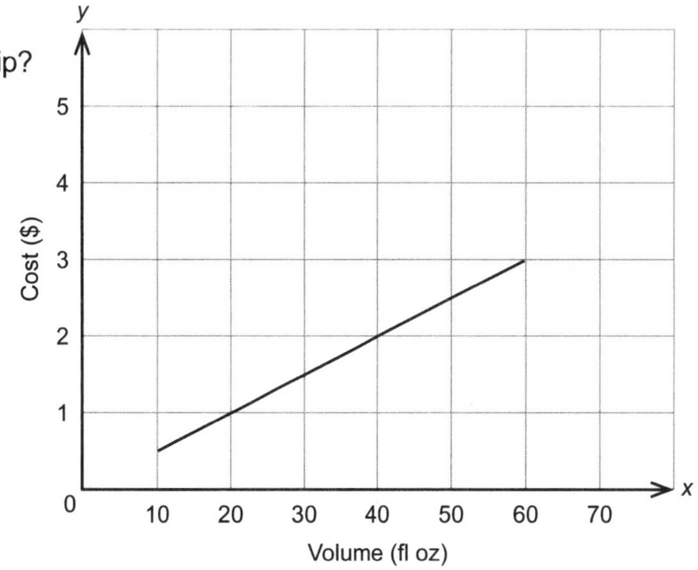

a) Does the graph show a proportional relationship? How do you know? Hint: Extend the graph.

____

____

b) Mark two points on the graph. Fill in the table for these points.

Volume (fl oz)	Cost ($)

c) Is the table in part b) a ratio table? Explain.

d) Find the unit rate for the table.

e) Tomato juice costs $3 for a 40 fl oz bottle. Which juice is cheaper by volume? Explain using unit rates.

f) Make a graph for the cost of tomato juice. Which juice is cheaper by volume? Explain using graphs.

4. Abdul wants to invest $10,000.

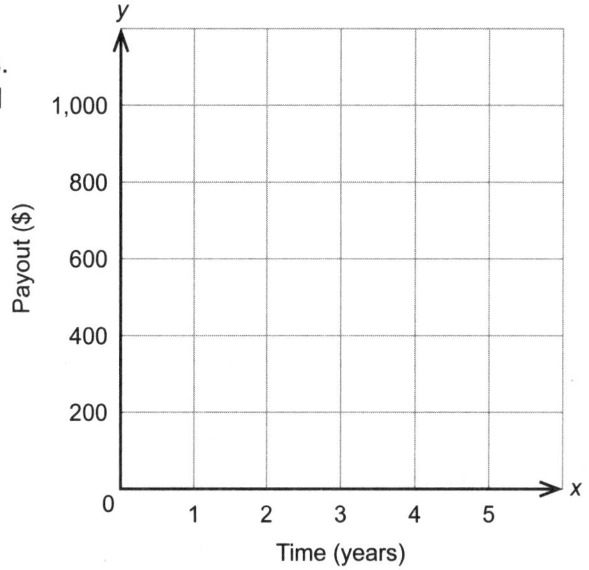

a) Program A will earn 2% interest each year for 5 years. The interest is paid every year, and Abdul will not add the interest into the investment.

Plot the points showing the total interest earned after each year. Join the points with a line and label the line.

b) Program B will earn $550 every 2.5 years. Abdul will not add the interest into the investment.

Graph the interest earned after 5 years. Join the points with a line and label the line.

c) Compare programs A and B. Which one would you prefer? Explain.

Bonus ▶ If you were to invest $10,000 for 10 years, which of the two programs would you prefer?

F8-1 Functions as Machines

1. For each input, find the output.

a) **Input:** 3

Times 2

Output: 6

Input	Output
3	*6*
2	
−5	
0	

b) **Input:** 3

Add 2

Output: 5

Input	Output
3	*5*
0	
7	
−4	

c) **Input:** 1

Subtract the input from 10

Output: 9

Input	Output
1	*9*
2	
3	
4	

d) **Input:** Sam

The first letter of the name

Output: S

Input	Output
Sam	*S*
Megan	
Kim	
John	

e) **Input:** 1

Divide 12 by the input

Output: 12

Input	Output
1	*12*
2	
3	
4	

f) **Input:** 2

Square the input

Output: 4

Input	Output
2	*4*
3	
−2	
0	

g) **Input:** triangle

The number of sides in the shape

Output: 3

Input	Output
triangle	*3*
rectangle	
hexagon	
rhombus	

h) **Input:** 1

Multiply by 2, then add 1

Output: 3

Input	Output
1	*3*
2	
3	
4	

i) **Input:** −2

Absolute value of the input

Output: 2

Input	Output
−2	*2*
1.7	
0	
2	

A machine has *exactly* one output for each input.

Examples:

Input: 3

2 more than the input

Output: 5

This is a machine.

Input: 3

2 away from the input

Output: 1 or 5?

This is not a machine.

2. Test with any input number to see if the picture shows a machine. Circle the machines.

a) 3 less than the input

b) 1 away from the input

c) Square of the input

d) Half of the input

e) Absolute value of the input

f) The input's classmate

A **function** is a machine—it assigns exactly one output to each input.

Example: The machine on the right is a function.

Input: 3

Double the input

Output: 6

3. Write the rule, then find the output for each input in the table.

a) **Input:** 3

Add 2 to the input

Output: 5

Rule: *add 2*

Input	Output
3	*5*
4	
0	
−2	

b) **Input:** 5

Square the input

Output: 25

Rule: ____________

Input	Output
5	*25*
3	
0	
−3	

c) **Input:** 2

Multiply the input by 2, then add 1

Output: 5

Rule: ____________

Input	Output
2	*5*
4	
−4	
0	

F8-2 Tables and Functions

Sally makes a table for a function with the following rule: Subtract 3 from the input.

The inputs are the first four prime numbers.

This is an example of a **function table**, because each input in the table has exactly one output.

Input	Output
2	−1
3	0
5	2
7	4

1. a) Circle the table if it is not a function table.

i)

Input	Output
−2	3
1	6
2	7
4	9

ii)

Input	Output
0	2
1	3
2	4
2	5

iii)

Input	Output
1	2
2	−3
3	1
4	1

iv)

Input	Output
0	0
1	3
2	6
3	9

v)

Input	Output
5	1
3	−2
2	2
3	3

vi)

Input	Output
1	−1
2	0
3	4
3	2^2

b) Explain why part iii) is a function table. ______________________________

c) In part vi) above, does the input 3 have more than one output? Is part vi) a function table?

2. Apply the rule to fill in the missing inputs or outputs in the function table.

a) Rule: Multiply by 3

Input	Output
−1	*−3*
0	
1	
2	

b) Rule: Divide by 2

Input	Output
4	*2*
10	
6	
−2	

c) Rule: Multiply by 2, then add 1

Input	Output
−2	
0	
1	
2	

d) Rule: Divide by −3

Input	Output
6	
	1
	0
−9	

e) Rule: Add −0.5

Input	Output
3	*2.5*
	2
−3	
	−2

f) Rule: Divide by 5, then add 2

Input	Output
5	
10	
−5	
−10	

3. The function was made by addition, subtraction, multiplication, or division. Find the rule.

a)

Input	Output
0	1
1	2
2	3
3	4

Rule: ____________________

b)

Input	Output
1	10
3	30
5	50
7	70

Rule: ____________________

c)

Input	Output
−2	−1
0	0
2	1
4	2

Rule: ____________________

d)

Input	Output
5	1
10	6
15	11
20	16

Rule: ____________________

e)

Input	Output
1	0.5
2	1.5
3	2.5
4	3.5

Rule: ____________________

f)

Input	Output
1	4
2	3
3	2
4	1

Rule: ____________________

4. Find the rule, then complete the function table.

a) Rule: ____________________

Input	Output
1	4
2	8
3	12
4	
5	
6	

b) Rule: ____________________

Input	Output
1	−3
2	−2
3	−1
4	
5	
6	

c) Rule: ____________________

Input	Output
1	1
2	4
3	9
4	
5	
6	

d) Rule: ____________________

Input	Output
1	0.5
2	1
3	1.5
4	
5	
6	

e) Rule: ____________________

Input	Output
1	−1
2	−2
3	−3
4	
5	
6	

Bonus ▶ Rule: ____________________

Input	Output
one	2
two	1
three	2
four	2
five	
six	

5. Make a function table for the rule, "Double the input, then add 3" using the inputs 0, 1, 2, and 3.

F8-3 Sequences and Functions

1. Extend the sequence. Start by finding the gap (the difference between each number and the next).

   a) 5 (+4) 9 (+4) 13 (+4) *17* , ____ , ____

   b) 12 , 21 , 30 , ____ , ____ , ____

   c) 45 (−3) 42 , 39 , ____ , ____ , ____

   d) 83 , 77 , 71 , ____ , ____ , ____

   e) 14 , 18.5 , 23 , ____ , ____ , ____

   f) 35 , 32.5 , 30 , ____ , ____ , ____

   g) 10 , 10 , 10 , ____ , ____ , ____

   h) 5 , 0 , −5 , ____ , ____ , ____

   i) 12 , 31 , 50 , ____ , ____ , ____

   j) 104 , 89 , 74 , ____ , ____ , ____

2. Extend the sequence using the given rule.

   a) Add 11: 2, 13, ____, ____, ____

   b) Subtract 7: 52, 45, ____, ____, ____

   c) Add −5: 32, 27, ____, ____, ____

   d) Multiply by −1: 6, −6, ____, ____, ____

   e) Subtract 1.5: 9, ____, ____, ____

   f) Add $\frac{1}{3}$: 1, $1\frac{1}{3}$, ____, ____, ____

   g) Add 3.5: 52, ____, ____, ____

   h) Subtract −3: 11, 14, ____, ____, ____

   i) Add 0.7: 2, 2.7, ____, ____, ____

   j) Double: 1, 2, ____, ____, ____

> Look at the sequence: 1, 3, 5, 7, 9, 11, 13, 15, 17
>
> The first term is 1, the second term is 3, the third term is 5, and so on.

3. Find the given term in the sequence in the box above.

   a) The 4th term is ________.

   b) The 9th term is ________.

   c) The 6th term is ________.

   d) The 7th term is ________.

4. The first term of a sequence is 1. The second term is also 1, and every other term is the sum of the two previous terms. Write the first 6 terms of the sequence.

   Bonus ▶ Is 144 in the sequence?

The position of a term in a sequence is called the **term number**.

Example: 2, 4, 6, 8, 10, 12, 14, 16, 18

10 is the 5th term in this sequence, so the term number of 10 is 5.

5. A function inputs term numbers and outputs this sequence:
5, 8, 11, 14, 17, 20, 23, 24, 27, 30, 33, 36, 39

For the given term number (the input), write the output.

5 → *17*   8 → ____   4 → ____   9 → ____   11 → ____

6. Make a table for the sequence.

a) 2, 5, 8, 11, 14

Term Number	Output
1	*2*
2	*5*
3	*8*
4	
5	

b) 17.5, 15, 12.5, 10, 7.5

Term Number	Output
1	*17.5*
2	
3	
4	
5	

c) 73, 61, 41, 50, 51

Term Number	Output
1	*73*
2	
3	
4	
5	

7. Circle the tables in Question 6 that are function tables. Are all of them function tables? ____ Explain why. ____________________

A **sequence table** is a special kind of function table with term numbers as inputs: 1, 2, 3, 4, and so on. You can think of the sequence as a set of ordered pairs (Term Number, Term).

Example: **2**, **5**, **8**, **11**, **14** ⟶ (1, **2**), (2, **5**), (3, **8**), (4, **11**), (5, **14**)

Any set of ordered pairs is called a **relation**.

8. Change the sequence into a set of ordered pairs.

a) 1, 3, 5, 7, 9

(1, 1), (2, 3), (3, 5), (4, 7), (5, 9)

b) 2, 4, 6, 8, 10

(1,), (2,), (3,), (4,), (5,)

c) 4, 7, 10, 13, 16

d) 3, 7, 11, 15, 19

9. Change the set of ordered pairs into a sequence of numbers.

a) (1, 0), (2, 4), (3, 8), (4, 12), (5, 16)

b) (1, 17), (2, 11), (3, 9), (4, 4), (5, 1)

c) (1, 2), (2, 3), (3, 4), (4, 3), (5, 2)

d) (1, 5), (2, 9), (3, 5), (4, 9), (5, 5), (6, 9), (7, 5), (8, 9)

10. a) The pairs are not in order. Reorder them so that the first numbers are in order.

i) (4, 4), (6, 2), (2, 9), (3, 6), (1, 10), (5, 3)

ii) (4, 7), (2, 6), (5, 6), (1, 2), (6, 5), (3, 8)

iii) (2, 4), (5, 7), (4, 4), (1, 7), (6, 4), (3, 7), (7, 7)

iv) (3, 7), (5, 9), (1, 5), (6, 10), (4, 8), (2, 6)

b) Match each sequence in part a) to a description below.

increases, then decreases ______

increases by the same amount ______

repeats ______

decreases by different amounts ______

> Remember: A function assigns exactly one output to each input. You can think of a function as a set of ordered pairs (input, output) in which no input has more than one output.
>
> Examples: (1, 3), (2, 6), (3, 9), (4, 12) — This is a function.
>
> (1, 5), (2, 6), (2, 7), (3, 9) — This is not a function.

11. Make a table for the set of ordered pairs. Do the ordered pairs represent a function?

a) (1, 2), (2, 3), (2, 4), (3, 5), (4, 6), (5, 7)

Input	Output
1	*2*
2	*3, 4*
3	*5*
4	*6*
5	*7*

not a function

b) (1, 1), (2, 2), (3, 3), (4, 4), (5, 5)

Input	Output
1	
2	
3	
4	
5	

____

c) (1, −3), (3, 2), (2, 3), (5, 2), (4, 11)

Input	Output
1	
2	
3	
4	
5	

____

d) (2, 3), (1, 2), (3, 4), (4, 5), (5, 6), (3, 1)

Input	Output
1	
2	
3	
4	
5	

____

e) (1, 5), (2, 5), (3, 5), (4, 5), (5, 5)

f) (1, 1), (3, 4), (2, 0), (5, 7), (3, 2), (4, 3)

F8-4 Functions and Mapping Diagrams

1. For the set of ordered pairs, draw arrows between the corresponding input and output.

a) (1, 2), (2, 4), (3, 3), (4, 5), (5, 1)

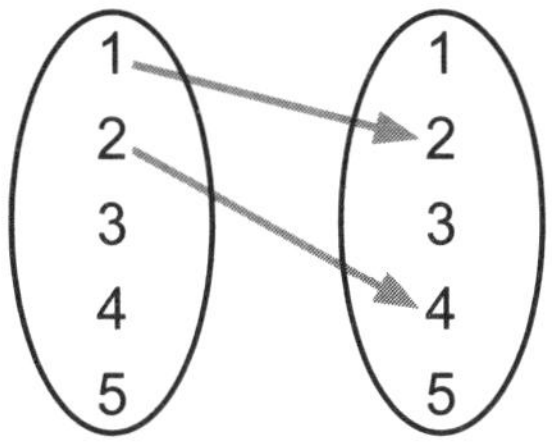

b) (1, 3), (2, 4), (1, 4), (4, 6), (6, 2)

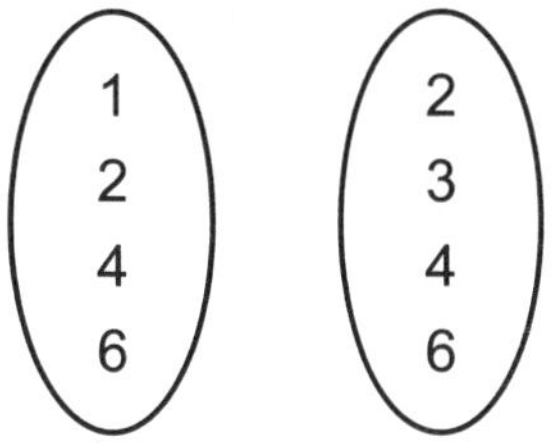

c) (1, 2), (2, 3), (3, 4), (4, 3), (5, 2)

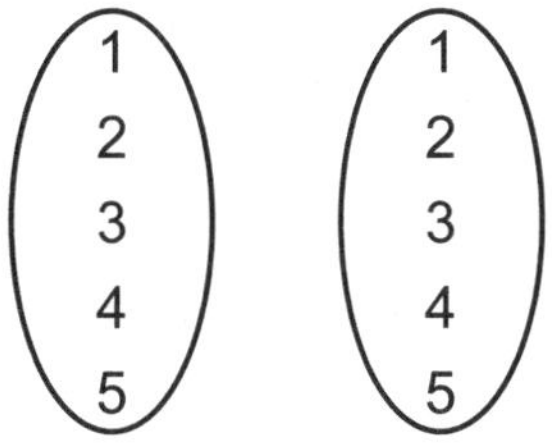

d) (1, 4), (2, 7), (3, 4), (4, 7), (5, 4)

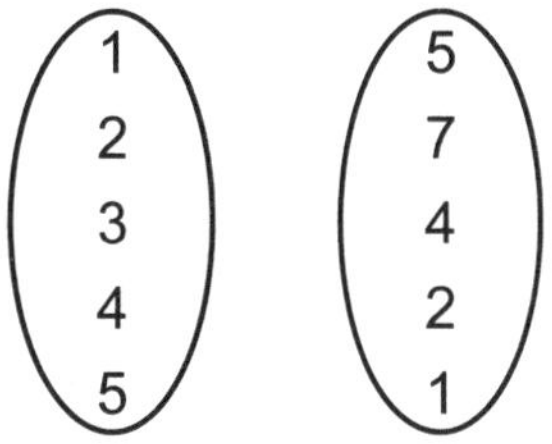

e) (1, −1), (2, −2), (3, −3), (4, −4), (5, −5)

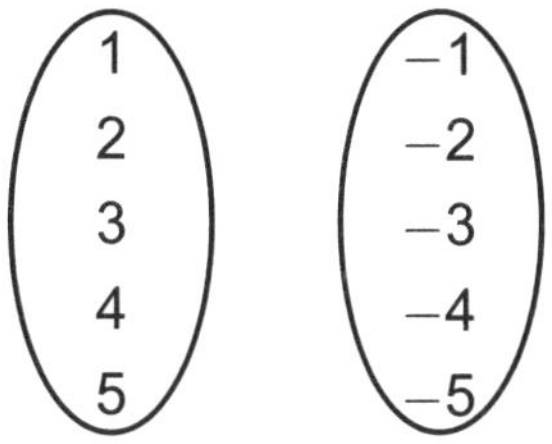

f) (1, a), (2, w), (9, w), (4, p), (6, n)

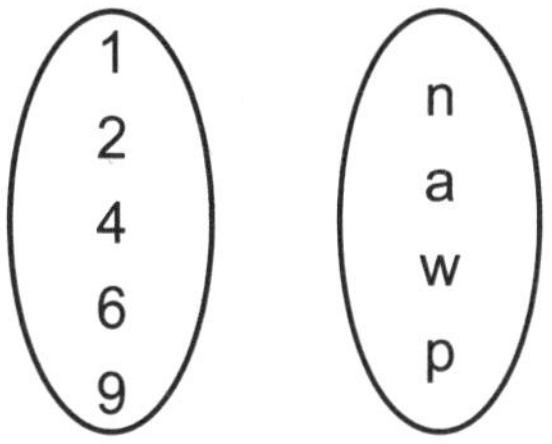

To draw a **mapping diagram** from a table of inputs and outputs, write all the different inputs on the left and all the different outputs on the right.

Then draw arrows between the corresponding input and output.

Input	Output
1	3
7	21
10	30
20	60

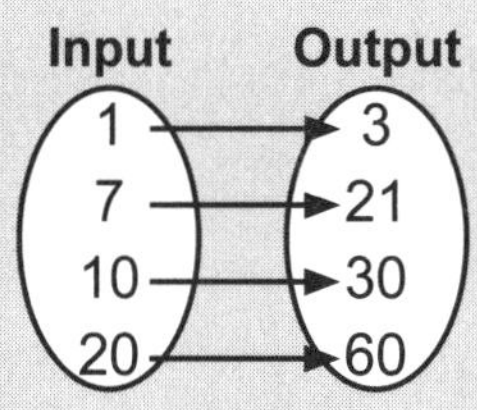

2. Draw a mapping diagram for the table.

a)

Input	Output
1	2
2	3
3	4
4	5

b)

Input	Output
1	1
2	0
3	1
4	0

c)

Input	Output
New York	USA
Paris	France
Boston	USA
Toronto	Canada

d)

Input	Output
Europe	UK
Europe	Italy
Asia	India
Africa	Nigeria

You can use a diagram to show any relation.

Example: (1, 5), (3, 2), (5, −1), (−1, −1), (3, 6)

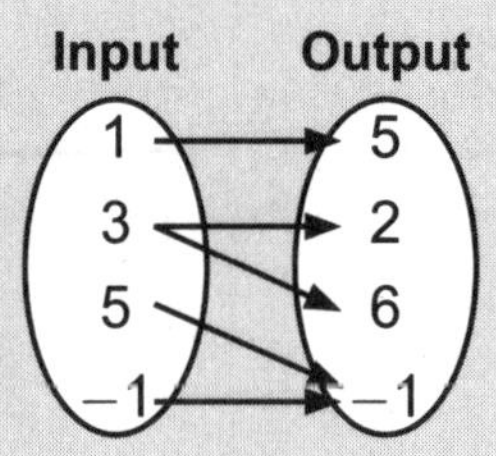

3. Draw a diagram for the relation.

a) (1, 2), (2, 4), (3, 6), (4, 8), (5, 10)

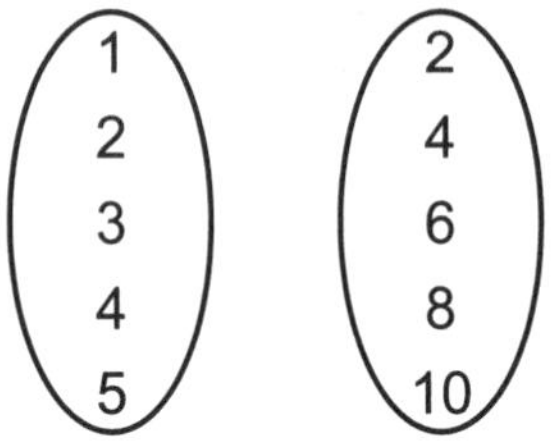

b) (1, 3), (2, 4), (1, 4), (4, 6), (6, 2)

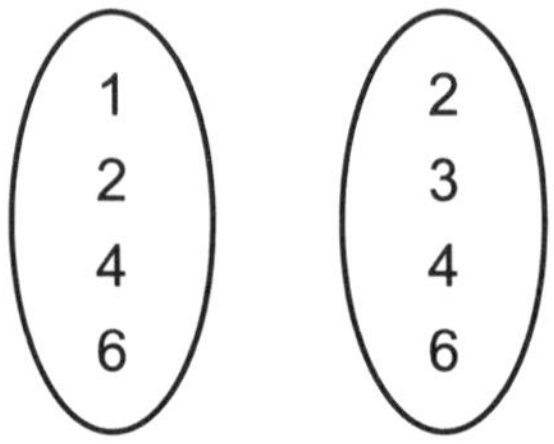

c) (1, 2), (2, 3), (3, 4), (4, 3), (5, 2)

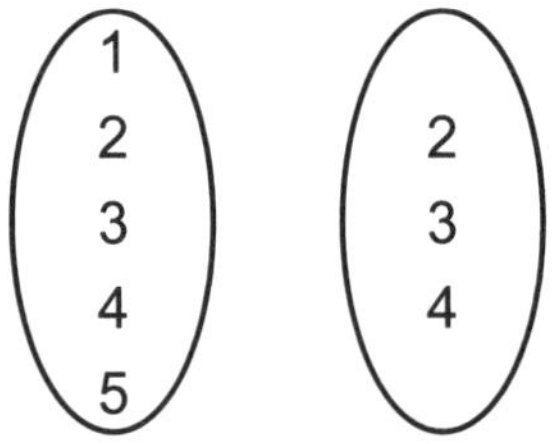

d) (1, 4), (2, 7), (3, 4), (4, 7), (5, 4)

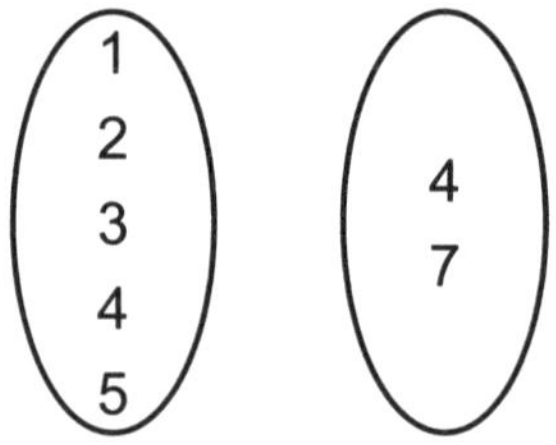

e) (1, 2), (2, 4), (3, 3), (4, 5), (5, 1)

f) (1, 3), (2, 4), (9, 4), (4, 6), (2, 5)

To determine if a diagram represents a function, check if more than one arrow goes from one input. If an input has more than one corresponding output, then the diagram does not represent a function.

Examples:

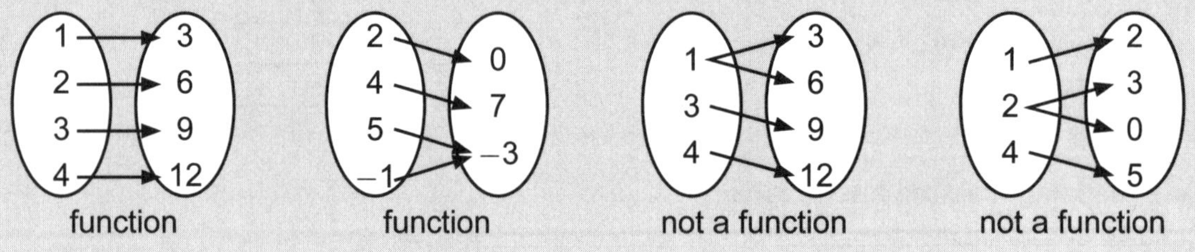

4. Circle the diagrams that represent a function.

A.

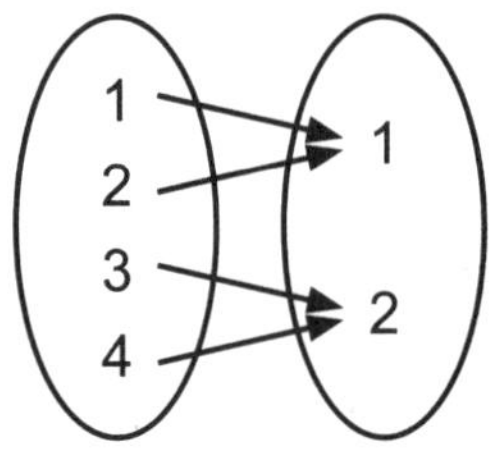

B.

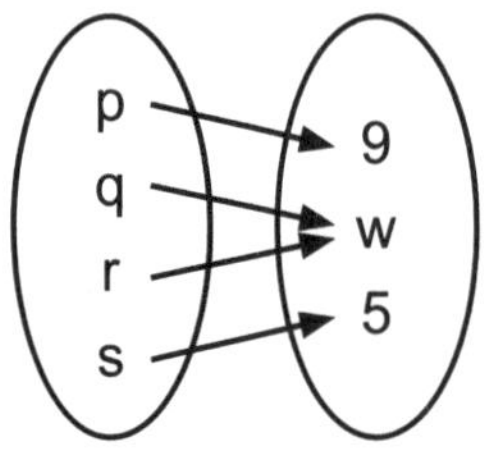

C.

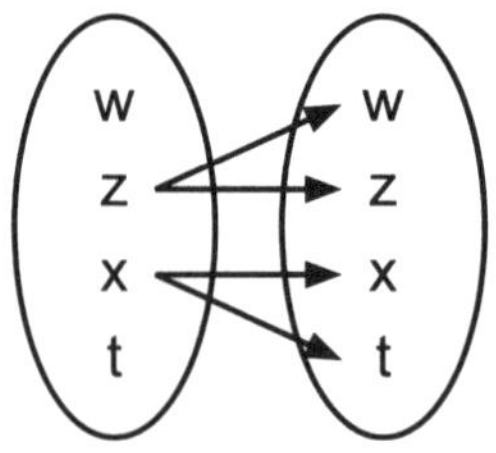

D.

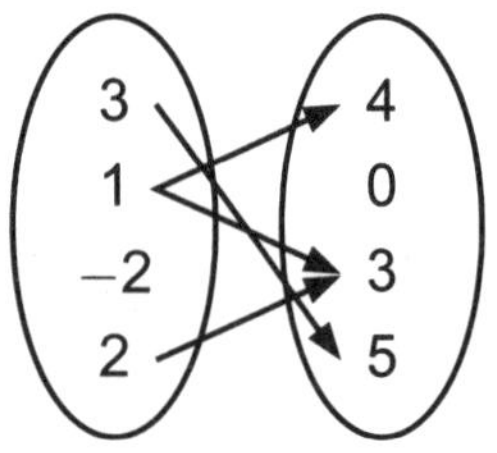

5. Which diagrams in Question 3 represent a function? ______________________

F8-5 Sequences and Graphs

To graph a sequence:

Step 1: Make a list of ordered pairs.

2, **4**, **6**, **8**, **10**

↓

(1, **2**), (2, **4**), (3, **6**), (4, **8**), (5, **10**)

Step 2: Plot the ordered pairs on a graph.

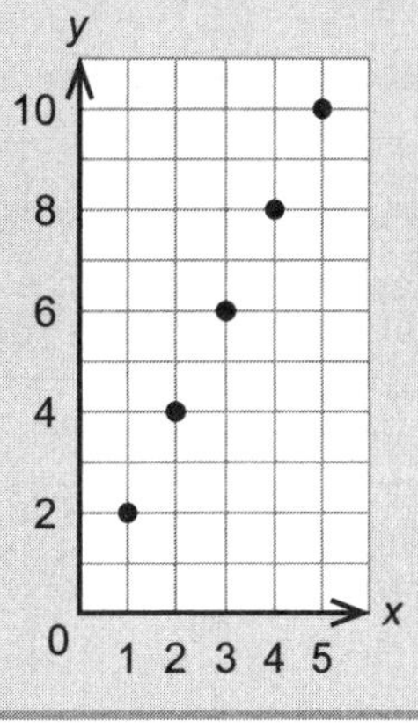

1. a) Graph the sequence of numbers by first making a list of ordered pairs.

i) 1, 4, 6, 12

(1,   ), (2,   ), (3,   ), (4,   )

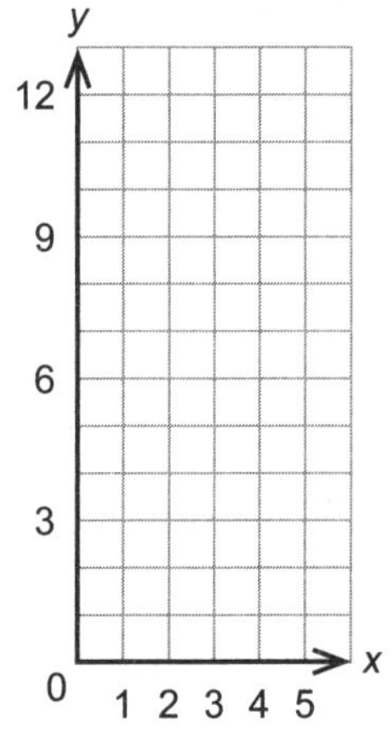

ii) 3, 6, 9, 12

(1,   ), (2,   ), (3,   ), (4,   )

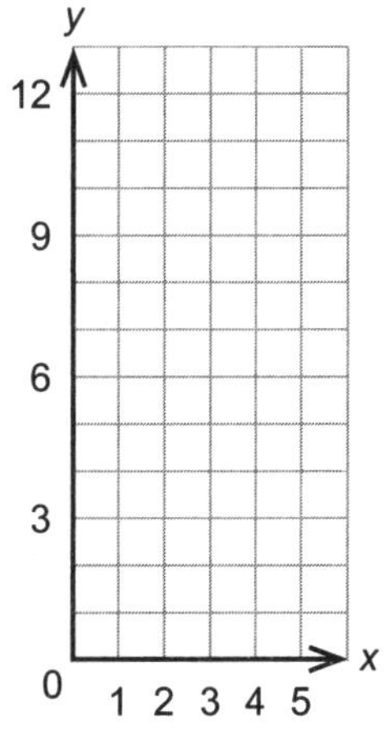

iii) 1, 4, 7, 10

(1,   ), (2,   ), (3,   ), (4,   )

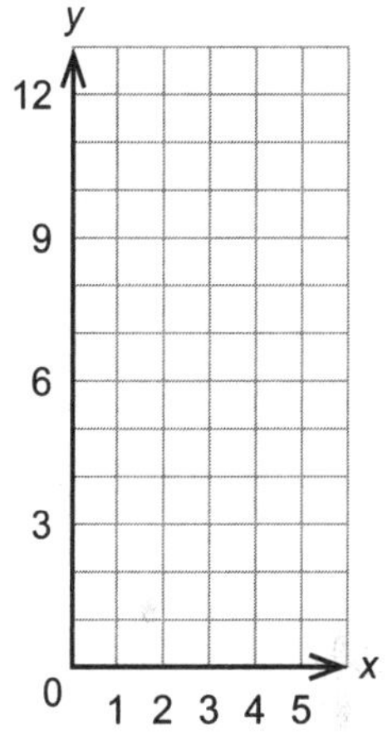

iv) 2, 3, 4, 9

(1,   ), (2,   ), (3,   ), (4,   )

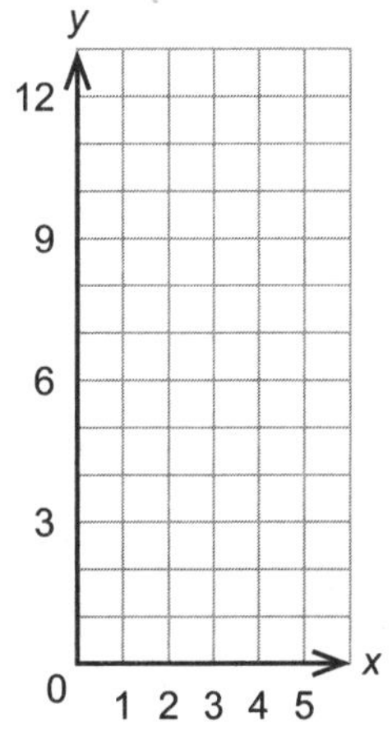

v) 11, 9, 7, 5

(1,   ), (2,   ), (3,   ), (4,   )

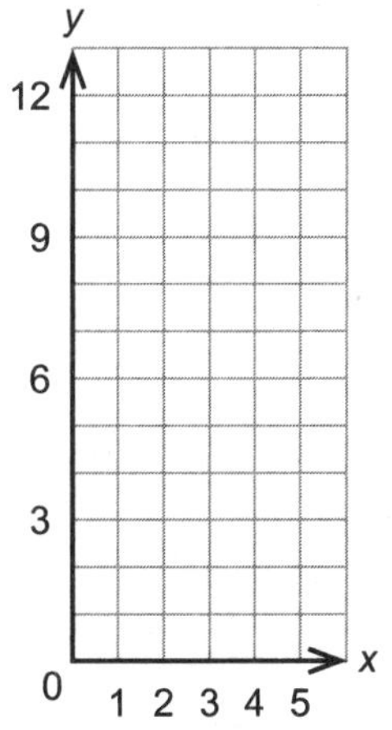

vi) 12, 10, 8, 4

(1,   ), (2,   ), (3,   ), (4,   )

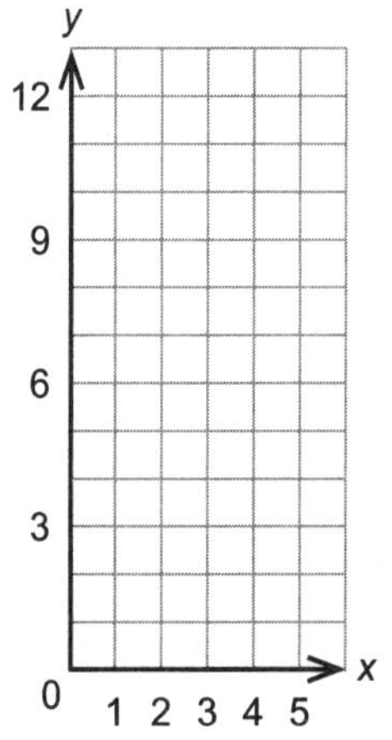

b) Look at your graphs from part a). Can the points be joined by a straight line?

i) ______ ii) ______ iii) ______ iv) ______ v) ______ vi) ______

A sequence is **linear** if plotting the points on a graph and joining them make a straight line.
If a sequence is not linear, we call it **nonlinear**.

Examples:

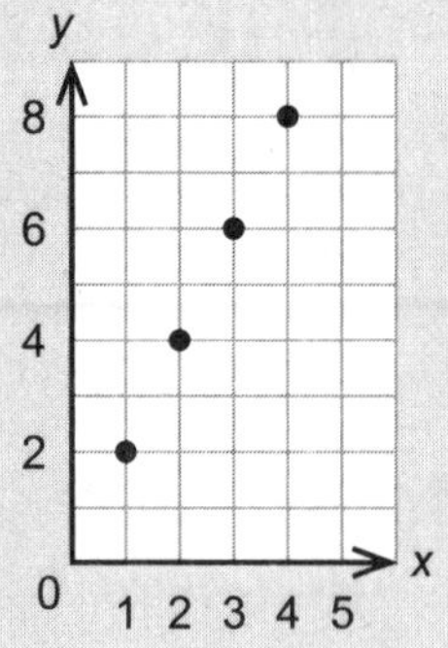

2, 4, 6, 8 is a linear sequence.

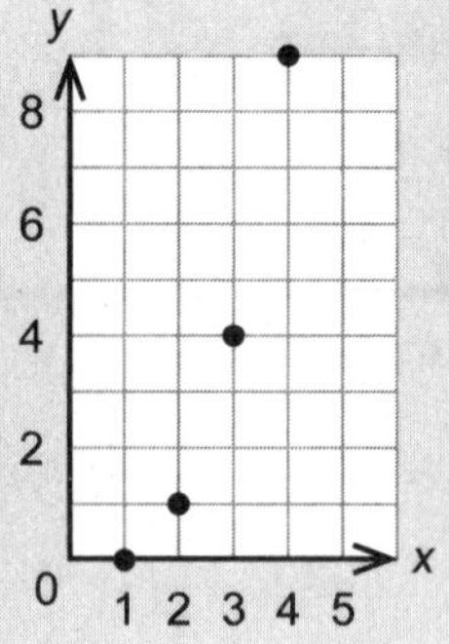

0, 1, 4, 9 is a nonlinear sequence.

2. a) For the sequence table, find the gaps between the terms.

i)

Term Number	Term
1	3
2	5
3	7
4	9

ii)

Term Number	Term
1	10
2	7
3	4
4	1

iii)

Term Number	Term
1	1
2	4
3	9
4	10

b) Plot the ordered pairs from each table in part a) on a graph.

i)

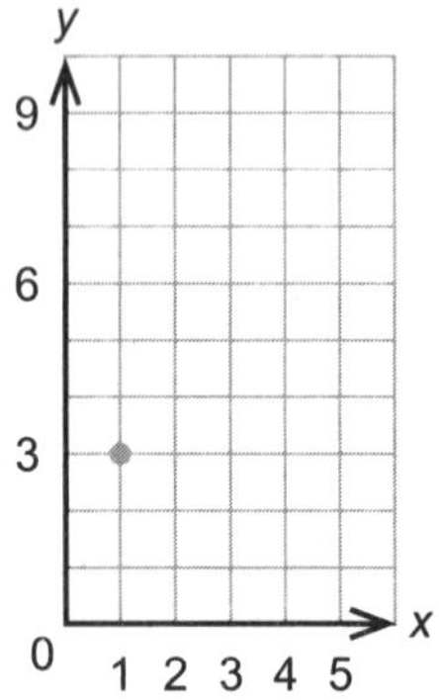

ii)

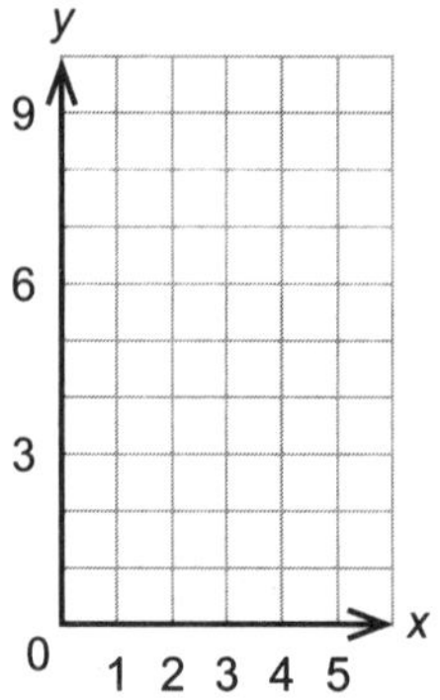

iii)

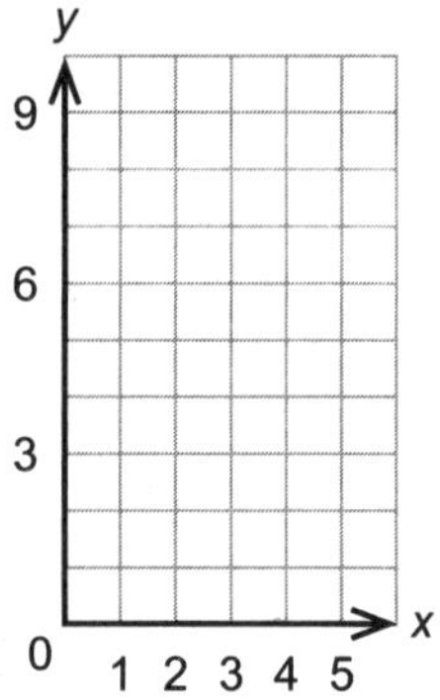

c) Which sequences from part a) are linear?

d) Which sequences from part a) have a gap that is always the same?

e) What do you notice from parts c) and d)?

REMINDER: In an **increasing sequence**, each number is greater than the one before it.
In a **decreasing sequence**, each number is less than the one before it.

3. a) Write the sequence for each table in Question 2, part a).

b) Which sequences from part a) are increasing?

c) Which sequences from part a) always have a positive gap?

d) What do you notice from parts b) and c)?

4. On grid paper, graph the increasing sequence.

a) 5, 7, 9, 11 b) 2, 3, 7, 9 c) 1, 4, 9, 16

5. On grid paper, graph the decreasing sequence.

a) 12, 8, 4, 0 b) 11, 5, 3, 2 c) 15, 12, 7, 0

6. Write if the graph represents an increasing, decreasing, and/or linear sequence.

a)
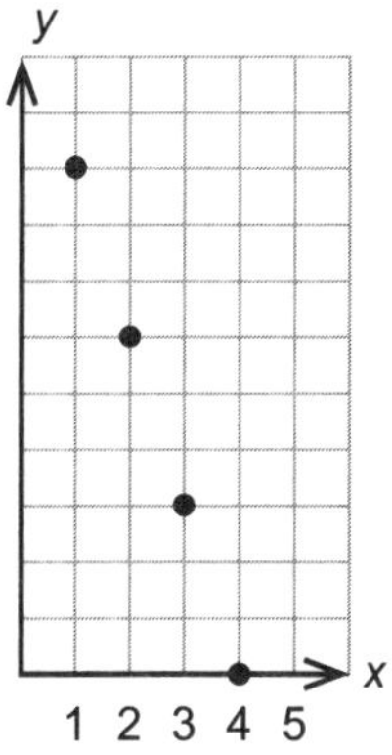

decreasing linear

b)
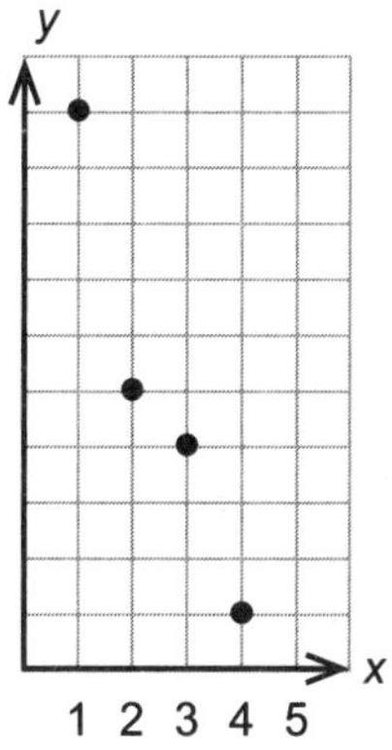

____

c)
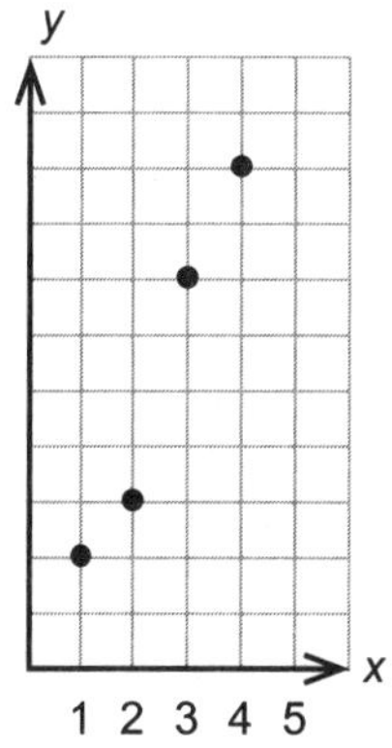

____

When the gap is ...	always positive	always negative	always the same
The sequence is ...	increasing	decreasing	linear

7. Find the gap and write the correct description for the sequence table.

a)

Term Number	Term
1	9
2	7
3	5
4	3

Gaps: −2, −2, −2

decreasing linear

b)

Term Number	Term
1	2
2	5
3	6
4	8

____

c)

Term Number	Term
1	0
2	2
3	4
4	6

____

d)

Term Number	Term
1	1
2	2
3	3
4	4

____

e)

Term Number	Term
1	1
2	4
3	9
4	16

____

f)

Term Number	Term
1	5
2	3
3	1
4	0

____

F8-6 Functions and Algebra

1. Evaluate the expressions for each value of x.

x	$3x - 1$	$2x + 3$	$2x - 1$
1	$3x - 1 = 3(1) - 1$ $= 3 - 1$ $= 2$		
2	$= 3(2) - 1$ $=$ $=$		
3			
4			

Mathematicians usually use the variable x for the input and y for the output.

Example: In this set of ordered pairs (x, y), for each value of x, there is exactly one output. $y = 2x + 1$ represents the **rule** of the **function**.

x	$y = 2x + 1$
1	3
2	5
3	7
4	9

2. Complete the function table.

a)

x	$y = x - 1$
1	
2	
3	
4	

b)

x	$y = -x + 2$
1	
2	
3	
4	

c)

x	$y = \frac{1}{2}x$
1	
2	
3	
4	

d)

x	$y = 4$
1	
2	
3	
4	

e)

x	$y = -2x$
1	
2	
3	
4	

f)

x	$y = x^2$
1	
2	
3	
4	

3. Finish the function table, write the ordered pairs, and plot the ordered pairs on the graph.

a)

x	$2x + 2$
1	
2	
3	
4	

(1,   ), (2,   ), (3,   ), (4,   )

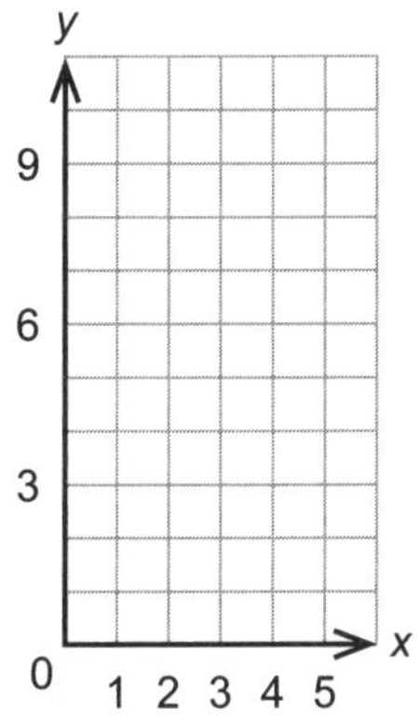

b)

x	$3x - 2$
1	
2	
3	
4	

(1,   ), (2,   ), (3,   ), (4,   )

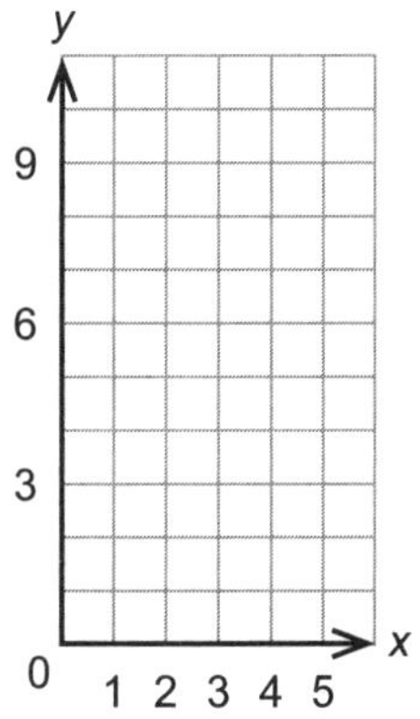

c)

x	$-3x + 13$
1	
2	
3	
4	

(1,   ), (2,   ), (3,   ), (4,   )

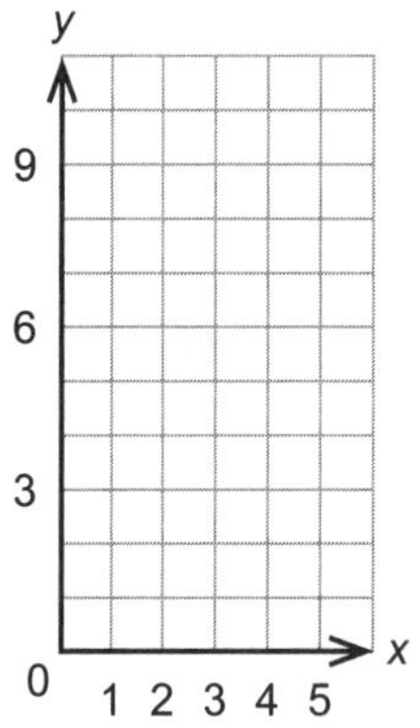

d)

x	$-2x + 3$
1	
2	
3	
4	

(1,   ), (2,   ), (3,   ), (4,   )

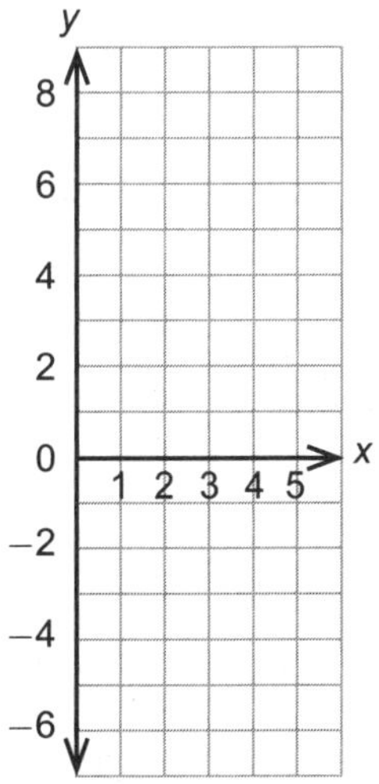

e)

x	$0.5x + 2$
1	
2	
3	
4	

(1,   ), (2,   ), (3,   ), (4,   )

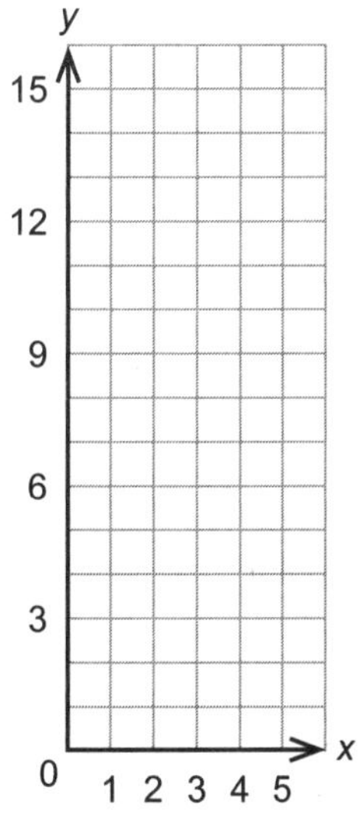

f)

x	$x^2 - 1$
1	
2	
3	
4	

(1,   ), (2,   ), (3,   ), (4,   )

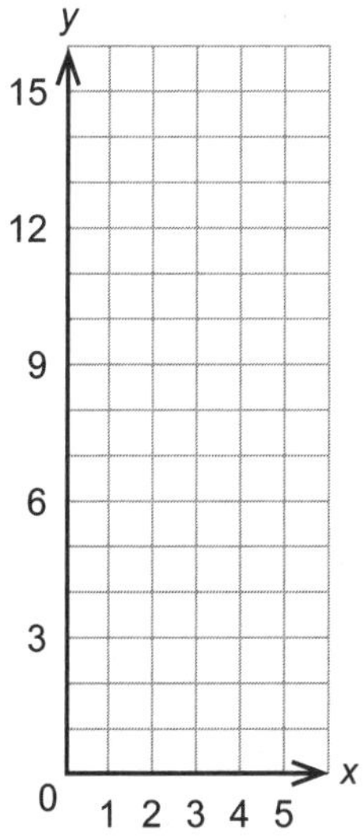

4. a) Determine the coefficient of x. Remember, a coefficient is a number used to multiply a variable. Fill in the table using the equation. Find the gap.

i) $y = 2x + 1$

x	y	
1	*3*	
2	*5*	*+2*
3		
4		

coefficient of x = __2__

gap = __+2__

ii) $y = 2x - 1$

x	y
1	
2	
3	
4	

coefficient of x = ______

gap = ______

iii) $y = -2x + 5$

x	y
1	
2	
3	
4	

coefficient of x = ______

gap = ______

iv) $y = \frac{1}{2}x + 1$

x	y
1	*1.5*
2	*2*
3	
4	

coefficient of x = ______

gap = ______

v) $y = -0.5x + 1$

x	y
1	
2	
3	
4	

coefficient of x = ______

gap = ______

vi) $y = -3x - 2$

x	y
1	
2	
3	
4	

coefficient of x = ______

gap = ______

b) Where do you see the gap in the expression? ____________________

5. a) Plot each function table in Question 4.a) on a graph. Use grid paper to for parts iv), v), and vi).

i)

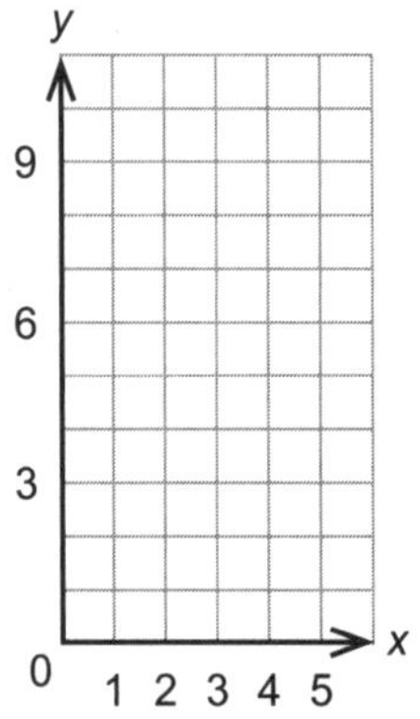

ii)

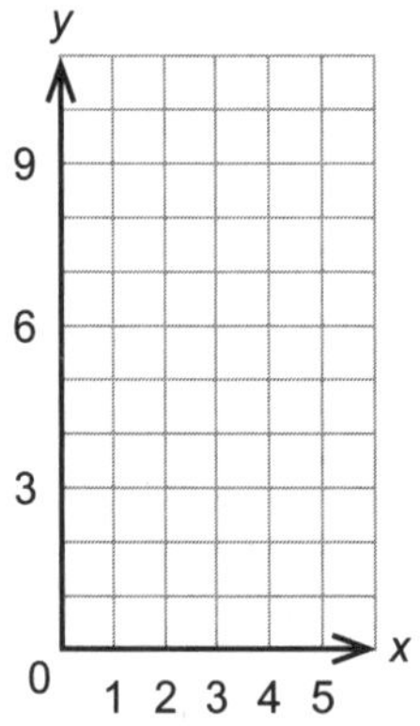

iii)

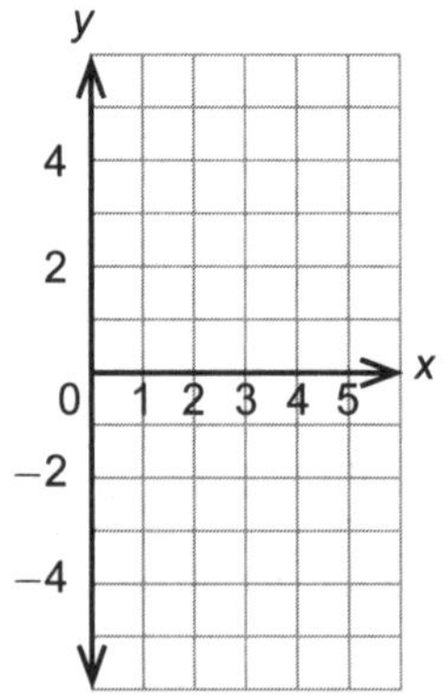

b) Which graphs from part a) are increasing? ________ Which have a positive coefficient? ________

c) Which graphs from part a) are decreasing? ________ Which have a negative coefficient? ________

d) How can you tell from the coefficient if the graph is increasing or decreasing? ____________________

____

F8-7 Formulas for Tables

1. Use the gap to complete the table.

a)

Input	Output
1	3
2	
3	
4	

Gaps: +2, +2, +2

b)

Input	Output
1	4
2	
3	
4	

Gaps: +2, +2, +2

c)

Input	Output
1	5
2	
3	
4	

Gaps: −3, −3, −3

d)

Input	Output
1	1
2	
3	
4	

Gaps: +4, +4, +4

2. a) Use the rule to fill in the table. Find the gap between outputs.

i) Rule: Multiply by 3 and add 1

Input	Output
1	
2	
3	
4	

gap = ______

ii) Rule: Multiply by 0.5 and add 2

Input	Output
1	
2	
3	
4	

gap = ______

iii) Rule: Multiply by −2 and add 10

Input	Output
1	
2	
3	
4	

gap = ______

iv) Rule: Multiply by 0 and subtract 4

Input	Output
1	
2	
3	
4	

gap = ______

b) Compare the gap and the rule for each table in part a). What do you notice?

____

____

To find the rule for how to get the output from the input:

Step 1: Find the gap between the numbers in the Output column.

Input (n)	$n \times$ gap	Output
1		5
2		8
3		11

(+3) (+3)

Step 2: Multiply each Input by the gap.

Input (n)	$n \times$ gap	Output
1	3	5
2	6	8
3	9	11

(+3) (+3)

Step 3: What must you add (or subtract) to each number in the second column to get the output?

Input (n)	$n \times$ gap	Output
1	3	5
2	6	8
3	9	11

(+3) (+3)

Add 2

Step 4: Write the rule for the table. Rule: Multiply the input by 3, then add 2.

3. Use the steps above to find the rule for the table.

a)

Input (n)	$n \times$ gap	Output
1		11
2		15
3		19

Add ______

Rule: Multiply by ______, then add ______.

b)

Input (n)	$n \times$ gap	Output
1		5
2		7
3		9

Add ______

Rule: Multiply by ______, then add ______.

c)

Input (n)	$n \times$ gap	Output
1		2
2		5
3		8

Subtract ______

Rule: Multiply by ______, then subtract ______.

d)

Input (n)	$n \times$ gap	Output
1		4
2		10
3		16

Subtract ______

Rule: Multiply by ______, then subtract ______.

4. Write the sequence for each table in Question 3.

a) *11, 15, 19*

b)

c)

d)

Which sequences are increasing? ______________________________

5. Use the gap in the sequence to find the coefficient in the formula. Then complete the chart to finish writing the formula.

a)

Input (n)	$n \times$ gap	Output
1	*5*	2
2	*10*	7
3	*15*	12
4	*20*	17

Gaps: *+5*, *+5*, *+5*

−3

Formula: *5n − 3*

b)

Input (n)	$n \times$ gap	Output
1		1
2		4
3		7
4		10

Formula: ____________________

c)

Input (n)	$n \times$ gap	Output
1		3
2		7
3		11
4		15

Formula: ____________________

d)

Input (n)	$n \times$ gap	Output
1		9
2		15
3		21
4		27

Formula: ____________________

> Once you know the gap—and hence the coefficient—you really only need to see how the first term compares to the gap in order to find the formula.
>
> Example: In Question 5.a), the gap is 5 and the first output is 2, so the formula is $5n - 3$.

6. Find the gaps in the sequence. Then write the formula for the sequence.

a) 3, 5, 7, 9

Formula: ____________

b) 9, 20, 31, 42

Formula: ____________

c) 12, 17, 22, 27

Formula: ____________

d) 2, 3.5, 5, 6.5

e) 53, 55, 57, 59

Bonus ▶ 10, 7, 4, 1

7. a) Write a formula for the number of toothpicks in the sequence shown below:

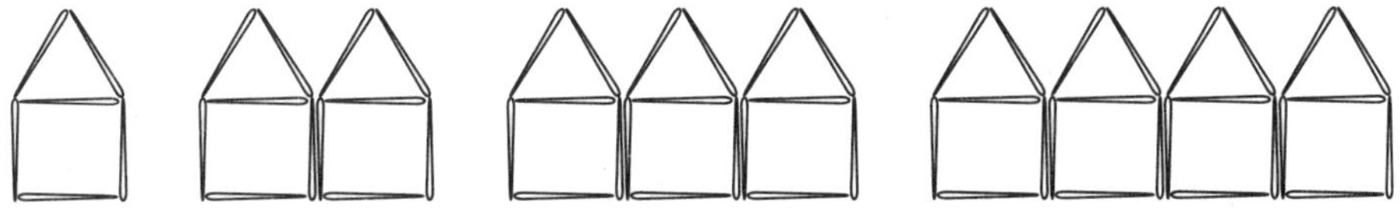

Figure 1 Figure 2 Figure 3 Figure 4

b) Use your formula to determine the number of toothpicks in the 30th figure.

F8-8 Sequences, Graphs, and Algebra

1. Without writing the sequence for the rule, find the gap in the sequence.

   a) Start at 15. Subtract 4 each time. -4

   b) Start at 3. Add 2 each time. ______

   c) Start at 15. Add 3.5 each time. ______

   d) Start at 23. Subtract 2 each time. ______

2. Without writing the sequence for the formula, find the gap in the sequence. Remember to include the sign.

   a) $3n + 2$ ______

   b) $5 - 4n$ ______

   c) $6 + 2n$ ______

   d) $5 - 3n$ ______

   e) $0.5n + 4$ ______

3. a) The sequence in the graph is nonlinear. Write the term values of the graph, and then find the gaps.

   0 ______ ______ ______

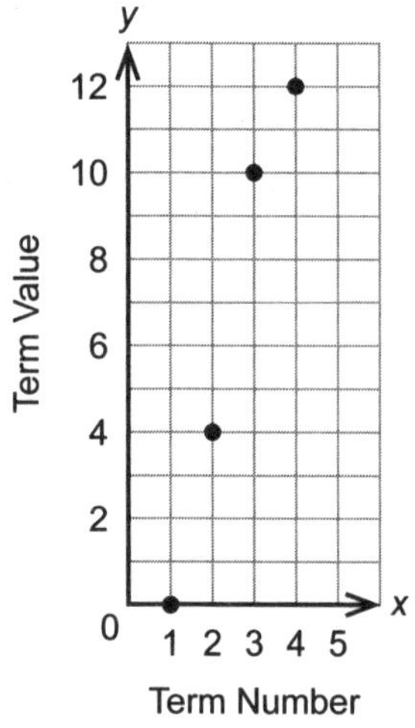

   b) Do the gaps show the difference between the term values or the term numbers? ______

   c) Should you look at the horizontal axis or the vertical axis to see the gaps between the terms of the sequence? ______

4. a) Without writing the sequence for the graph, find the gap in the sequence.

   i)

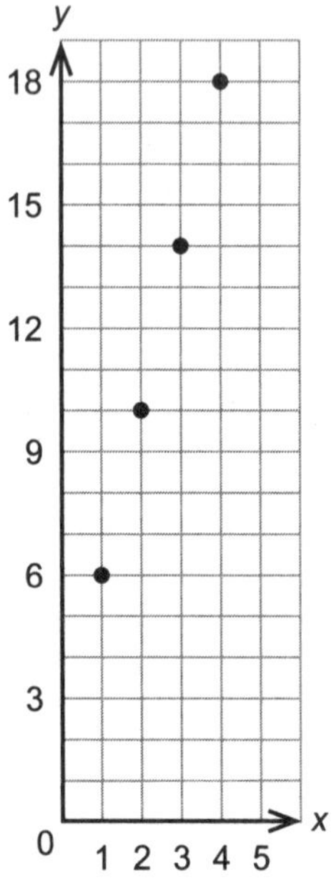

   gap: ______

   ii)

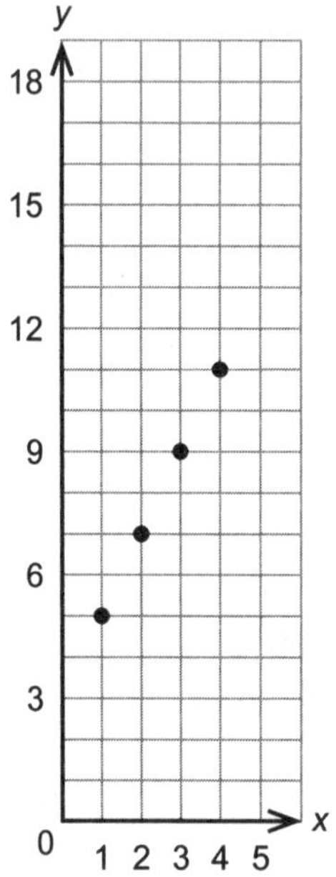

   gap: ______

   iii)

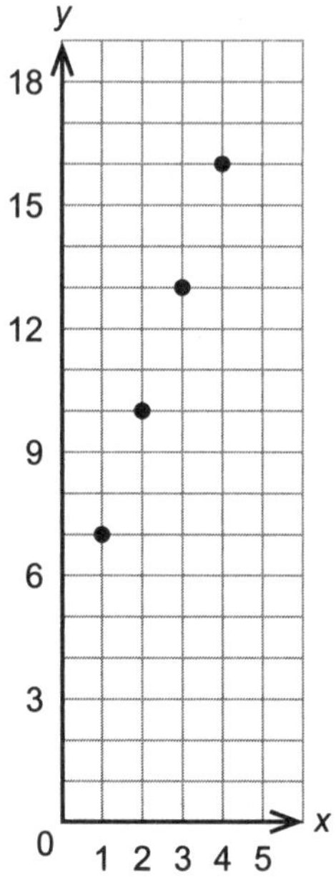

   gap: ______

   b) Sara wrote the formula for each graph in part a), but the graphs got mixed up! Match the graph to the formula.

   $3n + 4$ ______ $4n + 2$ ______ $2n + 3$ ______

5. a) The expression represents a sequence. Evaluate the expression with $n = 1$ to find the first term of the sequence.

i) $3n + 4$ ______ ii) $3n + 2$ ______ iii) $3n - 1$ ______

b) Each graph represents a sequence. Find the term value when the term number is 1.

A.

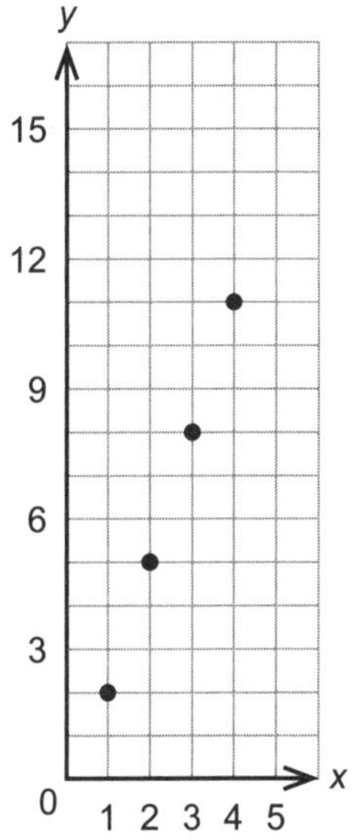

______

B.

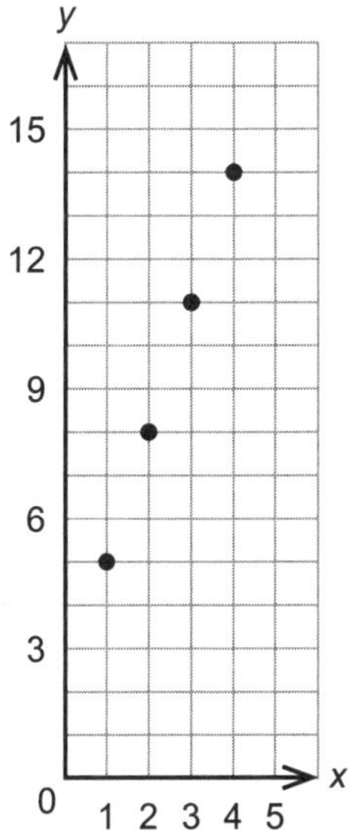

______

C.

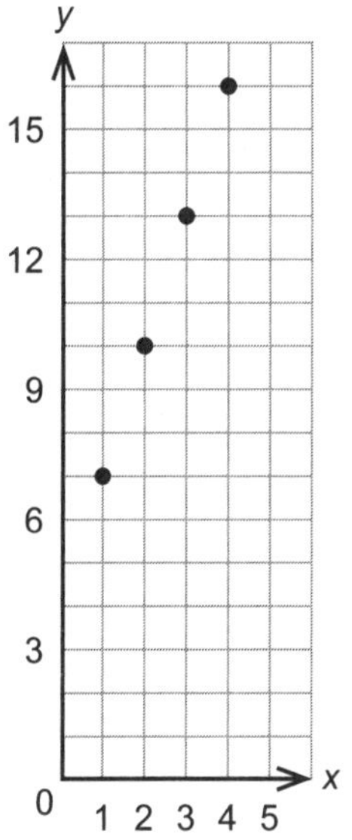

______

c) Match each expression from part a) with a graph from part b).

i) $3n + 4$ ______ ii) $3n + 2$ ______ iii) $3n - 1$ ______

6. Match the graph to the formula.

A.

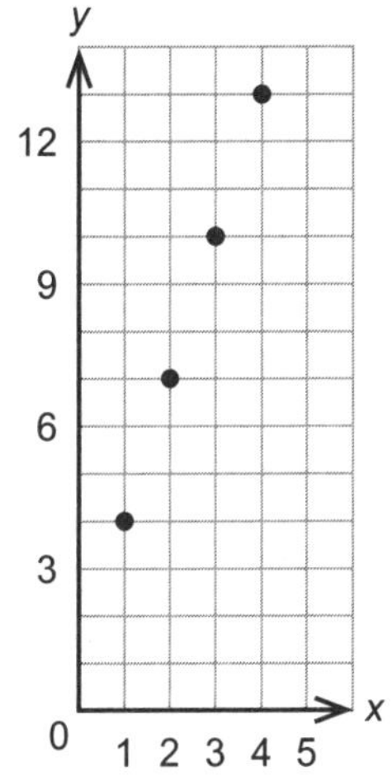

B.

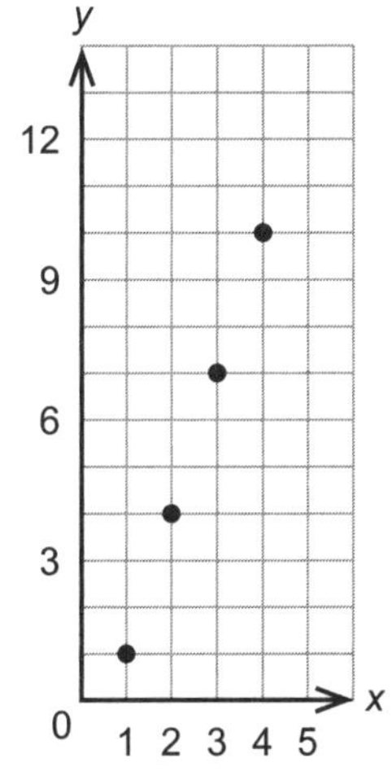

C.

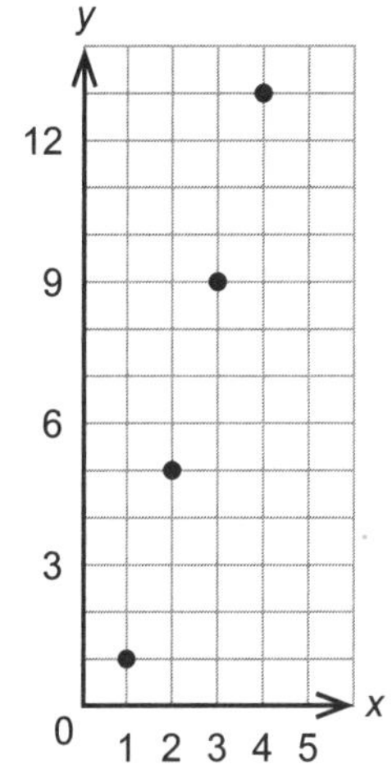

a) $3n - 2$ ______ b) $4n - 3$ ______ c) $3n + 1$ ______

7. a) Finish writing the expressions below with numbers of your choice.

$3n +$ ______ $2n +$ ______ $4n +$ ______ $3n +$ ______ $2n +$ ______

b) Draw a graph for each expression from part a) on grid paper in random order.

c) Have a partner match the expressions to the graphs.

F8-9 Linear Functions

1. The graph is linear. Join the points with a straight line to find the missing values in the table.

a)

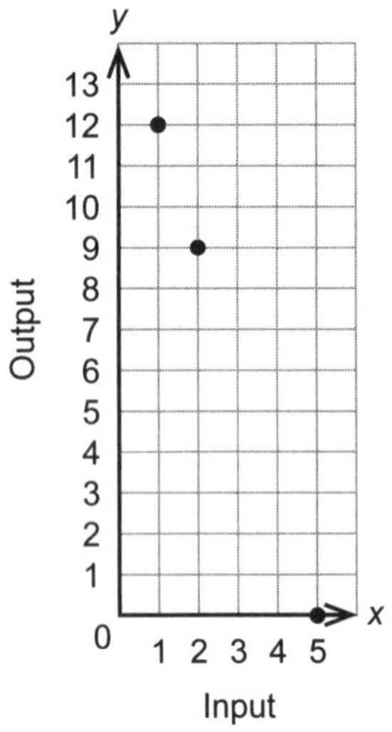

Input	Output
1	12
2	9
3	
	3
5	

b)

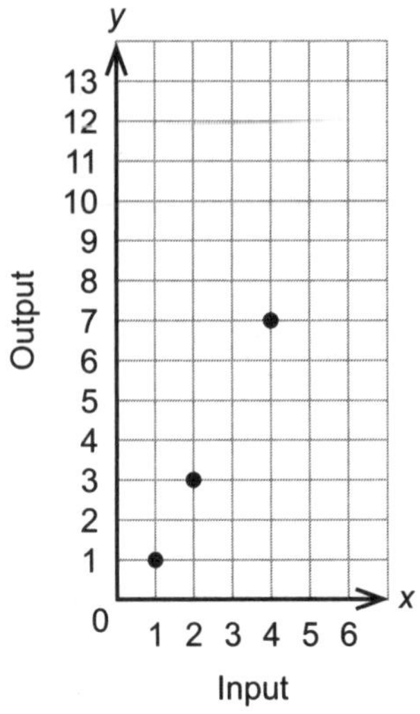

Input	Output
1	1
	3
4	7
5	
	13

2. Extend the line to find the output when the input is 11.

a)

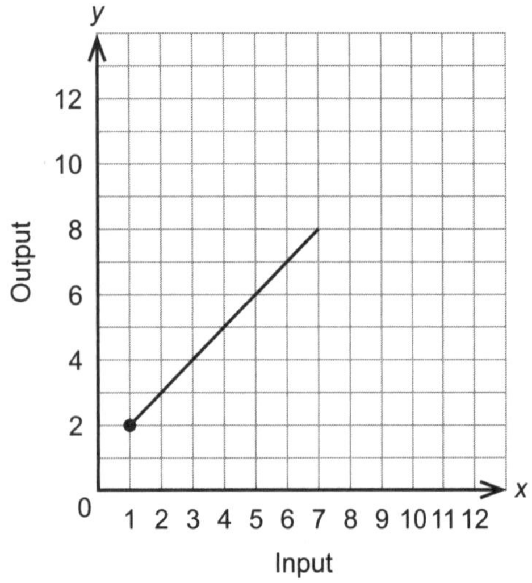

When the input is 11, the output is ______.

b)

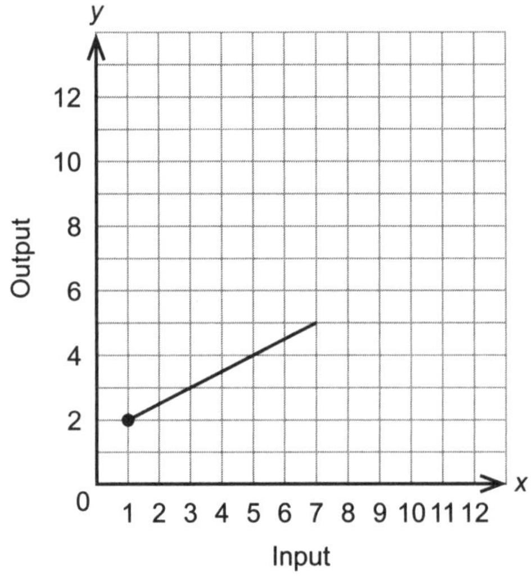

When the input is 11, the output is ______.

In a linear function, any number can be the input, not just a whole number.

3. For each graph in Question 1, find the missing values in the table.

a)

Input	Output
0	
1.5	
2.5	
3.5	
4.5	

b)

Input	Output
0.5	
1.5	
2.5	
4.5	
5.5	

4. Extend the line to find the output for each input.

a)

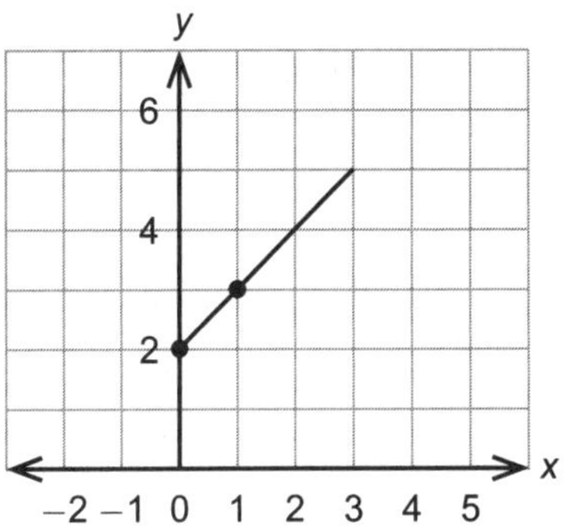

Input	1	0	−1	−2
Output	*3*			

b)

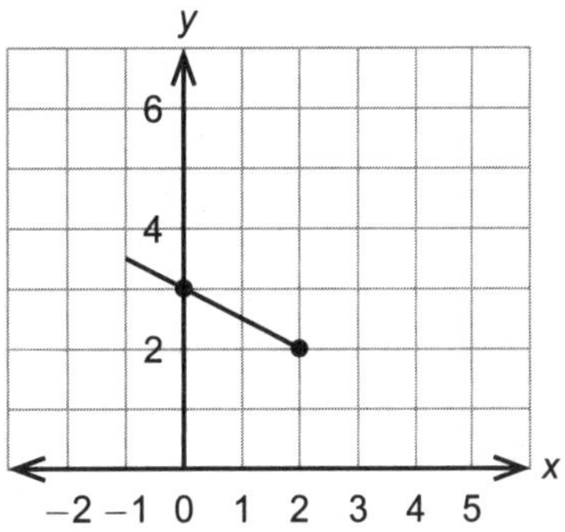

Input	2	0	−1	−2
Output	*2*			

5. A car is traveling at a constant speed of 60 km/h.

a) Write an expression for the distance the car traveled after *t* hours.

____

b) Create a table of values for the distance the car traveled after *t* hours.

t hours	Distance Traveled (km)

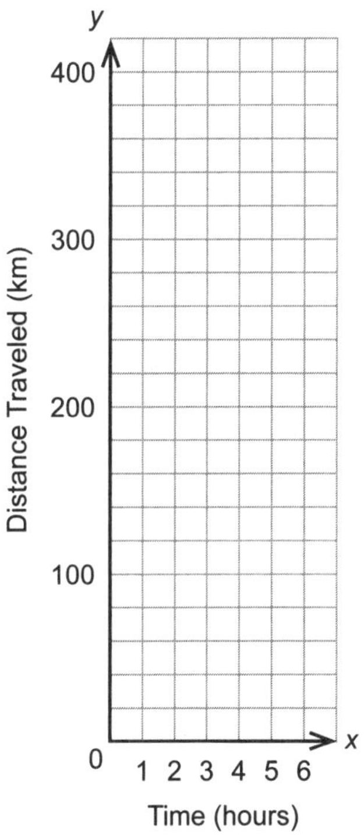

c) Write the ordered pairs from the above table of values. Then plot the points on the graph on the right. ____________________

d) Join the points on the graph with a straight line. If the car traveled for 3.5 hours, how far would it go? ____________________

e) How many hours would it take the car to travel 390 km? Extend the line to find out. ____________________

6. a) For the function, plot a graph for *x* equal to 1, 2, 3, 4, and 5. Note: Leave extra space on the horizontal axis to extend the graph.

i) $y = 4x + 1$ ii) $y = 5x - 2$ iii) $y = 3x + 9$

b) Extend the line on each graph from part a) to find *y* when $x = 6$. Then check your answer by substituting $x = 6$ in the formula.

c) Use the graphs to find the value of *x* when $y = 33$.

d) Write an equation and solve it to check your work for part c). Example: Solve $4x + 1 = 33$ to check your answer to part i).

F8-10 Rate of Change

Change in x is the horizontal change from the first point to the second point along the x-axis.

Change in y is the vertical change from the first point to the second point along the y-axis.

Example: From point A to point B: change in $x = 2$, change in $y = -3$

Change in x and change in y can be negative numbers.

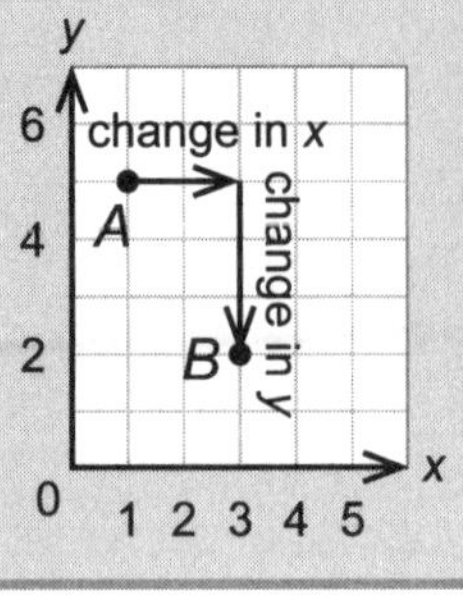

1. Find the change in x and the change in y from point A to point B.

a) 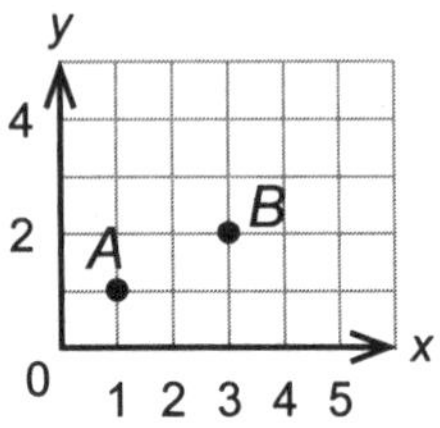

change in $x =$ ______

change in $y =$ ______

b) 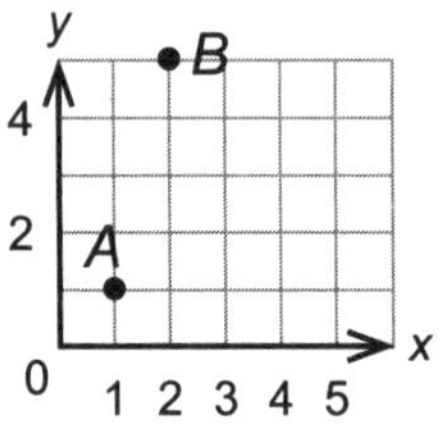

change in $x =$ ______

change in $y =$ ______

c) 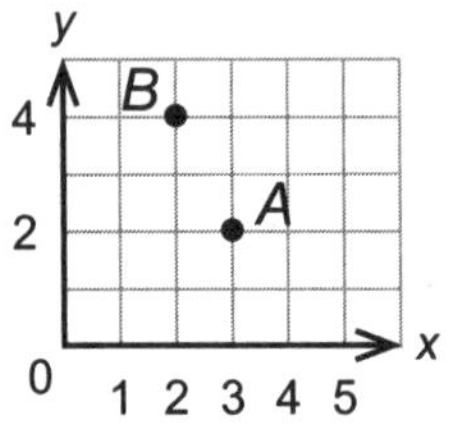

change in $x =$ ______

change in $y =$ ______

d) 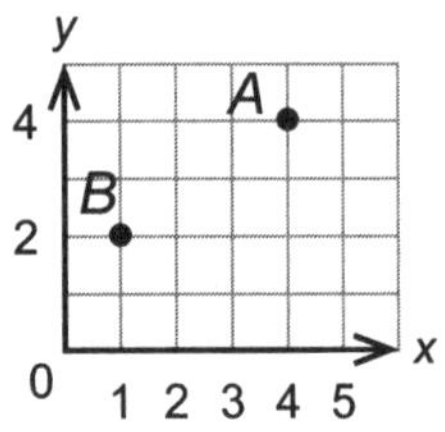

change in $x =$ ______

change in $y =$ ______

e) 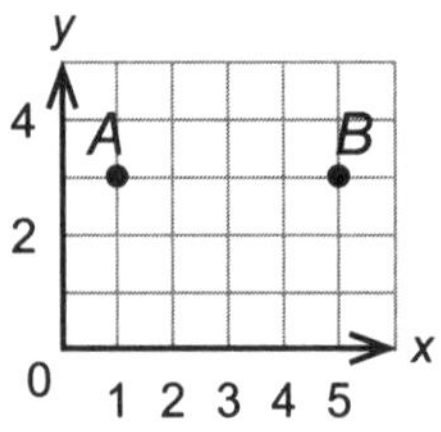

change in $x =$ ______

change in $y =$ ______

f) 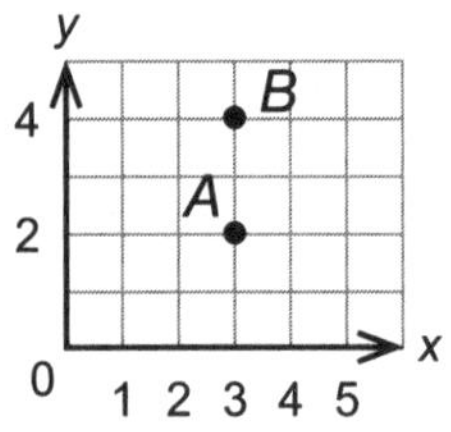

change in $x =$ ______

change in $y =$ ______

2. Find the change in x and the change in y from point A to point …

a) 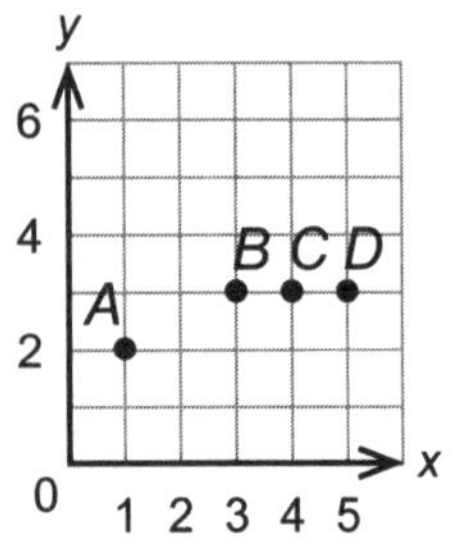

i) B: change in $x =$ ____, change in $y =$ ____

ii) C: change in $x =$ ____, change in $y =$ ____

iii) D: change in $x =$ ____, change in $y =$ ____

b) 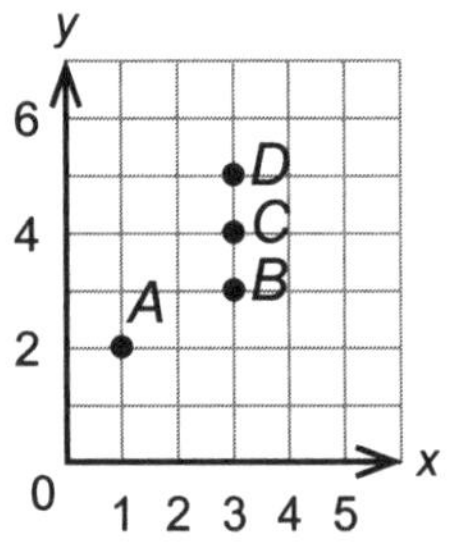

i) B: change in $x =$ ____, change in $y =$ ____

ii) C: change in $x =$ ____, change in $y =$ ____

iii) D: change in $x =$ ____, change in $y =$ ____

c) The change in ______ from point A to any point on a horizontal line is constant.

d) The change in ______ from point A to any point on a vertical line is constant.

3. Write the coordinates of points A and B in the table, then find the change in x and the change in y by finding the gaps.

a)

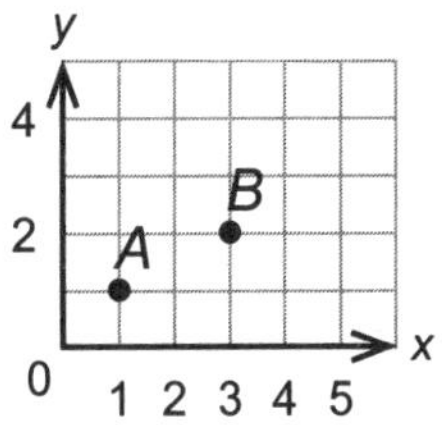

	x	y	
	1	1	
+2	3	2	+1

change in x = ______

change in y = ______

b)

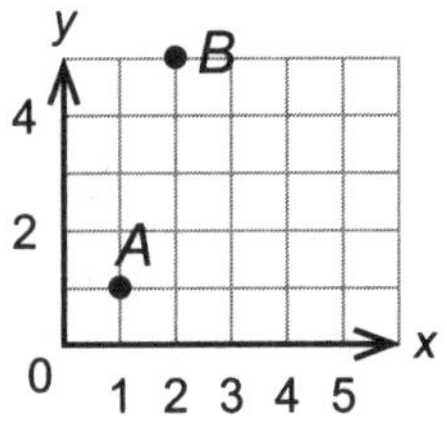

	x	y	

change in x = ______

change in y = ______

c)

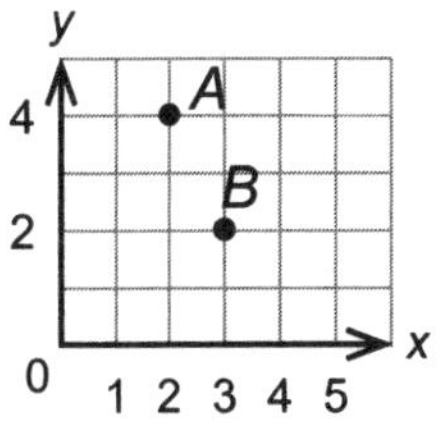

	x	y	

change in x = ______

change in y = ______

d)

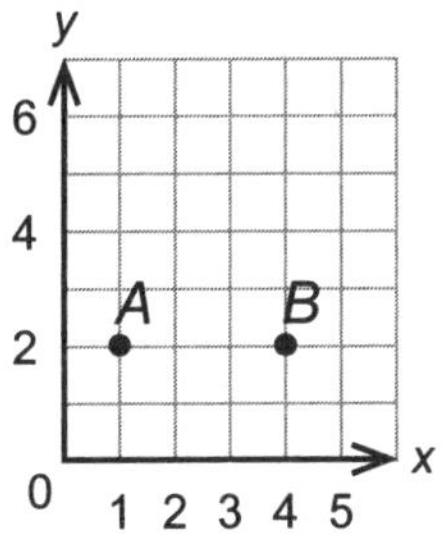

	x	y	

change in x = ______

change in y = ______

e)

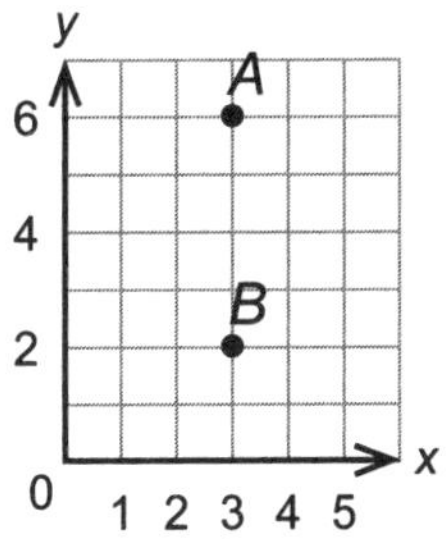

	x	y	

change in x = ______

change in y = ______

f)

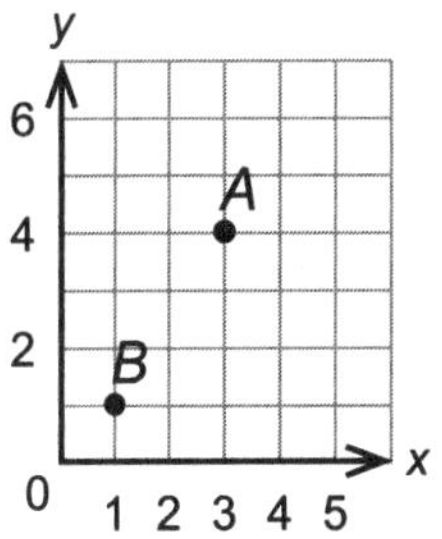

	x	y	

change in x = ______

change in y = ______

The **rate of change** is the rate of change in y to change in x. Rate of change = $\dfrac{\text{change in } y}{\text{change in } x}$

The rate of change is very important in mathematics and other sciences.

4. Find the rate of change from A to B.

a)

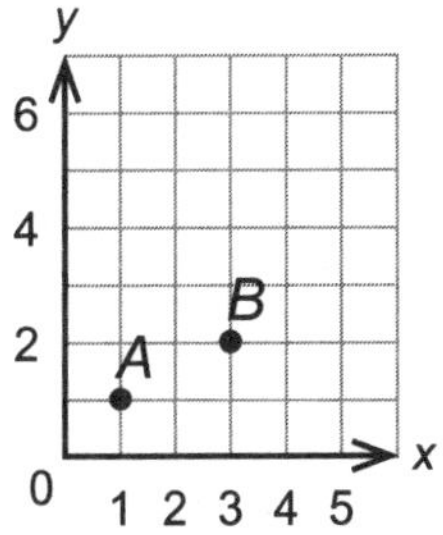

$\dfrac{\text{change in } y}{\text{change in } x} = \dfrac{1}{2}$

b)

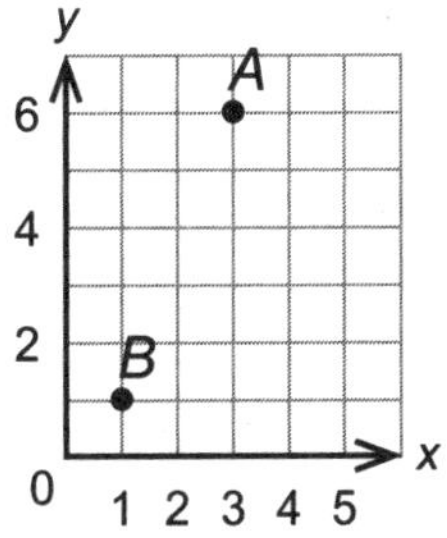

$\dfrac{\text{change in } y}{\text{change in } x} = \dfrac{\quad}{\quad} =$

c)

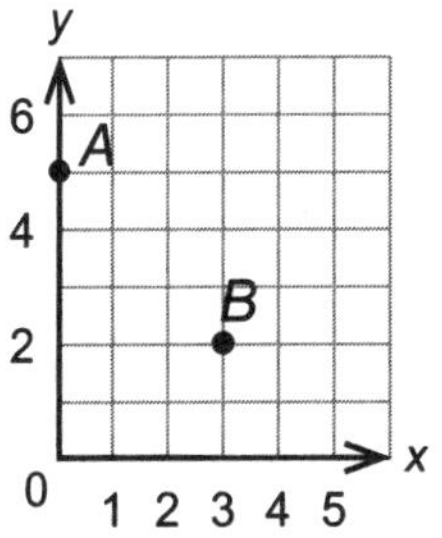

Rate of change = $\dfrac{\quad}{\quad} =$

5. Find the rate of change in Question 4 from *B* to *A*.

a) $\frac{\text{change in } y}{\text{change in } x} = \frac{-1}{-2} = \frac{1}{2}$

b) $\frac{\text{change in } y}{\text{change in } x} = \frac{\quad}{\quad}$

c) $\frac{\text{change in } y}{\text{change in } x} = \frac{\quad}{\quad} =$

d) What did you notice in parts a), b), and c)? ____________________

The rate of change from *A* to *B* is equal to the rate of change from *B* to *A*, so we can call this:

The rate of change between *A* and *B*

6. Find the rates of change between point *A* and the other points on the graph. Reduce to lowest terms.

a) 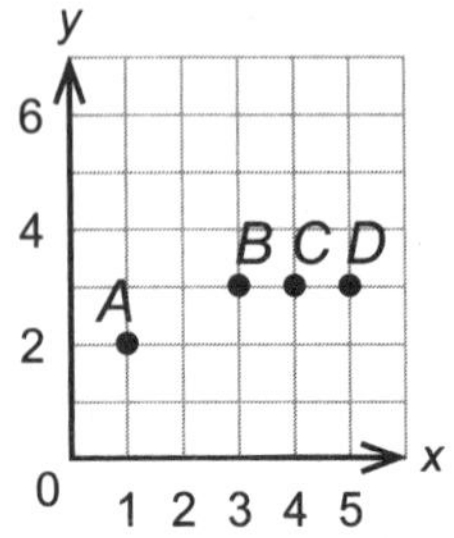

B: $\frac{\text{change in } y}{\text{change in } x} = \frac{\quad}{\quad}$

C: $\frac{\text{change in } y}{\text{change in } x} = \frac{\quad}{\quad}$

D: $\frac{\text{change in } y}{\text{change in } x} = \frac{\quad}{\quad}$

b) 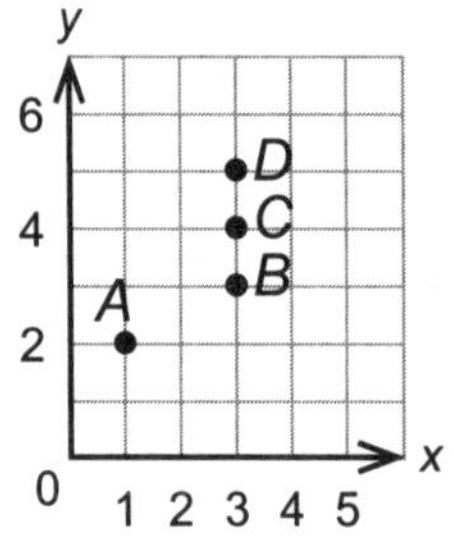

B: $\frac{\text{change in } y}{\text{change in } x} = \frac{\quad}{\quad}$

C: $\frac{\text{change in } y}{\text{change in } x} = \frac{\quad}{\quad}$

D: $\frac{\text{change in } y}{\text{change in } x} = \frac{\quad}{\quad}$

c) 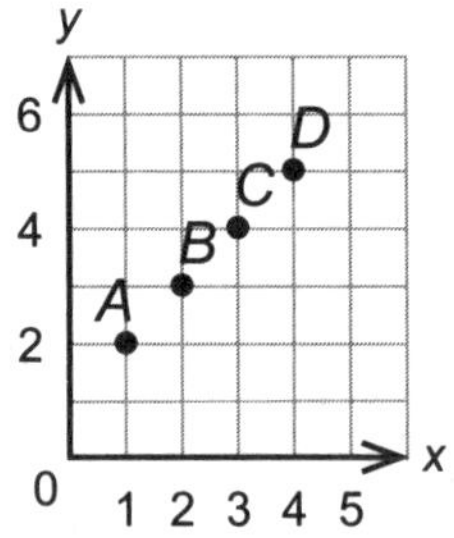

B: $\frac{\text{change in } y}{\text{change in } x} = \frac{\quad}{\quad}$

C: $\frac{\text{change in } y}{\text{change in } x} = \frac{\quad}{\quad}$

D: $\frac{\text{change in } y}{\text{change in } x} = \frac{\quad}{\quad}$

d) For the graph in part a), circle the biggest rate of change.

A to *B* *A* to *C* *A* to *D*

e) For the graph in part b), circle the biggest rate of change.

A to *B* *A* to *C* *A* to *D*

f) What did you notice in graph c)? ____________________

g) For the graph in part a), what is the rate of change between points *B* and *D*?

$\frac{\text{change in } y}{\text{change in } x} = \frac{\quad}{\quad} =$

What did you notice? ____________________

Bonus ▶ Explain why you cannot find the rate of change between points *B* and *D* in part b). ____________________

____

F8-11 Slope in Linear Functions

Mathematicians use other terms when they work with linear functions or straight lines.

Another name for the change in *x* is **run**.
Another name for the change in *y* is **rise**.

Another name for rate of change is **slope**, so slope $= \frac{\text{rise}}{\text{run}}$.

Example: From point *A* to point *B*, run = 2 and rise = 3, so the slope is $\frac{3}{2}$.

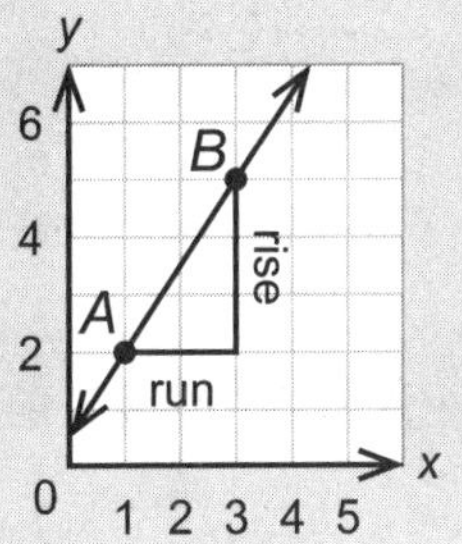

1. Find the rise and run from point *A* to point *B*. Then find the slope and reduce to lowest terms.

a) 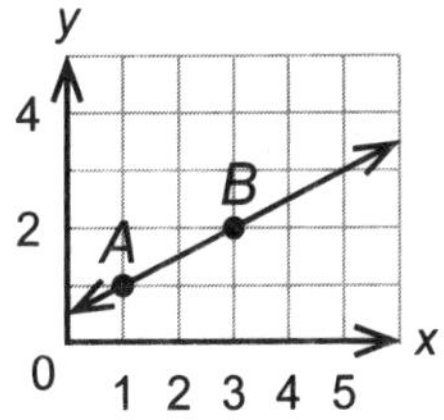

$\text{slope} = \frac{\text{rise}}{\text{run}} = \frac{\quad}{\quad}$

b) 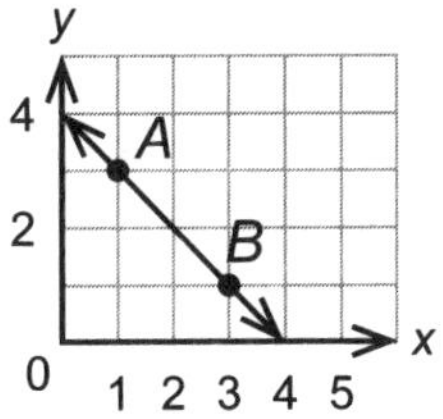

$\text{slope} = \frac{\text{rise}}{\text{run}} = \frac{\quad}{\quad}$

c) 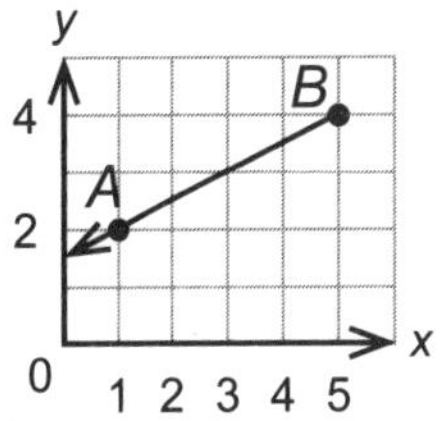

$\text{slope} = \frac{\text{rise}}{\text{run}} = \frac{\quad}{\quad}$

d) 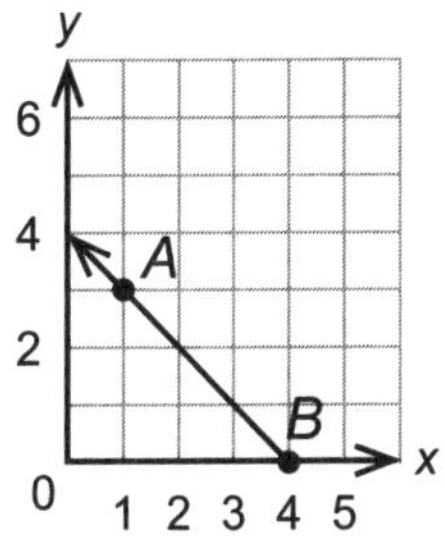

$\text{slope} = \frac{\text{rise}}{\text{run}} = \frac{\quad}{\quad}$

e) 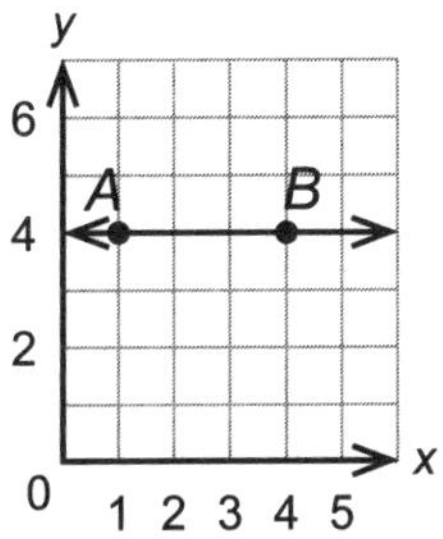

$\text{slope} = \frac{\text{rise}}{\text{run}} = \frac{\quad}{\quad}$

f) 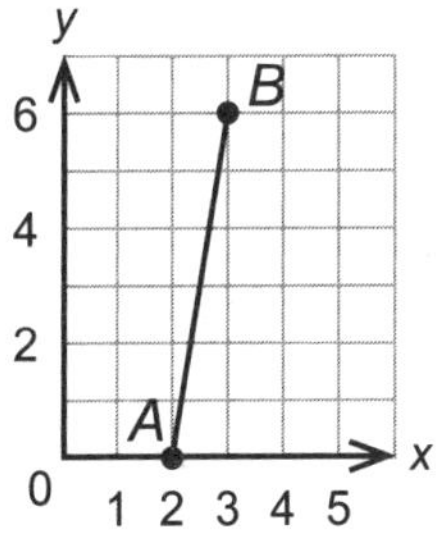

$\text{slope} = \frac{\text{rise}}{\text{run}} = \frac{\quad}{\quad}$

2. Find the slopes of the lines *AB*, *AC*, and *AD*. Reduce to lowest terms.

a) 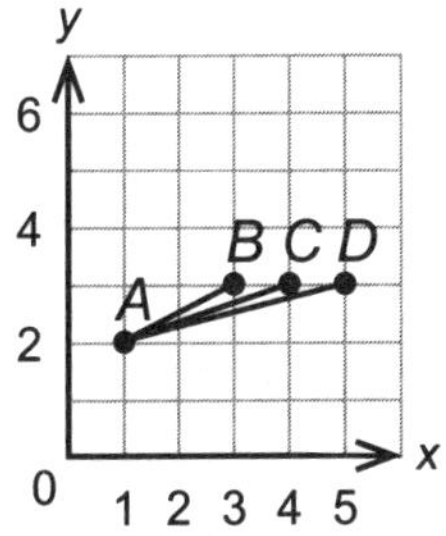

$\text{slope of } AB = \frac{\text{rise}}{\text{run}} = \frac{\quad}{\quad}$

$\text{slope of } AC = \frac{\text{rise}}{\text{run}} = \frac{\quad}{\quad}$

$\text{slope of } AD = \frac{\text{rise}}{\text{run}} = \frac{\quad}{\quad}$

b) 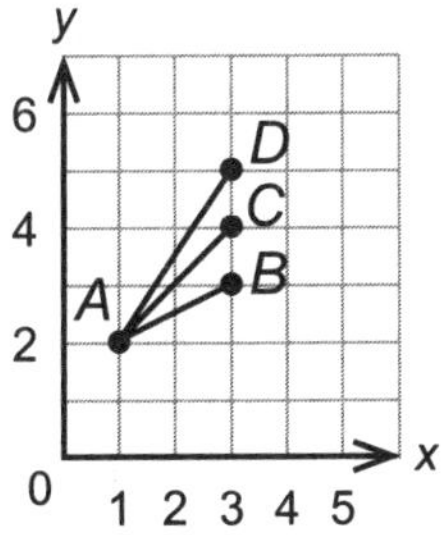

$\text{slope of } AB = \frac{\text{rise}}{\text{run}} = \frac{\quad}{\quad}$

$\text{slope of } AC = \frac{\text{rise}}{\text{run}} = \frac{\quad}{\quad}$

$\text{slope of } AD = \frac{\text{rise}}{\text{run}} = \frac{\quad}{\quad}$

c) 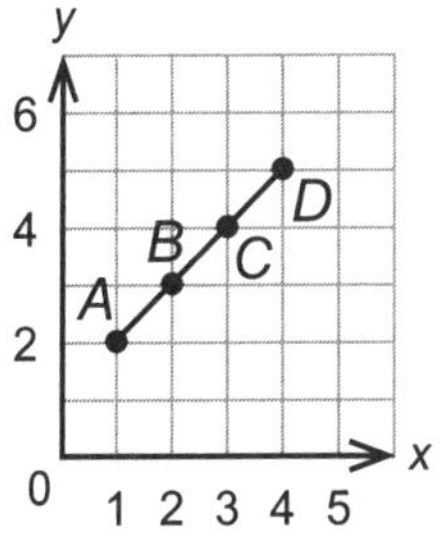

$\text{slope of } AB = \frac{\text{rise}}{\text{run}} = \frac{\quad}{\quad}$

$\text{slope of } AC = \frac{\text{rise}}{\text{run}} = \frac{\quad}{\quad}$

$\text{slope of } AD = \frac{\text{rise}}{\text{run}} = \frac{\quad}{\quad}$

3. a) For the graph in Question 2.a), find the slope of a new line, *BD*.

slope of $BD = \frac{\text{rise}}{\text{run}} = \frac{\quad}{\quad}$

b) Can you find the slope of a new line, *BD*, in Question 2.b)? ______

> For any horizontal line, rise = 0, so the slope of a horizontal line is 0.
>
> For any vertical line, run = 0.
>
> Mathematicians don't define the slope of the vertical line because we cannot divide a number by 0.

4. Write the coordinates of points *A* and *B* in the table. Then find the rise and run by finding the gaps. Then find the slope of the line *AB*. Reduce to lowest terms.

a)

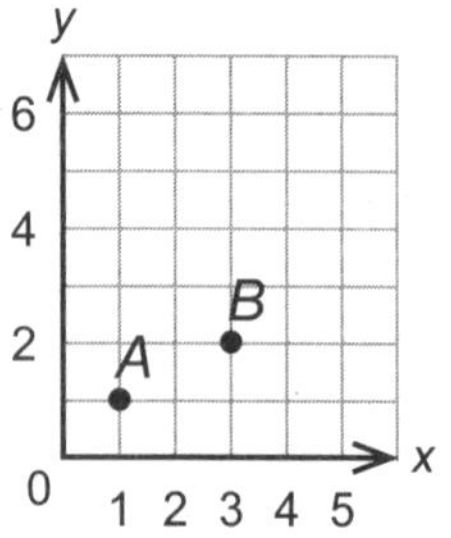

x	y
1	1
3	2

(+2) (+1)

run = ______ rise = ______

slope = $\frac{\text{rise}}{\text{run}} = \frac{\quad}{\quad}$

b)

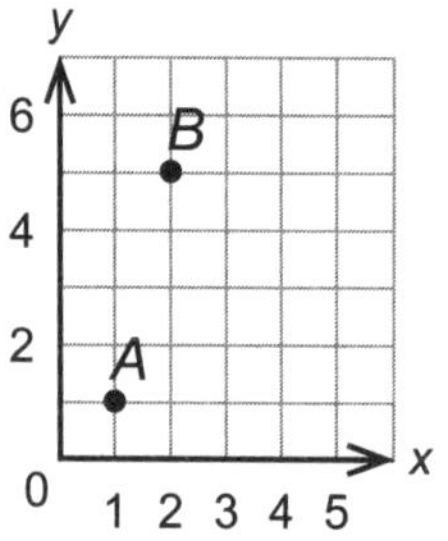

x	y

run = ______ rise = ______

slope = $\frac{\text{rise}}{\text{run}} = \frac{\quad}{\quad}$

c)

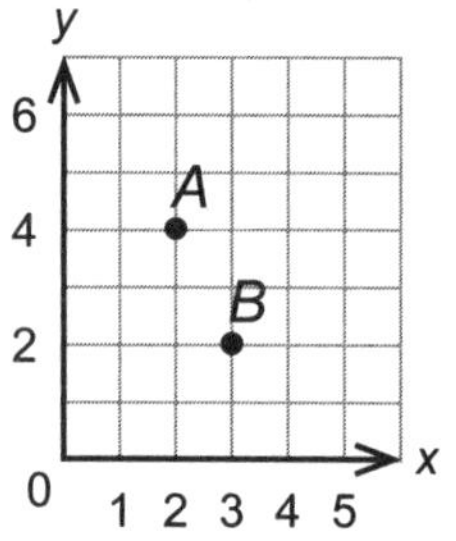

x	y

run = ______ rise = ______

slope = $\frac{\text{rise}}{\text{run}} = \frac{\quad}{\quad}$

d)

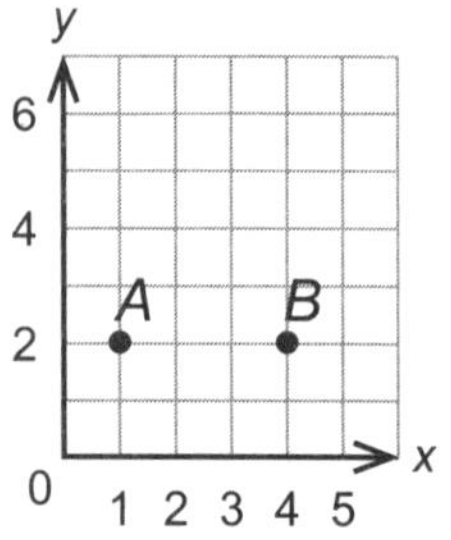

x	y

run = ______ rise = ______

slope = $\frac{\text{rise}}{\text{run}} = \frac{\quad}{\quad}$

e)

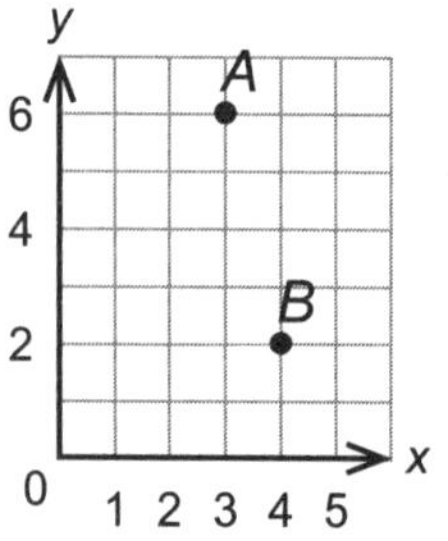

x	y

run = ______ rise = ______

slope = $\frac{\text{rise}}{\text{run}} = \frac{\quad}{\quad}$

f)

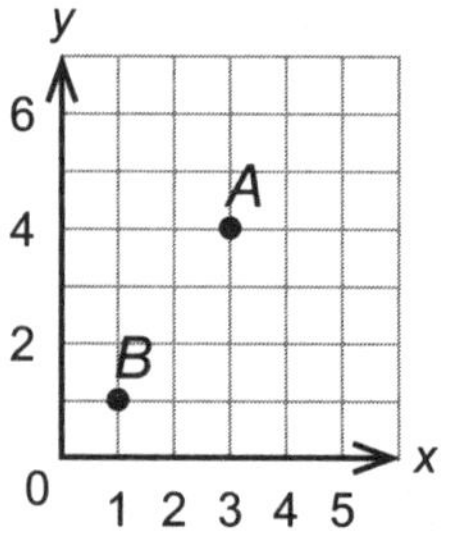

x	y

run = ______ rise = ______

slope = $\frac{\text{rise}}{\text{run}} = \frac{\quad}{\quad}$

5. Find the slope of a line that passes through the pair of points by filling in the table and finding the gaps.

a) $A\,(1, 2)$, $B\,(2, 5)$

x	y
1	2
2	5

(gaps: +1, +3)

slope $= \frac{\text{rise}}{\text{run}} = \frac{3}{1} = 3$

b) $A\,(3, 1)$, $B\,(4, 2)$

x	y

slope $= \frac{\text{rise}}{\text{run}} = \frac{\quad}{\quad} =$

c) $A\,(5, 2)$, $B\,(3, 3)$

x	y

slope $= \frac{\text{rise}}{\text{run}} = \frac{\quad}{\quad} =$

d) $A\,(0, 4)$, $B\,(4, 2)$

x	y

slope $= \frac{\text{rise}}{\text{run}} = \frac{\quad}{\quad} =$

e) $A\,(2, 0)$, $B\,(0, 2)$

x	y

slope $= \frac{\text{rise}}{\text{run}} = \frac{\quad}{\quad} =$

f) $A\,(3, 4)$, $B\,(7, 4)$

x	y

slope $= \frac{\text{rise}}{\text{run}} = \frac{\quad}{\quad} =$

g) $A\,(-1, 3)$, $B\,(2, 6)$

x	y

slope $= \frac{\text{rise}}{\text{run}} = \frac{\quad}{\quad} =$

h) $A\,(3, -2)$, $B\,(2, 0)$

x	y

slope $= \frac{\text{rise}}{\text{run}} = \frac{\quad}{\quad} =$

i) $A\,(-1, -2)$, $B\,(-3, -5)$

x	y

slope $= \frac{\text{rise}}{\text{run}} = \frac{\quad}{\quad} =$

6. Find the rise and run by finding the change in y and the change in x. Then find the slope.

a) $A\,(-2, 1)$, $B\,(0, -3)$

rise $= -3 - 1 = -4$

run $= 0 - (-2) = 2$

slope $= \frac{\text{rise}}{\text{run}} = \frac{-4}{2} =$

b) $A\,(2, -1)$, $B\,(1, 2)$

rise $=$

run $=$

slope $\frac{\text{rise}}{\text{run}} = \frac{\quad}{\quad} =$

c) $A\,(-2, -1)$, $B\,(-4, -5)$

rise $=$

run $=$

slope $\frac{\text{rise}}{\text{run}} = \frac{\quad}{\quad} =$

7. a) Find the slope of the line on the graph.

i) slope of $AB = \frac{\text{rise}}{\text{run}} = \frac{\quad}{\quad}$ ii) slope of $AC = \frac{\text{rise}}{\text{run}} = \frac{\quad}{\quad}$

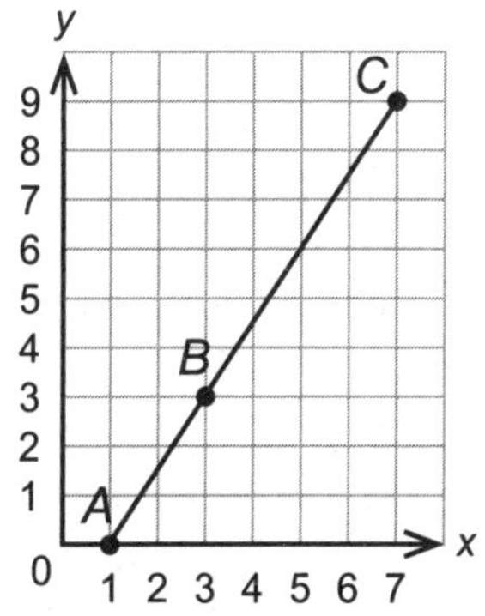

b) Mark the point $D\,(5, 6)$ on the graph and find the slope of the line AD.

slope of $AD = \frac{\text{rise}}{\text{run}} = \frac{\quad}{\quad} =$

c) Are the slopes between every two points on this straight line equal? ______

F8-12 Finding Slope Using Tables and Equations

1. Fill in the table using the rule. Find the changes in x and y and then find the slope.

a) Multiply by 2.5 and add 1.

x	y
1	*3.5*
3	*8.5*
5	
7	

(+2) (+5)

change in x = *+2*

change in y = *+5*

slope $= \frac{5}{2} = 2.5$

b) Multiply by 3 and add 1.5.

x	y
−1	*−1.5*
1	
3	
5	

change in x = ______

change in y = ______

slope $= \frac{\quad}{\quad} =$

c) Multiply by 1.5 and subtract 2.

x	y
2	*1*
4	
6	
8	

change in x = ______

change in y = ______

slope $= \frac{\quad}{\quad} =$

d) Where can you find the slope in a rule? ______________________

2. Fill in the table using the equation. The change in x is 1. Find the change in y and the slope.

a) $y = 2x + 1$

x	y
1	3
2	5

(+2)

coefficient of x: *2*

slope $= \frac{2}{1} = 2$

b) $y = 2x - 1$

x	y
1	
2	

coefficient of x: ______

slope $= \frac{\quad}{\quad} =$

c) $y = 3x - 2.5$

x	y
1	*0.5*
2	

coefficient of x: ______

slope $= \frac{\quad}{\quad} =$

d) $y = -2x + 1$

x	y
1	*−1*
2	

coefficient of x: ______

slope $= \frac{\quad}{\quad} =$

e) $y = -3x + 3$

x	y
1	
2	

coefficient of x: ______

slope $= \frac{\quad}{\quad} =$

f) $y = 1.5x - 1$

x	y
1	
2	

coefficient of x: ______

slope $= \frac{\quad}{\quad} =$

g) Where can you find the slope in the rule? ______________________

3. According to ski trail difficulty ratings in North America, ski slopes are rated by level of difficulty, as shown below:

Beginner hills: $\frac{6}{100}$ to $\frac{25}{100}$ Intermediate hills: $\frac{25}{100}$ to $\frac{40}{100}$ Advanced hills: $\frac{40}{100}$ to $\frac{100}{100}$

Find the slope and say if the hill is for beginner, intermediate, or advanced skiers.

a)

____

b)

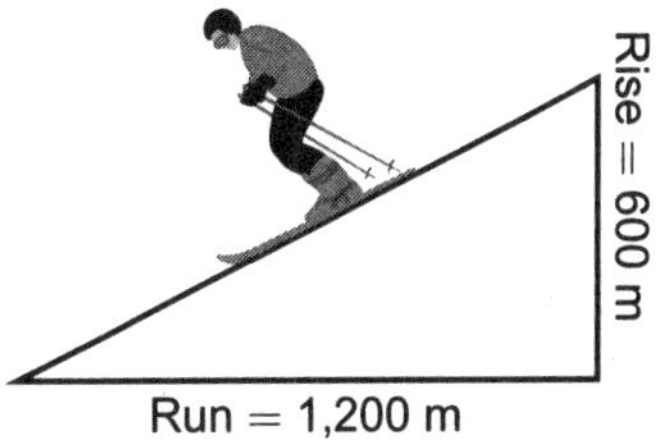

____

c)

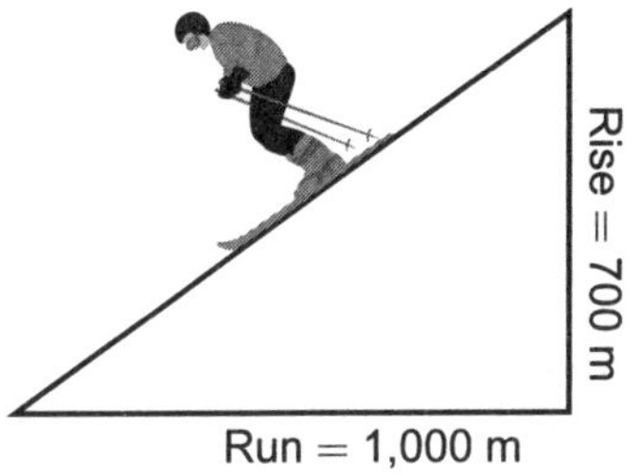

____

d)

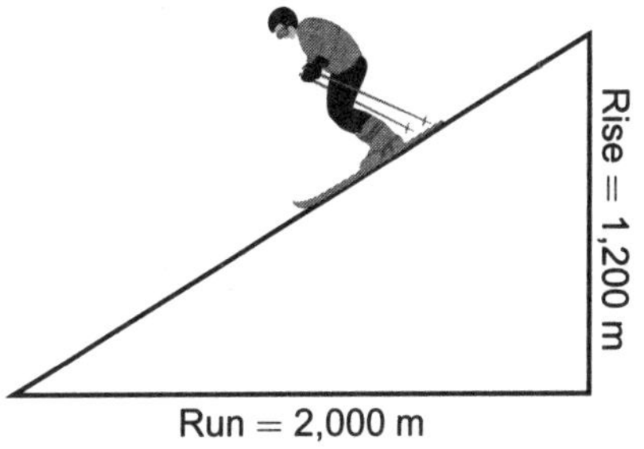

____

e)

____

f)

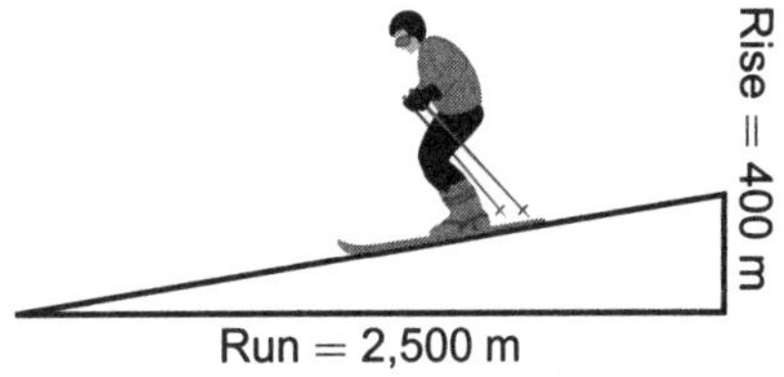

____

4. a) The four different linear functions below are represented in different ways. Calculate the slope for each.

i)

Input	Output
−1	1
0	2
1	3
2	4

ii)

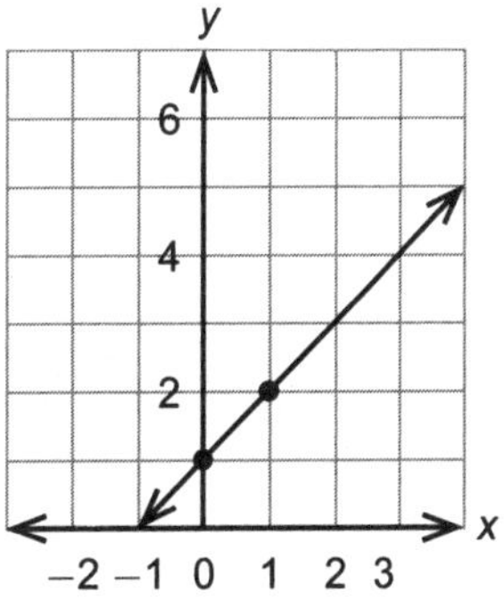

iii) $y = 3x - 4$

iv) (1, 1), (2, 3), (3, 5), (4, 7)

b) Which has the greatest slope? Are there any with the same slope?

5. A balloon is released from the top of a tower. The graph shows the height of the rising balloon over time.

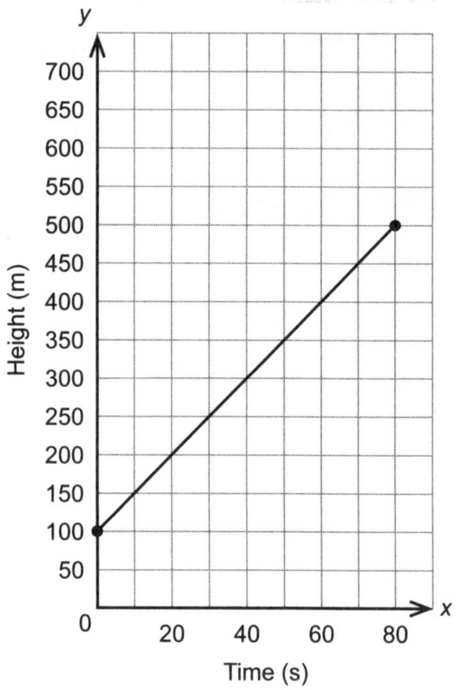

a) What is the height of the tower? ________________

b) Find the slope of the line.

c) Use the slope to find the height of the balloon after 65 seconds.

d) Check your answer to part c) using the graph.

6. A ramp in California must have a maximum rise of 1 foot for a 12-foot horizontal run.

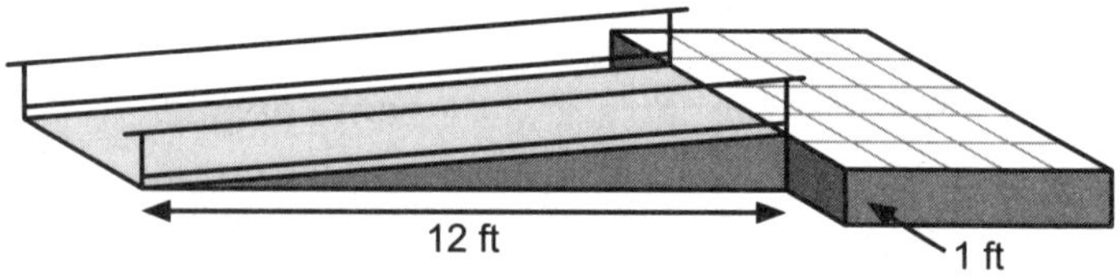

a) Find the maximum slope.

b) An exit door is 3 feet higher than the ground level. Determine the horizontal run needed for a ramp.

7. A shed has a square base and each side measures 15 feet. The roof has a $\frac{1}{6}$ slope. Find the maximum height of the shed roof from the ground.

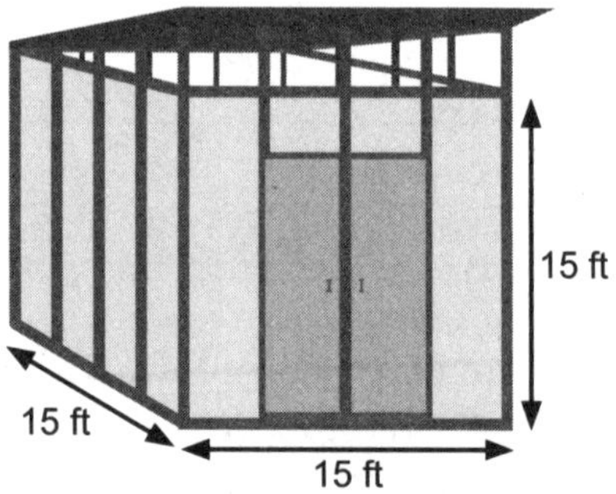

8. A ramp slopes upward from the sidewalk to the entrance of a building. The horizontal run of the ramp is 28 ft from the sidewalk. Find the maximum height of the ramp, if the ramp is 2 ft high when it is 8 ft from the sidewalk.

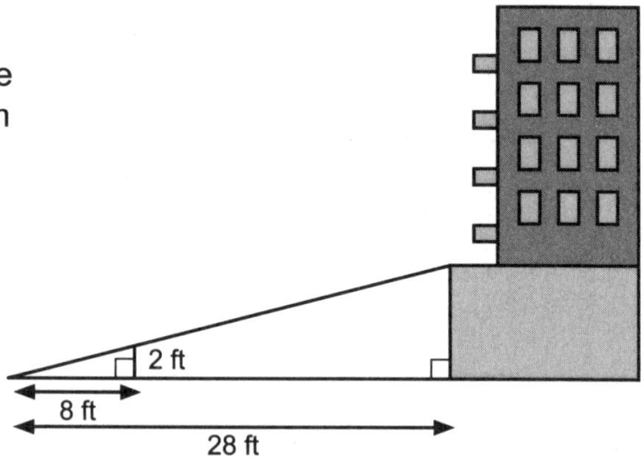

SP8-1 Drawing Scatter Plots

Bivariate data is data that has two variables. A **scatter plot** is used to show the bivariate data on a coordinate plane. Each dot on the scatter plot is an ordered pair containing the two measurements.

1. Five students recorded their ages and their heights, and made a scatter plot. Each dot on the scatter plot shows the data for one student. Because there are no students with a height less than 150 cm, we leave those numbers off the vertical axis.

	Age (years)	Height (cm)
Tanya	13	160
Mona	14	168
Kevin	13	154
Melanie	13	166
Zack	14	160

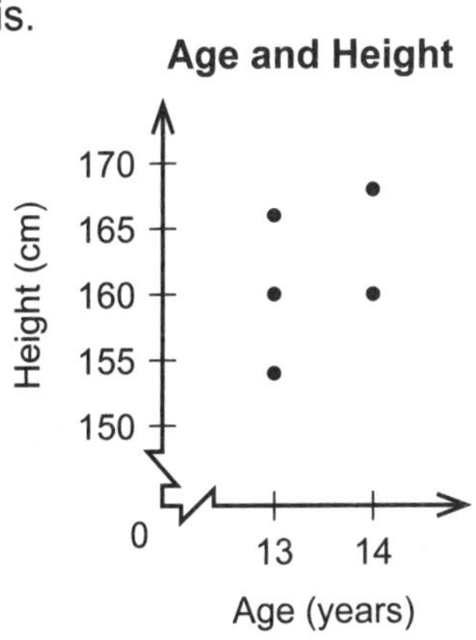

a) Write the ordered pairs (age, height) for the five students.

(13, 160), *(14,*   ), (,   ), (,   ), (,   )

b) Circle Melanie's dot.

c) Which two people are the same height? ______________________

d) How is this shown on the scatter plot? ______________________

When making a scatter plot, do not connect the points.

2. For the table, write the ordered pairs and then plot the points on the scatter plot.

a)

Years of Experience	1	2	3	4	5	6
Hourly Wage ($)	10	11	13	14	16	16

(1, 10), (2,   ), (3,   ), (4,   ), (5,   ), (6,   )

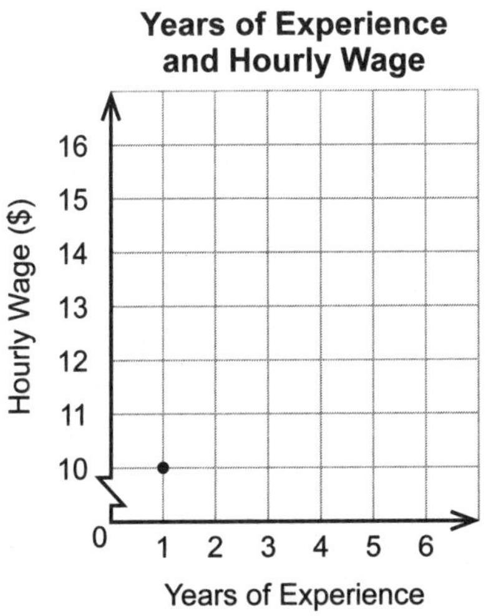

b)

Temperature (°F)	30	40	50	60	70
Number of Heaters Sold	12	11	8	2	0

(30, 12), (,   ), (,   ), (,   ), (,   )

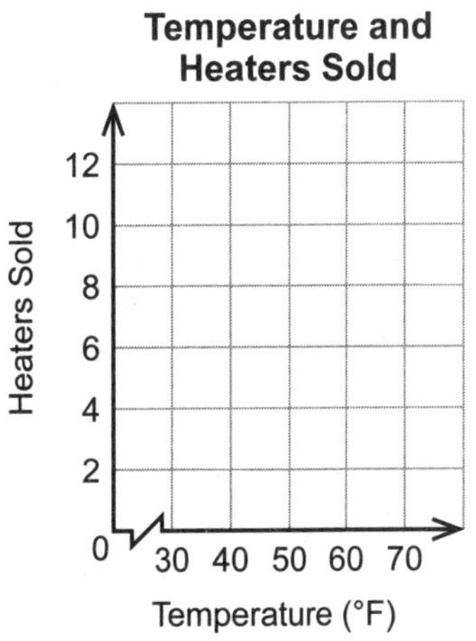

To draw a scatter plot:

Step 1: On grid paper, draw the horizontal axis and vertical axis, and label them. Give your graph a short, descriptive title.

Step 2: Mark an appropriate scale for the units on the axes. If some numbers should be left off a scale, show the break in the axis with ⌇.

Step 3: Plot the data points.

3. The table shows how many people attended theme parks in the United States, and the revenue earned, from 2001 to 2007.

Year	2001	2002	2003	2004	2005	2006	2007
Attendance (millions)	319	324	322	328	335	335	341
Revenue (billion $)	9.6	9.9	10.3	10.8	11.2	11.5	12.0

a) Make a scatter plot for the year and attendance.

Year and Attendance

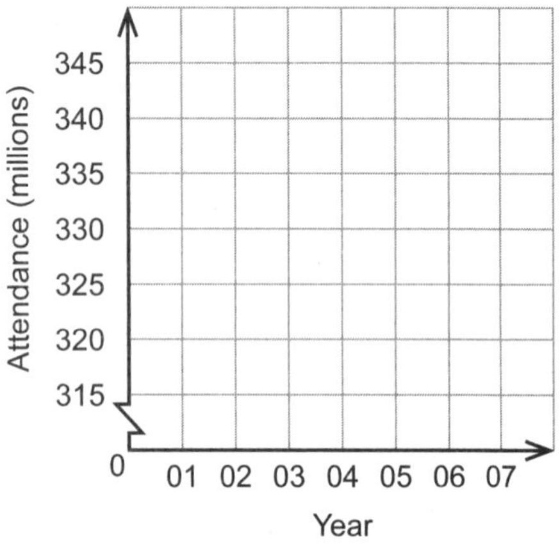

b) Make a scatter plot for the year and revenue.

Year and Revenue

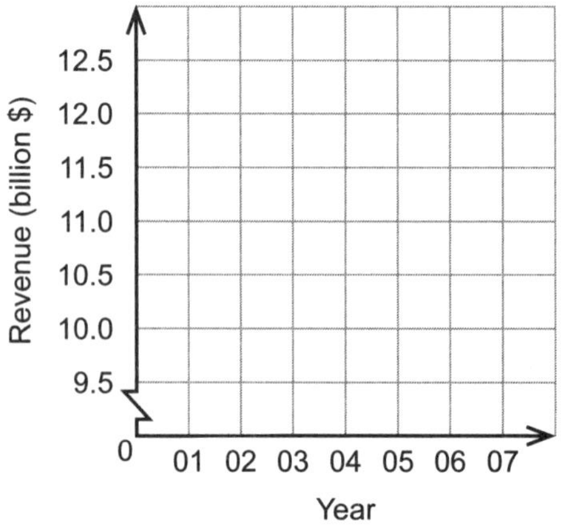

c) Make a scatter plot for the attendance and revenue.

4. The table shows the number of hours Dana spent listening to music over 10 days. Draw a scatter plot to represent the data.

Day	1	2	3	4	5	6	7	8	9	10
Hours	5	3	9	5	6	4	8	2	4	2

5. The table shows the number of vehicles that ran on alternative fuels in the United States from 2001 to 2011. Draw a scatter plot for the data.

Year	2001	2002	2003	2004	2005	2006	2007	2008	2009	2010	2011
Alternative-Fuel Vehicles (thousands)	425	471	534	565	592	635	596	776	826	939	1,192

SP8-2 Describing Scatter Plots

1. a) For how many 5-year-olds does the scatter plot show data?

b) According to the data, are 10-year-olds likely to be taller or shorter than 9-year-olds?

c) Was every 10-year-old taller than every 9-year-old?

d) According to the data, does height increase or decrease when age increases?

e) How does the scatter plot show what you described in part d)?

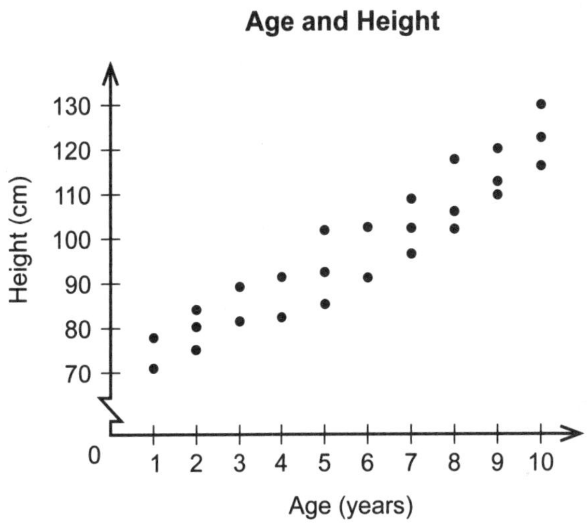

2. a) How many 55-year-olds are shown in the data?

____

b) According to the data, are 55-year-olds likely to be taller than 40-year-olds, shorter than 40-year-olds, or is it too difficult to say?

____

c) Explain your answer to part b) using the scatter plot.

____

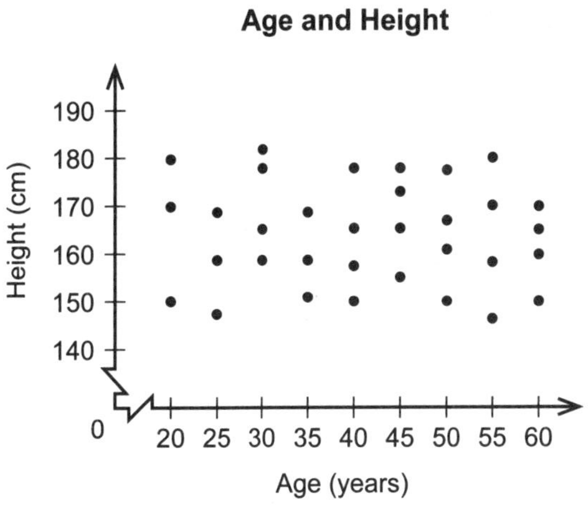

3. Based on the scatter plot, write "increases," "decreases," or "is not affected."

a)

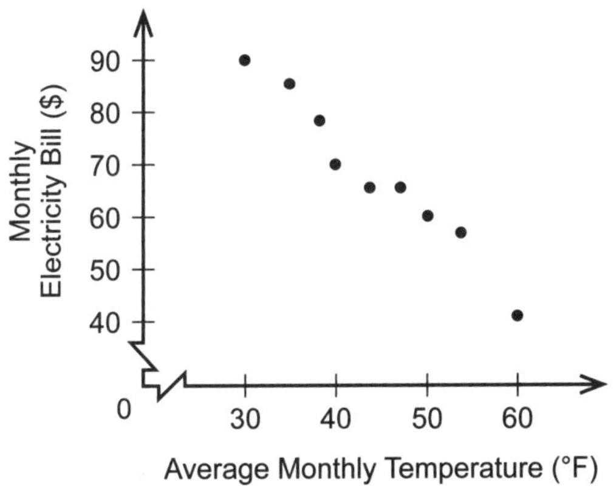

As the average monthly temperature increases, the electricity bill _______________.

b)

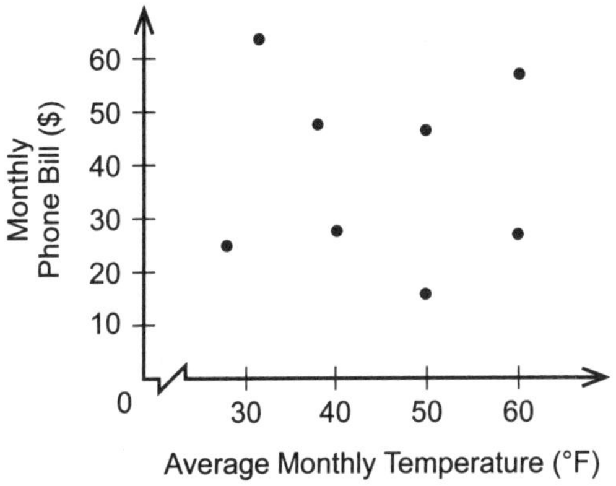

As the average monthly temperature increases, the phone bill _______________.

4. Explain why your answers to Question 3 make sense. _______________

____

There is a **positive association** between two sets of data if the values in the sets of data increase together.

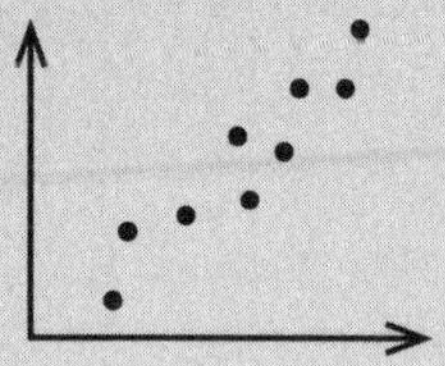

There is a **negative association** if the values in one set of data increase as the values in the other set of data decrease.

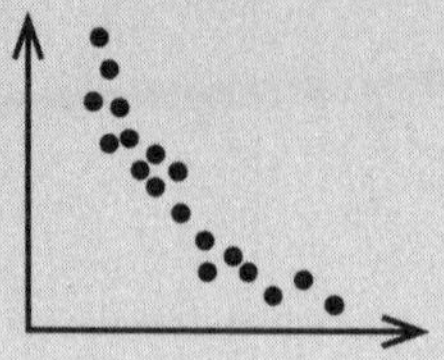

There is **no association** if there is neither a positive nor negative association between the two sets of data.

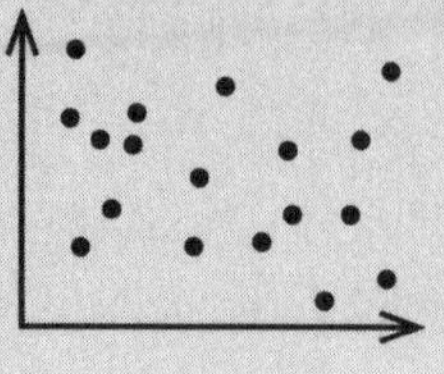

5. Write the type of association for the scatter plot.

a) 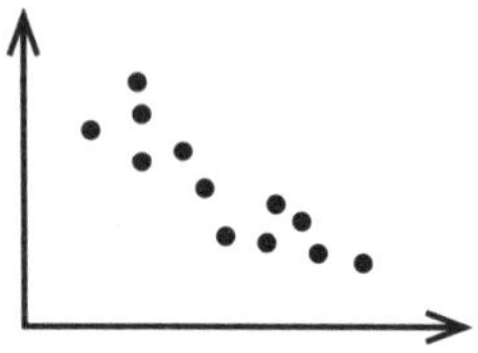

____

b) 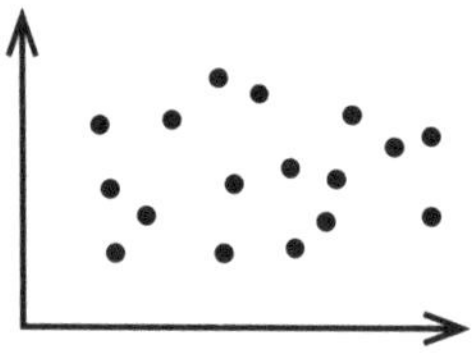

____

c) 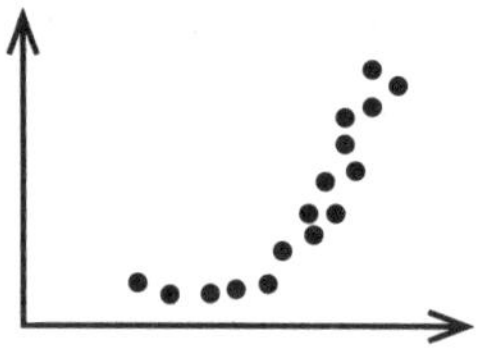

____

6. Nine students were surveyed about the hours they spent watching TV and about their math marks.

TV Watched Per Week (h)	12	14	6	13	17	5	9	11	19
Math Mark (%)	75	72	84	70	55	81	74	76	60

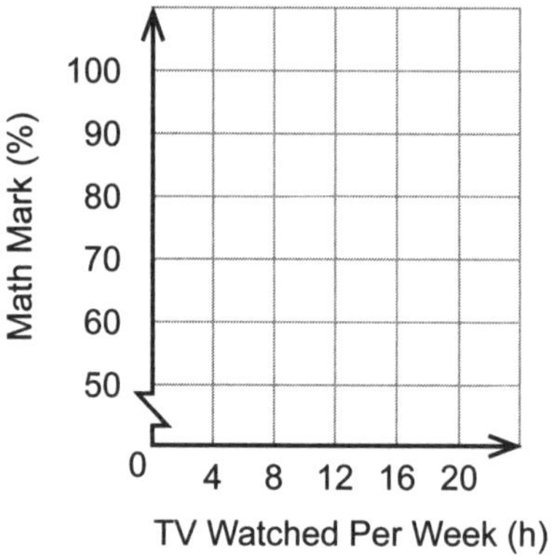

a) Write the data as ordered pairs and then plot the data points on the coordinate grid.

(*12* , *75*), (,), (,), (,), (,),
(,), (,), (,), (,)

b) Does the graph indicate an association between hours spent watching TV and math marks? __________

c) If so, describe the association. ______________

7. The table shows the marks of 11 students from two tests.

Test 1 Mark (%)	88	51	80	96	60	50	60	74	76	68	57
Test 2 Mark (%)	86	56	76	84	62	60	52	70	80	74	71

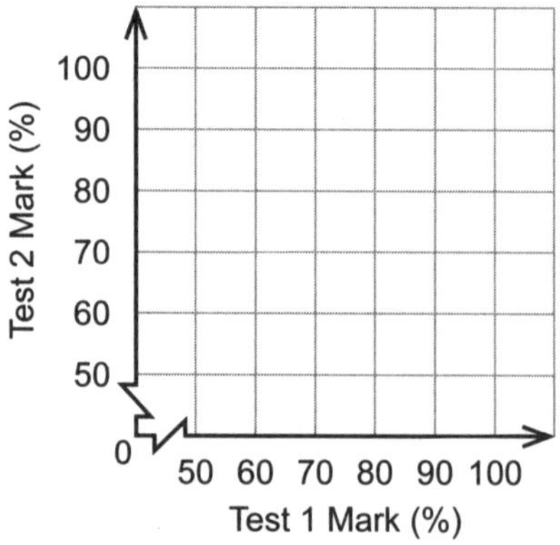

a) Draw a scatter plot for the data.

b) Describe the association. ______________

8. a) Draw the scatter plot based on the following data about a soccer team.

Age (years)	12	13	14	14	15	15	13	14	15	12	15	14
Height (cm)	141	162	174	154	166	174	150	168	182	156	160	152
Gender	F	M	M	F	F	M	F	M	M	M	F	F

i)

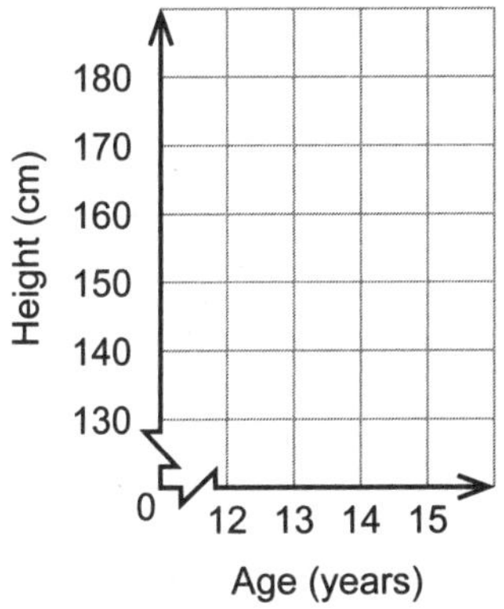

ii)

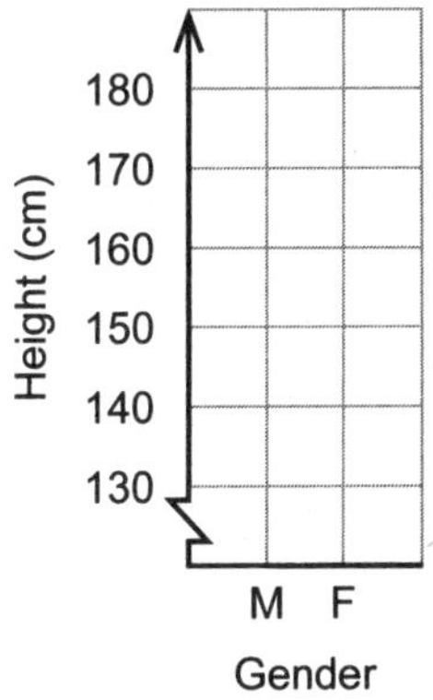

iii)

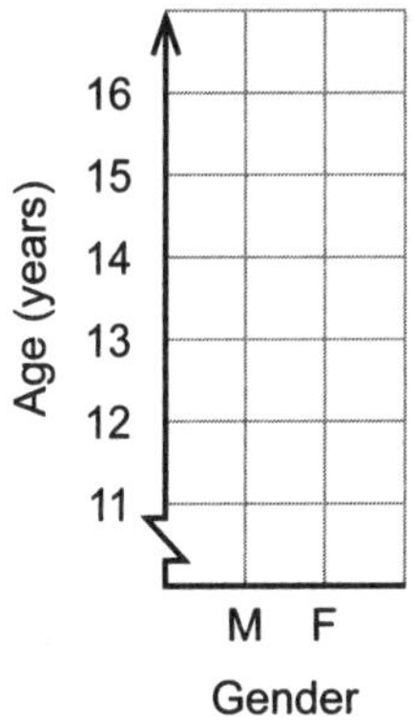

b) Circle the statements you agree with based on the data.

A. Males on the soccer team are likely to be taller than females.

B. Older people on the soccer team are likely to be taller.

C. Males on the soccer team are likely to be older.

9. The table shows the number of ice creams sold at a convenience store in the first half of April.

Day of the Month	1	2	3	4	5	6	7	8	9	10	11	12	13	14	15
Ice Creams Sold	45	38	51	55	42	39	44	58	41	49	40	53	36	45	43
Temperature (°F)	77	66	82	85	75	65	76	88	73	80	70	83	63	74	72

a) Draw a scatter plot for the data. Use the day of the month for the horizontal axis and the number of ice creams sold for the vertical axis.

b) Is there any association between the day of the month and the number of ice creams sold? Explain.

c) Draw a scatter plot for the data. Use the temperature for the horizontal axis and the number of ice creams sold for the vertical axis.

d) Is there any association between the temperature and the number of ice creams sold? Explain.

SP8-3 Interpreting Scatter Plots

1. Mark asked 15 students about their monthly allowance. The table shows the data he collected.

Age	10	12	11	8	12	9	8	10	13	13	9	12	11	8	13
Monthly Allowance ($)	40	80	50	10	100	75	20	30	60	70	30	20	60	30	90

a) Draw a scatter plot for the data.

b) Is there any association between age and monthly allowance?

2. The fuel economy of a car (how far it can travel using a unit of gas) is reported as miles per gallon. Sara recorded her car's fuel economy at different speeds. The results are shown in the table below:

Speed (mi/h)	20	30	40	50	55	65	70
Fuel Economy (mi/gal)	15	19	24	28	29	27	22

a) Draw a scatter plot for Sara's data. Record the speed on the horizontal axis and the fuel economy on the vertical axis. Use the same scale for both axes.

b) For speeds up to 55 mi/h, what type of association is there between speed and fuel economy?

c) For speeds over 55 mi/h, what type of association is there between speed and fuel economy?

d) For the scatter plot overall, can we say there is an association between speed and fuel economy? Explain.

3. Several people tested their cars the same way Sara did in Question 2. The results are shown in the table below:

Speed (mi/h)	20	20	30	35	40	45	50	60	60
Fuel Economy (mi/gal)	16	21	18	15	20	19	24	32	23

a) Draw a scatter plot for the data. Use the same scales for both axes.

b) Explain why this data is more difficult to interpret than the data in Question 2.

c) Split the data to draw two scatter plots, one showing that the fuel economy increases as speed increases and the other showing that the fuel economy decreases as speed increases.

4. The table shows the percentage of households with internet access in Lithuania from 2005 to 2014.

Year	2005	2006	2007	2008	2009	2010	2011	2012	2013	2014
Percent	16	35	44	51	60	61	60	60	65	66

a) Draw a scatter plot for the data. Use the year for the horizontal axis.

b) Is there any association between the year and percentage of households with internet access in Lithuania? Explain.

A **cluster** is a group of dots that are close to each other.

An **outlier** is a dot that is very different from others in the data set.

On the scatter plot, the outliers are far from other dots.

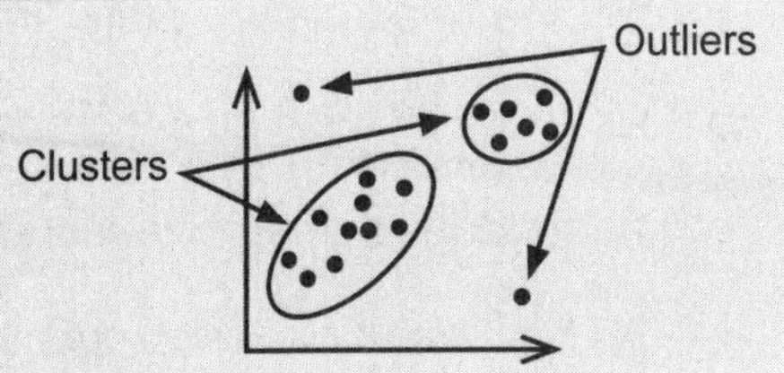

5. A student graphed data for the population and area of some countries in Europe.

a) What type of association does the scatter plot show?

Explain. ______________________________

____

b) Circle the cluster.

c) Are there any data points you find surprising? ________

d) Finland has an area of 338,000 km^2 and a population of 5.3 million. Circle the data point for Finland.

e) Poland is not yet shown on the scatter plot. Add a data point for Poland, which has an area of 313,000 km^2 and a population of 39 million.

Population and Area of 13 Countries in Europe

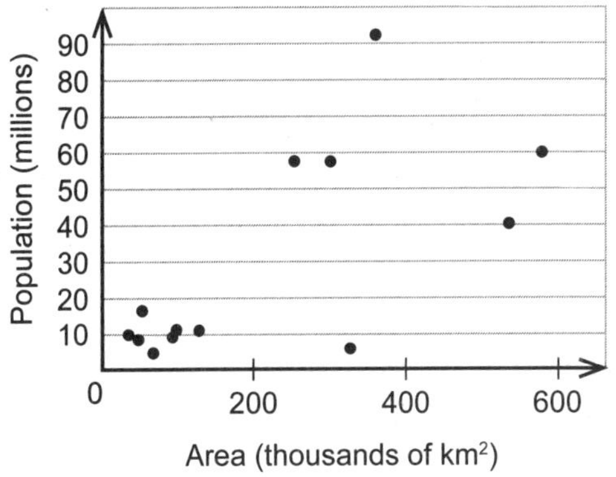

6. Which scatter plot best represents the association between the heights of people and their shoe sizes? Explain.

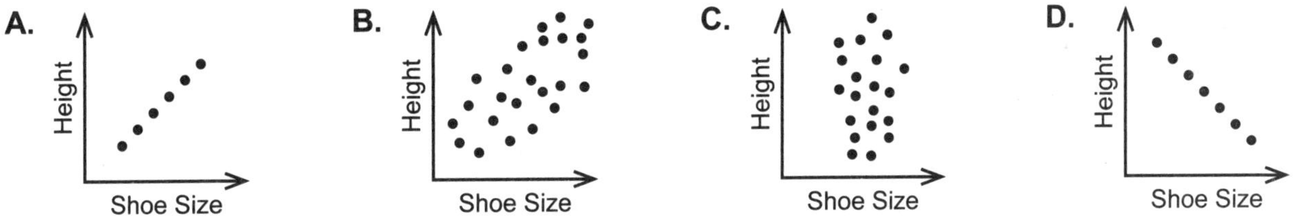

____

____

7. The table below shows the values of cars and their ages.

Age (years)	1	2	3	4	5	7	8	9
Value ($)	15,000	12,000	8,000	5,000	4,000	2,500	1,500	1,000

a) Draw a scatter plot for the data. Use age for the horizontal axis and the value of the car for the vertical axis.

b) Describe the association. ______________________________

c) Use the graph to estimate the value of a car that is six years old. ______________________________

8. Predict the relationship. Write "increases," "decreases," or "is not affected."

a) As a child's shoe size increases, the child's height ______________________.

b) As an adult's shoe size increases, the adult's monthly cable bill ______________________.

c) As the length of a rectangle increases, the rectangle's perimeter ______________________.

d) As a person's age increases, the length of the person's given name ______________________.

e) As the number of test questions left unanswered increases, the test score

______________________.

f) As the number of hours of study increases, the test score ______________________.

g) As a person's running speed increases, the person's heart rate ______________________.

h) As the denominator of a fraction increases, the value of the fraction ______________________.

i) As the fire gets bigger, the number of firefighters fighting the fire ______________________.

9. Choose three sentences from Question 8 that have different answers. Sketch what you think a scatter plot might look like for each sentence. Include the titles and labels, but no scales.

10. Linda and Michael are thinking about buying a house in Chicago. They each collected data about housing prices.

Linda's data:

Number of Bedrooms	0	1	1	0	2	3	1	2
Price ($10,000)	18	23	34	19	47	96	52	41

Michael's data:

Distance from the Subway Line (km)	1	4	7	11	8	9	6	2
Price ($10,000)	120	62	43	21	15	32	31	89

a) Draw a scatter plot for Linda's data. What type of association is there between the number of bedrooms and the price of the house? Explain.

b) Draw a scatter plot for Michael's data. What type of association is there between the price of the house and the distance from the subway line? Explain.

c) Michael looks at both scatter plots. He thinks that houses closer to the subway will have more bedrooms. How strongly does the data support Michael's thinking? Explain.

11. True or false?

a) A positive association occurs when the points on a scatter plot are in a straight line. __________

b) The association of a scatter plot is either positive or negative. __________

c) An association talks about the relationship between two variables. __________

d) If the graph shows no association, the graph is wrong. __________